PIMLICO

395

BIG JIM
THE LIFE AND WORK OF
JAMES STIRLING

Mark Girouard is a well-known architectural and social historian, who knew James Stirling for many years. His many prize-winning works include *Life in the English Country House, The Victorian Country House, Return to Camelot, Cities and People* and *The English Town: A History of Urban Life*. He lives in London.

BIG JIM

The Life and Work of
James Stirling

Mark Girouard

PIMLICO

Published by Pimlico 2000

2 4 6 8 10 9 7 5 3 1

First published in Great Britain by
Chatto & Windus 1998
Pimlico edition 2000

Pimlico
Random House, 20 Vauxhall Bridge Road,
London SW1V 2SA

Random House Australia (Pty) Limited
20 Alfred Street, Milsons Point, Sydney,
New South Wales 2061, Australia

Random House New Zealand Limited
18 Poland Road, Glenfield,
Auckland 10, New Zealand

Random House (Pty) Limited
Endulini, 5A Jubilee Road, Parktown 2193, South Africa

Random House Group Limited Reg. No. 954009
www.randomhouse.co.uk

A CIP catalogue record for this book
is available from the British Library

ISBN 0-7126-6422-X

Papers used by Random House are natural,
recyclable products made from wood grown in sustainable forests.
The manufacturing processes conform to the environmental
regulations of the country of origin

Printed and bound in Great Britain by
Butler & Tanner Ltd, Frome

CONTENTS

List of Illustrations   vii

Introduction   xiii

1.   Young Jim   1

2.   Jim in the Army   18

3.   Jim at Architecture School   27

4.   London in the 50s   50

5.   Jim comes to London   64

6.   The Leicester Explosion   92

7.   American Interludes   116

8.   After Leicester   137

9.   Marriage, Home and Travel   165

10.   Big Jim and Stuttgart   186

11.   After Stuttgart   211

12.   The Office   242

13.   Jim Regnant   255

14.   The Broken Chapter   274

Epilogue   294

A Note on the Sources   297

Chapter Notes   301

A Minimal Bibliography   312

Index   313

LIST OF ILLUSTRATIONS

Jim at the opening of the Stirling Foster Rogers Exhibition, Royal
Academy, Burlington House, 1986 (James Stirling Estate)   xviii

Colour plates, between pages 238 and 239

i   Engineering Building, Leicester University (James Stirling
      Foundation)
ii   History Faculty Building, Cambridge (Richard Einzig/Arcaid)
iii   The Florey Building, Queen's College, Oxford (Richard
      Einzig/Arcaid)
iv   Jim on the concourse at the Olivetti Training School, Haslemere
      (Charles Jencks)
v   In the sculpture court at the Neue Staatsgalerie, Stuttgart
      (Charles Jencks)
vi   On holiday in Italy in 1982 (Robert Kahn)
vii   The Library Building, Neue Staatsgalerie, Stuttgart (James
      Stirling Foundation)
viii Competition design for the National Gallery extension, London,
      1986 (James Stirling Foundation)
ix   The Entrance Hall, Neue Staatsgalerie, Stuttgart (Richard
      Einzig/Arcaid)
x   Number 1, Poultry, City of London (Dennis Gilbert/View)

Between pages 110 and 111

1   Louise Frazer, Jim's mother (James Stirling Estate)
2   Joseph Stirling, his father (James Stirling Estate)
3   Jim as a small boy (James Stirling Estate)
4   With his sister Oonagh (James Stirling Estate)
5   Jim holding birds' eggs (James Stirling Estate)
6   Liverpool School of Architecture, with Jim in front (James
      Stirling Estate)
7   In Black Watch uniform (James Stirling Estate)

8   In the early 1950s (James Stirling Estate)
9   Around 1955 (Paul Manousso)
10   Jim having a look (James Stirling Estate)
11   Detail of the flats at Ham Common, 1955-8 (James Stirling
     Foundation)
12   Assembly Hall, Dartmouth Park Primary School, Camberwell,
     1958-61 (Richard Einzig/Arcaid)
13   Jim outside the Engineering Building, University of Leicester in
     the early 1960s (James Stirling Estate)
14   The tower and laboratory block, Engineering Building, University
     of Leicester, 1959-63 (Richard Einzig/Arcaid)
15   Alan Colquhoun at Maisons Jaoul, photographed by Jim (Alan
     Colquhoun)
16   Barbara Chase-Riboud in about 1961 (James Stirling Foundation)
17   Creative tension: Jim Stirling and James Gowan outside York
     Terrace, Regent's Park (James Stirling Foundation)
18   Eldred Evans in her Rolls-Royce (Keith Manners)
19   The History Faculty Building, Cambridge, exterior from the
     south-west, 1964-7 (Ezra Stoller Associates)
20   History Faculty, looking down into the reading room (Richard
     Einzig/Arcaid)
21   Detail of Andrew Melville Hall, St Andrews, 1964-8 (Richard
     Einzig/Arcaid)
22   Detail of Olivetti Training School, Haslemere, 1969-72 (Richard
     Einzig/Arcaid)
23   Housing at Runcorn New Town, Cheshire, 1967-76 (Richard
     Einzig/Arcaid)
24   Jim with Mary Shand at the presentation of the Reynolds
     Aluminium Prize, 1965 (James Stirling Estate)
25   Jim and Mary in Greece (James Stirling Estate)
26   Jim with the newborn Ben (Mary Stirling)

Between pages 174 and 175
27   Jim with Ben, Kate and Sophie (Mary Stirling)
28   Mr Bush, a photograph given to Sophie by Mr Bush (Sophie Stirling)
29   Family lunch at Le Beausset with Marthe Moreau (Mary Stirling)
30   The Stirling family, photographed by Robert Kahn in the Vatican
     gardens (James Stirling Estate)
31   Jim and Mary in Cordoba in 1987 (Sophie Stirling)
32   The Neue Staatsgalerie, Stuttgart, from the terrace (Richard
     Bryant/Arcaid)

33   In the courtyard of the Neue Staatsgalerie (Richard Bryant/Arcaid)

34   The entrance hall, Arthur M. Sackler Museum, Harvard University (Timothy Hursley)

35   The Staircase, Arthur M. Sackler Museum (Timothy Hursley)

36   The Office: Jim and Michael Wilford (James Stirling Foundation)

37   Jim with models of the Florey Building and Dorman Long Headquarters, outside the office at 75 Gloucester Place (James Stirling Foundation)

38   With Cathy Martin and Jackie Simnet (James Stirling Estate)

39   In the partners' room at Gloucester Place (John Donat)

40   The Clore Building, Tate Gallery, London (Richard Bryant/Arcaid)

41   The courtyard of the Wissenschaftszentrum, Berlin (Richard Bryant/Arcaid)

42   Jim being interviewed in the courtyard (Marlies Hentrup)

43   Model of the proposed library at Latina, Italy (James Stirling Foundation)

44   The Cornell Center for the Performing Arts, Ithaca, USA (Richard Bryant/Arcaid)

45   Headquarters for Braun AG, Melsungen, Germany. The pedestrian walkway (Richard Bryant/Arcaid)

46   With Mary Stirling, receiving the Praemium Imperiale in Tokyo, 1991 (James Stirling Estate)

47   Jim's hands (Marlies Hentrup)

48   With Marlies Hentrup in the Museum of Modern Art, New York (Marlies Hentrup)

49   Jim at his desk (Marlies Hentrup)

50   The Bookshop in the Biennale Gardens, Venice (James Stirling Foundation)

51   Number 1 Poultry, City of London (Richard Bryant/Arcaid)

52   The empty table. Jim's worktable at the office in Fitzroy Square, photographed by him shortly before his death (James Stirling Estate)

Jim in Italy in the 1960s (Julia Bloomfield)   325

Drawings in the text

The statue of Queen Victoria in Liverpool (James Stirling Foundation)   49

Competition design for Sheffield University, 1953 (James Stirling
    Foundation)   76
Stirling and Gowan's competition design for Churchill College,
    Cambridge, 1958 (James Stirling Foundation)   103
Michael Wilford's drawing for glazing of the lobby areas,
    Engineering Building, University of Leicester (James Stirling
    Foundation)   109
St Andrews student residences (James Stirling Foundation)   141
Florey Building, Queen's College, Oxford (James Stirling
    Foundation)   143
Sketch drawings for the Florey Building (James Stirling Foundation) 143
Olivetti Training School, Haslemere, Surrey (James Stirling
    Foundation)   145
'Dad and Sophie', drawn by Jim for Sophie (James Stirling Estate)   178
Kate and blackbird's nest, drawn by Jim for Kate (James Stirling
    Estate)   178
Sophie's birthday card for Jim (Sophie Stirling)   179
Jim, Brian Riches and Leon Krier in the projected Olivetti
    headquarters, by Leon Krier (James Stirling Foundation)   186
Drawing of Jim by Ben, aged four (Ben Stirling)   191
Worm's-eye axonometric of the Florey Building, Oxford,
    by Leon Krier (James Stirling Foundation)   194
Derby Civic Centre competition: the arcade, by Leon Krier
    (James Stirling Foundation)   196
Sketch designs for the Dusseldorf Art Gallery competition
    (James Stirling Foundation)   201
The plan of the Wissenschaftszentrum (WZB), Berlin
    (James Stirling Foundation)   223
Proposal for roofing the courtyard of the Pallazzo Citterio
    (James Stirling Foundation)   233
A proposed terrace of houses in New York
    (James Stirling Foundation)   250
Drawings by Richard Portchmouth showing the proposed
    extension to the National Gallery, London
    (James Stirling Foundation)   251
Jim in outline in his chair (James Stirling Foundation)   271

To Elizabeth Manners, who saw behind the scenes

INTRODUCTION

The public knows little enough about contemporary architecture, and even less about contemporary architects. Those who are any good are so caught up in their work that they become a caste or race apart. They meet only with other architects, eat and drink with other architects, sleep with other architects, and usually marry other architects. Unless their buildings are unusually high or unusually large, or fall down, or are blown up, or are attacked by the Prince of Wales, they seldom receive much attention. Their personal lives, unlike those of royalty or pop stars, tycoons or footballers, jockeys or even novelists, are ignored by the media.

Yet architects are interesting people, engaged in interesting work, which impinges on people's lives in one form or another twenty-four hours a day. They are often creative and entertaining. They have their own methods of working, their own feuds, and their own traumas. They are in the awkward position of trying to be artists and practical men at the same time. One architect's office can be quite unlike another, but as a group architects' offices are unlike anywhere else. Designing a building and getting it built is a complex, absorbing, exciting, exasperating, tedious, dramatic and sometimes devastating business.

It is worth taking a look at their lives, and peering into their offices, and among contemporary architects none is more worth looking at than Jim Stirling. For over twenty years he was the architect best known in the world to other architects or to people interested in contemporary architecture; deservedly so, for his buildings were extraordinary and his personality and appearance unforgettable. Every architect has his favourite Jim Stirling story. His voice was and is still imitated, his massive profile caricatured, and his bright blue shirt, emerald-green briefcase and purple socks were as familiar in the architectural world as Winston Churchill's cigar or Neville Chamberlain's umbrella.

I first met Jim Stirling in 1972 when I was commissioned by the *Architectural Review* to write an article on his Florey Building at Oxford.

I came by way of that to look more closely at his Engineering Building at Leicester, and History Faculty Building at Cambridge, and I fell in love with all three of them, as so many architects and architectural writers did at the time. I found them strange and beautiful, and quite unlike anything else that I had ever seen. At the same time, as I worked on the article it became clear that the Florey Building had run into some serious practical troubles. I wrote about these perhaps rather too gingerly, because Jim had a reputation for being prickly about criticism. Prickly he was, but he accepted what I wrote, and perhaps because he saw that I was a genuine admirer, and because he liked my wife Dorothy, and we both got on very well with Mary Stirling, we became part of their circle of friends. We went to their dinners or parties in London, we stayed with them in France, and when Jim was given the Gold Medal at the RIBA Norman Foster and I were the two people whom he asked to speak at the ceremony.

In 1987 Stirling, Wilford's controversial design for No. 1 Poultry, in the heart of the City of London, was heading for a Public Inquiry. I vividly remember how we were showing Jim and Mary round a house that Dorothy had converted for letting in Holland Park, and how Jim came up to me and asked if I would give evidence for him at the Inquiry. The new building would involve the destruction of nine listed buildings, and I said that I could not support it. Jim was very hurt. He went over to my wife and said, 'He's my friend, isn't he?' He had strong and simple views about friendship. I did not give evidence for him, and what was worse, in the end and after much soul-searching, I wrote a letter to the Inspector opposing the building, on the grounds of the destruction which it would involve. He would not speak to me for over three years, and I do not blame him.

Then he came up to me at a party and made it up. A little later, when he was about to fly out to Singapore, I looked in at his house to lend him J.G. Farrell's *Singapore Grip*. He told me candidly that he thought it unlikely that he would read it, but I think he was pleased that I had taken the trouble to bring it round. He and Mary were sitting side by side in his library in their twin Le Corbusier chairs, and I sat and talked to them a little, and then left. It was a pleasant occasion, and I went home feeling happy that we were friends again. I remember, too, thinking how companionable he and Mary looked, sitting there. I did not fully realise at the time what strain their marriage was under, but even so I think that my impression was a true one.

A few months passed, during much of which time Jim was abroad, and then the telephone rang. It was Jim's partner, Michael Wilford, to tell us that Jim had died unexpectedly as the result of what should have been a minor operation. I went sadly to his funeral in Hawksmoor's St Mary Woolnoth, opposite the still-contested site of No. 1 Poultry. At Mary's request I was one of the people who spoke at it. Some months later she suggested that I write his biography, and I agreed to do it.

There proved to be problems in writing it, in addition to the inevitable problems of writing a biography of someone so recently dead. Jim almost never wrote personal letters, and outside his office correspondence never kept letters that were written to him. After the age of sixteen he never kept a diary. The kind of massive personal archive that some biographers can draw on does not exist. The biographer has to rely heavily on memories. I have taped or noted conversations with about 150 people, and wish I had the time or resources to talk to 150 more. To a large extent this book is an orchestration of other people's voices, and I am only too aware that memories are often unreliable, and a biographer's selection from them inevitably personal. I have checked against contemporary sources wherever I can and I have used Jim's own words wherever I have them. He very seldom wrote personal letters, but he often wrote postcards, of a very individual kind, and one way or another, in lectures, articles or interviews, he talked a good deal about his life, though, as I now realise, not always with accuracy.

I made occasional discoveries. One of the most important was finding the bird-watching diary which Jim had kept as a schoolboy, still sitting inconspicuously on the shelves of his library. Another was when Robin Bell, a friend of Jim's youth now living in British Columbia, disinterred and generously gave me the several-thousand-word letter which Jim had written to him from New York in 1949 saying, in effect, how ghastly New York and the Americans were, an opinion which he was not to hold to in later years.

But the discoveries were less rewarding than the slow emergence of a portrait of Jim and his work, as it built up as the result of my talking to more and more people, going through files and photograph albums in his home, his office archive and elsewhere, visiting his buildings, looking at his drawings, finding postcards and the occasional letter, and reading everything that I could find published by and about him.

A biographer must always worry that in the course of researching and writing he will come to dislike his subject. I am pleased that did not happen to me. I grew to appreciate Jim more, not less, as I worked on him. I also realised how little I had known him, and how remarkable he was. He was a man who kept himself private. I cannot pretend that I have explained him, but I hope that I have put across some impression of his qualities, and helped to bring them and him and his buildings to life for readers who did not know them already.

This is a biography, not a study of Jim's buildings. I have not felt able to discuss all his designs or projects, or to go into the kind of detail that one would expect of an architectural monograph. But of course buildings have to feature prominently in what I have written. Although people meant a lot to him, architecture almost always came first. The more I worked on the book the more I realised that his buildings and his life were all of a piece. Jim was complex and contradictory. As his great friend Colin Rowe put it at the American memorial meeting, he was 'brash, gentle, generous, modest, immoderate, candid, and things of that kind'. One might add, as qualities 'of that kind', that he could be subtle, prickly, abrupt, outrageous, naif and childish, and that he was always private. Almost all these qualities are to be found in his buildings.

I remember with pleasure the variety of places to which the biography brought me, the people with whom I talked, and the vividness and often love with which they recreated Jim for me. A medley of images remain: going in freezing cold with Magda Cordell, Jim's sharp-brained and invigorating friend of the 1950s, to the Niagara Falls and being unable to see them, owing to the spray freezing on my spectacles; being taken between eleven at night and three in the morning around the casinos of Las Vegas by Jim's Turkish friend and former student, Vefik Soyeren, and being told that Caesar's Palace, the biggest and brassiest of them, was inspired by Jim's competition design for a museum in Dusseldorf; recording Gretchen Dal Co against the burble of voices and the tolling campanile bell of the Piazza San Marco in Venice; talking to Colin Rowe, while he interminably sipped cold tea and the snow on the branches outside reflected a cold radiance into his tree-top Washington apartment; having dinner, along with Mary and Sophie Stirling and members of Jim's office, in the home of Herr Fecker, Jim's loyal and delightful patron for the Neue Staatsgalerie at Stuttgart; spending another genial evening talking to former members of Jim's office in a Dublin bar, as the Guinness flowed, and their memories of, and love for, Jim flowed with it; and being received far from genially by a hostile Paul Rudolph, amid the glass furniture of his amazing East River penthouse.

James Gowan would not talk to me on the grounds that he was sure that I would not be allowed to say anything derogatory about Jim. Peter Smithson would not talk because he said that he only liked doing so when he could be constructive. Both had a tricky relationship with Jim, and I would have liked to have heard their version of it. But on the whole people were generous with their time and their memories, and how much

I owe to them will appear in the course of the biography.

I must thank Mary Stirling, who suggested the biography in the first place, for helping me, talking to me and giving me access to her photographs and her archives. I am especially grateful to Jim's children, whose sometimes difficult but always close relationship with their father comes across so vividly and sympathetically when they talk about him; and to Michael Wilford, Catherine Martin, Russell Bevington and other former colleagues of Jim for talking freely to me, and making me aware how full of character Jim's office was, and how important a part its members played in the creation of the buildings that were designed in it. I owe much to Marlies Hentrup, for her patience and her help. Geoffrey Howe gave good advice, Phoebe Mason kindly sent her comments and, as with all my recent books, I had unfailing help from Elizabeth Manners. Dorothy Girouard's support of and belief in my work on the biography has meant a great deal to me. I am grateful to the Graham Foundation for Advanced Studies in the Fine Arts for a generous grant which made it possible for me to travel round America talking to people about their memories of Jim.

Jim was admired and loved by people of many types, ages and nationalities, but he was not a saint. His behaviour was not always creditable, and on a few occasions was outrageous. Some of his buildings had troubled histories, and his personal life could be complex. I do not think that he would have wanted to be whitewashed. To attempt to cover over these qualities, or to try to conceal what happened, seems deceitful and demeaning to him.

He always liked a building that could make him smile. He loved the furniture designed by Thomas Hope, and commended it for being 'extreme, over the top, eccentric and gutsy'. He told an architect about to design a detail in his Sackler Gallery at Harvard, 'Do whatever you like, as long as it's not in good taste.' He was talking about buildings and furniture, but with Jim it is difficult to separate architecture and life. I have included a number of stories that made me smile, including, for instance, ones told by Jim's secretary and associate Catherine Martin, whose vigorous personality he so much enjoyed, and on whose loyalty and support he so much relied. I have told one or two stories that are perhaps over the top and in bad taste, because they seemed redolent of Jim. My aim throughout has been to present him and his buildings as vividly as I can, if possible in the words of people who knew him better than I did. I have tried to write a true story of the life of an extraordinary man.

ONE

YOUNG JIM

James Frazer Stirling – to be known over the years as Blimey, the Bird-Watcher, the BW, the Beachcomber, the Seedy Viking, Jumbo, Lucky Jim, and finally, round the world, just as Big Jim – was conceived in New York Harbour around July 1923, on a cargo ship of the Liverpool-based Blue Funnel Line. So his mother told him. His father, Joseph Stirling, was a ship's engineer, and, as was the way in those days, travelled on the Blue Funnel ships for trips of many months, with no return home. In 1923 his wife came out to join him for a few days in New York. The birth of a son followed on 22 April 1924, at 125 Kent Road, Glasgow, in the tenement flat of Joseph's widowed mother, May. By then Joseph Stirling was away for a year's trip on the China run. He returned a few months after the birth, and saw his son for the first time.

The boy was named James after his paternal grandfather and great grandfather, and Frazer after the surname of his mother's family. The Stirlings had been, for three generations, an artisan family living in Glasgow. The first James Stirling, described as an engine-fitter, was dead by the time of the census of 1881. His widow Christina, born Marshall, was then living in a four-roomed tenement at 86 McAlpine Street, just off the Broomielaw quay in the centre of Glasgow. The tenement was one of three in a small tenement block. The other occupants were a seed storeman and a ship's carpenter, with their families. Christina's four rooms had seven occupants: herself; her son James, a brass-moulder, aged 22; her nephew William Walker, salesman, and Alexander Marshall, coal-miner, aged 32 and 22; her niece Maggie Marshall, general servant, aged 15; a boarder, Duncan S. Mitchell, shipping agent and outfitter, aged 26; and a second boarder, Janet McLean, aged 4 months.

In 1882 the younger James Stirling married May Bett. At the time of the marriage she described herself as a dressmaker, and was living with her people in a tenement at 26 Brown Street, a few blocks away from McAlpine Street. Her father was a foreman house-painter. The newly-married couple moved across the river to 12 Richard Street. This was a biggish block containing ten tenements. It was occupied in 1891 (after the Stirlings had moved on) by an iron-turner, an iron-moulder, a brass-finisher, a cabinet-maker, a seaman, and a steam engine fitter. Joseph Stirling was born there on 21 May 1883.

All these families were living in the old industrial quarter of Glasgow, located along the river as such quarters usually are. It had grown up on the edge of the medieval town. Broomielaw was so called from the broom growing along the river banks, but this had long been replaced by masonry quays and the district was one of warehouses, small factories and workshops on or near the quayside and crowded tenements further inland. The shipyards, the docks and the bigger and newer factories from which the great black city drew its wealth were farther down the river. 'Tenement', in Glasgow, is a term applied to flats and apartments of all kinds. Those where the Stirlings and Betts lived were towards the lower end of the scale, but certainly not slums. They have all disappeared under post-war development or motorways, but the tenement in Kent Road where Jim Stirling was born still exists. It is a quite handsome classical block near the Mitchell Library, in what was then a socially rather better area. Either Jim's grandfather, of whose later career nothing is known, had come up in the world, or his grandmother had established her own small dressmaking business.

In later life Jim sometimes enjoyed claiming that he was the son of a ship's stoker, and had been brought up in the Liverpool slums. In fact he was a respectable suburban child; and Joseph Stirling is unlikely ever to have been a stoker, and was certainly far from being one at the time of Jim's birth. He had been apprenticed as a fitter with the London and Glasgow Engineering and Shipbuilding Company. Either as part of his apprenticeship, or perhaps at evening class, he had a good technical education, and in later life made engineering drawings of high quality. He became a ship's engineer in the Merchant Navy, and by at least the early 1920s had moved from Glasgow to Liverpool and was working for the Blue Funnel Line, one of the shipping lines belonging to the Holt family. Through his friend Will Campbell, with whom he had studied engineering, he got to know a Mrs Inglis, living in Mossley Side, and her school-teacher lodger, Louise Frazer. She and Joseph Stirling were married in Liverpool on 4 August 1922. They had two children, James Frazer and Oonagh, born four and a half years after her brother.

Jim's mother came from a family of Irish Protestant farmers of Scottish origin, living at Killymaddy near Killyleagh in County Armagh; Oonagh was named after the river near the farm. Louise had left Ireland in her teens to be a pupil teacher in Norfolk, and then moved to

Liverpool, perhaps to teach under her father's cousin, Henry Frazer, who was the rector of St Peter's Everton, north of Liverpool. By the time of her marriage she was teaching at Mossley Hill, in the southern suburbs.

The Frazers were a family of high tempers, quick to flare up and die down, and not harbouring resentment. Henry Frazer was a campaigning teetotaller, who would storm into pubs in his parish and preach against the evils of alcohol. Louise was quieter, a strong-willed, intelligent, friendly and careful woman, who liked things properly done. Her ambitions for her son were to see him married to a nice girl and settled in a good safe job, with a pension. He loved her, and as a young man clashed with his father, perhaps partly because he resented the strain which his long absences put on her, but in character he was closer to his father.

Joseph Stirling was not easy. His daughter has fond recollections of him, but her husband and all Jim Stirling's surviving friends who knew him remember him with alarm, as 'not a very friendly type', 'a really rough type of Scotsman', 'terrifying at times'. 'Try and keep out of my father's way,' Jim would say. But if they did run into this dour, huge-chinned Scotsman, he would say nothing, let alone anything welcoming. He would merely emit a grunt or growl which girls found especially intimidating. He was probably the only person of whom Jim was frightened.

From modest origins, Joseph Stirling worked his way up to become the Chief Engineer of the Blue Funnel Line. He had travelled round the world on the company's ships, all with Greek names – *Ulysses*, *Autolycus*, and so on. When a Blue Funnel ship broke down with engine trouble in Vladivostok, he was sent out across Russia by the newly opened Trans-Siberia line to repair her engines and bring her back to Liverpool. Just after Japan came into the Second World War his then ship, the SS *Ulysses*, was damaged in a typhoon in the Pacific. He kept the engine going until it got to Australia, rather than take the easier option and put into Manila. Another damaged Blue Funnel ship did go to Manila, where it was impounded by the Japanese, and all its crew taken prisoner. Joseph Stirling survived to be torpedoed in the *Ulysses* off Charleston in America. All the ship's crew, including the cats, were rescued, sent up to Canada, and embarked in another ship which was torpedoed and sunk in the mouth of the St Lawrence River. He returned safely to England on yet another ship. It was his last sea voyage, and he finished the war in Liverpool, where he was commissioned by the Shipping Federation to set up a training school for firemen.

When Jim was a boy the war years were still in the future. His father's life was a steady pattern of long absences at sea, punctuated by shore leave. His return from a sea trip was always exciting: his daughter Oonagh remembers him coming into the house like Santa Claus, loaded with presents. The house filled up with mementos of his visits – carved ivory, elaborate oriental plates and vases, a clock, and other objects of what Jim was later to consider hideous design. Up in Scotland his mother kept a glass-fronted cabinet full of postcards sent to her by him from all over the world. More exciting and mysterious were the odd nicks and scars on his body. He was not forthcoming about these, but warned Oonagh never to wake him up suddenly, as he might react with violence.

In company which interested him – which did not include that of his children's friends – he could relax and talk. Occasionally he could become convivial and tell stories of past adventures and experiences. Sometimes he sang as he walked round the house, for he had a good voice, and had been a choirboy in Glasgow, although in later life he never went to church. Sometimes he played the fool to amuse his children or waltzed his daughter round the kitchen. He was good with his hands, made numerous pieces of furniture for the house, and carved models of ships. His masterpiece was an elaborate model of a three-masted sixteenth-century galleon, the *Santa Maria*. He used to take this on his sea voyages, and it was lost when his ship was torpedoed. Jim remembered 'being fascinated at the age of four or five by the beautiful drawings he did of engine and turbine parts, and so on, coloured blue and pink'. To his regret his mother threw them out when she moved to a smaller house after her husband's death.

The silences, the switching off company which did not interest him, the sense of potential anger which made people frightened of him, the sudden outbursts of buffoonery, the collecting instinct, the returns from abroad loaded with presents, even the long absences abroad – anyone who knew Jim will recognise these traits in his father. A photograph of Joseph Stirling playing the fool in the garden could almost be of Jim.

Liverpool in the 1920s and 1930s was still a mighty city. Its ships traded all over the world, and brought great wealth to its merchants and ship owners. The huge Cunard liners on the Liverpool-New York line were still regularly slipping in and out, and disgorging opulent passengers into the marble-lined Adelphi Hotel, the Ritz of Northern England. On the Pier Head the Liver Building with its skyline of flapping Liver birds, and the Dock and Harbour Board, with its swaggering baroque dome and cupolas, did not look out on a pathetically empty Mersey, as they do today. The huge, turbulent fast-flowing estuary was crowded with ships on their way to and from the docks. The massive granite walls of the docks stretched for twenty miles to either side of the Pier Head. The overhead railway, to be demolished in the late 1950s, was still running alongside them, and from its carriages passengers could look over the wall at the ships unloading, and huge warehouses of sombrely impressive architecture. Inland on the hills rising from the river were great public buildings, lavish banks and insurance offices, innumerable churches, Georgian streets and squares, areas packed with rows of little working-class houses, blocks of huge flats on the Vienna model, and public houses as lavish and elaborate as the banks. It was a city of fog and soot, of cliff-like walls of brick, of solid marble, brass and mahogany, of dockers and immigrants, of great wealth, great poverty, and occasional violence.

Jim Stirling had romantic memories of the Liverpool of his childhood and was correspondingly bitter about the financial collapse, demolitions and destructive town planning of post-war years. For this reason he almost always refused invitations to go back there. But although he made excursions as a boy, with his mother into the central city, or with his father into the docks, he lived and was brought up in a very different Liverpool, the clean, respectable, unremarkable suburban Liverpool of semi-detached villas which had spread out to the south-west of the city in the 1920s and 1930s. His parents, after a couple of moves, settled in 24 Childwall Priory Road, about three and a half miles from the city centre. It was one of a row of semi-detached houses like dozens of others in the neighbourhood. His parents remained there until his father died in 1957.

Jim lived the unremarkable life of a little boy in the suburbs, the only unusual feature being the long absences of his father. He made model aeroplanes, and rode around the streets on his bicycle, proudly sporting a Scottish flag. He teased his little sister, crawled under her cot and made noises, but came to her protection with an air gun when a rooster attacked her in the yard of the Frazer farm in Ireland. He went on holiday to the Frazers, or with his family to Anglesey, or to an 'aunt', in fact a cousin, who kept a commercial hotel in Bedford, and went often to his grandmother in Glasgow. She had moved further out of the centre to Knightswood, and he remembered being intrigued by the locks on the canals at Bearsden, and the City Art Gallery in Kelvingrove Park, a massive survivor of the 1901 International Exhibition. He went with Oonagh to the big Exhibition of 1938. 'When Granny told you to do something, you did it,' as Oonagh remembers; they went to Presbyterian Sunday School in Liverpool because she insisted on it.

The Stirlings were not a social family. Louisa's teetotal background and Joseph's Presbyterian upbringing meant that drink only appeared on special occasions. There was a little quiet bridge. Visitors were limited to relatives, or a small group of friends, among them Captain Davis, a Merchant Navy associate of Joseph's, and Will Campbell, his old friend from Glasgow days. He became 'Uncle Will', and had a son, Bobby, who was a few years older than Jim, and whom Jim hero-worshipped.

The new villas in the Childwall Priory Road area were interspersed here and there with the earlier green-field residences of opulent Liverpudlians. One of these, a rich timber-merchant's chunky neo-Romanesque mansion of about 1860, had been adapted and enlarged to become the Quarry Bank Secondary Day School. It was within walking distance of Childwall Priory Road, and in 1935 or 1936 Jim became a pupil there.

Quarry Bank was a school somewhat out of the ordinary, thanks to its headmaster, Richard Fitzroy Bailey. He was a bachelor, with a comfortable private income from his family interest in the Cyfartha Ironworks in South Wales, had been at Eton and King's College, Cambridge, and went on to become a housemaster at Shrewsbury. He seemed all set for the conventional career of someone of his type and background: headmastership of a prestigious public school, and beyond that, perhaps, by way of ordination, a bishopric, for he was a devout Christian and a Bible scholar. But Bailey, who once described himself as 'hating labels, but if pressed, I would say I was an old-fashioned Tory with a social conscience', went off in a different direction. Quarry Bank was one of half a dozen or so new secondary day schools started up around Liverpool in the 1920s. Bailey set out to bring public-school ways and values to day-school boys in the suburbs of Liverpool. So Quarry Bank had a house system, a crest, a motto (*'ex hoc metallo virtutem'*), a school song, prefects, caning, a magazine, a Boy Scout troop, an Old Boys' Society, and links with a boys' club in the Liverpool slums, where boys and old boys were encouraged to work. Its alumni were known as 'Ashlars'.

It was Tory paternalism, perhaps, but it worked, thanks to Bailey's personality and abilities. He was a kind, tolerant and good man, an old-fashioned bachelor never touched by rumour or scandal, who said that the school was 'wife and child as well as work' to him, and, when he retired, that 'you will find some of my heart in every room in the school'. He was nothing to look at, a small unimpressive man, whose trousers were too short, with a nicotine-stained moustache on a face like that of a rather frayed owl or cat. Ultimately he gave most of his money away, and during his life his kindness and generosity expressed itself in much financial help, given constructively and on the side. Every year he gave a Christmas party for the children of his staff at George Henry-Lee's restaurant in central Liverpool, and when members of staff married he invariably gave them a canteen of cutlery as a wedding present. The staff all had nicknames, of long-forgotten origin – 'Porky' Burrows, 'Tripe' Galloway, 'Nicko' Nixon, who had a lethal skill in chucking chalk at boys who displeased him, and 'Dippy' Dawson. 'Dippy' Dawson ran the Scouts. He was a kindly, lanky man, six foot five in height, looked a little ridiculous in his Boy Scout shorts, was a hopeless disciplinarian, but much liked by the boys.

Bailey's own interests were bee-keeping and rock-climbing, but he set out to find out what his boys were good at, and to encourage them to pursue it. Quarry Bank boys were, on the whole, happy at the school, and looked back at it with affection and some pride. Many of them were successful in later life: the old boys included two Labour cabinet ministers (Peter Shore and Bill Rogers, later, with Roy Jenkins, the co-founder of the Social Democrats), a sprinkling of bishops, professors and leading businessmen, the actor Derek Nimmo, John Lennon of the Beatles (but he was there after Bailey's day) – and Jim Stirling.

In later years, when Jim was beginning to make a name for himself, 'Dippy' Dawson reminisced with the English master, and they agreed that Jim was one of the worst pupils they had ever had, and the least likely to succeed in later life. Dawson described him as 'just a grubby little boy among a lot of other grubby little boys'. The only subjects that he was good at were Art and Handicrafts. There was an excellent art master, Jack Simmonds, who encouraged him. He was an unremarkable Boy Scout who never became a troop-leader, was never a prefect, did not play in any school team, could not spell, was always bottom of the class, and never passed an exam. His nickname, from his favourite expression, was 'Blimey'.

Jim was never one for organisations. What Quarry Bank did for him was to leave him alone, give him a stable background alongside his stable family life – and ultimately, by way of the art master and Bailey, get him into Liverpool Art School. But it was typical of Jim that 'Dippy' Dawson, his scoutmaster, was unaware of his ruling passion as a schoolboy. He kept it separate from his school life.

In the fifth (1940) volume of H.F. Witherby's magisterial *Handbook of British Birds*, the acknowledgements to 'those who have given information' include the names of J.F. Stirling and G.K. Robinson. Gerry Robinson had made friends with Jim in 1938, when they were both 14. He lived in Eldred Road, a few streets from Jim, and they were in the same class at Quarry Bank. He was towards the top of the class, and Jim at the bottom, but this did not signify much. Robinson had done so badly in the previous year that he had been kept back in the same class, and did well because he had been through all the work before. The two boys remained close friends until 1942, brought together by an obsessive interest in egg-collecting and bird-watching. The class duffers became, in however modest a way, professional experts whose observations were quoted in books and newspapers. Jim's genius and ambition was to bring him world-wide fame; his friend Gerry Robinson never left Liverpool, and is living in retirement in the same kind of house, and in the same neighbourhood, as that in which he and Jim were brought up. He is a gentle, charming man, who recollects that 'Jim was the one who led, you know. He was wanting to be off and do things. I suppose I must have followed, although I don't really see him as being the dominant of the two of us'. The two boys worked well and happily together.

Gerry Robinson cannot remember how their joint interest started. It perhaps grew out of the fact that they both had bicycles and used to go on outings together, Jim flying his Scottish flag, for he was, and remained throughout his life, intensely proud of his Scottish ancestry. A few streets away, in Woodsorrel Road, lived Eric Hardy, the founder and secretary of the Merseyside Naturalists' Association. The boys joined the Association, became Hardy's dedicated disciples, and by 1941 had become its joint assistant secretaries.

Hardy was a journalist, working on the *Liverpool Daily Post* and *Liverpool Echo*, wrote a regular nature column, and in 1941 published a little book on *The Birds of the Liverpool Area*. He was generous in acknowledging the work of others, and there were many references to the observations of the two boys between 1939 and 1942 in his book and articles. As he puts it today, 'they did a lot of good pioneering work in the ringing section', for ringing birds for scientific purposes, to trace their age and movements, was still in its early days. But they also carried out general surveys of nesting grounds in the Liverpool area and further afield for the Association. Much of their spare time was spent in long bicycle rides around Liverpool and in the adjacent countryside, and each Whitsun holiday from 1939 to 1942 they set out on a longer expedition, by bicycle, bus, train, foot or hitching lifts: to Great Orme in North Wales in 1939, to Puffin Island off Anglesey in 1940, to Denbigh Moors in Wales and Ravenglass and St Bees in Cumberland in 1941, to Pen-y-Pont and Llanwrtyd in Central Wales in 1942.

Observations made at St Bees earned them the acknowledgement in Witherby's *Handbook,* and two short entries in the London ornithological magazine *British Birds*. Their note that fulmar petrels bred on St Bees Head was picked up by the editor as 'the first record of definite breeding of the fulmars on the west side of England and Wales'. Jim's copies of the two issues are still in his library, along with a copy of Hardy's *Birds of the Liverpool Area*, with pencil notes by Jim of his own observations in the margin.

Their summer expeditions took them to famous and often dramatic nesting-grounds, on moorland or cliff-faces in wild and beautiful countryside, but the Liverpool area itself was sufficiently remarkable. In particular, the Wirral, the peninsula across the water from Liverpool, between the broad estuaries of the Mersey and the Dee, was fringed with rocks and marshes which were the first and last ports-of-call for huge flights of migrating birds. In contrast to the built-up areas of Birkenhead or the community or resort adjuncts to Liverpool, which covered much of the Wirral, there were lonely and beautiful places. One of the boys' favourite bicycle expeditions was to Red Rocks, between Hoylake and West Kirby on the northern tip of the Wirral, where, at the right time of year, the birds, packed in thousands on the rocks when the high tide drove them away from feeding on the sands, were an extraordinary sight.

Their attempt to photograph it was a disaster, however. Photography was not the boys' strong card. On their first expeditions they used 'an unsophisticated folding camera which was really no more than a glorified box camera'. Then Jim purchased a superior half-plate reflex camera. They constructed a portable hide out of sackcloth and wooden stakes, and set off for Red Rocks. The hide was only big enough for one, and it was agreed that Jim, as the owner of the camera, should occupy it. It was difficult to find sand among the rocks into which to fix the stakes, and the site chosen was below high-water level, so that by the time Jim had taken his photographs the water was up to his waist, and he had to wade back. As Gerry Robinson puts it, 'we lost the hide and the camera never worked properly after that'.

The Naturalists' Association was interested in observing, recording, ringing and photographing, not egg-collecting, but the two boys were also enthusiastic collectors, a hobby then still widely practised, although ceasing to be thought respectable by ornithologists. Jim built up a big collection, and his father made a cabinet for him to keep it in, much envied by Gerry Robinson, who had to keep his in cardboard boxes. Their egg-collecting mentor was a professional egg-dealer called Gowland, who lived in Pensbury Road in the Wirral. He was an attractive and knowledgeable man, who ran his own society, the North of England Zoological Society. He had a pretty wife, much younger than he was, who was later to run off with his solicitor. But he used his schoolboy contacts to buy eggs cheap and sell them at a good profit. On occasions he sent the two friends looking for rare pure white tern's eggs (the eggs are usually off-white and blotched with brown) on Burton marshes, a great nesting-ground for terns on the Wirral coast. They felt they were being exploited, and resented it.

Hazards of egg-collecting are mentioned from time to time in the diary that Jim kept of their Whitsun expeditions. In May 1941 on Puffin Island, for instance, he records 'climb up to the ruined tower to eat lunch and blow puffins' eggs – have to dodge the university girl who is no doubt a bird-lover and wouldn't think of touching their eggs . . . hid eggs in tins wrapped up in capes in case the keeper would want to see our packs on returning'.

They ate the eggs as well as collecting them, for gulls' eggs were necessary to keep them going as a supplement to tins, milk from farms, and post-office buns, lemonade and ice-cream, on their long outings, done on the cheap on schoolboy pocket money and with schoolboy appetites. Gerry Robinson remembers how 'we had gathered these gulls' eggs to have for our breakfast, and we cooked them on a hot stone over a fire, and thought we were going to have a fine breakfast, but when we ate them they had a very fishy and horrible taste . . . anyway, we ate them quite keenly, because that's about all we had for breakfast'. But these were herring gulls' eggs: black-headed gulls' eggs were delicious, and became a staple part of their diet.

And so they set out, with tent, rucksacks, cheap binoculars bought at a local pawnbroker, and a box camera. On later expeditions they took rope and climbing-irons, but though they were proud of these, they never became proficient in their use; Jim, however, was especially adept at swarming unaided up and down trees and cliff-faces, getting into precipitous situations, and sometimes into danger. In 1939 he had a serious fall on Great Orme, badly gashing his leg, but nevertheless bicycled into Llandudno with blood streaming to have it dressed in the hospital. On the same outing the boys earned a paragraph in the local newspaper. Great Orme drops almost sheer down to the sea below the lighthouse, and it is on ledges on this precipitous face that the gulls, razorbills and guillemots nest. They had climbed onto one of these ledges to look at the birds when a steamer came past close-in to the Head, on its weekend trip carrying holiday-makers from Liverpool to Anglesey. The boys waved frantically, as boys do, but the captain of the steamer took it to mean that they were in difficulties, and wheeled the steamer round to come back and investigate, much to their embarrassment. All they could do was stop waving, and in the end the steamer went away again.

Gerry Robinson got stuck on the St Bees cliffs in 1941, as recorded in Jim's diary. 'I return along the cliff to meet a chap with a long stick with a neck on the end for getting birds' eggs, he points with a mournful face and says "he's done for". I look and see G.K.R. stuck half-way down the cliff-face – darkness is gathering – I get a wire to try and help him up with, serious position!' But finally he managed to scramble up of his own accord.

Eric Hardy remembers Jim with appreciation as 'likeable', 'clean and well-spoken', 'a bit naive', on the whole a 'sensible, young lad', albeit capable of being 'a bit erratic at times'. Gerry Robinson was the steadier of the two. What he liked about Jim was that he knew his stuff, was potentially a professional zoologist, and was not sentimentally poetic about birds 'like many people today'. One can see these qualities in the diary which Jim kept of their outings. It is a down-to-earth record of their search for birds, and the events of the day, with not much in the way of picturesque descriptions of landscape or the birds themselves, but it is direct and readable.

The diary was probably started in 1940. Although the first entry in the list of contents is headed 'Great Orme's Head', and a space was left for this 1939 expedition, it was never written up. The title page is carefully and proudly set out: 'J.F. Stirling. G.K. Robinson', 'Bird-Watching Expedition', '1930-' – each entry well spaced from the others, and on the opposite page postage-stamp-size photographs of the two friends with their full names – 'Gerald Kirby Robinson' and 'Jammes [sic] Frazer Stirling'. The day-by-day record of each expedition is illustrated by postcards or the boys' own photographs, and followed by general notes under headings such as 'Eggs', 'Weather', 'Money', 'Food', 'Comment', and 'Remarks'. The spelling is erratic: 'supper' is always 'super', 'climbed' always 'climped', 'their' always 'there'.

Every now and then the war obtrudes. On 14 May they learn of the imminent fall of France from the farmer on whose land they are camping; at the end of this expedition Jim sums up that, 'At this time Britain was menaced by the threat of invasion. France was at the point of collapse, the evacuation of Dunkirk was in progress, all people are warned to stay at home, we would not have been surprised to have seen parachutists dropping out of the skies above Anglesey.' On the way to Denbighshire on 4 May 1941, 'Arrived at Woodside by boat at 3.35 – at back of que – entertained by spectacle of ballon at the dock going up, and for the rest of the time have to listen to cackling old housewives talking about there little evacuese.' Later on that day 'G.K.R. opens map in bus and we are regarded by almost all the occupants in suspicion'. On St Bees Head on 27 May 1941, 'guns start firing on Eskmeal point across the river, we witness a vivid display of bursting ack-ack shells, quite close, contemplate in taking cover'.

At St Bees Jim makes his only architectural comment. He finds the public school there occupying 'a very nice old building' but is more intrigued by the schoolboys: 'very amused by the specticle of full grown youths walking around in short trousers and light blue stockings, which proved to be the school uniform of the public school.' Occasionally landscape or atmosphere are briefly evoked. On the way to Puffin Island on 10 May 1940, 'Return to the point to look at the island in the gathering dusk – lighthouse bell ringing mournfully.' A longer extract, on Denbigh Moors in May 1941, gives the feel of the directness and at times vividness of the writing: 'get out of car and start walking up cartract [cart-track] road to Lyn-y-foel-fuch, the sky is a deep and dark colour, a storm is coming up, it is getting cold – see curlew running through grass to the left of the path, walk straight to the nest which contains three eggs – take them – see wheatears, notice agitated dunlin on the side of Lyn-Abd – cut of track over the moors to the pool guided by the calls of the gulls – flush a red grouse on the way – pitch camp on the north side of Lyn-y-foel-fuch – getting dark – corn beef for super – very cold cant get to sleep about 1300 feet above sea level – a red grouse flits around in the gathering darkness outside – the gulls call all through the night.'

In September 1939, when war seemed imminent, Quarry Bank School was evacuated to Wrexham. It was on Wrexham Station on 3 September, in the process of the move, that the boys heard that war had been declared at 11 o'clock that morning. They were then all taken to a cinema in the town when they were each given a bag of biscuits and a tin of condensed milk, and distributed in billets in and around the town. Jim and Gerry Robinson were sent to what the latter described in a postcard to his mother as a 'very nice lady' at Acton Park, on the outskirts of Wrexham. But she turned out not to be so nice, or at any rate did not get on with Jim, who felt frustrated and rebellious, and as a gesture took the light bulbs out of the sockets in their bedroom and threw them onto the road in front of the house, where they exploded. As Gerry Robinson put it, 'The lady didn't like that at all. We had to go.'

The pair were split up and sent to different houses. But in the quiet first months of the war – the 'Phony War' before the air-raids started, when nothing happened – the parents began to bring their children back to Liverpool, Jim among them. After Christmas a skeleton staff of masters came back too, and taught 50 boys or so in temporary accommodation. Later on in the year the whole school returned – just in time for the bombing, as it turned out, but the suburb where the school was was not much affected by this, and Quarry Bank remained in Liverpool for the rest of the war.

Jim left school at the end of the summer term of 1941. His father would have liked him to follow him as a Merchant Navy engineer, but, as Jim wrote in later life, 'I had no particular mechanical aptitude, nor – to his disappointment – any urge to go to sea. I think this may have been because I'd seen how long he was away from home, and how my mother was left alone.' He left school without educational qualifications. To get the School Certificate, the lower of the two public exams of those days, one had to pass in five obligatory subjects, and Jim, it seems, had passed only in Art and Handicrafts, which were not even amongst the obligatory five. In these he had passed with distinction, however, and R.F. Bailey, the headmaster, and Jack Simmonds, the art master, realised that he had talent, and thought of art or architecture as possible careers for him. It must have been through their efforts that Jim was accepted without qualifications at the Liverpool School of Art, which he entered in October 1941. However, he combined attending the School on day-release with working in an architect's office in Liverpool. Although the School may also have helped here, in later life Jim credited Bob Campbell with suggesting the idea: 'It was a cousin called Bob Campbell who saw some of my drawings and suggested I ought to become an architect . . . There was also, I think, a bit of Scottish puritanism in me, so that the idea of doing something practical appealed to me, rather than just being an artist.'

Jim's architectural beginnings were not glamorous. He found them so uninteresting, frustrating or even unpleasant that he censored out any reference to them in later accounts of this period of his life, where he only mentions the Liverpool School of Art. He worked in the one-roomed office of D.A. Beveridge, on the first floor of the Prudential Building, No. 36 Dale Street. Beveridge had had a moderate practice in the 1930s. His best-known building was Watson's Motor Show Room in Liverpool, stripped classical in style, but with a bit of zig-zag Art Deco ornament. He had entered various competitions, never with success, among them designs for an entrance to the Channel Tunnel, in the Egyptian style. The designs hung framed around the office. But in 1941 he had little work, and what he had was utilitarian. He was an elderly, humourless bachelor, who did not believe in spending money: he tore up all incoming envelopes and re-used them for drafting out letters or doing plans on; he was said to send the typewriter tapes to the cleaners. His staff consisted of 19-year-old Robin Bell, known as the senior draughtsman but in fact the only draughtsman, and 17-year-old Jim. Jim did little if any drawing.

13

Robin Bell drew out designs for adding women's lavatories to Liverpool factories, and Jim laboriously typed out the specifications.

There is no evidence that Jim had any great interest in architecture at this period, and if he had his job did nothing to encourage it. Even his work at the Art School does not seem especially to have engaged him. He made friends with Robin Bell, but what they explored together was neither architecture, nor art, but jazz, beer and girls. He was already into jazz, introduced to it by Gerry Robinson, who was an enthusiast for early jazz and had records of King Oliver, Louis Armstrong, and others; but beer and girls were new.

Robin Bell's family lived at West Kirby in the Wirral, and the Wirral was where Jim spent as much of his spare time as he could manage, in a circle that gradually extended to include George Hayes, Alec and Pat Parker, Tom Evans, the girls of the Carlisle and Dray families, and various extras and hangers-on.

George Hayes was the rollicking, hard-drinking but by no means stupid son of an Oldham architect who had a house at West Kirby. He was doing his first year at Liverpool School of Architecture, a curious experience in wartime, because 'we would arrive at Central Station from the underground railway to find trams upside down, Lewis's on fire, the sewers burst, total chaos. And we would go into the School of Architecture and they would carry on as if absolutely nothing had happened', and set him to work designing a church in the Romanesque style. At this time George's parents insisted that he have dancing lessons, and accordingly he went to Miss Bravington's Dancing School at the Blenheim Café, West Kirby. Encouraged by the fact that Miss Bravington's assistant was 'a most gorgeous blonde', he made a beeline for her, and danced with her. 'Afterwards, I was walking up the hill, because we lived at the top of Grange Hill, which overlooks the Mersey on one side and the Dee on the other, and a chap came up and said "I've been going to this jolly old dancing class for a few weeks, and I've not had an opportunity of dancing with that nice girl" . . . and anyway, we then started to talk about things in general, and I discovered that he was very interested in jazz music.'

The chap was Robin Bell, whose family house was a little further along Grange Hill. He told George Hayes of a friend whom he called the Bird-Watcher, who worked in the same office as he did and was also keen on jazz. This was Jim. He arranged for the three of them to meet up in Liverpool, to play Jim's records – not in Jim's house, because his parents were strict and would not stand for the noise, but in a place organised by a girl whom Jim knew, and who had a gramophone.

14

Over the next few years, the three young men joined the armed forces, were demobbed, studied, took jobs and changed them, moved around the country, but remained firm friends, three musketeers who met up and went around together whenever they could, on the Wirral and elsewhere. The trio was broken up when Robin Bell, who had left architecture for marine insurance, emigrated to Canada in 1947; he and Jim gradually lost touch, but Jim and George Hayes were good friends until Jim died.

The last of Jim's scribbled observations in his copy of *The Birds of the Liverpool Area* was made in January 1942: 'I saw a solitary fieldfare in the shrubbery at Abercromby Square after a heavy snow fall.' He was presumably in the square while attending the Art School or Student Union, which are nearby. He went on his last expedition with Gerry Robinson in May 1942, but never completed writing it up. Although he continued to notice birds all through his life, his days of serious bird-watching were over. Their legacy, he always claimed, was his visual memory and powers of observation, which were remarkable. His friendship with Gerry Robinson was a casualty of this loss of interest. Moreover, Gerry did not get on with Jim's Wirral friends. To George Hayes he seemed 'just the sort of chap you would expect who would go round looking at birds'; and to Gerry they seemed a bit of a jet-set, going in for all-night parties, and not at all his type. So the two young men drifted apart.

Jim arrived in the Wirral with the nickname of the Bird-Watcher, and it or its abbreviation, the BW, stuck to him for the next few years. It quickly acquired a double meaning, as Jim withdrew his interest from the gulls and cormorants on the Wirral rocks, beaches and marshes, and transferred it to another kind of bird inland. He was now tall, slim, athletic, good-looking and extremely attractive to girls and in George Hayes's nostalgic memories pretty girls feature as thicker on the ground in the Wirral than anywhere else he knew.

Among them were the Dray sisters, an apparently inexhaustible supply of whom lived opposite the Hydro Hotel in West Kirby: 'the elder girl would join the Services, go off in the Wrens or something, and then the next one would be there, and then we would go on to 1942, 1943, and then the next one would mature and Jim used to spend quite a lot of time at the Drays'.' Then there were Clarice and Molly Carlisle, living in a big Victorian house 'and the father used to hibernate in winter – literally! When it got to something like November, he used to take some crates of White Shield Worthington or whatever it was upstairs, and go to bed, and when we used to go round he used to holler down from the landing "What the hell's going on down there, you lot? Bloody well shut up", and that sort of thing. And there was a girl called Lynn, a long-haired blonde who looked like Veronica Lake, with whom Jim disappeared one night on the Royal Liverpool Golf Links' – but 'no one ever talked about sex in those days'.

Jim frequently came over to the Wirral for weekends, to stay with the Hayes or the Bells. The three friends had a regular evening routine: they started out with ten shillings each, went to the Ring of Bells, an old-fashioned pub at the old village centre of West Kirby 'with marvellous Burton Head Brewery beer', drank as much beer and bought as many cigarettes as they wanted, picked up some girls, and perhaps more friends, and went dancing at Hoylake, 'and somehow we would get home, and we always had some money left'.

Their Wirral circle expanded, and came to include more than pretty girls and noisy young men. They got to know Alec Parker, an insurance broker with an attractive ex-dancer wife called Pat, and Alec Parker's friend, Tommy Evans, who was the County Clerk of Staffordshire at that time, but often stayed with the Parkers. These two men were closer in age to their parents' generation, as were various other figures who appeared in the circle: 'a chap called Charley, who never spoke and had some ghastly job in the Town Hall; and there was another chap called the BFP – that was an abbreviation for the Big Fat Pig; he was a great sort of boasting type of individual . . . Robin used to bring along extraordinary characters – really with the intention, I suppose (because Robin was a great wit) of sharpening people off against each other.'

Alec Parker was lively, amusing and well-read, but the most interesting among these older friends was Tommy Evans. He was later to make a big impression on David Queensberry, the future Professor of Ceramics at the Royal College of Art in London, when Queensberry studied ceramics and industrial design at Stoke-on-Trent in the 1950s. He found Evans an outpost of civilisation in the Potteries; as he put it 'there were not many people in Stoke-on-Trent who had Wittgenstein on the table'. Evans was a good pianist who may have wanted to become a musician, but in the end qualified as a solicitor, and went into local government. Queensberry describes him as interested in literature, poetry and philosophy, disrespectful of conventional religion, apolitical, sad, cynical, with a savagely clear intellect – but 'he didn't want to persuade you'. As far as his northern life was concerned, he was a closet homosexual, but by the 1950s had a boyfriend in London, a ballet-dancer called Fred. At weekends he used to leave Stoke-on-Trent complete with bowler hat and umbrella and go down to London to unwind with Fred.

The two ultimately retired together to Hove, where they died within a few months of each other.

Jim had a sure instinct for quality and always liked the company of older men from whom he could learn whatever he wanted to learn at the time. He had learned from Eric Hardy, and now he learned from Tommy Evans. At this period of his life he started to read a good deal – Huxley, Proust, possibly Auden and Eliot, whom he was certainly reading in a few years' time. Robin Bell was a fan of Damon Runyon and Wodehouse, but Jim could never see the point of Wodehouse. Tommy Evans interested and impressed him, and so he talked to him, and he talked with his friends, but if he met people who did not interest him, or if he felt that he had nothing to say, he said nothing; on occasions this could make him seem rude. He never pretended to be knowledgeable about subjects about which he knew nothing, but whatever he did he wanted to do as well as possible. He was keen to extend his experience; Tommy Evans told him that he would not be satisfied until he had slept with the last girl in China. He never told funny stories, but had a laconic off-the-cuff wit which could be extremely funny. He could break out and be boisterously noisy, but much of the time he sat silently, absorbing impressions. There was a sense of latent power in him. So he already seemed to his friends, or so he seems in their memories of him, perhaps reading too much of the future back into the past. Even so, Jim was beginning to become formidable.

TWO

JIM IN THE ARMY

Jim enlisted into the army in November 1942. Both as an architect and a university student he was in a reserved occupation, secured against call-up, but he volunteered, as did many of his contemporaries in similar situations, George Hayes among them. One of the conditions of reserved-student status was that the student had to join the University Senior Training Corps or University Air Squadron, and Jim had joined the former. A mild whiff of egalitarianism had caused the Officer Training Corps to be renamed Senior Training Corps, but they were still a natural path to a commission. Jim was accepted as a recruit in the Black Watch and after preliminary training at Perth was at an Officer Cadet Training Unit at Mons Barracks by June 1943, when he features in a group photograph of No. 2 Platoon, A Company. He was commissioned into the Black Watch on 2 July, and moved to its barracks at Maryhill outside Glasgow.

At Perth he was a recruit at the Queen's Barracks. In the same barrack-room were Colin Rowe and Christopher Owtram (also known by his other Christian name of Dennis). Both had been at Liverpool School of Architecture and had volunteered at the end of their second and first years, respectively. Both were to go back to the School of Architecture and become friends of Jim. Colin Rowe, whose friendship was to become of especial importance to him, talked about these days after Jim's death.

'I first met him in the first week of December 1942. This was in a place called Queen's Barracks, Perth. It wasn't really in Queen's Barracks, but in a great big weaving shed in which we were obliged to sleep, which was about 700 feet long . . . And it was an inexplicable job to which Jim had been assigned. He was at the other end of the room from us. "We" were a guy called Bill Kidd, Dennis Owtram, and myself. Jim was at the other end, and he began each morning after breakfast sweeping up the floor of this appalling weaving shed. And by the end of the day, he would approach the area where we were hanging out. This was my first exposure to Jim. . . .

18

'And then of course we often used to go to dinner in the station hotel in Perth. It sounds grim but it's one of those elaborate hotels they have in Scotland. It had been built really for Queen Victoria to have breakfast in on the way to Balmoral, I think. And her breakfast service lined the walls and vitrines, etc. So we went to dinner there. Dinners were excellent. Everyone was supposed to be starving, but we had trout and salmon and venison and pheasant and everything that might be delicious and all very cheap. A charming old waiter opened up a special room for us with a Gothic sort of hammer beam roof and a huge fire. And he would say "Gentlemen, sit in here. Now it's nothing, sir, but you should see it in the summer, sir. Oh, it's lovely in the summer." . . .

'I see Jim again in Mount Pleasant, Liverpool. I imagine rather more than a year later. . . . The profusion and the jingle and jangle with which he was draped all over was quite something. It was sort of a military Christmas tree that one was looking at. There were epaulettes and the red beret and the sporran and the kilt and the dirk and all those funny things they have in Scotland. It was an extreme exhibition of an anthology of costume jewellery. Then of course there was the moustache, which was huge, intimidating, and spared neither, I suppose, the public sentiment nor private expense. And then Jim disappears from my vision for quite a time.'

Jim was indeed a dashing sight, as photographs of him taken at this time make clear: kilt or trews, a little skean dubh dagger, a present from his father, stuck into his stocking, and a natty moustache, first appearing in the OCTU photograph and more David-Niven-toothbrush in type than the huge one remembered by Colin Rowe. On leave in Liverpool he celebrated his commission with whoever of his friends were available. George Hayes remembers how they had started off with bottled beer at his house, and then went down to the pub as soon as it opened – 'and we were thrown out immediately, because Jim was pretty boisterous. And I thought, how extraordinary to be thrown out of a pub at opening time rather than closing time.'

Jim revelled in his Scottish blood, but any pride and triumph in winning a commission in one of the best Scottish regiments soon turned sour. Life in a conventional officers' mess proved to be everything that he most disliked; and possibly the officers' mess disliked him in return. He later described how 'I was appalled by the formality of regimental life in wartime. We had to dress up for dinner twice a week, and the Colonel would walk down the line of subalterns lifting our kilts with his crummack to make sure we weren't wearing underpants.' He hated the way in which the bagpipers played round the table at dinner and made conversation impossible. After a few months he obtained a secondment into the Parachute Regiment. The parachutists were looked on by the old-established regiments as buccaneers. Jim was more of a buccaneer than a Scottish officer and gentleman.

One bonus of his time at Maryhill Barracks was his first experience of the architecture of Charles Rennie Mackintosh, at Queen's Cross Church and Glasgow School of Art. He talked about it when he was up in Glasgow many years later: 'In the year before D-Day I was a 2nd Lieutenant in the barracks at Maryhill – with the Black Watch – and going backwards and forwards into the city centre by tram I became aware and I think obsessed by this funny building – the Church at Queen's Cross – so much so that I got off the tram and went all round it and inside, though I wasn't a churchgoer. The other thing in my memory from this period in the middle of the War was that we young lieutenants at Maryhill got asked by the Art School girls to the Saturday night hops in the School of Art and I remember several somewhat drunken parties up and down and around the staircase in the Art School and being fascinated by the building and getting to explore its nooks and crannies with the ladies who were somewhat adventurous with young officers on the eve of the second front.'

Jim had his preliminary training as a parachutist at Hardwick Hall in Derbyshire, quartered in a Nissen hut encampment down by the lake. The six-towered Hardwick-Hall-more-glass-than-wall looming at the top of the hill above the park remained vivid in his memory. He made his first drops at Ringway airport, outside Manchester. On one of them his parachute failed to open. As he dropped he saw the ambulances screaming out onto the runway, but by good luck the parachute caught in the guide ropes, and he was left suspended until rescue came.

By now George Hayes was going out with Barbara Bennett, whom he was soon to marry. She was an extremely pretty and vivacious girl, who came from the same area of Liverpool as the Stirlings, but did not know them. She met Jim for the first time early in 1944: 'George was in the Air Force when I met him so when he came home on leave he always organised parties, and I would see him, and then he would go back to the Air Force. He talked a lot about his three or four very close friends, and the only one I hadn't met was the person he called the Bird-Watcher. He used to talk about the Bird-Watcher very often, and then one day he rang me up and he said "I'm coming home for a weekend's leave, because the Bird-Watcher has finished his paratroop training, and he's got leave, and he's coming home, so my parents have invited you and the Bird-Watcher to come and stay for the weekend. We're having a big party on Saturday."

So I was quite looking forward to this, and on the day Jim arrived on the train and for once in my life I was speechless. This apparition got off the train, and he was wearing his uniform, and he wasn't wearing a kilt, he was wearing those tight plaid trews they wore in the Scottish regiments. He was very blond, very slim, very handsome, and I was just completely bowled over. I thought, George has never mentioned the fact that the Bird-Watcher looks like this. I had imagined someone grovelling around lying in bushes, which of course he used to do looking for birds.

'Anyway, we went back to George's house, and Jim was very, very lively at the party, and a great success with all the ladies there, as he always was. George's parents had a lovely garden, and the next day we were walking around the garden talking about this and that, and suddenly Jim veered off, and there was a sandstone wall about thirty feet high, and he rushed at this wall and ran up it like a fly. So it shows what state he was in. And I turned to George and said, "Why did he do that?" and George said, "Well, I suppose he must feel caged at the moment, because he's been training for weeks." And so of course he was incredibly fit. He was always charging around, and very exuberant. And very noisy really.'

Then Jim vanished for a few months. His mother, who was working in the Censorship Office in Liverpool, received regular letters from him, but inevitably they said nothing as to his whereabouts or plans. No one who knew him had very much doubt about what was brewing, however. D-Day came, and silence. A few days later a telegram arrived at Childwall Priory Road. Oonagh remembers how she waited in suspense as her parents opened it because 'you never knew whether it was injury, or missing, or killed'. It said that Jim had been injured in the D-Day landing, and was in hospital in England.

Jim had been in the section of paratroopers that were dropped behind the coast, to take and hold the bridge across the River Orne. He and his platoon were blasted early on, by a German armoured car. All but he and his sergeant were killed. He came to when he was half-way across the Channel, on his way back to England. He was shell-shocked, but appeared not to be seriously injured. He spent a short time in hospital, and on sick leave, and was then returned to his unit and to bloody fighting in the Caen bridgehead.

He wrote four poems at this period, the only poems that he is known to have written. The first is entitled 'Return to the Battlefront, 4th August, 1944'.

'Take off'.

The floor of the earth
Is dropping away,
The plain
Is empty now.
Its occupants are far away
But they will welcome us.

'Climbing for height'.

Higher and higher
Piercing the clouds.
We catch a last glimpse
Of green fields where we played,
But we shall play again,
More deadly.

'Crossing the Channel'.

Some of us smoke,
Some of us stare,
All are thinking,
All are silent.
Some of us shall see the moon tonight.
Some of us shall not.

'Crossing the Normandy Beaches'.

The yellow sands are pock-marked here,
Diseased and scarred,
And everything is dead and still.
Man's greatest hopes, effort, sacrifice succeeded here
Where men screamed.

The second is entitled 'Amfreville, 10th August, 1944. Written under intense mortar bombardment'. Oddly enough, considering the circumstances, it is more literary than the first one.

Stay with me God, this night is dark,
The night is cold, my little spark

Of courage dies. The night is long,
Be with me God and make me strong.

Help me oh God when death is near
To mock the haggard face of fear,
That when I fall – if fall I must,
My soul may triumph in the dust.

The third and fourth poems were tributes to the 6th Airborne Division in the Ardennes salient, written by Jim in January 1945, when he was back in England. Some time in August, while he and his men were clearing a building of Germans, and were on the ground floor, a machine gunner on the floor above had fired through the floor and hit him in the left hand and shoulder, disabling him. His active service was finished. Once again he was returned to England, this time to long weeks in various hospitals, followed by over a year's hanging around, until he was finally released from the army in April 1946, with a small disability pension which was paid to him up till his death. The pension was for 'disablement of 20% arising from gunshot wound left wrist with median nerve palsy'. One finger was badly paralysed for a time and never fully recovered. To begin with he had to be helped to dress. Moreover, when he was recovering from his injured hand, he started to get pains in his chest when he coughed, breathed hard or ran. It turned out that when he had been blown up the first time, a rib had been blown into one lung, and adhered to it. He had to be operated on to put this right. It was a sizeable operation, and it took him a good deal of time to recover.

Jim was proud to have taken part in the D-Day landing, but talked very little about his army experiences and his few days of active service. He told Eric Hardy that in one period of fighting he passed a dead German officer with a good Leica camera hanging around his neck. He went back and removed the camera. He told his friends Sandy Wilson and Paul Manousso that he had killed a man at close quarters, and found it deeply distressing. In January 1951 he sent a formal statement to Professor Budden, the head of the Liverpool School of Architecture, declaring that he had 'no intention of taking part in any future war, nor service relating to war'. Apart from Colin Rowe and Christopher Owtram, whom he met again at Liverpool, he kept no friends from his army years.

The tedious business of recovery from his injuries ended with a spell at Harewood House in Yorkshire, which during the war served as a convalescent home for officers. Robert Adam's magnificent state rooms were filled with rows of beds. The Earl of Harewood and his wife, the Princess Royal, still lived in one end of the house, and used to visit the wards. Jim liked to relate how, when lying flat on his back in the sumptuous Gallery at Harewood, 'I made the decision to become an architect. An education officer walked in and said I was going to be invalided out, and as my education had been interrupted by the War (I had been a student at Liverpool School of Art), I could receive a university education at the government's expense but I had to commit to what I was going to study within two hours. So, I looked up at the Robert Adam ceiling and thought about medicine, and law, and decided to become an architect – and I went to study at Liverpool University.'

Jim simplified the story, to improve it. The idea of becoming an architect was certainly not new to him: his mentors at Quarry Bank had suggested it, Bob Campbell had suggested it, his best friend was an architect, and he had already worked in an architect's office, however unenthusiastically. But no doubt Harewood played its part, and certainly Adam's polychromatic fireworks were more exciting than D.A. Beveridge's factory lavatories. At any rate, the decision was taken, and Jim was given a place at Liverpool. His year at the School of Art was accepted as a first year, and he was allowed to qualify as an architect after four years, instead of the usual five.

He was not in fact released from the army until April 1946. Some of this time he spent at the Parachute Depot, in Albany Barracks at Newport on the Isle of Wight. He seems to have been doing little more than marking time until he went to architecture school in September. He went to Liverpool a good deal, and met up with his old Wirral friends whenever possible. They all had a bit more money, and could splash out on occasions with dinner and dancing at the State Restaurant in Liverpool. George Hayes had celebrated his 21st birthday there on 4 March 1944, 'and everyone got absolutely stinking drunk, and on the train back to the Wirral, people got off to be terribly ill in one of the static water tanks that were supplied for the firemen during the Blitz, and then got back on the train, and it finished up so that almost the entire party were not on the train that they set off from, but arrived on the next train, or the next but one, leaving lost shoes and God knows what.' Jim's own 21st birthday took place on 22 April 1945, in the last dramatic months of the war with Germany, and eight days before Hitler shot himself. His parents for once relaxed their strictness, and went out for the evening, leaving the house free for a noisy party.

A few months before this George and Barbara had become engaged. George was 21 and Barbara 19. The engagement caused a temporary rift between the two friends, not at all because Jim disliked Barbara, but because he disapproved of early marriages. Barbara remembers how, at the party which they gave to celebrate their engagement, 'Jim sat in a terrible sulk, and a day or two later he asked if he could see me on my own. He told me what his objections were – he said "You are far too inexperienced." So I said "Well, what kind of experience does one need?", so he said, 'Well, it's just ridiculous – you have hardly been out with anyone else; you are very young. What about George's career? I think he'll be a very good architect. My intention is that I am going to finish my time at university, and then I'm going to travel, and become as good an architect as I can. If George ties himself down, perhaps has children, he won't be able to do any of that. He'll have to buckle down to it, and he won't be able to travel, and he won't be able to do the things I intend to do." He said, "I am going to marry when I am either 39 or 40", which seemed to me quite ridiculous. I said Thirty-nine or 40! Nobody will have you then. You'll be too old and decrepit." Well, of course, this is the way a 19-year-old thinks. So Jim said, "Well, I think it's absolute nonsense." So I said, "Well, George and I have been friends for some time. We want to get married. Of course I know you have a lot of girlfriends, mostly older than yourself. You disapprove of me, but I disapprove of you", and I mentioned the fact that I knew he was having an affair with a married woman. Well, Jim hit the roof at this, and he said, "How do you know? Nobody knows about this", and I said, "Well, you say I'm inexperienced, but at least I've got woman's intuition." So he said "This is absolutely frightful": it was a very closely guarded secret, and if people found out it would cause terrible trouble. So I said, "Well, I'm sorry about that", and he said, "Will you promise not to tell anybody?" and I said, "Well, of course. I suppose I shouldn't have mentioned it, but it is rather horrid to just sit being criticised", and of course Jim was only 20, you have to remember, and so anyway, it caused this terrible rift between us, and for about a year I didn't see him. During that year we got married, but my mother sent him an invitation to the wedding, and he didn't even reply, so I think George was a bit upset about that.'

The violence of Jim's reaction must have been conditioned by his own situation. His affair with a married woman was a serious one. According to his own account, given years later, he was very much in love with her. She was the wife of a friend. His desire to marry her and to face up to the divorce and scandal which this would entail competed with his driving ambition for his career, which he thought would be destroyed by an early marriage. His career won. George was doing what he had decided not to do. His affair continued, however, and led to pregnancy and an

THREE

JIM AT ARCHITECTURE SCHOOL

Brian Richards vividly remembers the eruption of the ex-servicemen among the students at Liverpool School of Architecture in September 1946, when he himself was a callow boy not far from his schooldays, at the beginning of his second year. 'The door was kicked open, and the toughies came in. They were still in uniform. They didn't behave like students at all. They wanted to qualify. They weren't going to muck about, and they worked like hell.'

In schools all over Britain the ex-service students knew what they wanted. They were going to build a new Britain, both literally and metaphorically. The same overwhelming idealism which had carried the Labour Party into office in the July election, largely on the service vote, filled them with the conviction that the Modern Movement was the only way by which architecture could escape from the past, and move into a new and better future.

This is how Jim saw it, when looking back a few years later, in notes written in the 1950s:

'Back to 1946 – end of a war is always start of something. The cities were bombed and devastated. From now on, everything could only be better. We assumed that from here on everything would be built as Modern Architecture. In the Schools of this time, the rightness of modern as against past styles was not even debated; the overpowering logic of modern architecture was completely accepted, and the pioneering stage was over.'

Perhaps the situation at Liverpool was not quite as simple as this. In the first place, 'Modern Architecture' was itself complex and at times contradictory; its message was not as simple as it seemed. In the second place, as Jim was to recognise in later years, he and his contemporaries were influenced, perhaps more than they recognised at the time, by the Beaux-Arts-inspired teaching of the School.

By 1946 the Modern Movement had thirty years of history behind it. It had developed different inflexions and rival masters, and could

inspire people for different reasons. For those who were socially committed it suggested a way of building which, by means of mass-production
and prefabrication, would make possible the schools, public housing and
hospitals that were the priority in the new Britain. They believed in planning. The hero of this group, if it had one, was Walter Gropius, with his
long history of commitment to public-sector architecture and rational
building in Germany in the 1920s and in America in the 1940s. But they
were not addicted to heroes, seeing architecture – as did Gropius himself
– as the product of teams working together with no place for the individual genius.

For the technically-inclined the Modern Movement was exciting
because it had produced structures in the great engineering tradition,
exquisitely assembled in steel and glass or boldly constructed in
reinforced concrete, with no superficial language of ornament to confuse
the clear expression of the structure. Their hero was Mies van der Rohe,
partly because of the great glass towers which he had designed, but never
built, in Germany in the 1930s, but even more because of the cool
controlled rectangles of steel, brick and glass which he was beginning to
produce in America.

But new technologies had suggested new forms of composition. As a
result of the development of curtain walling – which meant that the
external skin need no longer be load-bearing – and of huge spans and can-
tilevers made possible by reinforced concrete or steel beams, buildings
could seem to float instead of rising securely from the ground, and external openings instead of being placed one above another in the traditional
manner could be arranged at will, according to the convenience of the
plan or the visual preferences of the designer. The formal potentialities of
this were brilliantly exploited by some architects, to produce an abstract
architecture of solids and voids closely related to the abstract painting and
sculpture of the same period. The results were so far removed from the
conventional ideas of what buildings should look like that they were
found shocking and repellent by the majority, but intensely exciting by
the minority. The dominant figure – partly owing to his own genius,
partly to his tireless exposition of his work in books and articles – was Le
Corbusier.

It is an oversimplification to put these different groups and
approaches into water-tight compartments. There was, for instance, a
strong formal element in the architecture of Mies van der Rohe, and the
Modern Movement produced no more dazzling example of abstract
design than his Barcelona Pavilion. Le Corbusier was interested both in
town planning and mass-production, and his visual pyrotechnics always

derived creatively from the plan and function of his buildings, and were never purely wilful. Even so, he was not entirely trusted by the socially committed wing of the Modern Movement.

It remained a Movement, however, with a common language and common assumptions which overrode the differences. Certain axioms were taken for granted. Any imitation of past styles, or use of the ornamental language associated with them, was taboo. The form and treatment of a building should derive immediately from its function, without references to the past (the possibility that one of its functions might be to refer to the past was never considered). Ornament of any kind was suspect; it was a way of concealing absence of thought. Even architects whose buildings were carefully contrived for aesthetic reasons tended to talk or write as though the design of their buildings derived in some kind of inevitable way from their functions.

The chucking overboard of ornament and all the luggage of the past gave an exhilarating sense of release to those who had thrown them out. They were going to march unencumbered into a new dawn. They were converts who had found a new religion. Any suggestion that the Modern Movement was just another new style of building was anathema. They were escaping from style. They had discovered not one way of building, but the right way of building.

In the 1940s this idealism was now to be channelled into schools of architecture where the Faculties, in so far as they accepted the Modern Movement at all, saw it as just another new style or styles. By and large this was the position at Liverpool. Like most schools of architecture at the time it was heavily influenced by the Ecole des Beaux Arts in Paris. The Beaux Arts, which was the post-Revolutionary descendant of Louis XIV's Académie d'Architecture, had a long tradition behind it, and a formidable reputation. Essentially, it was concerned with an approach to design rather than commitment to one particular style. Its dominant concern was with 'composition'. Buildings had to cohere as three-dimensional entities, with plan, section and elevation all working logically together. The function of the building and its various parts had to be clearly expressed. They had to be designed in an ordered sequence: analysis of the site and brief; the conception of what was called the 'parti', a basic idea which gave unity to the design; and the working out of this in detail. They had, of course, to be well constructed, but the structure did not have to be revealed. The sense of clarity and order which Beaux-Arts architects tried to achieve was one of logical arrangement rather than clear structural expression. In any Beaux-Arts building you could be sure where the entrance was, and you would not lose your way. The tool used to produce clarity was one of symmetrical organisation along two axes, each acting as a major line of communication, set at right angles to each other. Architects showed their skill in fitting the functional needs of a building into this format in a sensible and logical way.

Once the basic concept and arrangement had been settled, an appropriate, ornamental treatment had to be decided on. Beaux-Arts architects had no *a priori* commitment to classicism, but because of the eighteenth-century roots of the Ecole, and the sense of order which its practitioners found in the classical style, classicism was for long the dominant language used by its architects. As a result, for most people Beaux-Arts architecture implied grand classical buildings symmetrical in plan and elevation. And since the Modern Movement had rejected the historic styles and distrusted symmetry, Beaux-Arts became a dirty word among its disciples, even though many Modern Movement architects were in fact strongly influenced by Beaux-Arts methods of composition and planning.

The Liverpool School of Architecture had been founded in a small way in 1894, but essentially it was the creation of Sir Charles Reilly, who was at its head from 1904 until 1933. He started with twelve part-time students, and turned it into one of the two leading schools of architecture, only rivalled by the Architectural Association in London. He had been an articled pupil himself, but believed in architectural education, and was a pioneer in establishing it as the superior alternative to articled pupillage.

He ran the school on Beaux-Arts lines but with an American accent. Liverpool was known in those days as 'the gateway to America', and its commercial and cultural links with America were strong: the great banks, company headquarters and insurance buildings built there between the wars were in the same competent and sumptuous classicism as was being practised in America by the architects who trained at the Beaux-Arts in Paris. Reilly established links with American firms like Carrere and Hastings (for whom he got the commission to design Devonshire House in London in 1924), and through his connections he was able to place his brighter students in American offices for five or six months' experience in their fourth year.

Reilly was an eclectic architect, who worked in various styles, but he was by no means hostile to the Modern Movement. His earlier buildings were beautiful exercises in neo-Greek. The Gilmour Hall at the Students' Union is an example. But in 1934 he had been associated with three of his former pupils in the design of Peter Jones's store in London, the first example of steel-and-glass curtain walling in England. More often he and his partner and associate in the School, Lionel Budden, preferred the kind of gentle modernism that was becoming acceptable in England in the 1930s, as an alternative to classicism: what was described at the time in phrases such as 'a successful application of modern idiom to a public building conceived in the classical manner' (metal windows in openings of vertical Georgian proportion) or 'an expressive functionalism while retaining the essential qualities of classical architecture' (the same metal windows put on their sides, or run in long strips along the façade). Their extension to the Students' Union was in the first manner, their School of Architecture building in the second.

By the time Jim arrived at the School, it was being run by Budden, in the tradition of Reilly, but with none of his panache. Eclecticism was the rule. Students learnt about the Modern Movement as one of a variety of possibilities, not as the final answer. Each year they were taken a little further along the four paths of construction (and materials), services, history (and theory), and design. Design started off with analysis of the programme, and ended with decisions on architectural decoration, which meant style. Students in their first and second years were set to design in the classical, Romanesque or arts-and-crafts styles. In their later years they could demonstrate that they were up-to-date by doing designs in the style of Perret, Gropius, Mendelsohn or Le Corbusier.

But though *Towards a New Architecture* was on the reading list, Le Corbusier was regarded with suspicion by the members of the Faculty. The abstract composition of his elevations, the *piloti* on which his buildings floated, ran foul of their notions of design. Students who embarked on Corbusian projects were liable to run into trouble. The types of modernism with which the Faculty felt happy involved buildings resting securely on the ground and openings placed with regularity one above the other. They could accept, and rather liked, the strip windows and semi-circular bays associated with 1930s German Expressionism. They felt at home with a new arrival, Swedish Modernism – the New Empiricism, as it was called at the time. Sweden, as a neutral country, had gone on building when the rest of Europe stopped, and its commitment to state schools and public housing seemed to make it a model for post-war socialism in England. But Swedish Modernism was much gentler than the German variety. It made much use of traditional materials; roofs could be pitched, windows were relatively small; it had a fondness for balconies and little porches. 'Cosiness is coming back', as the *Architectural Review* put it in 1948. The angry young men in the School did not take to cosiness.

Whatever the style employed, as in all Beaux-Arts schools presentation was all-important. Designs were first sketched on white detail paper and then drawn out on heavy Whatman or Kent papers, stretched for smoothness, coloured up with watercolour washes, and made three-dimensional with carefully-graded shadows. 'Sciagraphy', the science of shadows, was one of the subjects taught in the first year, along with lettering and perspective, the latter in great detail and variety.

The School was not run on the atelier system of the Beaux-Arts in Paris, where students attached themselves to one 'master' for the whole of their studies. At Liverpool each year had a separate year-master. But there were other features of Beaux-Arts origin. Every fortnight the students picked up a building programme in the morning and had to produce sketch designs on the basis of it by the evening. This was fun to do, and derived directly from the Beaux-Arts system of the *esquisse*. Also from the Beaux-Arts came the relationship between the years. It was a close one. The senior students criticised the work of the juniors. The juniors helped the seniors with their projects, especially with the fifth-year thesis which was the culmination of School work. In Paris the juniors added the colour washes and the shadows to the thesis drawings; the word used for this was *négrifier*. In Liverpool to do the same kind of work was to 'nigger'. To ask a junior student if he would nigger for one was considered a high compliment.

The School was in the odd position of having an enemy within the gates. A Polish School of Architecture had been founded in 1942, to train Poles in exile in England, so that they would be ready and waiting to build a new Poland after the war. It was given hospitality by Budden, and occupied one of the studios in the Liverpool School of Architecture. Its staff were all committed Modernists. They went their own way, and had little formal connection with teaching in the School. The Faculty treated them with courtesy and correctness, as guests and victims of the war, but were nervous about them. The brighter students got to know them, and were intrigued and influenced by them. They were beautiful draughtsmen, in styles quite different from those favoured by the School. A minimalist precision of thin black lines on white paper, without shadows, for instance, derived from Le Corbusier. They left Liverpool not long after Jim arrived there in 1946, but he bought the book published in that year to commemorate their Liverpool stay, and was influenced by their work.

But Jim later admitted the influence that the teaching of the School had had on him. His very first experience at Liverpool could be seen as a symbol of this. All freshmen had to undergo the traditional initiation or baiting from their seniors in the Gilmour Hall of the Students' Union. Jim's took place in 1941, in his first Liverpool year at the School of Art.

32

In 1983 a freshman of the same year, Bernard Wilson, wrote to Jim recalling how 'when I was called on to appear before them and respond to certain questions put to me, another fellow Fresher by the name of "James Stirling" turned to me and called out in a loud voice, to the effect that I should take no damn notice of their barmy questions – the attention of the students then turned to our Jim where they demanded for him to take off his shirt for his impudence and embrace a cold fluted stone column, which Jim did, much to his obvious discomfort. Now, would this Jim be your good self? Can you recall the incident?' Jim replied, 'Yes, I do recall that at an early age I embraced the orders.'

The anecdote is of interest less for itself than for Jim's laconic response to Wilson's letter. The order which he embraced was a classical column designed by Reilly. By the 1980s he was increasingly aware of himself as 'a product of later-day Beaux-Arts training'. As early as 1965 he had been able to write tolerantly about Budden's reaction to 'the furious debate' over Modern Architecture. He was 'a liberal without opinion in regard to the great argument. He believed that quality, whether neo-Georgian, modern etc. was all that mattered – an attitude that was maybe an asset to the School at that time.' In 1980 he wrote, 'I suspect I have always been an eclectic designer, and I now realise that with my background it could hardly have been otherwise.' Perhaps Jim exaggerated the influence of his schooling in the 1980s, just as he was over-dismissive of it in the 1950s. Even so, through the openings of the committed Corbusian façade which Jim presented to the world as a student and young architect, one can sometimes see unexpected things going on.

The School in Jim's time was dominated by ex-service students both male and female, although the latter were very much in a minority. They were older and more mature than the others. Some of them had suffered in the war. Lionel Budden treated their problems with sympathy, and was in general much liked. The atmosphere of the School was serious, and not especially noisy or high-spirited. Many of the students were married, some with children, lived in digs, and came in for crits or lectures. All the students tended to end up in digs, but single students could live in Halls of Residence some way from the School: University Hall at Wavertree for women, Derby House, on Mossley Hill near Sefton Park, for men. Derby House modelled itself on an Oxford or Cambridge college and the students had to wear gowns for dinner; Douglas Stephen, later to become a close friend of Jim's and a good architect, was expelled from it for writing 'fuck' in green peas (or, according to another version, in mashed potatoes) on the refectory table.

Liverpool was a good city to be in, still sufficiently prosperous, safe to walk in, full of fine buildings and handsome Georgian houses, even if in parts damaged in the war, with first-rate music and theatre, and excellent oyster-bars and Chinese restaurants. It did not feel provincial. The students tended to work in the evenings or at night, and spend the days shopping, having coffee or going to the movies. When the lights went up in the cinema they would look up and see the whole of their year in the auditorium.

Jim lived at home, in Childwall Priory Road, for the entire period he was at the School, except possibly for short periods in the rooms of friends. He was not good at looking after himself, and expected to be looked after. His few attempts at cooking were not successful. His sister Oonagh came in one evening with her boyfriend George Palin to find a note left by him on the hall table. 'Sorry about the mess in the kitchen. Had a slight accident.' He had put an unopened unpierced tin of baked beans in a saucepan of water to heat up. It had exploded. Fortunately 'he was half-way down the stairs when it went off with a bang. It would have killed him, probably, if he had been in the kitchen. When we went into the kitchen there was a saucepan, warped and torn, on the draining board . . . he did say he'd cleared it up as much as he could, but there were baked beans hanging from under shelves, under plates, and there was one cupboard door that was just slightly open and they had actually gone round the edge of the door, and were on the cakes and things. That was something we've never forgotten. You can't imagine how beans can cling to the underside of things. Did I take it well? Well, I suppose I was a bit mad at the time, but there wasn't a lot I could do about it, except clear it up. I think Jim took me a lot for granted.' But this was what sisters expected of their elder brothers in those days.

When Jim started at the School, he was still wearing uniform, complete with red beret and gleaming Sam Brown belt. He had never liked formal clothes, from the days when his father, each time he returned from a sea voyage, would march him off to Montagu Burton and buy him a suit. Jim told George Hayes that he hated these suits and refused to wear them. At Liverpool he soon relaxed with relief into the informal dress in which he was to remain, in one form or the other, until the end of his life. But he was not especially distinctive in dress at this period. He wore the tweed jacket, pullover, tie and flannel or cord trousers common to all students at the time. He became scruffy, and rather dirty. Anne Kerr, who was in his year, still has vivid memories of his long dirty fingernails. He took her out to a meal a few times, but 'I wouldn't have taken him home to meet my parents'. In his first year at the School he was still having his affair, but later he seems to have had no steady girlfriend, and no particular reputation as a womaniser.

He had made friends again with the Hayes, and saw a lot of them. George Hayes's father was in poor health, and George had had to leave the Liverpool School of Architecture, help him with his architectural practice in Oldham, and attend part-time at Manchester School of Art. He and Barbara bought a house in Oldham. Jim came to stay a good deal, and when George was away, in Manchester or at his father's office, he and Barbara 'were left for long periods on our own, and I suddenly saw a completely different side of him. I'd always thought of him as rampaging round – you know, drinking, girlfriends, and talking about architecture – and when he was with me he suddenly appeared very domesticated. By this time I'd started having babies. I had two very quickly, and Jim used to help me with the children, come out for walks in the park, help me with the shopping – George would never have done that – George was rather Edwardian about women's place, you see. I was at home doing all these things, and Jim was very helpful. I'm sure it wasn't just because I was his hostess, because he never ever covered his feelings. I could hardly believe this, and the strange thing about it was, perhaps we would have had lunch together, and we would be sitting having our coffee, and he would be chatting to me about the latest gossip amongst all his friends, and who was going out with who, and that sort of thing, and George would walk into the house, and immediately Jim would stop that, and talk about architecture. So I began to realise that although Jim seemed so hard, one day he would make a very good father.'

But by now talking about architecture, reading about architecture, seeing architecture, thinking about architecture, dominated Jim's life. George Hayes describes how, in his second or third year, Jim came over to Manchester, and 'brought over a suitcase which was almost full of books . . . we got a bus up to Hollingwood, and decided to go into a public house for a drink. It was a real working-class Lancashire public house – clogs, cloth caps, shawls, and Jim started to talk to the people, show them the books, and talk about the brave new world that was going to be built. People were buying us drinks – and his genuine enthusiasm . . . I mean, he wasn't just shooting a line, it wasn't like that . . . he started off by opening the suitcase and showing me something, people started to take an interest, and eventually there was a great crowd round . . . and then the pub closed, we missed the last bus, and had to lug this wretched suitcase the rest of the way – it was quite a long way, all uphill.'

Jim used to meet George in Liverpool, have lunch with him in an oyster-bar off Williamson Square, and then go round the bookshops, buying with what he could spare from his student's grant. Books were important to him. He wrote about them, as far as they concerned architecture, when he looked back on his student days from the 1950s:

'Modern architecture was to become the norm, the backcloth against which we could build; and if one was ultimately a better architect than the norm, it would be a matter of quality. But to be a better student you had to know more; the development of one's own ideas could, as with experience, come later. In the process of knowing more we pored through the pages of Corb's Oeuvre Complète, our designs were eclectic, a necessary stage to the formation of a personal style. The books of Corbusier were thus utilised as catalogues, as had been previously the books of Alberti and Palladio in the Renaissance. Thus one's first acquaintance with Corb's buildings, and also the work of Gropius and Mies and the other masters was through the medium of the printed page. The formative process was an intellectual one. The masterpiece buildings were on the continent, and not easily accessible on the limited money of a service grant. With the exception of buildings by Lubetkin, there were few others in this country which could be visited, and therefore assimilated emotionally.'

The books which he bought in this period and which survive in his library give some idea of his range. The identifiable ones are all hardbacks; paperbacks have disappeared or are not identifiable. In Liverpool he bought at Charles Wilson in Renshaw Street and the Medici Gallery in Broad Street. He also ordered books from Zwemmer's in London, and bought a good deal in New York when he was sent over there in his fourth year. His purchases formed the nucleus of what was to grow into a large and comprehensive architectural library. But Jim was not just buying books on architecture. He bought the collected poems of Auden and Eliot, Cyril Connolly's *Condemned Playground* and *Unquiet Grave*, Hesketh Pearson's *Oscar Wilde*, Denton Welch's *Maiden Voyage*, Henry Miller's *Cosmological Eye* and *This Life This Death* (1945), and poems by a forgotten young writer, Thomas Rahilley Hodgson. A copy of Sacheverell Sitwell's *Splendour and Miseries* is inscribed 'Jim from Betty, '45'. He bought Herbert Read's *Meaning of Art*, and sizeable illustrated books on Paul Klee, Max Ernst and Salvador Dali. He went carefully through the book on Max Ernst (*Cahiers d'Art*, Paris, 1937) and translated all the German picture titles. Now and later Jim had a somewhat unexpected interest in Surrealism, suggesting an appreciation of bizarre and unexpected combinations that went a little oddly with the rational functionalism professed by the Modern Movement.

Not surprisingly, books on or related to architecture form the largest section. They include books by Giedion, Mumford, and on or by Frank Lloyd Wright; Pevsner's *Pioneers of Modern Design*; the inevitable Banister Fletcher; Jiro Harada's *Lessons of Japanese Architecture*; Alberto Sartoris's *Encyclopédie de l'Architecture Nouvelle* (Milan, 1948); Alfred Roth's *New Architecture*; a book on Michelangelo in the French series *Collection des Maîtres* (with pencil notes by Jim on the meaning of 'terribilità'); and finally Le Corbusier's *When the Cathedrals were White* and the first four volumes of his *Oeuvre Complète*. Sartoris's book was an exhaustive anthology of Modern Movement buildings, and was much pored over by Jim. He valued it so much that he had it bound in white fur. This was a bizarre material for a Modern Movement binding, as if Jim the Surrealist was at work.

In 1948 Jim provided a correspondent with a list of 'books which influenced me most when I was a student at architecture school'. 'All of the following', he wrote, 'were of equal importance to me – but if I had to give an order of priority they might be as follows.' He then lists Saxl and Wittkower's *British Art and the Mediterranean* (1948); Le Corbusier's *Towards a New Architecture*; A.E. Richardson's *Monumental Classic Architecture in Britain and Ireland* (1914); Sartoris's *Architecture Nouvelle*; volumes 1 and 2 of Corbusier's *Oeuvre Complète*; *Gunnar Asplund Arkitekt* (Stockholm, 1943); and Roth's *New Architecture*. Not all these books feature in the previous list, and Jim may have read them in library copies.

Jim's interest in Le Corbusier dated from the beginning of his time in the School, and became increasingly important, but never exclusive. His earliest known architectural reaction of any significance is to the buildings of Bath. He was down there on a School outing in the summer of 1947, probably taken there by W.A. Eden, who was on the Faculty, and was later to become Chief Architect of the GLC's Historic Buildings section and to restore, with exemplary scholarship, Thomas Archer's St John's Smith Square as a concert hall. He was a committed classicist, and thought the Modern Movement an aberration. Jim's friend Bob Maxwell remembers him in Liverpool days as a 'thorough going Albertian and a Christian gentleman'. He took an annual trip of students to the south, to make measured drawings of selected buildings during the day, and drink generously in the evening: 'Eden didn't seem to mind; his theory was that you were learning even when just drinking and talking.'

Jim sent an enthusiastic postcard from Bath to Robin Bell and Alec Parker in Montreal:

'We are down here making measured drawings of some of the buildings. This is the most beautiful city I've ever seen. The scale of these

37

classical buildings is magnificent – smaller than I expected, intimate and human, they literally draw you in, makes one realise how big and incongruous such a thing as St George's Hall is. Colour too is marvellous, hot browns and buffs and the Regency light blues and reds. Modern architecture can learn a lot here. . . . Going over to Paris at the end of the month.'

Jim was later to describe how 'somewhere in the middle years at Architecture School, I had a passion for the stiff art nouveau designs like Mackintosh and Hoffmann, a little less so for their English equivalents like Voysey and Baillie Scott. This was supplanted towards the final years by Le Corbusier and the Italian rationalists such as Terragni and Cataneo.' Jim also remembered that at the end of his Liverpool time he started to look at and photograph Liverpool warehouses. It may have been at the same time that he became alive to the interest of Peter Ellis's two extraordinary 'pioneer-modern' office buildings in Liverpool, Oriel Chambers and No. 16 Cook Street, which were to influence his work in the mid-1950s. He had known of them for some years, for as a student at Liverpool School of Art in 1941 he had firewatched from Oriel Chambers. George Hayes also remembers how, just before or just after he qualified, he was driving with George in the Wigan area and saw 'I think it was a colliery – it was one of those marvellous conglomerations of industrial buildings, with gantries that crashed down, things going up – it was industrial architecture at its very best, and he stopped and took some photographs of it, and raved about it.'

For a few years Jim had a great admiration for Frank Lloyd Wright – an architect in whom he lost interest in later years. His interest almost certainly came from one of the most curious and remarkable of his fellow students, Christopher, or Dennis, Owtram. After a first year in the School of Architecture, Owtram had been with Colin Rowe and Jim as a Black Watch recruit at Perth, but has no memory of Jim at this period. He had disliked the Black Watch even more than Jim had, and was never commissioned. By the time he returned to Liverpool he was as neurotic as he was brilliant. His sympathetic memories of Lionel Budden have an autobiographical flavour. 'I think he had an understanding of those who had been to the War and had come back crippled. All of us bore scars, and some of us were almost hiding for our life.' He had long discussions with Jim, but barely communicated with most of the students. He would arrive at the School in a taxi, keep the taxi ticking over while he pinned up his drawings and placed his models, and go away again. He did brilliant designs, organic in style and deeply influenced by Frank Lloyd Wright. The students were fascinated by them, the Faculty disliked them.

Anne Kerr vividly remembers him: 'He was such a weirdo . . . I honestly wouldn't think he ever exchanged a word with anybody . . . Did I ever speak to him myself? . . . I think I tried, but it's no good trying to speak to someone who doesn't reply, is it really?'

Jim's closest friend for most of his time at Liverpool was Fred Thomas, a good draughtsman and a fellow fan of Le Corbusier. He was lively company and they got on well together because they teased and amused each other. Jim lost touch with both him and Owtram in later life. More important to him in the long run were others in the group who shared his interest in Le Corbusier, who became friends in his last year or two and with whom he was to associate in London: Colin Rowe, Douglas Stephen, Margaret and Bob Maxwell and Alan Cordingley. With the exception of Cordingley they were to form the nucleus of Jim's circle of friends for the rest of his life.

All these people went off to the army and came back again at different times, with results that are exasperatingly difficult to work out, and not especially important. The figure round whom the whole group pivoted was not Jim but Colin Rowe. Rowe had spent three years at Liverpool School of Architecture before joining up at the same time as Jim in 1942. He badly injured his back while training, was invalided out, and returned to the School of Architecture in 1944. After he qualified, he went to the Warburg Institute in London to study under Rudolf Wittkower, but returned to Liverpool in 1948 as a member of the staff, lecturing on the history of architecture. He had been a committed Modernist from the beginning, or almost the beginning, of his time at Liverpool. He was a brilliant lecturer, and a person of great charisma. Christopher Owtram describes him, in his Liverpool days, as 'a very magnetic figure, dashing, suave, very aristocratic in his ways'. As he lectured, Palladio, Michelangelo, and Italian Mannerism came alive to students, and above all were made to seem relevant to contemporary architecture: they were excited by his analysis of the mannerist elements in Le Corbusier and the mathematical or conceptual similarities between his work and that of Palladio. He suggested to them a mathematical and historical base to modern architecture that could carry it beyond functionalism. His own later assessment of the group and his position in it is convincing:

> I think it is without doubt that a certain number of students at Liverpool during the late Forties and very early Fifties did feel themselves to be, in some quite important way, avant garde; and I believe that I myself probably did have something to do with

39

crystallising this position. For this group of people sociological interests were at a minimum and Scandinavian meant virtually nothing. Nor was there the slightest level of tolerance for anything connected with townscapes.

There was indeed a strong contrast between the Liverpool and London students. The Liverpool students were design-obsessed and relatively apolitical. The students at the Architectural Association in the same period (or the livelier ones) were political, left-wing, committed to social service, schools and public housing, and at once shocked and fascinated by what they considered the formalism of their Liverpool contemporaries, when their work was exhibited at the Architectural Association early in the 1950s. They preferred Gropius to Le Corbusier. As John Miller remembers, 'we were highly moralistic and puritanical about what we produced, and there were these half-dozen projects all of which were very different to each other and using techniques which we repudiated completely – obsessive, rather excessive, rather florid drawings. We were rather jealous of them, nevertheless'.

In July 1948 Jim was one of three Liverpool students selected to go to New York and the United States, under the arrangement initiated by Reilly and continued under Budden. The other two were Fred Thomas and a student referred to as 'Ken'. Jim and Fred Thomas were to work for the New York firm of O'Connor and Kilham.

Although Jim was never political, at this time of his life he was, if anything, mildly left-wing, anti-American, and, in reaction, pro-Russian. This may have been due to the influence of Fred Thomas, whom Jim described as a Communist. Barbara Hayes remembers how (for reasons typical of Jim, that you should try everything once) he went with them and some of his fellow-students to the first post-war Grand National in 1949. 'There were masses of Americans there, and Jim was grumbling about "all these flashy Americans throwing their money around" . . . "Well, Jim," I said, "there's a horse running called Russian Hero . . . my goodness, if that wins the Americans will be furious."' Jim and Barbara (both broke at the time) put a joint five shillings on the horse, and won £50, which they blew on a dinner for the whole party at the Adelphi Hotel. Mrs Stirling, on hearing of the win, said 'Thank goodness for that, Jim will be able to pay his debts.' She was horrified when told how the money had gone, and George Hayes commented 'Let that be a lesson to you. Easy money never does anyone any good.'

This was just after Jim went to America, but a long letter which he wrote to Robin Bell and the Parkers six weeks or so after he had arrived suggests that his attitude had not changed all that much. It starts with a brief description of the crossing. 'We (Fred – a communist, Ken – queer, and myself) left Southampton on 28th July on the *Marine Jumper* – part bride, part-emigrant, part-student and part-tourist, comprising of about fifteen nationalities, about equal numbers of each, it was a most odd seven days! – completely immoral, so much happened, I'll tell you about it when I see you.'

On arrival 'Ken disappeared on the landing stage, haven't seen him since – we work for different architects.' Jim and Fred Thomas went to rooms in International House, a hostel for students at 500 Riverside Drive, not far from Columbia University. Harlem was 'our main drinking area', but 'I'm disappointed with the jazz joints – commercialised'. Jim had a room looking out over the West River, with Grant's Tomb, a Beaux-Arts version of the Mausoleum of Halicarnassos, in the near foreground. 'We . . . are the only Englishmen here . . . we serve afternoon tea in our rooms . . . There is an extremely nice atmosphere, not a bit like most student establishments.'

'You ask me what I think of N.Y.,' Jim asks, and then launches on a several-thousand-word tirade against the ghastliness of New York, in almost all its aspects. It is a scorching blast from Jim as angry young man, frustrated and lonely in his West River room, failing to make American girls and being cut out by Wasp boys, shaking his fist and his volume of Le Corbusier at the ghastly commercial city, letting off steam, and enjoying himself in doing so. It is not to be taken too seriously. He had been in New York for about six weeks when he wrote it, and had three months or more to go. Three months later he would have written differently, if he had time to write at all.

'This is a shocking egotistical, badly written letter,' he ends by admitting. Shocking and egotistical perhaps, but not badly written. In later life he complained that he found writing difficult, virtually stopped producing articles, and confined himself to office correspondence as brief as he could make it, to postcards or to the telephone. He became a master of laconic brevity. His New York letter shows that at this stage of his life he could produce vivid writing of a different nature – even if he still could not spell. What follows is about two-thirds of the letter, with the spelling corrected.

> You ask me what I think of N.Y. – it is so difficult to generalise
> – and I am repeatedly told not to judge America by New York
> – however I suppose one meets the best and the worst here, as
> in London.

The biggest surprise (or was it) – we began to suspect it on the ship, is the character and morals of the American. In England one judges Americans by Hollywood films, and the behaviour of the G.I.s during the War – from those two sources one receives the impression that Americans are essentially – happy go lucky – slap you on the back, rowdy, never serious, somewhat immoral – In actual fact I find that quite the opposite is the truth – they are deadly serious, frightfully hard-working, sober and moral to the point of perversion.

Leaving England, I said – thank God to get-away to bright lights and happy faces for a change – The people are even more miserable here than they are in England – though I think the city of N.Y. is more than partly responsible for this.

According to Hollywood, magazines, advertisements etc. – the American female appears luscious, lewd, and lusty – in fact – they are disgustingly priggish and as hard as nails! – I find this rather odd when I consider to what pains women go to make themselves attractive to the opposite sex – they paint and scent themselves, bare their legs, exaggerate their organs; and yet most important of all – femininity – they have completely lost (at least here in N.Y.) queer thing is that American males, completely agree with me on this point! – however, I fully approve of their figures, I think – physically they are very attractive – one rarely sees a woman with a bad figure, – but what is woman without a soul, one might just as well go to bed with a bathtub . . .

One cannot talk to a stranger, conversation is impossible without first being introduced – and the rigmarole of introduction! – they shake your hand, ask you out to dinner, write your name down on a piece of paper (throw it away as soon as you've gone) – Americans make many superficial (significant) friends, Englishmen a few lifelong friends – but such formality – and such conformity – here the man with an idea seems to have become an invidious reflection upon his many fellows who have none. Be unorthodox and be an outcast. Such a minor thing as my moustache causes panic wherever I go – long lines of giggling girls follow me about the street.

Along with their new-found wealth, has come a new set of 'Victorian' morals – and if it's like this in New York, God knows what it's like in the smaller towns and cities.

American culture, one can hardly dismiss it with a sentence –

(or can one?) – we have attempted, and I think succeeded in cultivating a fairly representative cross-section of New York. – 'Intellectuals' (all Americans who have been to college consider themselves 'intellectuals') – I find are completely superficial in their approach, – the knowledge (of which some have a considerable amount) is almost completely confined to literature and music – ignorance of the visual arts. They read the 'right' books as regularly as they eat their daily oranges, listen to 'good' music as regularly as they brush their teeth. But it's the ulterior attitudes which I find so sick-making – to be 'cultured' is to have a 'something more' – to be sought out as a reference when applying for a job – here 'culture' is conceived as a commercial expedient, or degraded to the level of a sentimental appliance business.

What is the reason for this frightful obsession that Americans have for their stomach, always making sure they are eating sufficient calories, getting the correct vitamins – Considering that they are the fattest and best-fed nation in the world – I find this nauseating – however, not only do the American humans over-eat, so do the animals – for instance, New Y. pigeons are shockingly overfed, their indulgence hangs about them in double chins, bleary eyes and dreadful paunches – they fly, it's true, but they make it look like hard labour. If you sit down in Central Park, pigeons join you, expecting an invitation to lunch or tea; they go through your pockets very carefully, and then when dreamy langour or indigestion calls a halt to their thieving, they lean against you and go to sleep – However, I can forgive the pigeons anything when I think of the squirrels. These animals are the delight of the English countryside – rare, charming fellows whose timidity and thrift make them universally popular, but here in N.Y. the squirrel is a rapacious, uncouth and prodigal exhibitionist. If you pause in your walk to read a paper, – they leap at your legs – bound away in a somersault – they work their way inside your trousers, and they climb on your back and try to read over your shoulder.

New York City – is a ghastly monstrosity. The wasteland, a harsh haphazard up-ended mass crowding in on the bewildered eye peering up from the shadows below. The shadow the sky-scraper casts is more significant than all beside, ancient shadow on the wall – sliding, edging, nicking and crowding – tier upon tier a soulless shelf – box on box beside boxes – black shadows below with artificial lights burning all day long in little caverns and squared cells – prison cubicles! Down in the dark shadows cast by this distortion of force lurks the human soul – out of scale! In other words complete inhumanity – (the exact opposite of Bath) – What of the skyscraper – that stupendous adventure in the business of space-making for rent – after six days one accepts, indeed, has forgotten about it – after all, it's only the first three floors which are important; one is never further enough away to take more in – but what about the top half – row upon row of cottage windows. The solid masonry book architecture – relentless commercial engine – architecturally the skyscraper is a nonsense. They really ought to get rid of either people or motor cars in this city – preferably people.

I was surprised by the amount of contemporary work in N.Y. – mainly shop and store interiors, architecturally Modern 'has arrived' – but what a mess they are making of it. Why is it Americans always do the right thing in the wrong way? My first reaction was 'Christ! If this is modern I am giving it up'. However, when one looks beneath the skin one realises it is not; here there is none of the philosophising and fanaticism which has motivated the 'new aesthete' in Europe; here only is constipated breath – yet another style – here today, gone tomorrow. I have only just realised that 'design' has become in America a vicious weapon in the hands of industrialists and businessmen; by deliberately stylising an object they date it, so that the dollar defied public to remain in the 'set' must always be in the fashion – constantly re-buying. No manufacturer would produce a really good design for fear that his future models would not be bought. As a consequence, nothing is beautiful nor would anything of lasting beauty be constructed under this system. Of course I knew of this before I came here – particularly as applied to American cars, but I had no idea that it was so completely all-embracing – everything, from the largest building to the smallest cigarette lighter.

'I must break off this tirade; you must think that there is nothing about America that I like,' Jim then understandably remarks. 'In actual fact quite a lot.' But much of what he likes he qualifies. He likes 'the systems whereby responsibility is given to men at a much earlier age'. He likes the clients 'who say "Modern of course, all the latest, you know", which gives you a free hand', but how frustrating to see so many meaningless buildings resulting. Then 'window display and fashion design generally has reached a very high standard', but 'it's logical that it should considering that it is concerned basically with the novel, superficial and ever-changing'. American men dress very sensibly. 'I desperately wore my tweed jacket for the first fortnight but had to give it up, finally with the recent warm weather I abandoned my tie and became completely Americanised.' Then 'Steel engineering is extremely fine. George Washington [bridge] is superb, so also are some of the road ways.' Above all, 'a fortnight ago we spent a weekend in a Frank L. Wright house on Long Island – it was really magnificent, the finest building I have ever been in (you can't see a FLW building you must be in). I have never felt such emotion before, it's really beyond description, it was worth coming to America for this style experience.'

There is a striking difference in tone, though not a straight contradiction, between the pasting which Jim gives New York in the letter, and his comment many years later. 'I recall my amazement, coming from Europe soon after the War, on seeing the bright chrome buildings and spotless pavements of New York. People forget how clean and bright and shiny New York was back then.' But between these memories, recalled in the 1980s, and the 1949 visit, were many subsequent visits, in the course of which New York became one of the cities in which Jim felt at home; and, above all perhaps, the discovery of New York and America in the circle in which Jim moved in London in the mid-1950s. In later life he took some pleasure in claiming that 'I was the first of several in that group to visit America in that post-War period', and that he had thus contributed to the 'considerable fascination with American popular culture' in his circle. The claim was correct enough in terms of dates, but it can be doubted if his American visit had much to do with the birth of London Pop Art in the 1950s. To judge from his letter, what John McHale and others were to discover and enthuse about a few years later was just what Jim, in 1948, disliked.

Initially, at any rate, he saw New York conditioned by the views of his hero Le Corbusier. In his *When the Cathedrals were White*, which was published in English just in time for Jim to buy it before going to America, Le Corbusier was ecstatic about the George Washington Bridge: . . . 'the most beautiful bridge in the world. Made of cables and steel beams, it gleams in the sky like a reversed arch. It is blessed. It is the only seat of grace in the disordered city . . . When your car moves up the ramp the two towers rise so high that it brings you happiness; their structure is so pure, so resolute, so regular that here, finally, steel architecture seems to laugh.'

Jim's contrasted pair – American engineering, good; American skyscrapers, bad – echoes the contrasting illustrations in *Towards a New Architecture*, and its aphorism 'Let us listen to the counsels of American engineers. But let us beware of American architects.'

Jim travelled out of New York to see other buildings, mostly mainstream Modern Movement, or by Frank Lloyd Wright: Howe and Lescaze's Philadelphia Savings Fund Society Building in Philadelphia; Wright's Suntop House at Ardmore; houses by Gropius, Breuer, Stubbins, Koch and Gropius's associates in The Architects' Collaborative (TAC) in and around Boston; Aalto's Baker Dormitory Building at MIT (which he did not like). He went to Princeton University to stay with a family whose Anglophile tastes he found absurd: 'to wear English clothes, talk with an English intonation, to have English connections, is the apex of all Princetonians'. The University buildings were 'sham sham Oxfordian Gothic'. He was in Princeton to work for O'Connor and Kilham on, as he later put it, 'a neo-Gothic library. My contribution, I'm glad to say, was simply the book-shelving system.' O'Connor and Kilham (formerly Morris and O'Connor) was a respectable Beaux-Arts firm somewhat in decline since the death of Morris. It contributed little to Jim except *Architectural Forum*'s 1948 special issue on Frank Lloyd Wright, which he borrowed from its library and did not return.

But by the time Jim left America, he had moved from his blanket dismissal of the New York skyscrapers. Colin Rowe remembers him on his return 'raving about largeness of scale and Fifth Avenue around Central Park and Eldorado Towers and the Palisades from Riverside Drive and the George Washington Bridge, and in that day, which is surprising, also the Chrysler Bulding.' The Chrysler Building is a masterpiece of Art Deco, and Art Deco, as the last style to rely heavily on ornament, was not considered respectable by the Modern Movement.

Towards the end of the year, Jim made the last of several visits to Montreal to visit the Parkers and Robin Bell. He went skiing, for the first of only two times in his life, on the slopes of the mountain behind the city, and was photographed by Robin Bell looking far from happy, the moment before he fell over. Early in the New Year he returned to England on an empty mid-winter sailing of the *Queen Elizabeth*.

Jim may have stored the Chrysler and other New York buildings in his omnivorous memory for future use, but there is no evidence that they had an effect on his design work in his last years at the School. One American product, however, he put to immediate use. He had discovered Zipatone, the ingenious American way for reducing the labour of drawing by attaching thin films marked with different shadings to the paper. It was still barely known in England. Jim introduced it to Liverpool. A postcard from George Hayes to Robin Bell, sent on 16 January 1950, reads, in red-ink capitals of varying size: 'ZIPATONE, ZIPATONE, ZIPATONE ZIPATONE – ZIPATONE. SEND THE NOS. BW WANTS TO ME!'

Armed with Zipatone, Jim returned to the Corbusian course that was to culminate in his final-year thesis, and his qualifying with distinction. In the summer vacation of 1950 he saw his first Le Corbusier building. He went with Fred Thomas to France, and visited the Pavillon Suisse in Paris. He sent Robin Bell postcards, from Paris between 10 and 19 July (the postmark is defaced) and from Avignon on 22 July. The Paris postcard ('a marvellous city') is of the Place de la Concorde, the Avignon one of the Bridge, and reads 'arrived en route through Alps and four days on the Riviera. Avignon is an entirely beautiful mediaeval town, there is a tolerable music festival taking place, going to listen to Mozart in the Palace garden . . . how about writing all the scandal?' He found the Pavillon Suisse 'disappointing'. In 1954, when he saw it again and was still disappointed, 'I found [it] again all too easy . . . at this stage Corb had obviously reached an end of a phase, as there is little real innovation. . . . This Corb (unfortunately) has had more influence on the English than any other.' But apart from this one visit to the Pavillon Suisse, and what he saw in America, Jim remained mainly reliant on books, slides and photographs for his knowledge of contemporary buildings.

In his remaining time at Liverpool, Jim's relations with Colin Rowe became much closer. It was almost certainly due to him that he became interested in the Italian rationalists Terragni and Cataneo, and immersed himself in Saxl and Wittkower's huge and splendid volume *British Art and the Mediterranean*. It was perhaps due to Rowe, too, that he read, or looked at, Albert Richardson's *Monumental Classical Architecture in Great Britain and Ireland*, and the Swedish monograph on Gunnar Asplund. He was becoming increasingly interested in the formal ideas behind Renaissance and later classical buildings as a basis for contemporary architecture.

In his last year Jim started a friendship with Robert Maxwell, which was to last to the end of his life. Bob Maxwell was an Ulsterman, who had come to the Liverpool School of Architecture in 1940. He had spent his first year under W.A. Eden, designing 'a monastery in ancient Ireland', 'a Greek propylaeum', 'a German baroque garden pavilion', and so on. In his second year he had been converted to modernism by Colin Rowe, and had upset his tutors by designing white abstract buildings in the manner of Corbusier. In his third year, he went over to Mendelsohnian

Expressionism. This was a success with the Faculty. He then departed for a spell in the Indian Army. He returned to Liverpool to do his thesis, had a disastrous year when he could not settle down, but returned to do a successful thesis project for a Warburg-Courtauld Institute on a site opposite the British Museum. Rudolph Wittkower, who had been Rowe's tutor at the Warburg, acted as an excellent 'client' for this.

Christopher Owtram remembers Maxwell as an 'enfant terrible', whose skill as a draughtsman was greatly admired by the other students. 'He was a great perspectivist ... and he would draw freehand, and nobody had seen anybody drawing freehand ... and we would see him fouling up a marvellous drawing with washes of colour, throwing on coffee and ... you know, everything, and somehow it could come off. We'd never seen anything so uninhibited. The Beaux-Arts school make their washes and presentation so clean; they're so nice, so controlled ... nothing ever goes wrong.' Besides being a great perspectivist, he was a great talker, bubbling over with ideas and theories about architecture.

Jim was in his fifth year by the time Bob Maxwell got to know him, and he himself had moved from the main School to do a postgraduate year at the Department of Civic Design, then being run by William Holford. He remembers Jim in those days as looking 'tough and very masculine but not coarse – with a certain refinement of his eyes – a very interesting person'. He was monosyllabic, and a jazz fiend. Jim seems to have left home for lodgings for at least part of his last year. Bob Maxwell visited him frequently. They used to meet up with George Hayes and Maxwell would play jazz on the piano (as he still does today). He was impressed by the determination with which Jim stuck to Le Corbusier, with no encouragement from his tutors, and flattered when Jim asked him if he would 'nigger' for him by doing the perspectives for his thesis.

The subject of the thesis was 'A New Town centre, including a community centre'. Maxwell and others helped Jim with the drawings, but the design was very much his own. It was impressively integrated, and had a sure sense of scale; Owtram called it a 'modern Versailles'. The community centre combined Mies and Le Corbusier in a way never to be repeated by Jim: a variety of functions and two courtyards enclosed in a simple rectangular block, in the manner of Mies, raised up on Corbusian piloti and with roof-top buildings in the manner of the Unité at Marseilles. However unenthusiastic the Faculty were about Le Corbusier, they could not deny the quality of the thesis, and on the strength of it Jim qualified with distinction in the summer of 1950.

The still slim young architect who left Liverpool to go to London in 1950 had an assured confidence, many strengths and some limitations.

He had acquired ideas from a creative thinker, in the person of Colin Rowe, and high standards of draughtsmanship and a methodical approach to design from the teaching tradition of the School. Ideas and methods remained with him throughout his career. Drawings, both as an aid to design and a way of explaining it, were to be of the greatest importance to him, far more so than models, and this reflected the Liverpool tradition. His knowledge of Modern Architecture came mostly from the printed page. He had never worked, or perhaps even been, on a building site, and had little knowledge of or interest in the way in which buildings were constructed or put together; he always had difficulty in passing the Structure papers in his exams. The concept of architecture as a social service did not mean much to him. Rather, he was caught up by the idea of a Modernism based on intellectual discipline with roots in the Renaissance, and of an architecture of striking forms, arranged with formal clarity but creatively derived from an analysis and understanding of the brief.

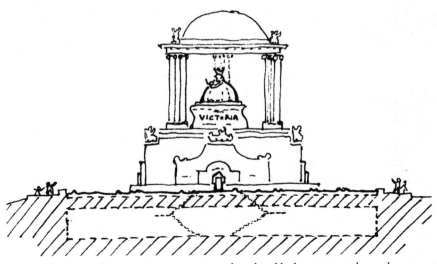

The statue of Queen Victoria in Liverpool, with public lavatories underneath.
A later drawing by Jim

He proudly proclaimed himself a Modernist, but with his sensitive eye and eager interest he had looked at or learnt about buildings of a variety of dates, styles and types. He repudiated the approach of his teachers that Modern Architecture was just another style or styles; but perhaps he was more influenced than he realised by Professor Budden's belief that in the end quality not style was all that mattered.

FOUR

LONDON IN THE 50s

The London to which Jim came at the end of 1950 was huge, dingy and dilapidated. Meat, butter and sweets were still rationed. New building was strictly controlled; iron and steel were rationed. Swathes of London had been flattened by bombing, and were still wastelands of flowering weeds and shattered walls. There were gaps in the streets everywhere, and the buildings between the gaps were down-at-heel. People looked dingy, too. No one had much money – or so it seemed. Few people had telephones or cars, no one had television. Foreign travel was difficult, even for those who had the means, because it was forbidden to take more than £50 out of the country. In clothes, in food, in restaurants, there was not much choice and little sense of style.

But there was hope and anticipation in the air. War was over, a new Britain was being built. Rationing was on the way out: rationing of clothes had ended the year before, of milk and petrol earlier in the year. Regulations limiting private-sector building were to be scrapped in 1954, and all remaining rationing ended in the same year. At the beginning of the 1950s, there was very little building in the private sector, but there were jobs for architects and engineers working, often with great social commitment, in or for the London County Council, local authorities, and ministries, on schools and housing. New building at the universities and polytechnics was just starting, and those with foresight could see an abundance of work on the way. With the lifting of restrictions the private sector was limbering up to build. All over London in the 1950s interlocking interacting circles of young people, still studying, looking for work or just starting work, with no money but plenty of hope and ideas, were meeting, talking, drinking coffee in the new coffee bars, drinking in pubs if they could afford it, talking and arguing as they drank, meeting at each other's houses, going to parties, giving parties, going to cinemas and jazz clubs, organising exhibitions, entering competitions, going to lectures and discussion groups, plotting, arguing, laughing, gossiping, making love, changing boyfriends and stealing each other's girls. 'London was full of people gathering in this way,' Mary Banham remembers, 'swapping notions and deciding how to change the world. It was the time when we were meeting people who were going to be our friends for life.'

The Banhams' flat in Oppidans Road, off Primrose Hill, was the centre of one of the intersecting circles. Peter Reyner Banham, born in 1922, had worked in the engine division of the Bristol Aircraft Company as a young man, had been stage manager, poet and local journalist in his native Norwich after the war, and then gone to the Courtauld Institute, where he graduated in 1952. He was a big man with, by the beginning of the 1960s, a big black beard, riding around London on a bicycle with wheels which seemed smaller than his beard. He was in the process of becoming a brilliant expounder, historian and journalist, smashing into Platonic concepts of stability, inherent order and proportion with arguments for built-in obsolescence and praise of popular culture and the 'throw-away economy' of American cars, 'vehicles of palpably fulfilled desire'. In and after 1952 he combined writing for the *Architectural Review* with working for the PhD thesis which was to develop into his book *Theory and Design in the Machine Age*.

He had married Mary Mullett in 1946. They had one small daughter and very little money. 'One of the things which we did regularly was to meet at our house on Sunday morning, because, well – it was somewhere for everybody to go on Sunday who didn't really know what to do with themselves, and it was a marvellous talking shop. Peter always loved to ask people to get together – I think he had the idea of a salon rather romantically in his mind. We could hardly do that – and we were housebound because we already had one child, so everybody came to us. We had a nice big room in one of those Victorian houses.'

The Banhams offered coffee, and little else, because that was all they could afford. Their Sunday mornings became a regular event, and any friend was welcome. The mornings started with two or three people looking in, and snowballed. The people who came were a mixture of architects, artists and art historians. The regulars lived locally, others dropped in from time to time. Bob and Margaret Maxwell, and Alan Colquhoun, lived down the road. So did the sculptor William Turnbull and his Austrian wife Cathy Wolpe, who was a pianist. Colin St John (known to his friends as Sandy) Wilson lived next door.

Wilson realised that the Banhams 'were involved in architecture, because booming farewell discussions took place on their doorstep, during which the names "Corb" and "Mies" floated up through my bedsit window. One night, when Peter Carter and I ran out of India ink while drawing up our project for the Coventry Cathedral competition, I thought I might touch my neighbours for a replacement bottle. No luck with the ink, but a most genial friendship began.' In those days, he had a motor-cycle, wore black leather 'with silver clips and things on it', as Bob Maxwell remembers, and 'his kitchen was painted black, which we all agreed was a bit mournful – he went as far as to change it to gloss black from matt black'. But under the black leather lurked a bishop's son, the future architect of the British Library, and a very serious person. He was working on housing in the LCC Architects' Department, and was interested in contemporary art. At the Banham coffee mornings he met Muriel Lavender, one of Peter Banham's young Courtauld students, and married her in 1954.

The dominant features of the Banham Sunday mornings were the big coffee-pot and the big pile of magazines. These were mainly architectural magazines, English, American and European, which Peter Banham brought back from the *Architectural Review*. 'Most of us would sit on the floor . . . you'd pour some coffee, and then we would look at the magazines . . . before we could even do two pages, someone would start something and say "Ah, look at this . . . oh my goodness! So and so's article . . . how can they?" Or "Look at this picture" or whatever. And so then we started to argue about it . . . everybody had an opinion. OK, it wasn't a "salon", it was a very relaxed, informal, comfortable place, and people could come in and go out and come late or come early.'

These are the memories of the painter Magda Cordell, a Sunday morning regular, and, when she was there, always the most decorative person in the room. In those days of little money or opportunity the men were wearing jerseys and shapeless grey flannels, the women 'anything that we could get hold of' (Mary Banham again). 'It was long before the stylishness of the 1960s. None of us had a penny piece. The person who changed all that around was Magda. She burst on the London scene like a bombshell – the most elegant woman I've ever met. She was Hungarian-Jewish. She lost her parents, then escaped with her sister to an arranged marriage in Israel. Then they were more or less on their own. They were seventeen and eighteen. Frank Cordell was the director and conductor of the RAF orchestra, and met her in Cairo where she was running a beauty parlour or something like that, and fell, ton of bricks. She was gorgeous. He brought her home with no papers, you know, across Europe – it's a novel, and it should be written. He took her to his parents in the outer suburbs somewhere, in the stockbroker belt, and – I don't know the details, but married her in order to give her some validity. But she always had this amazing elegance because she was brought up with lots of money. I think her father was in charge of all the grain business in Hungary, so they were very well off, and she went to finishing school. Then this happened. But she retained all that style. It was her that really made us think about the way we looked. And then it began to change. We made things, you see. We would somehow get hold of materials and make things as elegantly as we could.'

Magda Cordell did not need to make things. Her husband was writing music for films, and they had a little more money than the others. She could feed up her hungry friends at dinners cooked by her in her flat in Cleveland Square. She bought clothes from Jacinet in George Street, one of the few shops of quality in London of those days. Her slimness and dazzling elegance were in odd contrast to the swirling earth-mother torsos which she painted. In the early 1950s she made a threesome with Frank Cordell and the Scottish painter John McHale, both Banham habitués. Later it became a twosome when she and McHale emigrated to America in 1962 and married there. McHale had been on a previous trip to America, in 1955, as a visiting fellow at Yale, ostensibly to study colour values and the use of industrial materials under Josef Albers. In fact he got fascinated by American popular culture, searched out diners and Howard Johnsons as though they were Byzantine churches, and returned with a suitcase full of glossy American magazines, which circulated among his friends, and were cut up by him and them to make collages.

Among less frequent visitors to the Banhams, because they lived further away, were Richard and Terry Hamilton, and Peter and Alison Smithson. Richard Hamilton also came alive to American pop culture in the mid-1950s; his *Homage à Chrysler Corp* and above all his *Just what is it that makes today's homes so different, so appealing* (the latter drawing heavily on McHale's magazines) are the products of the group best remembered today. His long thin face and long thin nose stick in people's memory. Terry, his wife, was very pretty, and very bright. At meetings, if she did not like what was being said, she would stand up and go through the motion of pulling a lavatory chain. At one lecture or meeting someone on the platform 'looked down, and there, in the second row, were what looked like a couple of little animals moving about. They were Terry Hamilton's feet, in three or four pairs of Richard's socks, because she didn't even have decent shoes to wear.' She, Mary Banham and Magda Cordell were firm friends. On the whole, the women in the group were, as Mary Banham puts it, 'highly aware, and exceptionally strong personalities'. Even so, the men 'tended to be patronising'.

There was no question about the strength of Alison Smithson's personality, and it was impossible to patronise her. It is hard today, since their later careers as architects never fulfilled their promise, to envisage the position held by Peter and Alison Smithson in the 1950s. In their own estimation, and that of a good many others, they were the leaders. Eduardo Paolozzi, their friend and collaborator, burst into a meeting with them one day, announcing, 'Right! Make way for THE architects!' They were the only architects in the group who had built their own buildings. As early as 1949, when they were aged 26 and 23, they had won the competition to build a school at Hunstanton in Norfolk. The resulting building aroused strong feelings of dislike or enthusiasm, but no one could deny its impact. It was an exercise in exposed steel construction in the manner of Mies van der Rohe, the first in this country. Steel was combined with brickwork, exposed inside as well as out. Brick and steel, and very little else, were used together with ruthless simplicity and extreme precision and elegance.

In the actual construction of the few buildings which they built, the Smithsons proved themselves competent and practical. But their competence was accompanied by a flood of words and ideas, of manifestos, articles and lectures. As one of the group put it, 'they used to whizz from one thing to another': Japanese art was the only art that mattered; Greek art was the only art that mattered; northerners were the only people who mattered (the Smithsons came from the North). They invented the term 'the New Brutalism' to describe the movement which they saw themselves as leading.

Quite what 'the New Brutalism' was, or who it applied to, never became entirely clear, in spite of Banham's tireless efforts to explain and promulgate it. But it was a phrase which caught people's imagination, in America as well as England. Moreover, Peter Smithson's nickname was Brutus: the definition 'Brutalism equals Brutus plus Alison' may have been a good joke thought up by someone in America, but the Smithsons were not allergic to being so firmly put at the head of a movement.

Peter Smithson tempered considerable intellectual arrogance with a streak of dry humour. He had an endearing trick, when thinking, of unconsciously stroking his stomach with one hand and his bald patch with the other. Alison had no endearing tricks. She was opinionated, outrageous, convinced of her own and her husband's importance, by no means without humour, yet in some fields quite humourless. But as Mary Banham puts it, she 'had a touch of genius, there's no doubt about it. People would be worrying over a great problem in some scheme, and then one morning Alison would walk in and put her finger on it. I was terribly fond of her. I miss her terribly. And yet she was terribly difficult to get on with.'

Alison's clothes became famous in her circle. She made them herself.

Magda Cordell greatly admired them, although they were the opposite of her own style. 'She was a Mary Quant before Mary Quant even thought she was Mary Quant. She predated Mary Quant face make-up. She produced herself, and had the most incredible stuff on you ever can imagine. It was wonderful, because she could carry it off.' 'Nobody', remembers Mary Banham, 'would miss a party that Alison was going to, because they all wanted to see what she was wearing. She wore the most extraordinary things at that time. She had knitted herself a kind of green gnome suit, like a babygrow, with a hood, and she looked absolutely extraordinary in it, because she was always a slightly weird shape, and she would add to it for each party; it would have red bobbles on it, or something.'

Evelyn Hogge, one of Peter Banham's Courtauld students, was at the marriage of Sandy Wilson and Muriel Lavender, at St Peter's Vere Street, off Oxford Street, in 1955. 'Alison and Peter turned up in an open Jeep, and she was wearing what could only be described as an upturned chamberpot in mustard-coloured long-haired felt, and a sort of flowing gown. My children loved her because she used to come and visit us at Christmas in the country, and she always wore an extraordinary outfit every time she came. She was very good value for the children. But we all thought she was absolutely marvellous, she never paid the slightest attention, she was an extremely clever needlewoman, she made it all herself. She could create things. I think people thought that they were funny, you know, but they would never say anything. She turned up to me with a long dress in Black Watch tartan, with a sort of padded mermaid's tail floating behind her, and my children thought it was marvellous. Or else silver spacesuits, or – always extraordinary garments she wore, with great panache, I must say.'

Almost everyone who came to the Banham coffee mornings, including the Banhams themselves, were involved in one way or another with the Institute of Contemporary Arts – even if they only frequented its bar. The ICA had been founded in 1946, but the idea had already been proposed before the war by Roland Penrose, Herbert Read and Peggy Guggenheim, the last then briefly resident in London. They had in mind an English equivalent of the Museum of Modern Art in New York, to be based on Peggy Guggenheim's collections. Roland Penrose was still the dominant force in 1946, and became the first Chairman, but the ICA never had a permanent collection: it was a forum for exhibitions, lectures and discussions. It only acquired premises in 1950, when it moved into the first floor of 17-18 Dover Street, in Mayfair. These were not very spacious, and have been described as 'nondescript, and more suitable to the garment trade than to lecturing and mounting exhibitions'. But the ICA, as often happens in such cases, was livelier and more influential in Dover Street than when it moved to grander and larger premises on the Mall in 1968.

Roland Penrose was born in 1900. He was Surrealist painter, friend and biographer of Picasso, of Henry Moore, Ben Nicholson, Herbert Read, and all the first generation of Modernists in England. It was perhaps inevitable that the younger members of the ICA would revolt against the old guard which ran it. But since this old guard saw itself as being all about revolt, instead of throwing out the dissidents, it made them official, by forming them, in 1952, into the Independent Group (briefly at first called the Young Group). This operated within the ICA, but had its independent programme. It was run (insofar as anyone ran it) for a time by Reyner Banham, and then by Lawrence Alloway (living in Greenwich, and therefore never a Banham habitué) and John McHale.

McHale later described the Independent as 'a small, cohesive, quarrelsome, abusive group'. They were clever, arrogant and ambitious young people. They were cohesive for about five years, and then the divergent attitudes among them gradually – or not so gradually, in some cases – pulled them apart. Various topics, attitudes, and ideas came to the surface in their formal meetings at the ICA, in the exhibitions they put on there, and in their continuous informal get-togethers at the Banhams' and elsewhere.

An initial impulse came from their feeling shut out. Many of them had little work or were looking for work. They felt that they had come back from the war and were waiting in a queue, while the older generation had a stranglehold on the best jobs, and the best commissions. The fact that what they did say frequently upset, antagonised or even infuriated their elders was no disincentive to them. They were busy, as Mary Banham puts it, 'kicking Daddy'.

They found the modern art establishment and its products exclusive and elitist. 'What is needed', Alloway wrote in 1957, 'is an approach which does not depend for its existence on the exclusion of most of the symbols that people live by . . . All kinds of messages are transmitted to every kind of audience . . . We begin to see the work of art in a changed context, freed from the iron curtain of traditional aesthetics which separate absolutely art from non-art.'

Symbolic of the group was the pinboard, scrap-screen or occasionally entire wall stuck randomly with postcards, photographs, torn-out fragments from newspapers or magazines, diagrams, drawings, or whatever image had caught the fancy of the sticker-on, the more varied the better. These proliferated in this period, but could also, as it were, go public. The scrap-screen-transmitted resulted in Paolozzi's pioneering epidiascope lecture at the ICA in 1952, where a random series of images were shown with no apparent connecting theme or dialogue, other than the heavy breathing and painful sighing of Paolozzi as he operated the epidiascope. The scrap-screen-as-exhibit produced *Parallel of Life and Art* at the ICA, in 1953, an exhibition of apparently random photographs randomly displayed, chosen by Paolozzi, the Smithsons, and their photographer friend, Nigel Henderson. The scrap-screen-into-art produced the collage, the favourite art form of Paolozzi, McHale and Hamilton, in the 1950s. 'All human experience is just one big collage,' Paolozzi remarked.

What became known as Pop Art – popular mass-produced artefacts, especially in the communications media, advertisements, illustrated magazines, comics, science fiction, horror as related in magazines, books and movies – was considered by the art establishment as outside or beneath their notice. It was certainly not art. It became one of the 'symbols that people live by' most exploited by the Independent Group – especially American Pop Art.

The group had a split personality as far as America was concerned. The members were aware of this, and at times unhappy about it. As they were almost all politically to the left, they disapproved of America as a capitalist society. But they were fascinated by it. From drab London of the early and mid-1950s, America seemed like an El Dorado, where the streets were flowing with chrome. It was still against the regulations to import cars from America into England, but the occasional huge gleaming cars of American diplomats cruised round the London streets like visitors from outer space. The windows of newsagents in working-class areas displayed their American comics like banners. And one by one members of the group went to America, and returned with trophies, like explorers returning from El Dorado or the moon.

In a letter to the Smithsons written in January 1957, Richard Hamilton summed up the characteristics of Pop Art. It was 'popular, transient, expendable, low cost, mass-produced, young, witty, sexy, gimmicky, glamorous, big business'. The group were romantic about Pop Art and also romantic about technology. The barriers it wanted to break down included those between art and technology, as well as those between fine art and popular art. Art had to change because the world had changed. Modern technology bombarded the market with images and options. This was liberating, not overpowering: it made possible continuous change, adaptation, rejection, and replacement. A throw-away economy called for a throw-away art, the diametrical opposite of the permanent art based on supposedly permanent values promulgated by earlier generations.

It became clear, in the course of the 1950s, that the architects in the group were out of tune with the artists. They were in reaction too, but against different bogeys. Their symbol of what was wrong with British architecture was the Festival of Britain of 1951, which in their view stood for a watered-down, un-rigorous, prettified, whimsical and parochial modernism. They thought that this description could be applied to most post-war building in Britain. They hated what they called the 'People's Architecture', the Swedish New Empiricism practised in the 1950s by the LCC Housing Department in the huge new estates at Roehampton and elsewhere. They disliked the *Architectural Review* for reviving interest in the English Picturesque, and developing it into what the *Review* called Townscape. They thought this resulted in a purely visual approach, in which buildings were designed from the outside in, in order to fit informally and prettily into the landscape or townscape. They aimed to go back to the masters and the mainstream, to Michelangelo, Palladio and Hawksmoor in the past, and to Le Corbusier and Mies in the present. They read and admired Wittkower's *Architectural Principles of the Age of Humanism*, and Colin Rowe's articles which had developed out of it.

Their mouthpiece was a new magazine, *Architectural Design*, of which Theo Crosby, an active member of the Independent Group, was the Technical Editor. But Reyner Banham worked from behind the lines in the *Architectural Review*, where he was tolerated because he was such a good journalist, and could place occasional articles and letters from his friends. Sandy Wilson, Bill Howell, Alan Colquhoun and others ran a fifth-column cell in the LCC Housing Department, putting up reinforced concrete buildings inspired by Le Corbusier in one section of the Alton estate in Roehampton, and on the Bentham Road estate in Hackney, and being much persecuted by their 'People's Architecture' bosses for doing so. Battle was engaged in architects' offices, discussion groups and architectural magazines, and 'Empiricist' or 'Formalist' hissed by one side as an insult against the other.

But going to Le Corbusier meant going to him as he was developing in the 1950s. In the 1930s reinforced concrete had been stuccoed and painted white, so that it could look clean and machine-made. At the Unité at Marseilles and elsewhere, Le Corbusier revelled in exposed concrete, carrying the grain of its timber shuttering. He made it seem heroic. He called the material *beton brut*, and the adjective gave resonance to the term 'Brutalism', which in general stood for a no-nonsense no-compromise anti-pretty approach to design, in which raw concrete, exposed steel and exposed services were all a sign of redemption.

Beton brut was far from being technologically advanced. It was so obviously not machine-made that it helped start an interest, stimulated by Le Corbusier himself, in any vernacular architecture that was strong, peasanty and not too pretty. Villages in Provence and the Greek islands, sand-built Moroccan kasbahs, unsentimental nineteenth-century English warehouses and oasthouses all began to be admired and photographed by young architects. This had little to do with the glossy American cars or advertisements and other icons of the Pop Art movement, and Wittkower searching for principles was far removed from Richard Hamilton and others who were trying to escape from them. Admittedly Banham became excited by the idea of a throw-away, changeable, client-adjustable, mass-produced pop architecture, but he had to wait until the 1960s to find younger architects to follow him (although the Smithsons tried for a time).

The official meetings and activities of the Independent Group took place at the ICA. Their main unofficial gathering place was at the Banhams', but there were numerous other places where they, or some of them, and their friends, met, to talk or just to enjoy themselves, or both. The Smithsons in Limerston Street, and Paolozzi nearby in Paultons Square, became the focus of a Chelsea circle, the western equivalent of the Banhams in Primrose Hill, though never so regularised. There were meals and parties at the Cordells' in Cleveland Square, and in the Hamiltons' big garden in Highgate. The conveniently central bar at the ICA was a place where everyone dropped in or arranged to meet. The French House pub in Dean Street, off Shaftesbury Avenue, became the venue for Saturday morning meetings, as regular as the Banhams' Sunday get-togethers. Quite why this not very attractive little pub run by a decidedly unattractive Frenchman became the haunt of architects and artists is not clear, but it did. The location must have helped and the publican somehow managed to give it the feel of a French café; everyone was smoking Gauloises. The painters tended to congregate on the left side of the bar: Francis Bacon, his photographer friend John Deakin and an assortment of artists and sailors. The architects and their set were on the right, among them Sandy Wilson, Douglas Stephen, Bob Maxwell, Alan Colquhoun, Edward Reynolds, Cedric Price (still a student) and the engineer Frank Newby. 'We didn't have a great deal to do with the others,' as Sandy Wilson recalls. The artists' side had a strong homosexual flavour, the architects' side very much the reverse; Toni del Renzio moved from one group to the other. The Banhams and Smithsons did not frequent the French Pub. The architects usually walked over for lunch to a little Italian restaurant across the street.

Another of the interlocking circles in the 1950s centred on Sam Stevens's flat in Marylebone High Street. Thomas Stevens, always known as Sam, was in some ways a perpetual student, in some ways a perpetual teacher. He had been at Liverpool School of Architecture, where Colin Rowe remembers him as already amazingly knowledgeable about the Modern Movement, but he twice failed the first-year exam and left. He was at the Architectural Association, but never graduated, and at the Courtauld Institute, where he only just scraped through. For much of the 1950s he was working in the LCC Architects' Department. Much later he taught History of Art at the AA, and was a great success.

It is a pleasure to talk to people about him, because they always light up with affection and amusement at his memory. Since so many people remember him and are grateful to him, and since he was important to Jim, and, to the best of my knowledge, appears in no book on architecture or architect's memoir, it is worth relating at some length what his friends – mostly architects – have to say about him.

A great many of the habitués at Marylebone High Street were students, or had recently qualified, at the Architectural Association: among them Kenneth Frampton, Colin Glennie, Joyce Lowrie, David Gray, John Miller, Neave Brown, Joseph Rykwert, Patrick Hodgkinson and Paul Manousso. Bob Maxwell and Alan Cordingley came originally because of the Liverpool connection. Alan Colquhoun had been at the same public school as Stevens. Peter Banham had been working with him at the Courtauld. The Smithsons may first have met him when they were briefly working in the LCC.

Bob Maxwell had been with him in his first year at Liverpool. He became for a time a lodger, and then a frequent visitor, at Marylebone High Street. 'Sam had done his own thinking. He was aware of modern architecture before any of us. Rowe undoubtedly learnt from him. He had an independent mind; his weakness was that he couldn't produce. It was always conversation, he never wrote anything. He had a sizeable flat on the first and second floor above a bank. Everyone visited him. I stayed with him until I was shovelled off to become a lodger with his mother – a remarkable woman – who had a flat in Barnes. There was a bit of money in the family – a disincentive to work. The people who stayed with Sam didn't pay – but although he may have had family money behind him, he wasn't rich. He was a good cook; he gave me my first salad made with vinaigrette and peppers. For a provincial arriving in London, it was like Paris. He had a sizeable library. His chief interest was in his hi-fi. He

60

pioneered the use of woofer speakers, made by taking a drawing board and cutting holes out of it. He couldn't give his attention to learning architecture; it somehow went into music. He was after absolute fidelity reproduction – I learnt from him about using cane needles rather than steel ones. In every little step like that he was always ahead. In terms of architecture, he was extremely knowledgeable about the Modern Movement. He loved Corbusier, and white-wall, modern architecture. Also some aspects of the Renaissance, especially the history of families like the Medici. He could discourse on the rivalry of the popes, and talk for hours about biographical details. He was a walking encyclopaedia.

'His main architectural project was a house for himself, to be built on an inherited site near Reading with inherited money, in the style of Gropius or Oud. Its feature was to be a central well, with an electric baroque organ at the bottom. It was never built. Sam became an expert on organs, and was consulted about the organ at the Festival Hall; it was probably due to him that this is a true baroque one, not a heavy atmospheric nineteenth-century one.'

Mary Banham remembers him as 'shortish, rather stocky. Very big head, that was the thing you noticed about him. He had a big booming voice. Otherwise not particularly noticeable.' He was 'a key figure and an elusive figure too. He was almost an anachronism. He had a first-class old-fashioned education at Bradfield . . . Latin and Greek and so on, which most of the others certainly didn't have. And he was used almost like a reference book, was Sam. He was very anxious to communicate, because as a child he had . . . a mastoid infection, was it? It made him deaf for a time, which probably accounted for the booming voice he had, and the fact that though he could hear, he was out of practice with listening. So that made him slightly strange. But he had an off-the-wall sense of humour. He used to think things were absolutely hilarious that nobody else could see at all. At the Courtauld he was brilliant on anything that interested him, and simply would not bother with anything that didn't. So that he just passed, but he did pass. He couldn't not be passed, because he had this definite brilliance, but no application. Very strange . . . jumping from one thing to the next, but he was always worth listening to.

'He had a fantastic collection of records. We used to go to Marylebone to listen . . . and were stunned by it. He was one of those people who always had the best equipment. He was a wonderful cook, a great host, but there came a point with Sam where he was like a dog with a bone. He wouldn't let go. He didn't know when to change the subject, or . . . because of this inability to listen, he was not aware that people were then wanting to go on to talk about something else. People had to say to him "Shut up, Sam, we're talking about something else." I was very fond of him, but there were times when we had to be quite brutal. At the same time we all had a tremendous fondness and admiration for him. He was wonderfully generous not only with his material goods but with his mind.'

On Kenneth Frampton, he had 'an enormous influence. For instance, he turned me on to Hannah Arendt's book *The Human Condition*, which I'm still extremely influenced by. I'm entirely indebted to Sam for that. Sam was, I think, the unsung, nomadic, non-stop talking-machine intellectual of that time. With strange interests, organs, plumbing, arcane anthropological knowledge. Ex-Courtauld, screwed-up kid, but nice, very very nice. Vanished breed, really. So there was a person I think Jim loved, but probably had not had much contact with, after a while.'

As Patrick Hodgkinson comments, 'He never built – but he did some valuable work for the LCC. But he wasn't a job architect. He was a really great, tip-top plumber. He knew all about it, and he was a very important part of that London scene. He was always at the French Pub, and of course, the trouble with Sam was that once he got talking, you couldn't stop him at all, but it was fascinating. Everyone was in and out of his rooms all the time. He was always putting people up for a bit when they couldn't find a room in London. He wasn't married then.

'He married quite late. He'd known Mary, his wife, some time, and then everybody was surprised, because suddenly they got married. She was the sweetest, sweetest girl, completely looked after him, and asked for nothing at all in return. Just after he'd married, he rang us up one Sunday, and said that he and Mary and Alan Colquhoun were going to have a picnic at Audley End, and could they come and have tea with us in Cambridge afterwards? So we said "yes, of course", and at about half past four the doorbell rang. I opened the door, and there were Sam and Alan, but no Mary. I said, "Hi, but where's Mary?" And they both said . . . "Oh, she must be still in the field . . .". They'd talked their way through lunch, and then they got up and started walking up and down the field, talking, talking, talking . . . and managed to get in the car and drive to Cambridge completely forgetting about poor Mary. But of course they drove back and got her, and she was patiently waiting. She was just sitting reading a book on the rug, and hadn't worried at all.'

David and Ilse Gray were among the many people who stayed with Sam. As a young architect David Gray learnt all about drainage from him. 'Oh, Sam Stevens was a wonderful man. He was always old, I think, Sam, and he was always around. Ken Frampton used to say that he was like some wonderful information-giving machine; you would put your penny in the slot, as it were, and ask this machine a question about, let's say, drainage. And the machine would ruminate a bit, and nothing would come out, so you would give it a thump on the chest, and you would get a stream of information about early Bach organ music. Sam was like that. He was a great master of the non sequitur, but he was full of information, and fathered us all. He used to boast that, as he stood in a crowd on some occasion in Germany, he'd been patted on the head by a passing Adolf Hitler. He said he was eight years old, I think.

'He also was a very fancy cook. We all used to foregather in his kitchen, but he used to start at about eleven o'clock at night. Then he would bake a cake at about three o'clock in the morning. "I'm going to make a cake. I'm going to make a peach sponge", or something, he would say. "You've got to stay, because we're going to have this cake." This was sometimes when we were staying for a bit, in Sam's flat, but also when we weren't. We were always round there. Everybody was. It was a club for architects. It was like a club in the sense that if you were really stuck for a bed, you could get one for the night with Sam . . .'

FIVE

JIM COMES TO LONDON

Jim arrived in London in the autumn of 1950. In terms of work his first two and a half years ranged from the dull to the disastrous. It was common practice for the graduates at the Liverpool School of Architecture to do a postgraduate year or more studying Town Planning. Reilly had founded the Department of Civil Design at Liverpool for that purpose, and planning, considered an essential discipline for the reconstruction of Britain, was much in the air in the 1950s. It was perhaps for this reason that Jim followed this route. Or it may simply have been that he wanted something that would subsidise him in London with a government grant while he was looking out for work. The diploma course on which he embarked was not in Liverpool but in London, at the School of Town Planning and Regional Research in Gordon Square. He found the two-year course insufferably dull, and did not complete it. He was never to be seriously interested in planning. The standard monograph on Asplund, which he failed to return to the School library, is virtually the only memento of these years. His time at Gordon Square was followed by a job which may have developed out of it, in the Planning Department of the London County Council. Jim lasted five weeks there. Then followed six unsatisfactory months working on West African schools in the office of James Cubitt and Partners. It was not till he became an assistant in the office of Lyons Israel Ellis at the beginning of 1953 that he found a berth which suited him.

But socially, intellectually and sexually Jim quickly got under way. His Liverpool friends or contacts already in London led him naturally to the various circles in which they moved. He started London life in the flat of two ex-Liverpool architects, John Diamond and Robin Black, at 80A South Hill Park, close to Hampstead Heath. Here he moved into a mixture of architecture and jazz, of Douglas and Margaret Stephen, Bob Maxwell and other architects, and of George Melly and Mick Mulligan, who were good friends of the architect gang. 'They were attracted by jazz people', according to Melly, 'because we were considered rather exotic

64

and louche . . . We were very squalid. But we liked that, because we all came from bourgeois or suburban backgrounds. We thought jazz musicians had to behave as badly as possible.' Melly came from Liverpool, where his mother presided over Liverpool culture, and was a great giver of parties, specialising in musicians and homosexuals, from Malcolm Sarjeant downwards. He had a beautiful sister, Andrée, who was well known as an actress and film star, and a shabby flat full of Magrittes and Mirós; Jim liked both the flat and the paintings, not least because they were the antithesis of the Festival of Britain image. Mick Mulligan was the son of a rich wine-merchant, had been a model public-school boy, Captain of Cricket at Merchant Taylors, but rebelled against his background when he left school, and became a foul-mouthed, hard-drinking, atheistic, anarchistic jazz musician. But behind all the boozing and 'fucking cunts' he was intelligent and a good friend.

Melly and Mulligan called Jim Beachcomber 'because, as opposed to some of the other architects, who were rather smart, Jim wore a sort of white suit, à la Somerset Maugham expatriate . . . the figure, you know, lurking about in some seaport in the Far East. He wore sandals, I think. Not absolutely certain about that, but certainly a rumpled white suit; everything slept in, it looked, so we called him Beachcomber. You could imagine him walking along the beach, looking for anything washed ashore.' There were wildish parties at South Hill Park. Melly remembers one that 'seemed to go on for about three days. And we had to go away and play gigs, but we would come back and start all over again. We had all that stamina.' At the end of this or a similar party, according to another guest, everyone went naked onto the balcony, and waved at passing cars in the dawn light.

One of the people in the set was Anne Sharpley, a popular girl from Manchester and a successful journalist on the *Evening Standard*. Melly describes her as 'warm, funny, beautiful, I thought. And rather promiscuous, why not? She was a smashing girl, really. I wouldn't have a word to say against her. Generosity itself.' She liked Mick Mulligan because she found him 'deliciously grubby'. She may have liked it less when he pissed into her shoe, because he was too lazy or drunk to go to the lavatory. ('It was a toeless shoe, so it was a totally ridiculous activity,' according to Melly.) At one time Jim was playing darts at one end of the room, and George Melly was making love to Anne Sharpley on the floor at the other, and Jim came up behind them and threw a dart into his thigh – 'I think he may have been a bit jealous'. Both Jim and Melly were also attracted to Margaret Dent: at a South Hill Park party she made an assignation at Melly's flat, and made love there wearing nothing but black stockings and a row of pearls. 'This rather impressed me, you know . . . I was from Liverpool and I thought "this is really living".'

From the South Hill Park flat, Jim moved on to Sam Stevens's flat in Marylebone High Street, some time in 1951. He had a room there until he found a one-room flat of his own, in York Terrace, Regent's Park, at the end of 1953 or beginning of 1954; it was on the ground floor of a house in one of Nash's columned terraces. His circle expanded. He was involved with the ICA at least from June 1952, when a glass and steel table, which he had designed and had made for himself when he was a Liverpool student, was shown at an ICA exhibition, *Tomorrow's Furniture*. He became a member of the Independent Group, and a habitué of the Banhams' coffee mornings, the French Pub, and all the parties given by the circle.

In the early 1950s Jim was a big powerful and formidable man. He looked a bit of a bruiser. He still had his moustache, and had not yet put on weight. One could believe that he had been a paratrooper, but he no longer had a military air. Mary Banham remembers him vividly in those days. 'He was young. He had the added glamour of being a wounded paratrooper, and burst on the scene with all this reputation. Also a lot of people at Liverpool had known him, and obviously had a great respect for him, although they were all the same age. And he was an instant success with all the women. He was something that was very fashionable in those days. Peter used to call him the Seedy Viking. He was slightly tousled, blond, and – in those days – thin. He had this totally irresistible throw-away air about him. "Take it or leave it. That's how I am." And at the same time was obviously so intrigued and fascinated, and loved people. He never made any bones about finding somebody in the room attractive, and immediately going over and approaching them. I'll tell you what Peter overheard at the ICA one night, an AA student talking to her boyfriend . . . and he was obviously trying to persuade her to get into bed with him, and she was saying "Well, yes, dear, I will, but I really think I should sleep with Jim Stirling first". He was a kind of initiation.'

Magda Cordell recalls him at parties: 'Jim could drink very well. But even then, he could carry his liquor better than the others. Even in those stages, he was different. He was fun. I don't even know why I'm saying that, but when I think of it, I've a smile. He looked very, very sexy. That's number one. I was a young woman then, so I remember it. I didn't have a crush on him . . . but I guess if I had been unattached, I might have. He looked very sinuous, he was slim, broad-shouldered. His hair was slightly disarrayed, it wasn't licked down cold, you know, it was always a little bit in disarray. Boyish, strangely enough . . . and very sexy. He was a very nifty kid, I must say. I'm sure I wasn't the only one who thought he was a nifty kid.' At the same time, 'One felt like one knew him, and became friendly with him, and yet one wasn't. One didn't know him.'

Magda Cordell noticed that, however apparently scruffy, he was very conscious of the way he looked. 'Jim was a kind of quote unquote designer. Even the way he wore his clothes was more design. No matter what it was, he wore it with a certain style. He brought a sense of design to everything.'

The 'Seedy Viking' look took over from the Beachcomber look, and was partly due to the Banhams. Clothes were still rationed and hard to come by. Peter Banham had an ancient navy-blue Norwegian sweater, coming apart at the seams. Jim fell in love with it, and it fitted him much better than it did Peter, so Peter gave it to him.

What men immediately noticed about Jim was his belief in himself. Sandy Wilson first met him in the LCC. 'I recall this rather mysterious character padding up into our studio, and by our studio I mean me and Peter Carter and Bill Howell and so on. He had a funny droopy moustache, and we thought he looked a little bit like a Viking. He had apparently found himself in the Planning Department of the LCC, God knows why, and only lasted a few weeks there. But as a friend of Sam Stevens and Alan Colquhoun and so on, I then got to know him independently.

'I've never met anybody who was so completely convinced of his own significance – I wouldn't say importance, because that implies a pomposity. I can remember almost immediately being invited to go round to his place, and being very firmly shown his portfolio of his work, which of course at that time was mostly his student pieces, and one competition scheme that he'd done. And I also noticed that he had a pretty good library, because there were various books there that I had my eye on, and hadn't got myself.'

Jim and Sandy Wilson became good friends. They played squash together every Thursday, in the Fire Brigade Courts across the river from the Tate Gallery (Wilson had the right to use them because he worked for the London County Council). They walked on Primrose Hill together, and talked about architecture. They went together to see Hawksmoor's St George's in the East and Soane's Dulwich Gallery. They ragged together, and teased each other, quite brutally at times. In spite of their friendship there was an element of rivalry between them.

The rivalry was much stronger and less friendly between Jim and the Smithsons. They met often enough, with Sam Stevens, at the Banhams', at the Independent Group or at parties. Initially the Smithsons welcomed him as a fellow northerner. But Jim could not accept their claim to leadership, and was antipathetic to Alison. By the mid-1950s there was a lot of tension. Evelyn Hogge remembers one party at which 'Alison turned up in one of her extraordinary outfits, which consisted of a sort of pyjama-top thing, with a big collar, and Jim took one look at her, walked up, unrolled the collar, and tied it with a knot on top of her head, which didn't go down at all well. They'd had words about something and at the end of the party she got so annoyed that she threw a glass of red wine at him, just as I was walking between them, and I got it all over me.'

Jim's friends were intrigued, amused, and possibly touched when Jim the champion sleeper-around started up a Platonic relationship with an innocent young girl. It was to last nearly two years. Evelyn Hogge had been one of Peter Banham's Courtauld students. She was half-French, Lycée-educated, and her father was 'to the right of Mr Barrett of Wimpole Street'. She graduated in the summer of 1954, and about then began to frequent the Banham coffee mornings. 'I met Jim there. I was, I must say, exceedingly flattered because he immediately took to me. He told me later that he thought I looked like Audrey Hepburn in *Roman Holiday* – in fact insisted on taking me to it twice, just to show me. And I suppose in those days I did a bit. Anyway, we started seeing a lot of each other, but I was incredibly innocent. I had a very stern father, and it was never a sexual relationship in any way.'

Magda Cordell remembers her as 'a very young kid, very beautiful. She was speaking beautifully enunciated English, with a tiny little French accent behind it. She was very nice, very warm, very friendly, very pretty.' Mary Banham is more down-to-earth. 'She was a very good scholar. But infuriated Jim because she was such a good Catholic and wouldn't sleep with him. It didn't stop him being intrigued, in fact, I think it probably intrigued him the more.' Whatever Jim's initial hopes, he never put any pressure on her. 'He realised I was unsophisticated; he never forced me. I was more like a little sister, or a puppy that he took round. He was in York Terrace then, and I used to go there most evenings. I would either buy food and make a picnic for him, or we would go out to have dinner. Since we didn't have much money we tended to go to those places where you could put as much as you like on your plate, for whatever it was. There was one place like that, in Marylebone High Street, where we used to go – and we would go and visit Sam Stevens and that lot down the road. Then I used to be deeply embarrassed because on the way back, at that time, at the very top of Marylebone High Street there was a little turning to the right, just above a garage showroom, and they were building a terrace of houses there. He used to make me secrete two bricks in my shopping bag, because he was busy building a typical architect's bookcase with bricks and planks. I had never done anything like that. I used to be absolutely horrified.'

His flat was just one room on 'the ground floor of one of those terraces with heavy columns outside, and then opening onto gardens. But there was nothing there at all. I suspect that the people who owned the lease of the house . . . one was a Czech, and the other one was English, and then there was a harpsichord player who used to live in the flat above . . . went in for rather shady sublettings which were not supposed to take place. Anyway, Jim had just that one big room, with a tiny little stove hidden in the top of what must have been the service lift from the kitchen, and then there was a tiny loo and a shared bathroom in what had been the downstairs loo. It was very, very primitive, but absolutely marvellous. There was just that huge room, with three huge windows. He had his drawing desk in one corner, a table in the other, and a bed against the back wall. It was about all there was, plus the bricks and the planks for the books. I don't remember pictures or any art at all. He used to draw the whole time I was there. I used to lie on the bed and read his books, and he used to be at his drawing board, and we would talk, and we would always have music: either jazz or classical. Not so much records, he really only spent money on essentials. He was pretty short in those days. But the Third Programme was on almost continually, and he just listened to that as he drew. No, he was not a talkative man, not a chatty man at all. Sometimes we would go out, but he was working very hard because he was doing little jobs for himself. Anyway, he was always drawing, and also doing office work . . . I used to love watching him draw and do his plans, because with those enormous stumpy fingers of his he had skill . . . the way he held those small pencils and pens; it was fascinating. I used to watch him do it.

'I suppose his books covered half a wall of the big room. He let me borrow anything. He introduced me to a lot of books – like *The Screwtape Letters*, all that sort of thing. He also made me read a book about Aleister Crowley. He had a fairly catholic taste. But Jim wasn't a poetry man – whereas Sandy used to read Donne, and had all the books of poetry. The only book Jim never allowed me to read was *Tropic of Cancer*. He said I wasn't up to it. He was like that with me . . . it was rather nice . . . protective. It wasn't a lover relationship at all.

'He talked about his work a lot. Not that I was up to understanding everything that he was doing, but he did talk about it, and he used to come and make me do crits of his drawings, just to see what I was going to say. I wrote to Corb on his behalf once. I wrote in French. I mean, he wrote the letter, but asked me to put it into French. It was about how much he admired him. It's difficult to think of Jim, who people thought was so arrogant, to have been in the position of rather stage-struck admiration. I never knew if he got an answer. He was a great admirer of Corb, and when he found out that my father's family had a large house in Garches he said "Oh, you know Garches . . .". Of course I had no idea there was a Corb house there, so that was a big black mark against me. But I did do my homework after that. He taught me a lot.'

They often went to jazz clubs, especially the Hundred Club in Oxford Street. They saw a good deal of Mick Mulligan and George Melly. Mulligan was 'foul-mouthed, and drank like a fish'. His one ambition was to make Evelyn blush 'but I didn't understand him, and didn't blush'. They went with him to an Irish pub behind the Hundred Club, and another in a basement near Piccadilly, and to a pub like a huge barn near Marylebone High Street – rough, all-men pubs with sawdust on the floor. George Melly was 'lovely'. He told Evelyn 'you've got a lovely white face'. One evening there was a fancy-dress party at the ICA, at which everyone wore heads or masks as creatures of fantasy (but Jim refused). George Melly came with his sister as Beauty and the Beast, and Evelyn remembers him, very high on drink, singing through a lion's head.

They used to walk over Regent's Park from York Terrace to Banham coffee mornings, and Jim would point out the birds as they walked. They went several times with the Banhams to motor races at Brands Hatch. By now Sandy Wilson had graduated from a motor-cycle to a car and drove them, for Banham, in spite of his passion for modern cars (the reason for the outing), did not learn to drive until he went to Los Angeles in the late 1960s. On another occasion they drove with Sandy and Muriel Wilson to West Wycombe, made the climb up into the gold ball at the top of the church tower, and had a cream tea in the village afterwards. Jim and Sandy Wilson were good value together: 'they understood each other very well'. Wilson 'was very serious about what he was doing, but had a little boy aspect. He was always ready for a laugh, and a giggle and a joke. One of them would do something, and the other one would respond, and before you knew where they were the whole thing had escalated into an upheaval, wherever you were.' She remembers coming out of the cinema after seeing *The Seven Samurai*, and Jim and Sandy re-enacting the film together as they walked down the street.

'Then of course the great thing was Saturday morning at the French Pub. I was the only one who looked half-way respectable, so I used to be sent off to the restaurant to book a table, and then this hirsute collection of people used to turn up. But Jim almost strangled Paul Pot the People's Poet once in a restaurant, and I was deeply embarrassed. Sandy and

Muriel and he and I had gone off to have some cheap lunch somewhere, at the Corner . . . and Sandy's jacket was over the back of the chair and his *Times* was in the pocket. Paul Pot, who was one of the Fitzrovia characters, you know, leant over, and got the paper out of Sandy's pocket, and Jim took immediate exception to this, picked him up by the scruff of the neck (he was a little man), and shook him. It almost started a riot. He tended to do things like that. He was always embarrassing me. Of course, I realise now he was doing it on purpose. He wanted to see whether he was going to get a rise out of me. He thought I was far too much *comme il faut*, and he needed to ginger me up a bit. He was quite right. For a long time, the few times I was in the car I used to sit and wait for him to open the door, and he would just walk off . . . but I learned quickly. There was a terrible time when we were sitting in the cinema behind a man with a bald head, and Jim sneezed without any effort at screening his mouth, and the man made a great play of putting a handkerchief up and polishing his dome. I was mortified.

'He was gruff and rough. He could be rude and off-hand. He didn't suffer fools gladly, and was not shy of telling people to go to hell. But there was a very sweet side to his nature. He was lovely to be around with. But I knew him very much on the surface. He didn't share his thoughts. There was always a sort of shutter that came down if you intruded at all. He never talked about his family. He once said to me "Oh, you know . . . when you speak to your family – when you speak French over the 'phone your voice changes – you sound quite different." I said, "Well, possibly I am more expressive in French than I am in English, or perhaps my emotions come through better . . .". "But you speak to your family as though you like them!" I said, "Well, yes, I do". . . . Looking back, you could see that there wasn't a very close relationship at home.'

In April 1956, Frank Newby, a young English engineer, was at an evening of Charles Eames's films at the ICA. He had been in Los Angeles working with Eames, and had brought eight of his chairs back with him to England. He knew Sandy Wilson, who introduced him to Jim and Evelyn on that evening, and invited him to come to the French Pub on Saturday. He became one of the French Pub gang for Saturday morning drinking, followed by lunch, and one of the group in general. 'At one stage Jim, who always paid for Evelyn's lunch, stopped paying and I started . . . there was some kind of arrangement or discussion with Jim, and an amicable change from one to the other.' Frank and Evelyn got married in 1957, and Jim started up an affair with Janet Kaye, one of his students at the Architectural Association, where he had become a thesis tutor in 1954.

Drinking, party-giving, screwing and jazz were let-outs for Jim. There were wild parties at South Hill Park, but Bob Maxwell's dominant memory of him there is leaning over an inclined table, drawing until late in the night. Evelyn Hogge had the experience of subsequent girlfriends of Jim: lying on the bed while Jim drew and drew. In between he visited buildings, talked about them, read about them, and occasionally wrote about them. Sam Stevens lent or gave him books, and he bought as much as he could afford. Stevens in Marylebone High Street and the Banhams in Oppidans Road provided talking-shops. At Marylebone High Street discussions would go on into the small hours. Jim was never verbally very articulate. He would sit and absorb, a presence in the background, and then start needling a speaker with whom he disagreed – he was very good at that – or come out with a short sentence, projected with enormous force. 'That's not right.' 'That's crap.' 'Let's face it, William Morris was a Swede.' 'Corb's gone soft.' He came to some of the Independent Group's meetings at the ICA, but seldom spoke at any of them. As Sandy Wilson puts it, he was always a bit of a lone ranger.

In congenial company, however, with not too many people there, Jim could relax and talk as much as anyone except Sam Stevens. He and Stevens got on very well together. Through him he struck up a friendship with Paul Manousso, the first of many friendships with architects younger than he was. Manousso was about ten years younger than Jim, and a third-year student at the Architectural Association when he first met him with Sam Stevens in 1951 or 1952. He had met Stevens through the AA, and through him got to know Alan Colquhoun as well. Colquhoun had made friends with Stevens at public school. They had both been at Bradfield, of which Stevens's forebear had been the founder.

Manousso took part in many 'long conversations into the small hours in Sam Stevens's flat, always with Jim and Alan Colquhoun, and sometimes with Kenneth Frampton or some others of the set there as well. We spent most of our time talking round the kitchen table, with Sam making cups of tea. Sam was also very fond of cooking, and would cook elaborate meals for us.' Or they had biscuits and coffee, but never alcohol.

Stevens was 'interested in relating architecture to philosophical concepts, particularly the Platonic quality of Le Corbusier. He used to say that the Villa at Poissy was a Platonic object that was placed in the landscape, as opposed to Frank Lloyd Wright, who he said was Aristotelian. We used to discuss that kind of thing a lot. But the conversations were very wide. We used to talk about French literature and about music, and about modern art, and Jim had wide interests, and was highly cultivated. He was reading quite a lot of French literature translated into English, because he couldn't understand French ... a lot of Stendhal, André Gide, he was interested in the poetry of Paul Valéry, particularly the one that's called "Eupalinos or the Architect". He was reading early novels of Anthony Powell. ... Ken Frampton put us onto books. I think he was the first person who talked to me and Jim about Borges, the Argentinian writer. And Jim was interested in developments in modern painting. He particularly liked Picasso – Juan Gris – Ecole de Paris, rather than the more decorative side of things. He loved Léger, for instance, and he liked the paintings of Corbusier very much.

'He was interested in the plans of castles, and became very excited by Pliny's description of his house and garden. I remember how we went through it together, and tried to reconstruct it. He got very interested through Sam Stevens in the writing of Moretti, who was the editor of an Italian mazagine called *Spazio*, and had developed some rather fine buildings in Rome, including a Fencing Academy for Mussolini, which is a beautiful building, that kind of Italian Fascism that borders on the surreal, and is in a sense very exciting. Sam Stevens put us onto *Spazio*, and knew Italian and would translate. There was an interesting article which put forward the idea that in ancient architecture mouldings were an abstract architecture, or abstract sculpture, that the ancients achieved abstraction through their mouldings, which was, of course, an exciting idea. Jim was extremely interested in all the developments that were going on in Italy, because in a sense Italy at that time was in the forefront of architecture. France, apart from Corb, had died. Nothing was happening in Spain. And the Italians were producing a great spate of quite interesting architects.'

For Manousso, 'Jim was very much a renaissance man, in the sense that he wasn't like Smithson, who was much more just interested in sociological ideas. Jim very rarely mentioned the sociological background of buildings. He was interested in their formal and their aesthetic qualities. He never discussed the technical side of architecture with me at all. I don't think it interested him, and I think that possibly it didn't interest me either.'

Colin Rowe (whose brother David was one of Stevens's lodgers for a time) came down from Liverpool on occasions. 'Jim and Alan and Sam and I used to sit round him as if he was a guru, who was imparting the essence, particularly of Le Corbusier, to us. He spoke, and we all listened. Insofar as Sam could listen to anything. But I think even he was silenced by him.' Manousso made his own contribution, too, and 'may have had something to do with Jim's interest in Russian constructivism, because I discovered a lot of books that were actually published at the time in Russia, and remember enthusiastically showing them to Jim, who borrowed them, and I think he was very interested.'

Another meeting place nearby was the Doctors' Restaurant, a Hungarian restaurant off Marylebone High Street which served terrible food very cheaply. A lot of doctors used to go there, because it was convenient for Harley Street, and it was also handy for Sam Stevens's flat, and for Jim in York Terrace. He and Paul Manousso often met for lunch there, and other habitués included Alan Colquhoun, Patrick Hodgkinson, Ken Frampton, Neave Brown, Douglas Stephen, Sandra Lousada (becoming a good photographer and 'Jim had rather a penchant for her, although I don't think they had an affair'), and, later on, Janet Kaye, coming with Jim. Reyner Banham also ate there from time to time, but 'I don't think he and Jim got on terribly well'. Sandra Lousada has vivid memories of how the architects would come piling in, pull tables together, and start arguing and drawing on the table-tops. She became something of a mascot to them. They enjoyed having a pretty girl sitting at the edge of their circle, absorbing what they said and not speaking herself. They would slap her on the bottom and get cross if she did not join them.

Jim took Manousso to his office to look at his drawings, but very rarely looked at buildings with him. However, 'there was a ludicrous episode when . . . because for my final thesis I was designing a Turkish Bath, I took him to the beautiful Turkish Bath in the Imperial Hotel in Russell Square. It was staggering. I said, "Jim, even if you don't enjoy the Turkish Bath, you must come with me and see the architecture", and I remember he didn't feel the heat as much as I did. We were in the very hot room, and he was excited, and I said, "Jim, if I don't move out of here I'm going to faint", and he kept saying to me, "I think this is all a little self-indulgent, isn't it?" Not the architecture of the bath, the whole system. He had a very strong puritanical streak in him. He was both puritanical and not puritanical. So when he said it was all a bit self-indulgent, it was semi-serious, yes, but I felt he wasn't totally light-hearted."

'He was wonderful company. He would laugh very easily. He liked ragging people. He didn't rag me so much, but he used to rag Colquhoun for being too serious, and Stevens for talking too much. He used to make rather ribald comments about Alan Cordingley because he was gay, which was a shame because he's a very nice chap, and it's neither here nor there. I would agree with whoever it was who said that he was a "curious mixture of naiveté and sophistication". The naiveté showed in the way he dealt with other people. He was no diplomat. There was a kind of uncouthness to other people if they weren't on his wavelength, or he found himself in deep waters. He would register incomprehension, and he would become inarticulate. He was never smooth.

'Though Jim appeared an extremely bluff figure, he was quite extraordinarily sensitive. Sensitive to slights, and sensitive to tremors of change in art history, to an extraordinary degree. He was an introvert, who appeared to be extrovert. I think he was pretty introverted. He certainly could be very touchy when his ideas were attacked, and would get quite worked up about that, and go on and on about it. One felt him to be very ambitious. But he never talked about his ambitions. One just instinctively felt that he would do very well. I don't know what it was about him, but he had this quality of a Rolls-Royce. He also worked very hard. He had tremendous powers of work; it was quite astounding. . . . One always sensed a power behind him. That he was built in a gigantic mould, so to speak.

'He was always very friendly, though he always bore himself with a certain reserve. One could never actually feel one could be totally intimate with him. Of course there was an age difference: he was a fully-fledged architect (though when I met him he hadn't, I think, built anything). I was a student, and slightly in awe of him. . . . He never discussed himself. I can't imagine him doing so. He might have discussed himself with women. He was much more interested in discussing ideas than in analysing his own feelings. There was a kind of privacy about his relationship with other people, insofar as he never really revealed himself. In a sense one didn't really need him to. He was so fascinating that it didn't enter one's mind. He made one feel totally relaxed.'

When Bob Maxwell saw Jim drawing at South Hill Park, he was probably working on competition drawings for Poole Technical College in Dorset. This was judged in 1952. Jim's was not placed, and the competition, being for a relatively minor building, aroused little interest. The competition for additions to Sheffield University, which took place in 1953, was a different matter. Jim drew up the designs with the help of Alan Cordingley, but again they were not placed. The winners were the firm of Gollins, Melville and Ward, whom Jim described as 'the best of the "safe, understandable moderns"'. But the competition was a major one, for one of the first big post-war university projects. The entries were exhibited at the Architectural Association, and aroused great interest among architects. They included designs by Sandy Wilson and the Smithsons. Jim described his reactions to the entries, and analysed his own design, in a big hard-cover note- or account-book which he bought from Rymans at the end of 1953 or very beginning of 1954. He entered jottings on architecture, buildings and other subjects into it for about two years. On the title page he wrote, carefully and stylishly, '*Very important. If found return to 37 YORK TERRACE, REGENTS PARK. LONDON NW1. James Stirling.*' One is reminded of the title page of his birdwatching diary; the spelling in the diary is, if anything, slightly better. But 'James Frazer Stirling' has become 'James Stirling'. Like Oscar Fingal O'Flaherty Wills Wilde, Jim no longer needed to bolster himself up with secondary names; he had less to remove than Wilde.

Jim's Sheffield entry is the first design by him which is distinctively personal, even if it is still much under the inspiration of Le Corbusier. As at Le Corbusier's Villa Stein at Garches (but on a much larger scale), the design is based on a regular structural grid of posts and slabs: and as at Garches, within this grid, and the long rectangular block which it produces, there is much freedom in the arrangement of partition walls and spaces. But Jim shows, to a greater extent than Le Corbusier, a commitment to revealing what was going on inside the building: each different function is given a different expression. It was a design principle which remained crucial to his buildings throughout his career. He was impressed by the competence of the Wilson design, but criticised it because it disregarded this principle. 'Sandy's scheme is impressive but for me is distasteful in the matter of principal . . . i.e. inasmuch as it is regarded entirely legitimate to give an overall single expression to a block which has such highly diverse accommodation – by running a glass curtain wall in front of the stanchions so "disguising" the nature (function) of the accommodation behind i.e. staff-rooms – ramped lecture theatres – lavatories etc.'

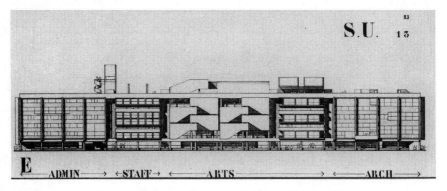

Jim's competition design for Sheffield University, 1953

Jim's design is divided into five sections. Each section has a different use. Each main section is separated from the next by a short recessed section containing lifts or staircases and each main section is given a different expression. The most striking is the central section, containing the lecture theatres. Each lecture theatre, complete with its sloping floor, is expressed as a separate box, and these boxes, eight on each façade, are threaded in four lots of two on pairs of concrete columns. But each pair is on a different level from, and running in a different direction to, its neighbours. A kind of syncopation results, played out in front of the glass walls of the central corridor, through which is a view to the silhouettes of the lecture theatres on the other façade. It is a brilliant piece of juggling, the first of many by Stirling, and a satisfying one, because it grows out of the nature of the building. There is nothing like it in Le Corbusier's work. The idea of showing the shape of the lecture theatres externally comes without doubt from the Constructivist architect Melnikov's Workers' Clubhouse in Moscow (1926). Jim certainly knew of this at this date, although there were occasions when he claimed that he did not. It is illustrated, for instance, in Bruno Zevi's *Architecture Moderne*, which he owned, and he had worked through Manousso's Russian books on the Constructivists, who had developed their own brand of Modernism in Russia in the 1920s. But the tightly organised way in which Jim arranged his theatres owed nothing to Melnikov.

Some time in the first half of 1954, Jim went down to Kent to visit his old Liverpool fellow-student Christopher Owtram. His studio was in a converted oasthouse, next to an Elizabethan barn and manor house near Tonbridge. He was living there in a state of creative excitement. He had cut what he described as a 'great Zeppelin window' in one side, and plastered the walls himself with 'the most creamy gorgeous plaster you could ever imagine', inspired by Frank Lloyd Wright, and made of cowhair and sand – 'it was like . . . sort of cow dung, cows from heaven, but you couldn't get it much higher than your own height, and the wattles were exposed after that . . . I'd raided an abandoned manor house in a hidden valley, and in the ancestral garden patch where they'd buried all their ancestors there grew the most wonderful tumbleweeds, about nine feet high, with great fronds and pods, and they dried, and I dragged them all back, and the whole of this oasthouse was full of moonlike podded things, and a huge drawing-board, everything manipulated out of tea chests . . . it was very romantic.' In the middle of the pods were models of his extraordinary designs.

Jim was fascinated by what he was doing (with no prospect of getting anything built) and wrote about it at length in his notebook. He found that Owtram had moved on from what he had been doing at Liverpool – straight Frank Lloyd Wright – and developed his own style.

His work compared to FLW is definitely more abstract, geometric, intellectual, but just as romantic (basic conception). 'Conceived in 3 seconds, worked out in 3 months' – remark regarding a recent project. Thus an expressionist phase occurs and he begins – but his architecture does not end at this point (i.e. Mendelsohn) but then proceeds to go down a geometric-ising 'production line' – I imagine the conception might completely alter during this phase – plans, sections, elevations, spring from a series of triangles or a selection of angles, which he gets from an analysis of the planes that occur in the platonic solids, octohedrons, detrohedrons [sic] etc. – This gives him a variety of angles (how many? – I guess 15) to which every plane in his architecture conforms. Thus a building is grouping together of a number of points (or intersections) from which all his angles depart (or converge). By doing this on the vertical, as well as the horizontal and in depth, he maintains he is truly 3 dimensional and a step beyond FLW. Instead of one angle 45°, which I have in my vocabulary, Owtram has a whole series – I would never be able to grapple with the mathematics involved. Therefore I consider what he is doing infinitely more difficult therefore would he find what I do all too easy? Perhaps not, as his architecture is expressionist in basis, all his best work is the 'one volume theme'. Therefore he would have done a better Coventry Cathedral or Crystal Palace than either Smithson or Entwistle, but how would he have faced up to Sheffield University? To quote him 'Architecture and mathematics are the same thing'. He says that FLW (and Corb) are falling behind through not being able to exploit up to the moment technology – I had not suspected such an attitude in so romantic an artist, but the basic thing about his work is that it is scientific, mathematical and un-arbitrary . . . I have always believed that 'there is nothing new in modern architecture' – but on encountering his work I have to retract this statement as there has certainly been nothing like this in the past, and *if* the future *is* going to be different? perhaps it will be more like this.

Jim spent two or three days staying with Christopher Owtram, looking at and talking about his drawings and models, about Jim's work and about architecture generally. He found Owtram 'as a personality . . . much less of an aesthete, almost easy to get on with and quite tolerant to "other" architecture'. The main model was 'marvellous . . . in this moon-like setting', as Owtram recalls, and Jim said 'Christopher, you're going to be the first architect of our generation to get national or international acclaim'. In fact, in less than ten years Jim was to have an international reputation; and shortly after their meeting, Owtram emigrated to Canada, and to a career of disappointment and frustration.

Jim was much exercised at this time about the future of architecture, and wrote about it at some length in his notebook. He agreed with the assessment of the architectural historian Bruno Zevi that the 'programmatic' buildings of the Modern Movement had been erected in the early 20s and 30s, in Jim's opinion almost entirely by Frank Lloyd Wright, Le Corbusier and Mies van der Rohe. From their buildings 'almost the entire vocabulary of modern architecture has descended'. The second generation had merely diffused, refined or watered-down this language. But he disagreed with Zevi's assumption that this was justifiable and that 'the programmatic period of modern architecture *is over*'. The lack of development had led to apathy and lack of vitality. It was up to the third generation 'to continue (we hope) programmatic development'.

He was concerned at the current split in contemporary architecture between what he called academic 'art' architecture, and technological 'non-art' architecture. A page of his notebook is filled with a diagram to illustrate this. The two streams had run separately in the nineteenth century: the Crystal Palace on one side, Mackintosh the culmination on the other. It was the achievement of the early Modern Movement to bring the two streams together, even if without total success. At Le Corbusier's villas at Garches and Poissy, at Mies's Barcelona Pavilion, perhaps at Wright's Johnson Wax Building, art and technology had been integrated. Now they had split again. Le Corbusier and Wright had turned their backs on technological development. Mies looked technological but wasn't (in his Seagram Building the steel of the exterior was pure decoration, fixed to a concrete frame). On the true technological side was the Lever Building in New York and a whole American School of mass-produced curtain wall buildings, factories in Italy and America, and Buckminster Fuller's geodesic domes. As technologists in England he listed 'AA tendencies', the 'Darbyshire group' (that is, the prefabricated school movement) and the buildings of John Winter. 'Smithson would claim to be (but isn't?).' But 'the greatest architect of them all would be the one who could solve these two tendencies which are splitting the modern movement.'

Frequently I wake in the morning [Jim wrote] and consider how it is that I can be an architect and an Englishman at the same time, particularly a modern architect. Since the crystallisation of the modern movement around about 1920 – Britain has not produced one single masterpiece, and it must be practically the only European country which has not produced a 'great man'. ... Indeed, the number of great Architects which this country has produced since the Gothic can be counted on one hand – Mackintosh, Archer, Hawksmoor – Vanbrugh, Inigo Jones, and perhaps Soane.

Jim's driving ambition was by now transparently obvious to everyone who met him. He was not interested in making money, although he was to have no difficulty in spending any that he earned. In a straightforward, old-fashioned way, he was going to be a great architect. Although he never specifically says so in his notebook, there is no doubt that, aged 30 and without a single building to his credit, he hoped that it would be he who would design a new programmatic building, he who would reconcile art and technology, he who would produce the first modern British masterpiece. Meanwhile, while he was feeling his way, he continued to learn from the first generation, prepared to accept that 'until we create our own theories or arrive at a new philosophy, it is better to understand our heritage than to try to produce in a void without direction.'

Jim made two voyages to France, in 1954 and 1955, mainly to look at buildings by Le Corbusier. Up till then he had only seen the Pavillon Suisse. In September 1954 he went to Paris, armed with a typewritten 'Paris Corbfinder' giving him directions how to find 11 buildings by Le Corbusier, and a number of others by other architects; 'Maisons Jaoul' is added in pencil at the bottom of the list. On 7 September he sent Sandy Wilson his reactions on a postcard of Juan Gris's *Petit Déjeuner*. 'Cook terrible disappointment – just like Connel Ward and Lucas – not as good (externally) as their house at Hampstead. Garches absolutely magnificent – scale heroic, geometry and penetration everywhere apparent – painted same white inside and out – otherwise De Stijl decoration (by Corb) with floors/blocks – black (externally) yellow (internally) too much concrete – knee level furniture on 1st floor – otherwise no criticism – Side walls casual compared to the stress of the long elevation – but they cant be seen for trees. Roll up Cook – Lipchitz – La Roche (except for town planning) – Molitor, and send them down the river – no good – in any case you cant see them for TREES.'

His reaction to the buildings – and to others which he saw later during this visit – are written up at greater length in the notebook. 'The Paris Corbs are disappointing, one knows them so well from the books, it is a sad shock to see them in their natural habitat.' The disappointment was for various causes; Maison Cook should have been an isolated villa but was part of a terrace; other houses had been spoiled by alteration or seemed tentative in their design; the Pavillon Suisse showed little real innovation, was arbitrary and 'too picturesque': Jim always disliked fanciful features unless they grew out of the brief. But three buildings gained his largely unqualified admiration: the Maison du Salut (or Cité de Refuge) in Paris, the Villa Savoie at Poissy and the Villa Stein at Garches.

The Maison du Salut was 'the toughest Corb I've seen yet', and he found 'masterly' what he called its town-planning: the entrance porch, bridge and circular rotunda which led in progression from the street, involving a 90-degree turn in the axis of approach.

As to Garches and Poissy, 'It is a toss up', he wrote, 'to say which is the better', but Garches caught his imagination in a way that Poissy did not. 'Socially one wonders for what sort of person this 20 cent palace was built, and what sort of people can inhabit it in the future – to succeed domestically it would certainly have to be occupied fully and with grand personality individuals, nobody petty or introvert would suffice – For a small family there would be a temptation to camp out in upper bedrooms and to allow the timeless and devastating of the lower floors to flow on, with only periodic visits to the bridge to see that all is well.'

He expounded on the nature of the ideal inhabitants for Garches when he wrote up his notes for an article in the *Architectural Review* in September 1955. 'It is difficult to imagine Garches being lived in spontaneously except by such as the Sitwells, with never less than half-a-dozen brilliant and permanent guests.'

The 'construction of the house', he went on in his notes, 'is superb – no cracks – no flaws in the RC, though the mastic of the windows has deteriorated in places, presumably with long neglect. The machinery i.e. boilers – plumbing are very high power and Rolls Royce. For instance the gates at the concierge's lodge are solid iron and it is with some effort one pushes them back, in fact they are the sort of barriers one would expect to find on the boundaries line of two countries – it is an event one is crossing the frontier. In this Architecture there is not one inch which is accidental – control is absolute. Corb must have felt like God when it was finished.'

Having seen Garches and Poissy Jim had to qualify his assessment of them as integrating art and technology. They were metaphors for technology, not technological. 'The earlier works are only in a special way results of a "machine aesthetic", it would be a mistake to think they are compiled of machine elements or built by a machine process. They most

81

decidedly are not – the construction is traditional almost antiquey, the machine elements which are incorporated are products of railroad engineering and steamship fabrication. But what is 20th century modern art for instance at Garches, besides the influence of cubism, is the spiritual presence of machine power – the whole atmosphere is charged with a silent dynamism (the silent machine perpetually in motion). The inside of Garches is more similar than any contemporary power plant, to the Mumfordian prophesy as to the end product of 20th century technology – "The silent staffless power factory" . . . Corb of the machine aesthetic is in anticipation of a society and its architecture which has not yet arrived.'

Jim went with Alan Colquhoun to see Le Corbusier's Maisons Jaoul at Neuilly at the end of his Paris trip, or just possibly on a separate visit. In the summer of 1955 he visited Ronchamp and the Unité at Marseilles. That summer Evelyn Hogge was staying with her parents near St Tropez 'and he turned up in incredible sort of football shorts, striped T-shirt, and socks, and black plimsolls. Just him, and penniless. He had remembered where I was and had come to ask my father to lend him some money. He'd been jumping trains, I think, already quite a bit. Whether he had gone to Italy as well I can't remember, but he had certainly been to see the Unité and things like that. He borrowed money from Daddy, who paid up like a lamb, and got home that way.' He stayed a couple of days: Evelyn took him into St Tropez and they ate grilled sardines in a cheap restaurant, which he enjoyed.

He must have detached himself from the group of AA students with whom he had visited the chapel at Ronchamp. He had sent a postcard of it to Sandy and Muriel Wilson, married that year. 'Building seen with Gowan students, most appropriate – surprising lack of solidity, due to festival type surface finish, colour etc., appalled by bad taste of RC trappings, certainly exploits the situation. Superb acoustics, marvellous sculptural (form) integration – no anti-climax (i.e. bad corners) but surface finish frequently in bad taste – i.e. coloured glass to windows (Anelau) also murals [will date] form will not.'

It is not a rapturous postcard. Jim's very mixed feelings about what seemed Le Corbusier's change of direction in his recent buildings had already been expressed in what he had written, were, if anything, increased when he saw them, were written down at length in his notebook, and were finally published in two articles in the *Architectural Review* (where Reyner Banham was still on the staff): 'From Garches to Jaoul' (September 1955) and 'Ronchamp – Le Corbusier's Chapel and the Crisis of Rationalism' (March 1956). Evelyn Hogge corrected their spelling, and edited their language: 'I contributed nothing to the ideas, but I did make them intelligible. I would say "Well, what exactly do you want, what are you trying to say?" He didn't always take kindly to it either. It was very difficult to make him realise, no, no, you really couldn't say that – it didn't make sense.' But in fact the articles draw heavily on the ideas already written out in the notebooks, and often on their language as well.

Jim could not but be impressed by the dramatic mass of Ronchamp: 'handling of form superb – no mistakes anywhere'. But he was not captivated by it (he changed his opinion in later years); it was too remote from anything that he admired; he found it difficult to appreciate sculptural form without any apparent geometric, proportional or functional base. He confessed his puzzlement in his notes: 'there is something about it (the idea in Corb's mind, I think) which I have failed to grasp. With considerable on the spot study I feel it might eventually communicate something of great importance – what?' This honest avowal is left out of the article; so is a more dismissive judgement: 'the form of this building will not date, as like the Johnson Wax by FLW it is outside the mainstream of the modern movement.'

There were other aspects of Ronchamp which Jim actively disliked, above all what seemed to him the dishonesty of its construction. The curving walls had originally been intended to be constructed by spraying concrete onto a wire framework. This, as it seemed to Jim, innovative technique had proved impractical; the design had not been changed, but instead the same effect had been gained by rendering over a mish-mash of traditional walling and frame construction. Jim found this distasteful.

At Maisons Jaoul Jim was similarly impressed by 'the sheer plastic (artistic) virtuosity of Corb', and the excitement of the vaulted internal spaces: 'they are encountered suddenly as one turns a corner, or passes a slot revealing an unexpected vertical . . . they are surprising and a little inexplicable (mystery) and they reminded me a little of FLW (also the finishes . . .).'

But – the houses 'are very exciting but the worst condemnation is that they are anti-mechanistic and unregional . . . they are against the machine, in fact, arty-crafty – they are handmade with unskilled labour . . . they are south and peasant.' The rough, handmade quality which so excited many of his contemporaries left him unmoved. He noted without comment that the concrete was 'deliberately crude'. As for the brickwork: 'if the finish had been harder i.e. blue Staffordshire English bricks with definite joints between wall and RC – the appearance would have been more mechanistic and I think that better (?) – not certain.'

Jim always lived in the present. He may not have liked the way that things were going, but he accepted what was in the air and recreated it in his own way. Thanks to Le Corbusier peasant culture and vernacular architecture were in fashion with architects. Jim was later to contribute an article on the subject, 'Regionalism and Modern Architecture', to *Architects' Year Book 8*, edited by Trevor Dannatt, and published in 1957. It was mainly illustrated by his own photographs, of Liverpool warehouses, Kentish oasthouses, a Staffordshire tile kiln, and so on, taken in the previous few years. Prefabrication and mass production of low-cost housing, he wrote, was no longer acceptable. In Europe, as opposed to America, the building industry was not prepared to go along with it. It was wedded to traditional methods. Architects had reacted by going back for ideas to 'anything of any period which is unselfconscious and usually anonymous'. The New World was 'inventing techniques', the Old World was 'exploiting and contorting, traditional ways and means. ... As a nation, we will probably get the architecture we deserve, and at this stage, we might reconsider these new trends which may ultimately be recognised as standing apart from the mainstream of modern architecture.'

Meanwhile, the tenth meeting of the CIAM (Congrès Internationaux d'Architecture Moderne) had taken place in 1956 in Dubrovnik. The theme was 'Habitat', and the contribution of the English architects was a series of projects for rural housing. The meeting had been prepared by Team X, a group of young European architects, including the Smithsons and Bill Howell from England. Many architects believed, Jim perhaps among them, that Jim should have been on the team but had been kept out by the Smithsons. Anyway, he did not attend the congress, but did send in a project, as did Howell and the Smithsons, who attended it. The congress resulted in violent rows between the younger and older architects, and CIAM never met again.

All three English entries, prepared in 1955, were for linear village schemes, of traditional brick or masonry load-bearing construction with mono-pitch roofs; the mono-pitch roof was, for some reason, the type of vernacular roof in fashion among young architects. Jim's entry was, as he put it in the accompanying explanation, 'to be built of local materials by local and, if necessary, unskilled labour'. But there was nothing random or 'arty-crafty' about it. The houses were ingeniously linked together on a staggered linear plan, and tightly composed in modules of 7 and 10½ feet, and angles of 30 and 60 degrees. It was rural housing polished up to crystalline perfection.

In the same year Jim was preparing the working drawings for a small house at Woolton Park, on the edge of Liverpool. The commission had come to him in the previous year. This, too, was based on mono-pitched roofs, set at different heights, running in four different directions and mounting up to the highest roof above a single bedroom on the first floor. There was a functional justification for all the roofs; but what ended up was a tightly controlled formal composition of roofs, each one setting off the other. The commission fell through in the final stages, and the house was never built.

In 1956, the Independent Group attained its culmination, and also what proved to be its dissolution, in the exhibition *This is Tomorrow*, held at the Whitechapel Art Gallery in August. This had been nearly two years in germinating, with members of the Group involved all the way along. The exhibition was made up of twelve separate booths or areas in which twelve different groups did separate things; each group was composed of people working in different disciplines. Artists outside the Independent Group were invited, as well as most of the people who have featured in this and the previous chapter, but the tensions which accompanied the preparations for the exhibition and the very disparate nature of the final exhibits made clear how little unity of approach there was in the Independent Group. In terms of publicity and public enjoyment, the show was stolen by the exhibit of Group Two – Richard Hamilton, John McHale and John Voelcker. It was almost pure Pop Art, and included, among much else, a giant bottle of Guinness, a jukebox, and the 16-foot-long Robbie the Robot, borrowed from MGM's film *Forbidden Planet*. Robbie, or rather an operator speaking from inside him, opened the exhibition. At the other end of the spectrum Sandy Wilson, Frank Newby, Peter Carter and Robert Adams in Group Ten created a large and impressive piece of architectural sculpture, through which visitors could walk, which was pure homage to Ronchamp.

Jim worked with two sculptors, Michael Pine and Richard Matthews, in Group Eight. Sandy Wilson calls their exhibit a 'funny little sort of sculptural object', and it was curiously unambitious compared to what many of the other groups produced. It took the form of a piece of sculpture inspired by taking photographs of soap bubbles, and was made by pasting slips of newspaper onto chicken wire, and painting the result white. The technique might be seen as a kind of kitchen version of the technique that Corbusier had hoped – but to Jim's disappointment failed – to use at Ronchamp, but it bore little relationship to anything else he ever did. Long afterwards he wrote 'I knew I was involved with something a bit off-track for me; far from having any burning convictions, I was a bit casual and tongue-in-cheek about the project.' According to

85

Sandy Wilson, 'When the catalogues appeared and nearly all of us were showing off in it, by putting in examples of our work and so on, I can remember him being very annoyed because he hadn't been aware that there was an opportunity in which he could have advertised himself, nor was he in any way interested in what he had done there. He hadn't grasped the significance of the whole thing.'

In fact, Jim's most significant contribution was what he wrote in the catalogue: 'Why clutter up your building with pieces of sculpture when the architect can make his medium so exciting that the need for sculpture will be done away with and its very presence nullified?' By the time the exhibition opened he was at last working on a building of his own, and this concerned him far more than the exhibition. He was never again to show the slightest desire to collaborate with artists or sculptors.

All this time Jim was working for Lyons Israel Ellis. He had gone there at the beginning of 1953, probably on the recommendation of Peter Smithson (still friendly), who had been taught by Ellis as a 5th-year student at Durham University. The firm was low-profile, hard-working and highly professional. Lyons and Israel had been partners since the 1930s. Their practice had started on the strength of their winning the competition for Wolverhampton Civic Halls in 1934. This was in Swedish moderno-classical style, with a rather elegant entrance portico of slim octagonal Ionic columns. The practice restarted after the war, and was joined by Tom Ellis; he became a partner in 1949. For a few years they had very little work, but then they benefited from the great surge of school building in the 1950s. There was more work than the architectural departments of local authorities could cope with, and private firms got the overspill. Lyons Israel Ellis established a reputation for schools, and had all the work the firm wanted from 1953 and through the 1960s, mainly though not entirely on schools.

The office was old-fashioned and formal. Everyone but the partners wore white draughtsman's smocks. Christian names were not used. Lyons and Israel worked in the front room; Ellis, when Jim was there, was working in the back rooms with the assistants. All drawings were done precisely and unshowily with lead pencil; ink was not used. All three partners had drawing boards, and were constantly working at them. The rattle of T-squares from the partners' room would be broken by a crash, as Israel's T-square shot onto the floor, and he came in to see the assistants. Then it would be 'Mr Yarker, a little point has revealed itself, and will have to be watched with care.' According to James Gowan, who came as an assistant in the year before Jim, 'there was an unwritten rule of silence in the office – heads down, and at the end of the day everyone

86

was black with pencil dust'. Frank Newby was the engineer for several of the schools, and when he came to the office, 'Lyons would nod to you, but what I couldn't do was talk to the assistants. I wasn't allowed to waste any time. I would come to see Tom and I just talked structures and that was that – a "cheerio" as I walked out. Quite different from other practices at the time, where you chatted away and had lunch.'

Lyons mainly did his own work, and stylistically looked back to what he had done in the 1930s. Israel and Ellis worked together. Israel was the down-to-earth, tough-minded partner. According to Neave Brown, who came into the firm in 1957, 'he held the finance and organisation in the palm of his hand, literally. Given a question, a small notebook would appear, minutely tabulated, hieroglyphic, subject to interminable erasings and revisions, always complete and up-to-date.' According to David Gray, who ultimately became a partner, 'if you ever had an idea which needed testing, he would apply an icy douche of common sense to it. He could say why it wouldn't work quicker than anyone I've ever known – like a mechanic in a garage – he didn't care about the lines of the car, he just told you if the carburettor was working. He chose the secretary, who was always good to look at.'

Tom Ellis was the enthusiast and the partner with new ideas. He had discovered Le Corbusier in the library of Lancaster College of Art when he was a student there in the 1930s, and was still a devotee. Jim described him as 'interested in intellectual and aesthetic matters, and in architecture outside this country. He was always flashing books in front of one's nose, was enthusiastic and wanted to talk.' Ellis's son John remembers how 'Jim would visit our house and he and Tom would pore over the latest volume of Corb like Talmudic scholars analysing plans and sections. As a young kid it made me aware of how exciting architecture could be.'

Previous to Jim and Gowan the assistants had been recruited from the Regent Street Polytechnic. They were self-effacing technicians, made precise drawings, and knew all about detailing and drainage. Ellis began to recruit a different type, more academically-minded and interested in design. He said that he liked to surround himself with officer material rather than other ranks; there was a certain amount of tension between the two. He used Smithson to put him in touch with promising young architects, several of them trained at the AA. Gowan and Stirling were to be followed by Alan Colquhoun, Neave Brown, John Miller, David Gray, Keith Manners and others. Draughting smocks gradually disappeared, but not in Jim's time.

For Jim, 'what impressed me was to find three partners who were all drawing, all with pencils in their hands, sitting at boards with T-squares going up and down. After the partners at Cubitts it was really quite incredible. You hardly ever saw them with a pencil in their hand, and you never saw Lyons, Israel and Ellis without one, although Ellis seemed to leap around a bit more. What I will be forever grateful for was that they made me the assistant in charge of the Peckham comprehensive school, which I administered, including site supervision. I learnt how to build a building through that experience, which lasted for about a year and a half. Whatever practical knowledge I acquired was during that period. It was a marvellous prelude to breaking into one's own practice. I felt confident about design when I was at school, but I was totally ignorant about putting a building up.' The advantage of a school for learning was that, unlike an office block, it was full of variety; one had to deal with classrooms, laboratories, and an assembly hall, as well as offices.

Under the influence of Ellis and his young men the look of the firm's work changed. Trescobear County Secondary School in Cornwall, which was won in competition in 1955, used exposed beams in board-marked concrete clearly inspired by Corbusier's Maisons Jaoul. Here the firm was a pioneer in England, and board-marked concrete and the influence of Le Corbusier were to be prominent in its work for the next fifteen years or so. Jim never claimed to have had anything to do with Trescobear, and the school at Peckham had been designed before he was involved in it. It used in situ concrete but this was generally plastered and painted. Jim could make an input into some of the detailing, however: a water-tower with a frame of board-marked concrete, and a rather crazy concrete stair crawling like a spiral worm up the side, is perhaps his first executed work.

Jim got on well with Ellis and he and Israel respected each other. He always spoke his mind to the partners, regardless of the fact that he was just an assistant. According to David Gray, 'Israel's reminiscences about Jim were quite amusing, because he'd got somebody as tough as himself. He was going to recruit somebody whom Jim had known, and Jim came in and said, "No, you absolutely can't have him" as if it was his, Jim's, verdict that should stand on this – but I think Israel probably took him anyway.' On such occasions 'they would have a terrible row, and Jim would go out of the room with his employment not quite secure, but then later they would make it up, and Jim would come up with photographs taken on his holiday, and it would be all right.'

The only assistant with whom Jim became friendly was James Gowan. Gowan had not only been born in Glasgow but, unlike Jim, brought up there and had a strong Scottish accent – all points in his favour as far as Jim was concerned. He had qualified at Kingston School of Architecture, and had worked for Powell and Moya on the Festival of Britain Skylon, before going to Lyons Israel Ellis. He and Jim had interests in common – English baroque, castles, vernacular housing, warehouses, and industrial buildings. They photographed these and showed slides of them at what became called the NW1 group, at which Stirling, Gowan, David Gray, Paolozzi and others used to meet and talk about art and architecture. Gowan had a dry sense of humour, but was quieter, more self-effacing, and also better organised than Jim. He was sometimes described as 'canny', sometimes as 'dour'. He didn't get drunk or sleep around. Jim took him along to Sam Stevens, where Paul Manousso remembers liking him but 'he was a much less definite character to me, at any rate, than Jim'. He never became a full member of Jim's set, and their friendship was largely a professional one.

Jim, like all ambitious young architects, wanted to get a good commission and start his own practice. He was doing his own work while he was at Lyons Israel Ellis, but it was all small stuff or abortive: possibly the Sheffield competition, though this may have been just before he joined the firm, the house in Woolton Park, which came to nothing, and little jobs which Evelyn Hogge remembers him working on. 'A shop-front which had one of those keyhole windows, and he also had something to do with the South African Airlines at the bottom of Albemarle Street.' The big opportunity came towards the end of 1955, when he was asked to design a small housing development at Ham Common, in the western suburbs of London. At the same time, or soon after, Gowan got the commission for a house on the Isle of Wight, and on the strength of the two jobs they set up in partnership together in 1956. David Gray thinks that perhaps Jim 'saw James potentially as the workhorse, as it were, of the partnership, in the form that so many partnerships do take; the extrovert and performing partner, and the one who stays in the background and keeps the wheel oiled.' If so, he was underestimating Gowan.

The Ham Common commission came to Jim through Paul Manousso. His father, Luke Manousso, was Chairman of Maybrook Properties, a sizeable firm of developers which did work all over England, and in Belgium and France. Manousso says that Jim had no idea of this. Jim had been helping Manousso with his final-year work at the AA and 'I talked about him a lot to my father, and I said how very stimulating and helpful he was. My father asked me if he would be interested in doing this scheme for flats in Ham Common, and they met, and they got on quite well.'

The site was the long narrow garden at the back of a Georgian house on Ham Common. The development was for thirty flats, strung out in three blocks, each with a rather skilfully staggered plan. In notes for a lecture Jim wrote that the inspiration for the plan came from De Stijl, for the 'scale and exterior contrasts', from English nineteenth-century functional architecture, and, for the brick and concrete finishes and textures, from Corb, 'and I hope some personal contribution of our own'.

In fact much the most obvious inspiration was that of Maisons Jaoul, but it was the Maisons Jaoul without the characteristics that Jim had criticised when he was there in 1954. Far from being neo-peasant-vernacular built by Algerian labourers, the flats were very precisely detailed and constructed by a good English contractor. Instead of the 'poor brickwork' which Jim had noted at Maisons Jaoul, the bricks followed his queried suggestions there: 'if the finish had been harder . . . the appearance would have been more mechanistic, and I think better.' The concrete beams were much less massive. The concrete was left board-marked, but had none of what Jim had called the 'deliberate crudity' of Maisons Jaoul. Instead of Le Corbusier's chunky protruding beam ends there were shapely concrete 'gargoyles' for drainage, to obviate down-pipes. The whole development could reasonably be described as elegant.

Inside there were no concrete vaults, but many of the walls were of exposed brick. There were carefully designed concrete mantel shelves over the fireplaces, and rather romantic concrete-walled access bridges to some of the flats. The kitchens had very solid chunky built-in fittings, in contrast to other kitchens of the time, which were still in the spindly Festival-of-Britain style.

Mr Manousso liked Jim, but according to his son, 'found him a difficult person to work with. He kept telling me, "Your friend's a terrible prima donna. You know, it's very irritating, because he's terribly touchy and won't make the little changes that I want, as a developer. He has a very feminine side to him. He's rather like a dressmaker producing a dress, and there are terrible scenes if I want the windows to be two inches lower or higher, because I don't think that the people buying them would like it." He found James Gowan a great deal easier to deal with than Jim. I think he was much more business-like, and understood the problems of a developer or financier much better. But he liked the scheme when it was finished, though I should add that it was an incredibly difficult scheme to sell.' The flats didn't look like anything that people were used to. Mr Manousso didn't employ Jim again, 'I'm afraid because he was difficult. But they certainly parted as friends, and I must say that he always, throughout his life, showed great appreciation both to my father and me.'

The flats aroused a good deal of interest. Reyner Banham claimed them as New Brutalist, much to Jim's annoyance; he disliked the label and thought, perhaps correctly, that the term would put off potential clients. But the architectural world was intrigued by the idea of Brutalism at the time, and the flats got coverage in the Italian, French and German architectural press, as well as in England. They established Stirling and Gowan's reputation.

SIX

THE LEICESTER EXPLOSION

The years from 1956 were ones of extraordinary achievement for Jim. At their beginning he was admired as an architect and talked of as a coming man, but only in a small circle. The Engineering Building at Leicester made him internationally famous. It and its successors were given top billing in architectural magazines everywhere, and architects and architectural students came from round the world to visit them. Le Corbusier was getting old and his star was on the wane. His last buildings received comparatively little attention, and he died in 1965. Architects and, perhaps even more, architectural students, were looking for a new god, and in Jim, more than in any other architect of his generation, they found one.

In these years Jim stopped writing, except for postcards, stopped talking, except in gruff laconic phrases, stopped reading, except for books on architecture, and put all his creative energy into building.

In these years he continued at first to work with Gowan, but it was Jim who attracted the bulk of the publicity.

In these years, he began to teach and work in America, and established a cult and a reputation there, for a variety of reasons, some of them scandalous.

In these years, he quietly moved his birth date from 1924 to 1926.

In these years he put on weight. The glamour-boy of the early 1950s did the opposite of melting away. His friend Sandy Wilson claims responsibility. In mid-1956 he left London to work with Leslie Martin in Cambridge, and his weekly game of squash with Jim ceased. By the end of 1956 Jim's students at the Architectural Association had nicknamed him 'Jumbo'. He began to be described by girls as 'cuddly'.

In 1964 Jim was driving slowly through Soho, rather drunk after a party. He was heading the wrong way down a one-way street. A policeman stood in the middle of the road and signalled him to stop. Jim continued, and scooped the policeman up on his bonnet. He did stop, eventually, and got out of the car to talk with the policeman. The latter's deposition described Jim as leaning 'heavily' on the bonnet. The case came to court and he lost his licence for a year. The adverb 'heavily' amused his friends.

In 1965, Mary Shand, soon to become his wife, and Mary Banham, sitting together in a London hall, watched him go up to receive the Reynolds Aluminium Prize. Mary Shand said in alarm, 'I must put Jim on a diet.' He was ceasing to be cuddly and in danger of becoming gross.

For Jim and his circle the 1960s were, as David and Ilse Gray put it, 'absolutely wonderful'. Austerity was over. London was bursting with life. All the circle had jobs, or were getting work and reputation. They had more money, and were young enough to enjoy spending it. Most of them owned cars. They drank more. Pretty students or au pair girls in mini-skirts enlivened their parties.

The French Pub continued to be a meeting place, and so did Sam Stevens's flat in Marylebone High Street. The Banham coffee sessions moved from Sunday mornings to Friday evenings. Magda Cordell and John McHale went to America, Sandy Wilson went to Cambridge. In the 1960s Peter Banham became the guru of a younger group of architects, who took up with enthusiasm his idea of a disposable 'pop' architecture, and propagated it in brilliant drawings in their broadsheet *Archigram*. Jim's friendship with the Banhams continued but he went to them much less often.

Towards the end of the 1950s, the London and country homes of Michael and Cynthia Wickham became new centres for the architects and others in Jim's circle. Michael Wickham was a photographer, and Cynthia Blackburn, his wife, was a journalist. Both worked for a time for *House and Garden*, which in those days took contemporary architecture seriously, and publicised it. Michael Wickham had photographed the flats on Ham Common, and buildings by other young architects, and friendships developed. Wickham was a flamboyant figure, ex-Marlborough, a gentleman Bohemian and Communist. He went around in a broad-brimmed hat, and gave the impression of wearing a cloak, even if he was not. Earlier, in 1947, he had shocked the conventional by escorting Princess Elizabeth around the Council of Industrial Design wearing bright pink socks and a brown bowler. He worked through four wives. His third marriage, to Cynthia Blackburn, broke up in 1979, and shortly afterwards she married Keith Manners, who had been one of their architect friends, and was briefly an associate in Lyons Israel Ellis, along with David Gray.

As far as Cynthia Manners recollects, 'we first met Jim in 1956 or 1957. At that time we happened to know a lot of architects. Both my husband and I had worked for *House and Garden* magazine, and had been involved with design and architecture. I suppose because one met the architects they all became friends, and they were always coming round to our house in London, in Mansfield Road. It was a sort of house with an ever-open door, like Dr Barnardo's. It was in Gospel Oak, grandly called NW3, but in fact it was Kentish Town. Gone now, I'm afraid; it was a dear little Victorian house with a garden full of apple trees, and fishing rights on the River Fleet, which ran under the garden.

'Jim was lovely. Not very talkative. Just lovely and friendly, and relaxed. It was so nice that he used to turn up without being invited, and feel happy, and have coffee or tea or whatever happened to be going on. I suppose he was beginning to put on weight. He was a little older than all the other architects who used to come, because they were still thin, and some of those have put on weight now. But he was plumpish, very good-looking: a lovely face; just . . . cuddly. He used to talk about how when he was a boy in Liverpool, and I was a little girl in a pram. He was just delightful. He could be funny, in a dry sort of way. He'd stand there without saying much, but you were conscious of his presence, and then some sort of dry remark used to come out. He had a rather nice laconic attitude. But he was never the life and soul of the party, in a noisy way.'

'Amongst the others who came were Kit Evans, Adie Gale, David Gray, Sam Stevens, Ken Frampton, Cedric Price, Ted Cullinan, John Miller. Ernö Goldfinger used to come, not at the same time, as far as I remember, as Jim. It wasn't only architects, though it seemed like it sometimes. There were designers, and journalists as well, because, as I said, we had both worked on *House and Garden*, and I was still freelancing for various other journals, doing interiors and so on.

'We used to go to the Duke of Cornwall, a pub round the corner in Lismore Circus, with Jim and anybody else who was there, to play shove-halfpenny. People used to come to tea, and then it was time to go to the pub, and then it was time to have supper. So they would come back to us. Very often there were twelve or thirteen people for supper. Goodness knows how one managed. We ate in the living room, at a big table. Various people used to take turns in cooking. I don't remember Jim ever doing so. Sam Stevens used to sometimes. He used to carve too, because in those days we could afford large joints of meat. Amazing, isn't it? People used to bring them, of course, as well, which was very kind of them, and David Gray said he'd never had such a small portion in all his life as he had in Mansfield Road when Sam was carving. Occasionally people rang and you spoke to them, and said, "Come and have supper", but sometimes they just happened to be there, and you said "Oh, carry on . . . let's have supper." Which was lovely.'

According to Michael Wickham, 'We immediately liked Jim very much. We found him a highly accessible character. He fitted into our scene very rapidly, and he came very often. But all his life he was a man of relatively few words. What he did say was said in a toss-it-off kind of way. He was never rude to people – though that nice tough Liverpool way of talking could seem to be rude, in a way, but it never was, because it was always done with such amiability. Invariably when he expressed an opinion it would be accompanied by a laugh, to indicate that "it doesn't really matter – I'm only just throwing it off". He was great value at a party, because he liked everybody. He was always a jolly fellow ... slightly backslapping kind of bonhomie. He loved gossip. He laughed at himself, you know. I don't remember ever engaging in a serious conversation with Jim, that didn't dissolve finally into laughter and general disorder.'

In 1961 the Wickhams leased a house at Coleshill in Berkshire from the National Trust. It was what had been the stables and laundry blocks of the great seventeenth-century house, designed by Sir Roger Pratt, which had been destroyed by fire in 1952. At first they went there for weekends, but in 1964 they sold the house in Mansfield Road and moved full-time to the country. Michael Wickham started to make furniture for Habitat, commissioned by his friend Terence Conran, and set up a workshop at Coleshill. Cynthia continued to run an open house for architects and others: 'They all came. It was a big old house, you know; naturally they all wanted to have a look at it, and tell us what to do. Being architects. And argue. We had a party there once, and someone had bought a sort of Indian tent or canopy. There must have been about six or seven architects in the kitchen ... there was Kit, there was David, there was my stepson Julyan Wickham, and Keith ... and I think Jim was there. They argued about how to put this tent up for about three hours, and any two women could have done it in about ten minutes. It was a wonderful example of architects ... they all said "Oh, well, we'd need a drawing, you know ... we've got to draw that." We were killing ourselves. Only a little canopy, in the garden.

'People would come for the day, because from London it was quite easy for the day, or occasionally they'd come and sleep on the floor, or on camp beds or in tents outside. It was very empty and very big, and there was plenty of room. At first we thought that it was far too big just for us, so Kit and Marsha Evans took a wing. Often Jim used to come down and see Kit and Marsha, and come over to us in the older part of the house. Which I think he quite enjoyed, because it wasn't quite so modern as Kit's bit. He quite liked the crumbliness. He used to say so, anyway. It was a change, you know, from neat modern architecture.' He felt at home, perhaps, in the kitchen with its six-foot-diameter kitchen table, made in elm by Wickham: 'Huge though it was, it always seemed to be overflowing with flowers, home-made jams, olives, wine, French china, other people's children and visitors.'

Jim was perhaps on the look-out for surrogate homes. Another place where he used to drop in, not all that far from Mansfield Road, was the house of Bill and Gill Howell, in South Hill Park, a few doors away from where he had lived when he first came to London. Bill Howell had been in the LCC Architects' Department with Sandy Wilson, as one of the pro-Le Corbusier, anti-People's Detailing anti-Swedish group. In the 1960s he was in partnership with John Killick and others, and the firm was beginning to make a name with tough, chunky concrete buildings of which the University Centre in Cambridge (1964-7) is perhaps the best known. Jim was never easy with architects whom he saw as competitors, and there was always a little awkwardness, though no dislike, between him and Bill Howell. But he got on well with Gill, and used to appear at South Hill Park unannounced with his current girlfriend 'to display them, perhaps', as she puts it.

Various girls passed through Jim's life in these years, and were brought to Gill Howell's, or taken up to stay with George and Barbara Hayes. There was Brit Bakema, the exotic daughter of a well-known Dutch architect. There was a dazzling Australian who survives only in a vaguely-remembered story that she had run away from home to London and that her father came to bring her back, and in a press photograph taken in Sydney with an inscription on the back: 'To you darling, I know you'll hate it, but just keep it for the time being. In a month or two you can throw it out. Poppet.' There was a New Zealand girl, whom Jim took up to the Hayeses' and talked of with fondness in later life. There was Santa Raymond, who met him when she was an architectural student at the London Polytechnic, and took him on as crew racing at Cowes in her father's boat. He was much in love with her for a time, and they remained good friends in later years. But these were all relatively short relationships, and not always affairs. His affairs with Janet Kaye and Eldred Evans both lasted several years.

Jim struck up a friendship with Janet Kaye in the autumn of 1956, when he was tutoring the first term of the fifth year at the Architectural Association. He was in his vernacular period, and illustrated a fifth-year project by her for a 'Bird Observatory, Scilly Isles', a kind of spiral sand-castle, in his 1957 article 'Regionalism and Modern Architecture'. She was lively, pretty and dashing. At the AA Carnival pantomime she sang a song dressed as a Brie cheese, with not all that much on except an enlarged cheese box around her waist: 'I am a Baby Brie, Sink your teeth into me. I will reward you and tickle your taste, Even my skin is too luscious to waste.' Her previous boyfriend had just gone off to the States to work, and in the course of the year she saw more and more of Jim. 'My gang were charmed by him, and also made fun of him a bit. We called him Jumbo, and didn't take him terribly seriously. He was a curious mixture, sincere and sensitive but also rather blunt and gauche. He sometimes could be slightly embarrassing because he was so straightforward and so unabashed by anything, so he would come out with things which we sophisticated little Londoners might not have. But he was enormously good fun, always very interested and extremely friendly. Right at the end of my AA career, at the beginning of August, I was suddenly diagnosed diabetic. I was just twenty-three, and it seemed like something really nasty to have for the rest of your life. I was a bit shattered by it, and Jim completely organised me. He took over my move: I was moving from Earl's Court to Lawn Road Flats in Belsize Park. He painted the whole place out for me, and was unbelievably helpful. It's something I will never forget, and will always be really grateful to Jim for.

'I think it was in the summer of 1957 that he went on a three-week tour of Europe, to Italy, and he asked me to go with him, but for some reason I was very reluctant, and didn't go. I suppose it was because I really wasn't sure of my relationship with him, because I had this other guy in the background, in America. Anyway, I think he went with Margaret Dent. Then I started with Architects' Co-Partnership, my first job. I certainly was going steady with Jim at this point. I had a Vespa, and I used to take him on the back, which was quite a challenge. He wasn't as sizeable as he became, but he was certainly not a slender youth.'

Cynthia Manners remembers the Vespa, and Janet 'with her very tight short skirt and her really high-heeled stiletto shoes, with a huge square shopping basket on the back, or Jim. She was very glamorous; she had long hair: occasionally it was up, but sometimes it flew out. They made a fine-looking pair.'

For fifteen months or so they went everywhere together. They made frequent outings to Ham Common. They went up to Liverpool, where Jim showed her Oriel Chambers and the Docks, but did not take her to see his family. They went to stay with the Paolozzis, at their cottage at Thorpe-le-Soken in Norfolk. They went to Jim's usual jazz haunts, and to the cinema, especially to science-fiction films. 'He took me to one called *The Fly*. It was about a man who by doing an experiment of some sort, had turned into a fly. Little by little on the huge screen you saw his various limbs turning into a fly's, until only his little face was left. It was gruesome, and I was absolutely repelled by it. Jim thought it was absolutely hilarious, and terribly funny that anyone could be intimidated by it. He was a very bold character, a curious combination of boldness and sensitivity.'

They went to Banham coffee mornings, on one of which 'Bucky Fuller came along, with his own decaffeinated coffee'. They went frequently with the gang to the French Pub, and lunch afterwards. 'Jim would talk a lot and drink a lot and stand on one foot and wave about, and then stand on the other.' At one lunch, 'I suppose there were fifteen or so people there. Douglas Stephen was sitting next to me, larger than life, very sharp, very naughty, always centre stage, and trying to say something precocious to upset people – but really a very nice chap. I was a fairly naive youngish person. Douglas said to me, "There's one person sitting at the table who's slept with everybody round it," and I said, "Gosh, it's not me!" I remember being horrified, and he said, "No, no . . . guess." I looked around, thinking, couldn't think who it could be, and he said, "It's Jim." I don't know whether he meant girls, or boys as well, so that will remain a mystery.'

Douglas Stephen deserves a paragraph because Jim, like many others, was fond of him, and was extremely upset when he died not long before Jim's own death. He was born in Scotland, brought up in China, and trained in Liverpool. He was married to Margaret Dent, whom he met in Liverpool, and later to Sandy Boyle. He was a card-carrying Communist who enjoyed high living, frequented race meetings, sported a bowler hat, suits with cuffs, a natty moustache and an E-type Jaguar (he said, 'Well, you have to operate guerrilla tactics, you know'). He was a good architect, European rather than English in his Modernism, with an eye for talent. He was often deliberately outrageous in his remarks, but was a loyal friend and, as Ed Jones, who worked for him, puts it, 'an immensely charming, witty and lovable man'.

Jim at this period still had very little money. He and James Gowan were living off their fees from Ham Common, from a small new house on the Isle of Wight, and from a little teaching. Janet and he 'went a lot to Indian restaurants, which were cheap at the time, and Jim was always hungry, and ate a great deal. I remember that because when I had undiagnosed diabetes I was eating twice as much, because none of it was doing me any good, and I would be keeping up with Jim. Which meant eating two lots of everything. He didn't notice how he looked after himself. He always looked slightly dishevelled. He was just so interested and preoccupied with what he was doing. York Terrace was a very dour place to live, I can tell you. As I recall, it was dark hardwood panels all the way round, drawing boards, and this little divan bed in the corner. It was definitely an office. I don't remember anything comfortable there at all.'

In December 1958, Janet Kaye went to the States 'to get some experience as a young architect, but also to sort myself out with this previous boyfriend'. Jim wrote to her, but his letters have been lost or destroyed. She worked for six months or so in Chicago, with Harry Weese, an architect whom Jim had suggested, and then for I.M. Pei in New York. In the autumn of 1959 Jim came out for his first session as visiting critic at Yale University School of Architecture. They met up. She went to Yale with him, and to see Philip Johnson at his house at New Canaan, and Louis Kahn in Philadelphia. By now she had resolved the situation with her boyfriend. She got engaged to Jim in New York in December.

Max Gordon, the English-born architect and interior designer, and a friend of Kit Evans, was living in New York then, in a minimalist apartment. 'There wasn't one item that you could see in his living room. I can't remember if there were any chairs, the impression I have is that there was nothing there. There was tracing paper, or some film of translucent stuff, over the window. Everything he possessed was in a huge cupboard, and the room was just pristine. Totally white.' They told him of their engagement, and he said they must get married in Las Vegas. As Las Vegas is the place for quick divorces, as well as quick marriages, the remark suggests an element of cynicism. It was justified. On 16 December they flew out to San Francisco together for Christmas, to stay with the Schicks, razor-blade millionaires with whom the Stirling family had a connection. Janet Kaye broke off the engagement in San Francisco, about two weeks after it had been entered on in New York. 'I just didn't see myself being married to him. He was cast down for a while, but I think he had a very good system with women. He had clear periods of attachment to one woman at a time, and when that was over, it was over.'

In 1960 Jim had a passionate and turbulent affair with Barbara Chase, a black postgraduate student whom he met at Yale (of which more later), and then found a new girlfriend in London in the summer of 1961. Eldred Evans had just graduated at the Architectural Association. Jim met her at a party given by Georgina Cheeseman at a house on Regent's Park. Malcolm Higgs, who was working in Jim's office at the time, was at the party. At some stage he went up to the bathroom, and found Jim and Eldred sitting in the bath together, both very drunk.They remained together for nearly three years.

While in her last year at the AA, Eldred Evans had been persuaded to enter a major competition for a Civic Centre at Lincoln, and won it. She bought herself a black Rolls-Royce out of the prize money. Her design had been developed out of her final-year thesis, and Jim, with others, spent a good deal of time helping her to prepare the necessary competition drawings. Gowan did not take too kindly to this. The news of her success came through when she and Jim were at Yale School of Architecture, he as visiting critic, she doing the Masters course there, along with Richard and Su Rogers and Norman Foster. She cut off her time at Yale, and came back to England to work on the Lincoln design. In London, she had a flat on the first floor of a big late-Victorian house in Hampstead, on Frognal. Jim's office was still in York Terrace, but he was living in the Lawn Road Flats, the pioneer modern building designed by Wells Coates in the 1930s, where Alan Colquhoun had a flat, and where Janet Kaye also lived for a time. Jim had a one-room service flat at Lawn Road, and when he returned to England was often in Frognal.

Those who knew Eldred Evans at that period all say the same two things. She was indisputably the best student of her year at the Architectural Association, as committed to excellence in architecture as Jim was. And she was 'very wild'.

The Wickhams and others also remember her whiteness – accentuated by the fact that she normally wore dark glasses. 'She used to lie about on the lawn, always dressed in black, and looking extremely pale, as if she hadn't seen the light of day at all for ages and ages . . . She was as white and as pale as a ghost, very slim, smoked like a chimney, and drank very heavily too.'

Richard Rogers was 'in the same year as Eldred at the AA, so I knew her very well. She was an amazing person, first of all because she had won the Lincoln Competition as a student, which made her an extremely important person to any young student. She was the bright spark of her year at the AA. In the Masters year at Yale the brightest student there was Eldred, and not Norman or I. She had a very strong character, probably more formed than we had. Jim and she were intellectually well linked, wonderfully well. She was quite a lady – she could drink well, swear well, etc., so they made a striking couple.

'In a sense she was somewhat of a goddess in her period. Good-looking in a slightly Scandinavian . . . Nordic . . . way, short hair, blonde, touched up, dress slightly masculine, very alluring, extremely . . . with a great laugh, and no patience whatsoever for anything that wasn't absolutely top. Absolutely nil. She enjoyed life, but her interest was very much about architecture and quality. And music. One of her parents was a musician, and one was a considerable painter. Both worked in schools, and I think their relationship with her was rather close. This gave her an exotic background to us younger people. She was a star in her own way, but not a flighty Marilyn Monroe character . . . very much more Nordic . . . a Marlene-Dietrich-like lady, at times introverted, but a very powerful personality.'

The impressions from her contemporaries pile up: 'Had this wonderful petulant indignation about things of which she didn't approve. And that usually included most other architects' buildings. Had very strong views about those indeed. "Absolutely disgusting. How can they publish this tripe?" But you got the feeling that a lot was for the moment, slightly play-acting, going over the top for an effect. . . . She was one of the most totally committed and hard-working architects I have ever come across. She was an absolute workaholic. She would never rest until, for her, something was absolutely perfect. She was quite an awe-inspiring student to teach, from that point of view. One's lasting impression is of always trying to keep her self-esteem high enough. She used to descend to the depths of despair if something didn't work out.' . . . 'She was slightly austere, but capable, when provoked, of laughing quite a lot. Could turn giggly, which was very disarming, going from the serious to the giggly.' . . . 'She has become a very sober person. She wasn't sober then. She was a wild kid who was always drinking, and carrying on, and being outrageous, and laughing a lot.' . . . 'As to the relationship with Jim, on an architectural level . . . I'm sure she would have been quite stern with him, she wouldn't have let him get away with anything. She was quite a hard-liner architecturally. Very much a purist . . . but a very warm person, a softie, really, on the other side.'

Keith Manners moved into the ground floor of the Frognal house, immediately underneath her flat, in about 1963. 'Not many of us had televisions at that time, and I hired a black and white set. Jim used to sneak downstairs to surreptitiously watch this set, much to Eldred's disgust. She used to occasionally come down and put her head round the door, and abuse Jim roundly, and then go back upstairs again.

'There was a restaurant somewhere on the north side of Oxford Street, incredibly busy at lunchtime, where, I suppose uniquely at that time, you could get marvellous steamed puddings, of which Jim was inordinately fond. He used to eat these things at lunchtime, and Eldred used to berate him when he got home to Frognal in the evenings. "Jim, Jim, you are disgustingly fat. Absolutely disgustingly fat, and I know you've been eating steamed pudding again."'

Eldred Evans's father Merlin was a painter, and lived in a house and studio on South End Green, not far from the Lawn Road Flats. His wife (Eldred's stepmother, not mother) was a concert pianist of some distinction. Jim got on especially well with the father, as did Keith Manners, who recollects how 'we used to drink an awful lot of whisky, and Merlin used to play his trumpet. Rather bad jazz trumpet. It was just a very enjoyable time. It was a nice old converted Sunday School down at South End Green, where he had two enormous etching presses. They must have been, I should think, two of the largest presses in London. It was a lovely spot.' Jim often looked in, and bought two of his etchings.

Jim and Eldred travelled round together, to Liverpool, to Leicester, to Paris, to Le Corbusier's monastery at La Tourette, to Barcelona, and to various places from Yale. They went to Ireland, to see the celebrated Celtic hermitages on Skellig Michael Island. They never got to them. The sea was too rough to land, the ship's engine broke down, and they spent several unhappy hours tossing up and down, in some danger of being wrecked, before the engine was mended. They went to parties, where they were often very drunk and very much together. But, as she recollects, 'most of his time was spent working. He worked seven days a week, and that's it. We were rather antisocial. . . . He was generous, kind, very friendly, very warm, very supportive, very amusing. Everything. I've got nothing to say against him. He was reserved with people he didn't know, but he enjoyed drinking and eating, and he had many wild moments.' But 'people always came second to his work'.

Although Ham Common gave Stirling and Gowan considerable *réclame* in the architectural world, it was a relatively small commission. It was accompanied by a small house on the Isle of Wight, followed by a small conversion in London, and a sizeable mixed-development housing scheme in Preston. This was passed on to them by Lyons Israel Ellis, who kept the point blocks for themselves. Stirling and Gowan did the rest, Stirling concentrating on terrace blocks and Gowan on an adjoining group of pavilion-type housing. It was useful bread-and-butter work but, like all new firms, what they needed and hoped for was the big breakthrough of a really prestigious commission.

The opportunity came in 1958, when they were invited to be one of twenty practices competing for the new Churchill College in Cambridge. Here was a plum indeed, if they could only get hold of it. In 1958 the *Architects' Journal* could comment that 'there are no notable post-war buildings at Cambridge'. In fact Cambridge, like all British universities, was about to embark on a massive campaign of building. Churchill College was one of the first projects, and one of the most ambitious: a new college for over 500 resident students and 60 fellows, on a 42-acre site, founded in honour of the greatest living Englishman, with all the prestige that brought, and lavishly supported by public and private funding.

Stirling and Gowan owed the invitation to Sir Leslie Martin, one of the assessors of the competition. He had gone to Cambridge as Professor of Architecture and head of the School of Architecture there in 1956, after eight years as Deputy and Chief Architect to the London County Council. At Cambridge he also had his own private practice. He brought Sandy Wilson in to work with him both at the School and in the practice, and he left much of the design work to him.

Martin was a phenomenon. His knighthood in 1957 underlined his position as the most powerful figure in the architectural establishment. He belonged to the cream of Labour's intellectual and cultural aristocracy, civilised, dedicated, socially committed, a good writer and talker,

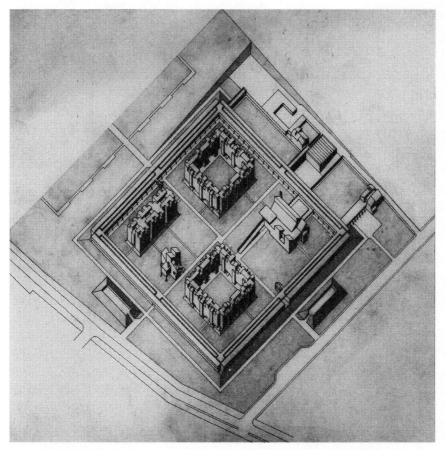

Stirling and Gowan's competition design for Churchill College, Cambridge, 1958

effortlessly dealing out development plans to cities and universities (which, if carried out, would have demolished large stretches of the cities). In addition to his own work – and he was never greedy about getting this – he was the great dealer out of work to other architects. It was something he both enjoyed doing, and was able to do, because he had his finger in so many pies. The extent of his influence would make a remarkable study. He was always on the look-out for talent, and used to ask Sandy Wilson, 'Are there any people who we ought to be trying to find work for?' Sandy brought Jim Stirling up to Cambridge for crits, and introduced him to Martin. He never especially liked Jim, whom he found too brash for his taste, but he proved a good friend to him. Jim was well aware of his power. He told Janet Kaye that it was important to meet him, because he would recommend him for a project, and went with her out to the converted mill, filled with drawings by Ben Nicholson and Moholy-Nagy and with sculptures by Gabo and Hepworth, where the Martins lived in some style near Cambridge.

The two partners threw everything that they had into the Churchill College competition. Their entry was dramatic in its strength and simplicity. The site was large, flat and featureless, on the outer edge of Cambridge. They designed what was in effect an ideal city. Four ranges of two-storey student rooms, each over five hundred feet in length, defined and enclosed the college, like the city walls. The analogy to walls was increased by the fact that the flat roofs provided a perimeter walk, and that the ranges rose from high turfed banks, as did the castle walls of Restormel in Cornwall, which Gowan had photographed.

Inside this great outer square was an enclosed court on the same grand scale, with a cloister walk all the way round at the base of the perimeter ranges. Spaced out in the big court were the library, the refectory and small courts of five-storey lodgings. From the outside these would have been seen rising above the outer walls like towers or a cathedral in a city.

The Stirling and Gowan entry was one of four selected to go through to the second stage. The others were by Howell, Killick and Partridge; Sheppard, Robson and Partners; and Chamberlin, Powell and Bon. Sheppard, Robson won with a scheme at the opposite extreme to the Stirling and Gowan one: twenty small courts (ultimately whittled down to ten) loosely scattered around a central space. Colin Rowe weighed in in praise of the Stirling and Gowan entry, and in denigration of most of the others in an article in the *Cambridge Review*, titled 'The Blenheim of the Welfare State'. 'It seems to have been agreed', he wrote, 'that a college implies a courtyard, and that the more courtyards a college possesses, the more collegiate it is likely to become . . . most competitors seem to have been satisfied to take any number of courts, to press them into either complicated or casual relationship, to flavour them all with an aroma of Cambridge (understood to be a demure charm) and to complete the whole with reminiscences of Le Corbusier or Scandinavia.' The title of the article was not, as is sometimes assumed, a commendation of the Stirling and Gowan scheme, but a denigration of the Sheppard, Robson one; Rowe was no friend to the Welfare State. Stirling and Gowan's entry was a Blenheim, perhaps, in its grandeur of conception, but its monumental simplicity owed more to the Renaissance or, most of all perhaps, to neo-classicism. Colin Rowe thought that the initial idea came from the small Mexican town of Chiapas de Cozo, an example of Spanish colonial town planning which he once described to Jim.

Gilbert Scott consoled himself for his loss of the Foreign Office by transferring his repertoire to the Railway Hotel at St Pancras. Jim worked out his disappointment over Churchill College on a school hall at the Brunswick Park School in Camberwell. The resulting mini-Blenheim for children is an amalgamation of the Churchill College library and of Jim's Woolton Park house: three spiralling mono-pitch roofs and one flat one are set on four squares and joined to form one big square. The building rises from turfed banks, as in the Churchill College scheme, and the area around the banks forms a still larger square, proportionally related to the smaller ones. The grand little building stands free, and rises from its banked podium like some ideal building of the Renaissance. Even the boiler chimney, at the outer angle of the flat-roofed square, assumes a heroic quality.

Leslie Martin tried again on Stirling and Gowan's behalf in 1959. Selwyn College at Cambridge wanted a new residential building, and Martin recommended them. The College was given a design as striking in its different and more modest way as the one for Churchill College. The building, also to be raised on a banked podium, was designed to form an S curve along the perimeter of the College garden, to which it would act as a wall, giving privacy to the garden and screening it from adjacent developments. The outer side of this wall of rooms was to be of brick, and virtually windowless. The inside was entirely of glass. Jim's principle of expressing internal arrangements externally was applied by faceting each stack of rooms in a slightly different direction, so that the building would have rippled like a jointed snake of glass. In 1965 Jim wrote that 'College members walking in the grounds would have seen reflected in the glass a shattered Cubist image of the trees in the garden.' The first stage was intended to include only a portion of one curve of the S. But lack of money or differences of opinion among the Fellows intervened, and even this was never built.

At the end of 1959, Martin was finally in a position to give Stirling and Gowan a firm commission, in a situation in which he was virtually in control. He had been asked to provide a development plan for the University of Leicester. His projected new buildings were mainly in a rectangular site on the edge of the existing campus. But there was also a small regular triangle to be filled, between the older university buildings and the adjacent public park. This was allotted for a new engineering building, and in September 1959 the University, at Martin's instigation, offered the commission to Stirling and Gowan. It is unlikely that either Martin, or the University, or Stirling and Gowan, realised what was to be the outcome of this modest commission in an obscure corner of what was still a minor provincial campus, only recently raised to full university status.

It was the beginning of a period of great expansion in the university world. New universities were being founded, old university colleges, such as Leicester, were being upgraded. New departments were being opened in existing universities, especially on the technological side. Leicester was chosen as one of them, and a new department of engineering was set up there. Edward Parkes, the first professor and head of the department, had something of a reputation as a radical. He was appointed towards the end of 1959, at much the same time as Stirling and Gowan. He was, in fact, in America on a year's sabbatical from Cambridge, and it was agreed that he would take up his appointment in September 1960. Initially he communicated with Stirling and Gowan from across the Atlantic, but he returned to England in March 1960, and came to live in Leicester, though still teaching at Cambridge for a few months.

It was a new department, a new university, and a young team. Parkes and Gowan were both aged 33, Jim 35. Frank Newby, who was the engineer (as he had been for the Camberwell school hall), was aged 33. Michael Wilford, whom Stirling and Gowan now took on as their first full-time assistant, was aged 22. Professor and architects got on very well together. They tended to regard the Vice-Chancellor as representing the stick-in-the-mud older generation, and had rows with him from time to time. But on the whole they were given their heads, and allowed to do what they wanted on their little patch of land. Money was not too tight. They were not saddled with any supposed Oxford or Cambridge tradition. Rather the reverse, for the younger universities were looking for a different and, if possible, a more progressive image. A building for a technological department could be expected to look, in some kind of way, technological. Parkes provided a comparatively short functional brief. 'I think they were slightly taken aback by this, because they said – though obviously they were going to ignore it, whatever I said – "Don't you have any idea what it should look like?" And I said "No, that is your business. I am concerned that it should do its job, but how you achieve that result is up to you".'

The architectural team was young and it was also small. The building was drawn up and designed in Jim's one-room flat at York Terrace. In the early stages, before Jim went off to Lawn Road, he was still sleeping there, and if he had had a night out, Michael Wilford would arrive and find him in bed. At first Wilford was the only full-time assistant. Malcolm Higgs was already there working part-time, and later became full-time. David Walsby worked for a period part-time, as did one or two others, including Quinlan Terry and Julian Harrap. Harrap, like Michael Wilford and others who worked for Stirling and Gowan at this time, was qualifying by studying at evening classes at the North London Polytechnic, and working in an architects' office at the same time. Stirling and Gowan liked using these Polytechnic students, because they had good practical experience. Harrap was sent to them by Eldred Evans, for whom he had made a model of the Lincoln Civic Centre scheme. 'She was a particular support during my training. She was immensely understanding of the poverty of students. I used to sleep under one of her drawing boards at a time when I didn't have anywhere else to go.'

The partners sat at their drawing boards by the left and right hand of the three windows, Wilford sat at the centre window and anyone else sat at the back of the room. Wilford's position 'was good because I had a good light, but they would argue with each other across me, so there was I in the middle, busily trying to draw, with this verbal salvo criss-crossing backwards and forth.' The exchanges could get more and more heated. At first it would be 'Jim' and 'Jamie', but as they became more worked-up, 'Jim' and 'Jamie' both became 'James', and it was, 'Noo, James', 'That's not so, James', 'Och, noo, noo, noo, James', volleying to and fro. 'It was pretty unpleasant at times . . . nevertheless, for someone who certainly wasn't biased either way, it was a design education. The tension was creative, but I'm sure one can have a creative tension that doesn't resort to such verbal ballistics.'

There was a concert pianist living and practising below, and strains of Beethoven came up through the floor. The use of the room as an office was against the lease, and became progressively harder to conceal as the room grew fuller; Wilford and others were instructed in the right misinformation to give if they were ever questioned. Office administra-

107

tion was minimal. Wilford waited for a letter of appointment prior to giving notice at his former job, and it never came. 'I remember phoning them up, and they said, "Oh, you want a letter?", so I said, "Yes, please."' To begin with there was no secretary, and Jim typed out the letters. Quinlan Terry recalls with pleasure the following dialogue:

> Jim: 'How do you spell "exception"?'
> Terry: 'e.g.s.e.p.s.o.n.'
> Jim types it out.

Later, a secretary came two afternoons a week.

Wilford's role 'was to organise the drawings into a coherent set that we could base a tender on, and start construction with. I found myself thrown in at the deep end, dealing with situations and the use of materials which were quite unusual, in a very experimental, very intense situation. Also, we were working through that job only about two or three weeks ahead of the contractor. The drawings were being done literally hand to mouth, and passed out. In some cases I remember going up to Leicester and measuring stuff up, in order to come back and draw it, so that we could do the next detail. So, all in all, for a young architect, it was an amazing experience. Yes, it was a big assignment for a very small firm, but I don't think any of us thought of it quite like that at the time. Certainly it didn't faze me at all. One was using materials in ways that had never been done before, pushing contractors and subcontractors to the limits, but it all seemed quite natural. And with Jim it was all matter-of-fact. It was obvious, somehow, that that was the way to do it. It couldn't be done any other way. It was Gowan who dealt on a day-to-day basis with the contractor and was always very tough. The contractor would complain about the late drawings. . . . Gowan taught me to write the one-line reply to a six-page letter of complaints. Basically dismissing it. I learned a lot from Gowan, in terms of contract administration and relationships with contractors.'

According to Jim's invariable principle, the different uses of the building were clearly expressed externally: workshops, laboratories, offices and seminar rooms, lecture theatres and circulation spaces. The workshops needed much the biggest area, and also top lighting. Parkes had asked for a big undivided space, which could be adjusted as needs changed. They were put into a rectangular block, with the heavy-machinery workshops at ground level, and smaller aerodynamics and electrical workshops on the first floor at one end, above the boiler and maintenance rooms. These projected above the service road to allow machinery to be lifted up through openings in the floor.

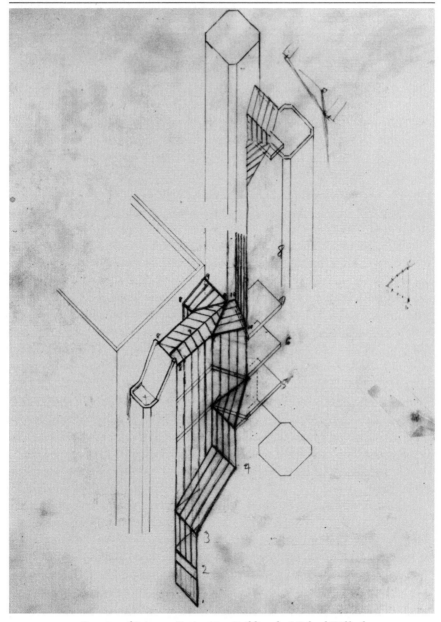

Drawing of Leicester Engineering Building, by Michael Wilford

Parkes required a water tank 60 feet above ground, for pressure experiments in hydraulic tanks at ground level. This suggested a tower, which could be an office tower, to support the tank. As built this was actually 100 feet up. Next to this was a lower, wider pavilion, containing four floors of laboratories. The lecture theatres projected, in Russian Constructivist fashion, from the first floor of the tower and pavilion. The tower was supported on very slender legs, which ran to either side of the lecture theatres. The circulation space was between the offices and the laboratories, with two staircases and a lift tower enclosed in slender turrets, and lobbies in between.

The north lighting required for the workshops ran at 45° across the workshop building. The laboratory block had to be fitted into the remaining triangle of the site, which meant one corner had to cut off at 45°. Set off by this, a 45° motif appears throughout the building. The office tower, for instance, has 45° splays at the corners. The grids of the laboratory ceilings are set at 45°. It is a pleasure to look at the shapely and disciplined plan that results.

The bones of the design were all in the drawing which Gowan presented to the client in March 1960. Stirling was away teaching at Yale in November and December 1959 and February and March 1960. But the design which finally emerged between the end of 1960 and the autumn of 1961 was in a different spirit from this drawing. It had become crystalline, gleaming and delicate. The differences all came from refining the original elements, but the resulting changes were dramatic. The strip windows on the laboratory block now protruded, like the frills on the neck of a lizard. The vertical divisions on each face of the tower had been doubled. The entrance lobbies on each floor were reduced in size as they went up, on the logical premises (in terms of function, perhaps not of cost) that the numbers of people circulating decreased as the building went upwards. As a result the glazing of these areas, instead of being a simple vertical, spilled down like water running over a series of projections. It had always been a problem how to devise a satisfactory junction where the structure of the workshop roofs hit the outside walls at 45°. It was finally achieved, neatly and with sensational visual effect, in a long line of squares resting on triangles, like giant crystals, with the line of the upper workshops banked up above the lower ones.

The whole complex was expressed in a consistent language of glass, steel, and glowing red tiles, the last internal as well as external, and applied in a continuous smooth skin to floors, walls and ceilings. The tiles were supplemented in places with bricks of the same colour. In the circulation spaces this combination was clear and workmanlike. The metal rails and pipes (the plumbing was left exposed) were exquisitely detailed, and had something of the gleam and glamour of a well-kept engine-room. They were also spatially enticing, for almost every floor was different, and off the main spaces there were straightforwardly romantic

Louise Frazer, Jim's mother

Joseph Stirling, his father

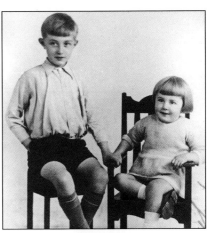

Jim as a small boy

With his sister Oonagh

Jim holding bird's eggs

Liverpool School of Architecture,
with Jim in front

In Black Watch uniform

In the early
1950s

Around 1955

Jim having a look

Detail of the flats
at Ham Common,
1955-8

Assembly Hall, Dartmouth Park Primary School, Camberwell, 1958-61

Jim outside the Engineering
Building, University of Leicester
in the early 1960s

The tower and
laboratory block,
Engineering
Building,
University of
Leicester, 1959-63

Barbara Chase Riboud in about 1961

Alan Colquhoun at Maisons Jaoul, photographed by Jim

Creative tension: Jim Stirling and James Gowan outside York Terrace, Regent's Park

Eldred Evans in her Rolls Royce

The History Faculty
Building, Cambridge,
1964-7, exterior
from the south west

History Faculty,
looking down into
the Reading Room

Detail of Andrew
Melville Hall,
St Andrews, 1964-8

Detail of Olivetti
Training School,
Haslemere, 1969-72

Housing at Runcorn
New Town, Cheshire,
1967-76

Jim with Mary Shand at the presentation of the Reynolds Aluminium Prize, 1965

Jim and Mary in Greece

Jim with the newborn Ben, 1967

vistas, along corridors, up and down stairs, and through the glass skin to the outside world.

The building was sensational in the daytime, and even more sensational at night when its tower and prisms glowed from within, so that the children at the school across the park called it the 'fairy palace'. Jim was delighted by this, and loved to walk out, by himself or with visitors, to look at it when it was lit up. Photographers loved it too, so much so that, as Parkes says, 'we reached a stage, with cameramen, television crews and whatnot wanting this building illuminated at night for their benefit, when we felt like billing the two Jameses for the electricity bill.' In general, Jim was ravished by his and Gowan's creation. He constantly brought visitors up to see it, partly for publicity, partly because he enjoyed it so much. He brought journalists, visiting architects from abroad, and all his own friends. He brought Philip Johnson, who loved the building, but found Jim 'inscrutable'. He came often with Eldred Evans, whose Rolls-Royce appears in the foreground of a reproduced illustration of the workshops, much as Le Corbusier's car was photographed in front of his buildings. He came with the Banhams, and repeated to them with enjoyment Colin Rowe's comment, as he looked down on the workshop roof from the top of the tower, 'Oh, Jim, it's like the sea coming in.'

He loved it that until the water tank was filled the pipes running down from it acted as organ pipes and produced perfect chords (a member of the staff who was a cellist used to come and accompany them). Mary Banham remembers how 'We sat at the top of the tower, and Jim was saying "listen to this . . . listen to this". It was one of the most magical experiences I've ever had. Jim said, "It's got to be changed, unfortunately, but I wanted you to hear it."'

Jim liked to take people to the base of the glazed spiral staircase running up into the lecture theatre, to watch the women students climbing up it. Or he walked them across the park, to get a good view of the building lit up at night. It amused him to see his friends scared by the vertiginous effect of looking down the main stairs at the top of the tower through the sheets of unprotected glass to the fall below. Possibly this reminded him of his parachuting days. It was not an effect that he was allowed to keep. The tiled steps could get slippery in wet weather, and there was a possibility that the person slipping would go through the glass. So Parkes and others said to him: 'You know, this will not do. There will have to be a horizontal bar.' Jim reacted with 'utter shock, and said "but the whole concept of the tower is verticality, and you will be able to see those bars from the outside through the glazing, which will spoil this.

Try it for a year or two, and see how you get on." We felt that he felt that if you don't lose more than a couple of undergraduates a year, it's all right.'

In the Leicester Engineering Building, there is an obvious shift away from buildings which, like Churchill College and the Camberwell school hall, could reasonably be described as monumental, to abundantly glazed, faceted, delicate buildings. There are earlier indications of the way in which Jim's mind was going. Some time in the 1950s, when he was walking with Sandy Wilson on Primrose Hill, Wilson recollects him 'talking about doing a building all in glass and it was something to do with the fact – which isn't strictly true, but partly true – that in this country there wasn't so much sun, and this meant that buildings were not modelled in terms of shadow and light coming up – the Italian thing – and that by using glass you could show the form by faceting because glass reflecting the sky in different facets was going to convey shape more brilliantly than shadow on solid would do.' And in pre-oil-crisis days, when no one bothered too much about heating bills, Jim was attracted by glass as a cheap, flexible material.

In 1955 or 1956 Jim renewed his interest in Peter Ellis's two office buildings in Liverpool, and made a synopsis of Ellis's work and career in his notebook. The buildings are remarkable not only for the street façade of Oriel Chambers, with its rows of delicate glass and iron oriels recessed between iron shafts, but because of their rear façades, which are almost entirely glazed. His office building in Cook Street has a glazed spiral staircase which is reminiscent of the little staircase which rises up into the base of one of the lecture theatres at Leicester, and was used to give inconspicuous access to late arrivals at lectures. There are other heavily glazed unornamented rear façades – the utilitarian façades – of nineteenth-century Liverpool buildings, at least one of which Jim photographed, probably at this time.

In 1958 Jim went with Colin Rowe and another ex-Liverpool friend to see Pierre Charreau's Maison de Verre in Paris, the façade of which is a continuous wall of glass bricks. He was intrigued enough by it to take Eldred Evans there two or three years later. And, of course, the faceted glass façade of the Selwyn College design, made in 1958, was something new in the Stirling and Gowan practice.

The Constructivist elements in the Leicester building are undeniable, and Stirling did not deny them: not only the Melnikov-style lecture theatres, but a flavour of the sharp outlines and sheen of glass of Alexander Vernin's project for the Pravda building in Moscow. Leicester is very much not in Corbusier's sculptural or primitivist style of the

1950s, but its precision and delicate shapeliness pay tribute to Jim's loves, Corb's villas at Garches and Poissy. There are suggestions, too, of the sleek modelling of the tower of Frank Lloyd Wright's Johnson Building. There is an obvious influence from the many utilitarian railway-siding or individual buildings which both Stirling and Gowan enjoyed photographing at this time, with their stilt-like legs and striking geometric shapes. In 1957, Edward Reynolds, a gifted AA student and French Pub crony of Alan Colquhoun's and Jim's, whose career was cut short by early death, had done a project in his fourth year in which single-storey workshops with an elaborately geometrical roof are combined with an office tower at one corner. Both Stirling and Gowan would certainly have known of it, for both were teaching at the AA at the time. Another remarkable faceted design by Reynolds and Paul Drake for a concert hall, and Christopher Owtram's extraordinary model which Jim saw in 1954, may also have suggested the idea of moving to more faceted buildings and a more elaborate geometry.

The building owed a good deal to Frank Newby. Newby saw his job to be to 'give architects the feel that they can design what they want and that they don't have to worry too much about the structure. I give them the confidence to design – that's the role of the structural engineer.' When he first became involved at Leicester, in 1960, the main form of the building had already been fixed. He made the structure work, and in doing so contributed visual elements. The elegant chamfer that transfers the octagonal office tower to its four columns is due to him. It was he who suggested that the ceiling beams of the laboratories should take up the 45° grid which provided the geometric base of the building. To Jim's delight he was able to take out as redundant the columns which Jim had put in to support the overhang of the lecture theatres. The impression that the tower and its lecture theatres give of a delicate balancing act is no more than the truth. The weight of the tower holds the lecture theatres in position. Jim used to like telling people that if the tower were removed the whole building would collapse.

All this is to say no more than that no architects, and no artists, work in a vacuum: they take ideas from whatever sources are to hand, and it is in how they use them that they show their quality – and it is why they use them that is the interesting question. As far as concerns Jim, he was always ready to try something new. An engineering building was a new type of commission, and seemed to require a new image. Moreover, Jim was sensitive to changes in atmosphere. He knew the Pop Art of the Independent Group. He must have savoured the movements in the 1960s of which it was the precursor. Richard Hamilton had described

Pop Art as 'popular, transient, expendable, low-cost, mass-produced, young, witty, sexy, gimmicky, glamorous, big business'. The Engineering Building could at least be described as young, witty, sexy, gimmicky and glamorous. The tower is delicately feminine, and much smaller than it looks in photographs. It is an architectural equivalent of the slim long-legged girls who were in fashion in the 1960s. The sheen and the bright colours are reminiscent of Mary Quant talking about PVC: 'designers on both sides of the Channel were as bewitched as I still am with this super shiny man-made stuff and its shrieking colours.' Quant and others were setting in orbit what they called fun fashion, in a market ready and longing to be entertained, and entertaining.

The Engineering Building, on its functional basis, was fun architecture. Colin Rowe, when he got out of the car and saw it for the first time, commented 'That's a nice little toy that you've had made for yourself here, Jim.' Tom Muirhead, who was to work with Jim on his later buildings, remembers what a revelation it was to him, as a young man, to be made to realise by Jim's buildings that architecture could be enjoyable. Craig Hodgetts, as an architectural student at Berkeley in 1964, came across an article in *Domus* on the Engineering Building: 'I thought architecture was a rather boring thing that one did for a living, and that it was certainly nothing to excite the soul, or the emotions. I said, "Holy Cow – this is like Brendan Behan. This is like some mad crazed eruption," and I knew right away that I must go and find out something about it.'

In 1954 Jim had written about the need for a new 'programmatic' building for modern architecture, for a reconciliation of art and technology, such as Le Corbusier had essayed in the 1920s, and for a modern British masterpiece. The Engineering Building answered all three needs. It received, over the succeeding years, an international acclaim unequalled by any previous British building since the Crystal Palace. It was the 'something different' which had been waited for. Perhaps it reconciled art and technology only in the same metaphorical way as Le Corbusier had. The patent glazing systems used at Leicester had been used in greenhouses for many years. The traditions of tiles, internal and external, on walls and floors though perhaps not on ceilings, dated back a century or more. Apart from the glazing systems, the building was hand-made on site, not factory-produced and prefabricated. The structure was ingeniously devised by Frank Newby, but in no sense revolutionary. But some kind of fusion had taken place. One can see this by looking at what is happening in today's architecture, when art and technology have gone their different ways again.

114

But the architects of the Engineering Building were Stirling and Gowan, not just Stirling. Gowan has always felt bitter that he has not received proper credit for his share. Everyone who saw them working together agrees that the tension between them, however uncomfortable, was creative. Parkes is emphatic about Gowan's qualities, and his share in the building. 'Because of Stirling's subsequent eminence, a lot of people in retrospect may have felt that Gowan was the chap who sharpened the pencils, and did the detailing, and so on. It wasn't actually like that; they were both equal contributors at the time. The other thing was, and this you may find surprising in view of the fact that they broke up after the Leicester affair, that actually they were a good team. They worked well together.' When Parkes came to build a house for himself in Wales in 1965, it was Gowan whom he asked to design it, not Stirling.

The two partners made an approximate division of responsibility: Jim looked after the tower block and laboratories; Gowan looked after the workshops. All the internal detailing of the workshops is Gowan's, and he and Newby worked out the structure of the roof between them. But the division was not a hard-and-fast one. Gowan was better than Jim at finding a feasible and good-looking way of solving practical problems, in both parts of the building. He contributed to the design of the tower by insisting on its having patent glazing, in face of Jim's advocacy of plate glass; his reasons were primarily financial, because patent glazing was much cheaper, but visually the change was an improvement. The much stronger vertical stress of the narrow widths of patent glazing added greatly to the tower's elegance. On the other hand, according to Frank Newby, 'I would go and see Jim to talk about one end, and having seen Jim talk to James about the other. But once we had sorted out the tower block, then Jim tended to take over the workshop block. Then I started to talk to Jim and James on the workshop block.' Newby has no doubt that Jim was not only the stronger personality, but the principal designer.

SEVEN

AMERICAN INTERLUDES

In 1959 Jim started his long connection with Yale School of Architecture. He was there as visiting critic for several weeks at the end of 1959, and again at the beginning of 1960. He returned for similar sessions in 1961-2 and 1963-4, and was Davenport Professor of Architecture there from 1966 to 1983.

For his first three sessions, Jim came at the invitation of Paul Rudolph, who ran the School from 1958 to 1965, and in that period made it the leading architectural school in America. Rudolph was formidable. He was the rising star of American architecture. He was a Southerner from Alabama, a Methodist minister's son, puritan by upbringing, homosexual by nature, incisively intelligent, buttoned-up, ambitious, and as dedicated to architecture as Jim was. He had a big practice of his own, and all his buildings were getting top publicity. He made a huge impression on his students. As Jacquelin Robertson, later to become an architect of distinction and a good friend of Jim's, puts it: 'he was the hottest thing on the American scene at that time, as an architect. He was not a formal teacher. He was a superb studio critic. He would come to your boards late at night, and he would give you a fabulous crit. He was a very good juror. He brought really interesting visitors into the School, and they came from very very different places. The entire life of the School was twenty-four hours, and it was all about architecture.'

For M.J. Long, who was at Yale in the mid-1950s, 'he was tough as a critic, but he was very quick. Whereas most critics would sit around waffling, trying to find their way into something, he would very much more quickly than anybody say not only "I see exactly what you're trying to do, which is this, but in your own terms you're inconsistent, here, here and here". He also was a very accurate reader of drawings; he would say "That stair doesn't correspond in plan and section". Nobody else would be doing things like that. He could also be very nasty, particularly if he was goaded on by the presence of somebody like Philip Johnson. There were occasions when they were totally destructive at crits. They would

116

egg each other on, and be clever at the expense of students, and that, I think, nobody ever admired very much. But on his own, and generally, I think he was very good.'

Rudolph lived in style, in an apartment that seemed to English visitors like something out of Hollywood: a double-height main room, marble steps coming down into it, a huge wall of glass, and a Steinway grand. A few hundred yards away a new building for the Schools of Art and Architecture was rising to his design. Its completion was awaited with as much suspense as the birth of a royal baby. It was to be his masterpiece, a dramatic sculpture in concrete, proclaiming what critics called the architecture of 'form for form's sake', which he, Saarinen, and others were launching in reaction against the low-key curtain-walled blocks of so-called International Modernism. In the meantime, however, the School of Architecture was happily ensconced in one very large space occupying the top floor of Louis Kahn's Art Gallery. The School was not at all a big one – only about a hundred and fifty students, including the graduate year.

One of the features of Rudolph's time at Yale were the visiting critics. They came one at a time, and Rudolph picked them internationally on the basis of quality and variety, not necessarily because they were of his own architectural persuasion. Amongst other Englishmen he brought Sandy Wilson and Peter Smithson, as well as Jim. He had admired Stirling and Gowan's Ham Common flats. His own Married Students' Housing at Yale showed their influence. He remained impressed when the partners moved off in a different direction with the Leicester Engineering Building.

Jim moved happily into an ambience where architecture was eaten, drunk and dreamt twenty-four hours a day – but for occasional breakouts. He and Rudolph respected each other, but their tastes, friends and characters were different, and the fact that they were both stars and showmen did not help to bring them together. Vincent Scully, whose lectures on the History of Architecture were one of the highlights of Yale at that time, thinks that they were 'in a funny way very much alike, which both would have hated. They were both High Modern performers. Each one, each time, tried to do something that had never been seen on land or sea before, and to knock your eye out. They were natural rivals.'

For different reasons, Jim made little contact with the Yale faculty, with one or two exceptions. Everything that the word 'Wasp' stands for was not so much antagonistic as incomprehensible to him. He got on well with some of the artists in the Art Department, with Vincent Scully, and with Charles Brewer, a young and slightly rebellious member of the architectural Faculty ('I was told at one time, when I had a motor-cycle, that Yale people didn't ride motor-cycles'). But on the other hand, the Faculty rather enjoyed Jim. They knew all about England's new culture of angry young men, irreverent, working-class, vital, saying 'sod you' to the Establishment. There was nothing like that in America, and now they had a real live Lucky Jim in their midst. They even called him that. Jim was neither working-class, nor especially young, nor in the least angry, but he was not averse to the image. In fact, in his first visits to Yale he was relaxed and amiable, and out to enjoy himself. His career was on the up, his office worries were across the Atlantic, and he had no concerns over money. As Norman Foster puts it, his behaviour there even at its most outrageous was 'more a celebration than offensive'.

Above all, Jim got on well with the students. He was by general agreement one of the best tutors that the School of Architecture has had. He brought his own drawings and his own projects along with him, explained how he came to his solutions, and then set the students to work out the same projects for themselves. This evolved as his distinctive way of teaching, and, as Charles Brewer puts it, 'It was surprising and unique that he was able to use that as a teaching device, and they understood about solving problems related to design programmes, but they never came up with the same answers that he did.'

He did not impose his own predilections. Like Rudolph, he had the gift of seeing what a student was trying to do more clearly than the student saw it himself, and helping him to order his ideas. But Stanley Tigerman, who was one of his students, thinks that he also encouraged them to develop a certain complexity and richness. Rudolph's approach was much more simplistic. Tigerman found him 'a very disciplined guy' as an architect: 'Students are always disarmed by people who have restraint and discipline, and don't impose themselves.' To George Buchanan, who was another of his students, 'If Paul was head, then Jim was heart.' Rudolph could be withering, and he seemed aloof and a little frightening to those who did not get past his barrier of shyness. He did not socialise with students at all. Jim was gentler with them. He enjoyed their company, and he relaxed with them rather than with the Faculty. As Buchanan puts it, 'Our conversations with Jim were usually over a bottle of beer at a local pub, and went on and on and on.' He and his students moved naturally, still discussing architecture, from the studio to the Old Heidelberg, a bar across the street from the School where you could get steak and potatoes with your beer, or the United Diner, an all-night Greek diner where Kahn's Yale Center for British Art now stands. Jim seemed always to be in the same dirty black sweater, rather than the three-piece suits which were standard uniform for the Yale Faculty at the time. He became 'Jim' to the students, whereas Rudolph was always 'Mr Rudolph'. He was only doing what he did, and wearing what he wore, in London, but in the 1950s the Yale Faculty did not behave or dress in that way. The students thought it wonderful. They valued him, loved him, laughed with and at him, worked extremely hard for him, and where necessary protected him.

Jim misbehaved a good deal in these early years at Yale. As Tigerman puts it, 'He was restrained in everything but drinking and womanising.' A legend was created, which succeeding generations of students handed on and elaborated. One noisy and drunken party was raided by the police when Jim and a girl were making love on the floor. The students prised them apart and dumped Jim in a cupboard just in time. There was a Vice Squad in New Haven in those days, which called itself, without irony, the SS Squad, and patrolled the town raiding motels to winkle out misbehaving businessmen: one of their discoveries was Jim, in bed with a black girl. Another incident may have occurred during Jim's third visit in 1964, when Paul Rudolph's new building had been completed. A big table in the refreshment room on the top floor was known to generations of students as the Stirling table. The room had originally been part of an apartment for visiting academics, and Jim was said to have been discovered making love to one of the Faculty on the table.

In addition to whatever he may have enjoyed in the way of one-night stands, Jim had three serious relationships during his first two Yale sessions. The end of his affair with Janet Kaye has already been described. She came to see him when he was at Yale in November or December 1959, met Paul Rudolph with him, and they went together to visit Louis Kahn and Philip Johnson, and to Chicago. Kahn took them round his half-completed Richards Medical Research Building at Philadelphia. Janet remembers him as 'a funny little wizened chap, with a very bright, moving, mobile face, absolutely infatuated with his latest building'. Kahn was a hero to Jim, and to his students. Philip Johnson was not, but he was still one of the big names of architecture, and he was welcoming and hospitable to architects and students who came to his glass house at New Canaan. Jim and Janet Kaye came with a group, and they all sat round the great man in the separate Garden House '. . . in a very quiet circle, cross-legged on the floor. He very definitely was holding court. We had to take off our shoes at the door. Jim had very holey socks, very very smelly, and it was the one thing you were conscious of in this Holy of Holies.' Jim described his visits to Chicago and to Kahn in two postcards sent on the same day to Sandy Wilson:

Spent week-end with Louis Kahn – his lab: building is marvellous, best recent thing I have seen here – also very English –
though he seems to be a natural descendant of Louis Sullivan,
he talks just like the kindergarten chats. . . . Terrible routine of
continuous parties, I've seen pretty well everything but always
with a hangover. Next best thing I've seen is the Johnson wax in
Chicago which is extremely eloquent, marvellous use of
materials. The Oak Park houses are like dolls houses, Crown
Hall & Seagrams by Mies are very good but you can keep the
rest. We had dinner with Mies, he was in marvellous form – full
of jokes about Neutra in England – and how you must 'built
well' – also funny stories about the 20s in Germany. Philip
Johnson is a fantastic creep – though his house is good – but that
is all. The Yale boys are well informed though the standard of
the salons is not high. They know all about your school
extension and are full of questions. They like it. They are
reacting against ballet arch: i.e. Johnson, Saarinen, Rudolph etc.

Jim paid a second visit to New Canaan during this American tour,
uninvited, according to his new girlfriend, who came with him. She was
Barbara Chase, a black graduate student in the School of Architecture,
later to become well known as Barbara Chase-Riboud, and to make a
reputation as a sculptor and writer. Visually she was the most sensational
of the many women who passed through Jim's life. She had already
travelled in Europe for a year as a Whitney Fellow, and was more
sophisticated than most of the American students of the same age. She
was 'Miss Chase' to both students and Faculty. 'I took it in my stride,
neither as a compliment nor as an insult.' Kenneth Frampton, who met
her a few years later (again with a group of architects at New Canaan),
remembers her as 'very tall, very assured, very reserved . . . pleasant,
ironic, rather aristocratic . . . not a lady to be trifled with.'

Jim was always just 'Stirling' to her. He never taught her. 'He was
surprised to see me at Yale, and followed me round for weeks without
speaking. Finally he asked: "Who are you? What are you doing here?" He
was fascinated, and so was I. It was a *coup de foudre*.' There were no
women undergraduates at Yale, and very few women graduates. Black
students were only just beginning to be accepted, and there was only one
other black woman student on the campus. To have an affair with a
student, even a graduate student, was, as she puts it, 'a slap in the face of
all Yale establishment conventions'.

Jim left for England early in 1960, and she came to London to join him after graduation. She lived there until the winter, and it was all 'hazily romantic and intense'. Of his friends, she got on especially well with Douglas and Margaret Stephen, but she never felt at home in London, or found her way around there. Jim took her up to Cheshire to stay with George and Barbara Hayes. They liked her, but the first meeting was something of a shock because, as Barbara Hayes puts it: 'He rang up – oh, the usual thing – said he'd like to bring a girlfriend for the weekend, and he didn't mention the fact that she was black. I mean, in Cheshire in those days I don't think anybody had even seen a black person – it wasn't like Liverpool or London.'

Jim and she went for a summer trip to the châteaux of the Loire, which was a failure. 'At first he was enthusiastic, but soon completely lost interest. The whole thing bored him. He threw a tantrum.' A short winter visit to Morocco was more successful. They went to Marrakesh and Fez, and Jim 'loved the desert architecture of the Northern Sahara, the "sand castles", as he called them'. Jim must have stored up memories, and possibly re-used them, but he never referred to this visit in later life.

By the winter 'I wasn't sure I understood Stirling any more. In other words, I was confused. I left England alone to visit friends in France. Was I really going to live out this great love with a man who was a heavy drinker, melancholic, an artistic radical, ruthless in his pursuit of his art, and who expected so much from me? At 24, after running away with him against the will of my parents, I found myself basically alone, with the responsibility of a psychologically, intellectually and affectively demanding personality which I hadn't a clue how to handle. Rule: never fall in love with a person outside his own country. Both sets of parents seemed to be real obstacles. I worked for the *New York Times* in Paris, coming "home" for weekends. I got a loft in Paris on the Place des Thermes, and we took turns flying over. Either I would go to London, or he would come to Paris.

'Stirling was very different in the United States than he was in England, and very different in Paris than in London. He hated most Parisian architecture, especially the Louvre, but loved the city life and urban plan. We would roam the streets at night in the Latin Quarter, walk along the Seine in the moonlight, or sit in the Tuileries or the Parc Monceau.'

She continued her job as art director at the Paris bureau of the *New York Times*, and in the spring of 1961, through a Magnum photographer whom she had known in Egypt, met the French photographer and protégé of Henri Cartier-Bresson, Marc Riboud, whom eventually she decided to marry. She returned to London several times to tell Jim this without having the courage to do so. They had made plans to take a trip at Easter. She broke the news finally by telephone, and did not see Jim again until four or five years later. 'I learned through friends that he took the break-up very badly, drinking more heavily and putting on a lot of weight, but his architecture flourished.

'I look back on my relationship with Stirling as an important, even decisive one in my own life, and perhaps in his . . . highly romantic and turbulent, full of emotion and extremely enriching. But he built a psychological wall around his inner self, which was difficult for others to penetrate. Except for his hands, which looked like two hams – he hated his hands – he was extremely attractive with devastating aquamarine eyes. He was dyslexic, I am convinced. He hated to write letters and avoided it if humanly possible. He once sent me a clipping of a poem entitled "Like a Black Angel on the Snow":

> Today you were like
> A Black Angel in the Snow
> And it's difficult to keep this secret.
> God's seal is upon you
> So strange an honor
> Granted by Heaven
> That you seemed to stand
> In a church, in a niche.
> May it be that love not of this earth
> And love of this earth will intermix.
> May it be that storm-blood
> Will not appear on your brow
> And magnificent marble will set off
> All the deceptions of this wrath,
> All the nakedness of your softest flesh
> But not your burning cheeks.'

Jim kept very few photographs of old girlfriends, but he did keep a large photograph of Barbara Chase-Riboud, and a sheet of contacts of a roll of film which he must have taken himself. He recovered from the break-up in his usual way. He almost immediately started an affair with Eldred Evans. He was seeing her all summer, and in the autumn of 1961 she, Jim, Norman Foster, Richard Rogers and his then wife Su (later to marry Jim's friend John Miller) all went to Yale, Jim to start his second tour as visiting critic, the others to do a Masters year there. Jim's predecessor before his first tour, the Viennese architect Wilhelm Holzbauer, had spent the whole of a two-year spell at Yale, trying – apparently with success – to conceal from the Faculty the fact that the lady with whom he was living was not his wife. Jim never made any attempt to conceal his relationship with Eldred.

Stories had preceded him from his previous visits. Charles Gwathmey, who was his student, remembers how he 'had a pre-reputation of being an iconoclast, totally unique and self-sufficient, and very much a presence, so there was a huge expectation about him coming'. Eldred Evans also made a big impact in her one term at Yale. They couldn't manage her Christian name and called her Millie. Both Charles Gwathmey and George Buchanan have vivid memories of her: 'She was scary to us. So tough. Boy! Well, those were the days. Tough, assured, extraordinarily confident, unbelievably facile and . . . basically unapproachable. But she was very highly regarded as a designer . . . In the Architecture School we felt that we were at the epicentre of architectural thought and practice. You know, we thought a great deal of ourselves. We were a pretty arrogant lot. We were heavy-drinking, heavy-working . . . and Millie was right in there with the rest of us.'

Su and Richard Rogers 'lived in a very old lady's house in Eady Street. We lived there free, in a flat at the top of the house, on the basis we were meant to look after her . . . be there at night, in case she fell down, or something like that. Eldred lived in an unbelievable flat, which was basically just an attic, but heated – vast, completely white, but no windows and very low ceilings. She got this for very little rent. It must have had one or two roof lights, but it wasn't really a habitable space, but she lived there, and we had very nice parties there, although I'm sure it wouldn't have met any regulations. Jim used to go there, and he'd work on her drawings for her all night long.'

There were twenty students in the Masters year and it became remembered as 'The English Year', because five of them were English: Evans, Foster, the two Rogers, and Allen Cunningham. They went around together, alternatively making fun of America, and being impressed by it. Although they worked very hard, in a sense they were on holiday, and they were cheerfully irresponsible. Su Rogers remembers that 'we were flippant about the American lifestyle, all the time'. They used to walk about saying 'tomayto' and making fun of supermarkets, which hadn't yet come to England, motels and the car-culture, and their fellow-students, whom they found too serious. 'The students all had these massive American cars, and we couldn't believe that, having come from the AA, where people rode on bicycles . . . I really did love America, just loved it. But we did take the mickey out of it, at the same time.'

Jim was often with them, both with Eldred and after she had left.

'Especially Friday evenings, after the studios, we used to go and have onion rings and whiskey sours. We seemed to drink a lot of whisky sours.' Jim enjoyed gossip, and was as ready to take the mickey out of America as they were. They travelled around a certain amount. 'Jim had a bit more money than we had, and he was very generous to us.' The Rogers had hired a small car, and they drove down to New York for weekends, with Jim, Eldred, and sometimes Norman Foster. 'We used to joke a lot, and fool around a lot. The great New York thing was go to the Four Seasons and sit there, probably drinking bullshots and whisky sours. The Four Seasons is in the Seagram Building, designed by Mies, but Philip Johnson did the interior. He still eats there every lunch. It was an incredibly elegant place, full of rather elegant people. One day we were sitting there on a Saturday afternoon. We'd had at least six rounds. Each round came on a tray with an ashtray on it. Every single round, Jim took the ashtray off the tray and put it in his pocket. They were little ashtrays, with orange leaves on, for the Four Seasons. So Jim was getting more and more pleased with himself, really chuffed about these ashtrays. No one said anything, but finally the bill came. We got this massive bill, and it just said "Six ashtrays" on the bottom.'

They met up several times with Philip Johnson in New York, and went out to see him in his glass house at New Canaan, where Jim explained to the others that Johnson had misunderstood Mies van der Rohe. The house should have been raised up above the landscape instead of set on the ground. The way the landscape came flooding in at New Canaan did not mean much to Jim. Jim and Eldred went to New York on their own, and to see Louis Kahn in Philadelphia, and went with the Rogerses to Chicago, where they saw Frank Lloyd Wright's houses, and buildings by Sullivan and Root. At some stage on this tour Jim went to the West Coast to lecture at Berkeley and San Diego. It was probably on this trip that he saw the Charles Eames house in Los Angeles. Jim met two West Coast architects, Craig Ellwood and Rafael Soriana, and put them in touch with Richard Rogers, who was to be influenced by Soriana.

Between studies there were a good few parties at Yale: parties in the Rogerses' house when their old lady was away in Florida; parties in Eldred's attic, parties given by other students, and above all a big party given by Paul Rudolph for Jim, which has become legendary. Richard Rogers vividly remembers the crucial episode at it: 'He had this amazing modern, real extreme modern, slightly Hollywood apartment, with steps coming in at the higher level, marble steps cantilevered off the wall. At the end there was a double-height wall of glass, and outside this there was probably seven foot of open space before a big white wall. The wall had a great light on it so you looked at it as though it was the screen of a cinema, and the light reflected back into the room – absolutely white. And everybody else was there. There was a piano, and let's say a hundred people. An hour later, still no Jim. No Eldred. Door opens up at high level, there's a commotion, yells and giggles and so on, and then suddenly there come Eldred and Jim, down these cantilevered slightly marbly steps, giggling because they're canned, literally just rolling down these goddamn steps, drunk. It was a great entry. Paralytic. And like a lot of these paralytic situations, they didn't hurt themselves. A few minutes later Jim says "Where's the loo?" Somebody says, "Oh, it's upstairs." Jim says, "Fuck the loo" or something, goes into the space outside, in front of this unbelievable white screen, turns round and pisses against the glass, with about a hundred people who could look nowhere else. Like on a cinema screen.'

This story is endlessly retailed. It is the best known of the many stories about Jim. All the versions are a little different, not surprisingly, as everyone was well stocked up with drink when it occurred. It has been improved on – it seems likely, for instance, that the people at the other end of the room remained unaware – but it happened. Rudolph hated to talk about it. Other people have different theories about why Jim did it: Rudolph had flayed Jim at a crit, as was sometimes his way with critics as well as students, and this was Jim's way of getting back at him; it was a 'sod you' gesture against the Yale establishment; it was just because Jim was drunk and happy. Perhaps it was a bit of all three, perhaps mostly the last. Explanations vary, but the basic image remains: Jim, with a big grin on his face, peeing against the glass.

Jim had one more tour as visiting scholar before Rudolph left. He came again in 1966, by which time Charles Moore had become the Dean: first in the spring term as visiting critic, and then in the autumn as Charlotte Shepherd Davenport Professor of Architectural Design. This was a post which Moore had thought up specially for Jim, although he shared it, as joint professor, with Robert Venturi. Both, in theory, were to come to Yale for ten weeks a year in two sessions, alternating with each other. It was a five-year appointment, but it was renewable, and Jim held it until 1983. Essentially, it involved teaching the thesis year.

All Jim's later visits were based in the Paul Rudolph building into which the School had moved in 1954. It proved amazing and impractical: an exterior like a great fortress, board-marked concrete inside and out, a great galleried hall for the studios, orange carpets and huge modern pictures everywhere, cargo-netting hanging against the windows (and casting impossible shadows on the drawing boards). Nikolaus Pevsner had been invited to open it, and made a speech at the opening ceremony, at which he effectively said 'I think this is a terrible building to put architectural students in.' M.J. Long, who was a student at the time, and who was shortly to work for Jim, found the ceremony 'fascinating. I think very few people actually listened. You know the way openings are. Everybody was sitting there smiling, and Paul Rudolph was getting pinker and pinker. He absolutely was listening.' Jim was critical of the building, but in a way admired it for being so positive. After all the anticipation it had a controversial reception. Charles Moore hated it. It was half burnt out in mysterious circumstances in 1969, and Rudolph's interiors were largely destroyed when it was restored. Its sad history coincided with Rudolph's own fall from his pinnacle of fashion as an architect, one of the tragedies of post-war American architecture.

Jim was put up in the Visiting Fellow's apartment in the new building in 1966, but on later visits stayed in a seedy hotel in the town, where he probably felt more at home. He was progressively less at New Haven as his contacts and life in New York developed, but he was still socialising a good deal, with the students rather than the Faculty. In 1966 he made three long-lasting friendships with much younger people. One of them was not actually at the School. Katrin Adam was a young, newly-qualified architect who had arrived recently from Germany, and was working in New Haven for Eero Saarinen. Her boyfriend, Keith Godard, was in the Graphic Design section of the Yale School. She and Keith gave a dinner-party in her large unfurnished apartment, to which Jim came. For lack of a table, they had raised sheets of plywood a foot or so off the floor, and put cushions around them. Jim, who was already getting big, was not too happy about this, but he enjoyed the food and the young company. As Katrin Adam puts it, 'we were all there with our little golden plastic dresses, mini mini mini, with Courrèges boots. I think he was just amused by the whole thing', and a friendship started which lasted till his death.

So did his friendship with Craig Hodgetts. Hodgetts had been at Berkeley under Charles Moore and, as described earlier, had virtually fallen in love with the Leicester Engineering Building on the strength of an article in *Domus*. When he heard about Jim's professorship at Yale, 'I promptly got on the plane, went to New Haven, left all my belongings in Los Angeles; my wife had to trail behind. I persuaded Charles to let me into the School, and got into one of Jim's classes.' He got on with Jim immediately, and was captivated by what he calls his 'quality of daring. The sense of daring which I think that he brought to nearly everyone was a bit "Up the Establishment", a little bit of that, but it was really much

126

more about probing very deeply beneath the surface to find first causes.'
He saw a lot of Jim. 'Now I think of it, we were incredibly privileged,
because Yale had got him as a prisoner in a way. I mean, when he came
he was there; there was NOTHING else to do in Yale, I can tell you.
There weren't even good-looking girls, really.'

One of the reasons why Jim had accepted the professorship at Yale,
and why Charles Moore had offered it to him, was that Jim wanted to
establish an architectural practice in America. It was frustrating for him,
constantly shackled as he was to underfunded buildings in England, to
observe the potential lavishness of expenditure in America: a good
American practice was a chimera which he was to pursue all his life.
Charles Moore wrote to him on 10 September 1965, clearly following on
earlier conversations or letters:

> I understand all too well the problems of exchanging a known
> practice for an unknown one. I can find or even imagine no way
> of guaranteeing a practice here in advance . . . But I wonder
> whether the following arrangements wouldn't be the best
> procedure: would you come as a Visiting Professor (we could
> stick a fancy name on that) for say 10 or 12 weeks each year
> (more if you would like) for the next 5 years (or more or fewer
> if you would like) so that we and you could advertise the
> connection? If the period were not so long that it disturbed your
> existing practice but long enough so that it gave you the
> opportunity here to nail down the available jobs, then we would
> seem to have achieved some modest measure of simultaneous
> cake-eating and -having.

A job came along in 1967, through Jim's former student Jacquelin (Jack)
Robertson, who was now working in the City Planning Commission. Jim
was asked to do a Redevelopment Study for the West Side of New York,
along the Hudson River from 42nd to 57th Street, and inland as far as 8th
Avenue – the area known as Clinton. The possibilities were being
discussed in May 1967, and he and his team started work in the beginning
of September, in advance of his contract which he signed on 31 October.
The contract was with the Commission, but the money came from the
New York Port Authority.

It turned out to be a fairly ridiculous story. The Port Authority
wanted to build a grand new terminal and pier to dignify the arrival of the
great passenger and cruise liners, both of which in fact were soon to cease
arriving at all. They wanted the City to grant them road closures for the

World Trade Center, and the planners used this as a lever for the closure of several roads. The City were into planning under Mayor Lindsay, and did a deal with the Port Authority: 'Help sponsor a planning study of the feasibility of opening up this run-down area of the city, and integrating the Terminal with it, and you will get your road closures.' A possible extra benefit, as far as the City was concerned, was that the dim terminal already designed by the Port Authority's Design Department might be improved or redesigned by a good architect. Another benefit, according to the cynical, was that a rubber stamp for the terminal would get votes for Mayor Lindsay.

The planning issues meant little to Jim, but he was interested in the possibilities of designing the terminal, and also the Convention Center, hotels, maritime museum, housing and other conceivable spin-offs of a revitalised Clinton. The City Planning Commission wanted a good Planning Study, a respectable name to attach to it, and some new public housing arising out of it. The Port Authority wanted their road closures, and their new building. It is unlikely that they ever had any intention of involving Jim with this, although initially they gave him some encouragement.

Jim set up a team. His chief assistant was an old acquaintance from French Pub days, Arthur Baker, who was now living in New York. Under him were Mike Wormfield, recently graduated from Princeton, who had got to know Baker through Kenneth Frampton; M.J. Long, who had been working for Sandy Wilson after leaving Yale, and had returned to America to escape from a situation which was to end in her marrying Sandy, as his second wife, in 1972; and Craig Hodgetts, who came straight from Yale to work on the Study. Wormfield was the only native New Yorker. Baker and Jim celebrated getting the job by buying banners from the Betsie Ross Banner Company, which transferred designs by well-known artists onto felt. Jim's purchase was Roy Lichtenstein's design of a giant hand holding a pistol. He brought it back to London to face visitors as they came into his house.

The others were all full-time, but Jim only appeared sporadically. It soon became clear that he was going to get no buildings to design, and the main element that now interested him was a proposed bird's-eye view of the area as it could be replanned. The situation in the office is described by M.J. Long: 'We had very disparate people. Arthur is a very nice person, and he was anxious to do what Jim wanted done, but I don't think he was quite sure what Jim did want done. Craig adored Jim, and wanted to do exactly what Jim wanted, but he wasn't sure what it was either, because it wasn't really clear. Mike and I were going through an

128

unfortunate phase of being fascinated with Chris Alexander – you know, giving a series of options – and we kept saying "Jim, you can't just do a pretty picture; you've got to do something that's a useful tool." I mean, how boring can you be? Sort of twerp kids. Jim would get off the plane and come into the office, and say "What the bloody hell is this all about?" And we would say "Well, you see, Jim, we're trying to make this useful thing." So there was Mike and me trying to do this network of available options and decisions, and in the end the report did have the network, but it also had an aerial perspective. I doubt that anyone did anything with it other than put it on a shelf.'

The pay-off of the Study, for Jim and the rest, was being in New York, and in their particular bit of New York. After a month or two at 419 Park Avenue South, the office moved at the beginning of 1968 to the seventh floor of 33 Union Square West, and remained there until June or July. No. 33 was a late nineteenth-century building, a narrow vertical strip about twenty foot wide and eighteen storeys high, with a truncated top where there had once been an elaborate cornice. It had a cramped lobby, a shabby elevator, and the occupants included the New York office of the *Daily Worker*, a manufacturer of paper novelties, a dealer in rags, shredded cloth and wallpaper, Sol Steinberg the cartoonist, and, briefly overlapping before the Stirling office closed, Andy Warhol's Factory. This had moved there in the spring from East 47th Street. Jack Robertson remembers going up in the elevator and 'there would be these people in dynel purple wigs and knocked-out girls, and Warhol who looked like he was from outer space.

'Jim had been worrying about the profile of the towers for the bird's-eye view, and one day there were some card sheets that had contained Christmas-tree light bulbs in the bins belonging to the dealer of waste paper. Jim pulled out a sheet, looked at the negative half punched-out shapes where the bulbs had been, and said, "We'll make the towers look like this."'

Jim and his office used to eat, when they had the time, at Max's Kansas City on Park Avenue South. If they had had a rough morning, they would have three Irish coffees there after lunch. Hodgetts has vivid memories of its black-painted interior, crude black furniture, good hamburgers and clientele of 'singers, poets, sculptors, artists etc. – not a soul in the whole place with a dime'. The clientele was soon joined by Warhol and his Factory, who were to make it famous: 'a big table of the Warhol Factory people,' as M.J. Long puts it, 'sometimes Warhol himself, just being pale and sitting there, but more often the younger people, making a big show of "we're the Warhol gang". They made a lot of noise, and wore amazing clothes. I hadn't ever seen anything like it, and it was fun to watch.'

Jim was something of a pioneer in moving into the area: he loved it, and he loved going to see Keith Godard and Katrin Adam, who had now moved into New York and taken an apartment at the Chelsea Hotel, then at the height of its life as a slightly raffish centre for artists, writers and Bohemians. It was around this time that he first acquired a lasting taste for New York. M.J. Long is probably right that 'a chance to spend some time in New York, and find out a bit about how it worked' was one of the main reasons for his taking on the Study.

He had an uptown life as well. He usually stayed at the Biltmore, across the street from Grand Central Station – then a rather seedy, old-fashioned hotel, with artificial canaries singing from cages in the hall, which used to intrigue Jim. He got to know Arthur Drexler, the neurotic, endearing curator of the architectural department of the Museum of Modern Art, who was projecting an exhibition of Jim's work. Through Drexler he found himself going to dinners in smart restaurants, given by or for rich New York ladies who were into culture. He came into the office one morning laughing uproariously, and explained why to Long and the others: 'He'd got drunk at one of the two or three big deal restaurants. It was a private party, and a black tie thing. He was sitting next to . . . I can't remember if it was an Astor or Vanderbilt, but it was somebody who was a patron of something, and she was wearing a handmade Belgian lace gown with long lace sleeves. He said "You'll never guess what happened. I spilled some brandy on her sleeve, and I was leaning over saying 'Oh, sorry', and brushing at it, and I set it alight with my cigar." So he had this woman with her flaming Belgian lace. I said, "Well, did she think it was funny?" and he said, "No, she didn't think it was funny."'

Jim had the greatest difficulty in getting paid for the Study, not through any unpleasantness or unwillingness, but because of the slow working or inefficiency of the City bureaucracy. He wrote a plaintive letter to the Chairman of the City Planning Commission on 19 February 1968. His letters of 31 October, 24 November, 12 December, 1, 9 and 29 January, and 8 February had all been unanswered. He was committed to spending $60,000 and had only received $28,000. 'During the years I have been teaching at Yale I have been able to save several thousand dollars. Unfortunately these have been consumed in financing this project, and I have nothing left in that bank either.' In fact he was not finally paid off until April 1969.

Jim was back in England by the late spring of 1968. The exhibition of his work, 'Three Buildings', opened at the Museum of Modern Art in June, and was well received. Its main feature was a big model of the History Faculty Building, suspended from the ceiling with the floor removed, so that one could look up into the great glazed library. This presided over giant colour transparencies of Jim's three buildings at Leicester, Cambridge and St Andrews. The exhibition must have done more to boost his reputation than the Study, which had caused Jim and his team continual frustration, a good deal of bewilderment, but a little entertainment as well.

All through the 1970s Jim was away at least nine weeks a year in America, teaching as Davenport Professor at Yale. His popularity and success as a teacher remained undimmed. His studios were the ones most sought after by the students. After Charles Moore had given up being Dean in 1975, the reputation of the School to a large extent rested on his presence there. He was a star, but a reliable star. As Cesar Pelli, who became Dean in 1977, points out: 'That was not always true of the star professors who were invited to come to Schools. Jim took his responsibilities seriously, not so much to the institution – that probably didn't count for much – but his responsibilities towards the students were extremely important to him.'

In Pelli's view 'he was not just a good teacher, he was a great teacher', yet what made him so is not easily communicable. When, in recent years, Robert Kahn, who had been his pupil in 1978, was working on a posthumous exhibition of Jim's teaching at Yale, and it was suggested that it should have something to do with his methodology, he and Michael Wilford agreed that 'there was no methodology'. As Kahn puts it, 'He just showed up, and because one had so much respect for him, you produced a lot of work, and he would make very direct and astute comments about the project: "Well, you could do this and you could do that", and then move on. Near the end of the semester, for some people, he would start to draw things that actually looked like images, or make concrete suggestions about how to change something, but not until near the end.'

Different people have different memories. Fred Koetter, who was teaching at the school from 1972 (and who was later to become Dean), was impressed by the way in which he would encourage students to give their buildings an identity derived from some aspect of the brief or site. Alexander Gorlin, one of his students in 1978, felt encouraged to do the unexpected: 'His critiques of my projects always in the end involved inversions, or taking something that was familiar, and turning it around, or shifting it in some way that would pull it together, but in a very unexpected way.' Ulla Wilke, who was Jim's student in the same year and later went into his office, 'liked the fact that he didn't talk much. He sat beside you at the drawing board, took the pen and drew. I learnt from him to reduce an idea to the bare essence, and then experiment with that. He didn't hesitate to sketch what he would do; he started from what you were presenting him, but he would almost say, by drawing it, "Look, how about that? What do you think about this?" '

Jim ran his studios in very much the same way as he ran his office in London. The schemes he set were usually the same schemes that were being, or just had been, worked on in his office. He went round the drawing boards working with his stubby pencil to suggest possibilities or alterations in the same way as he went round the drawing boards in Gloucester Place. He kept his students to a rigid programme and time schedule, as in an office: from plans to sections and elevations, from sections and elevations to details. At the end of the semester, he would present one of his ties or a pair of his socks to the scheme which he liked best, or which turned out to be most like his own; it varied from year to year. But what is remarkable is that no one who was in his studios seems to have felt pressurised to do work or design in Jim's way. For Gorlin, 'He was a kind of gentle giant. Physically you would think he would be very intimidating, but he wasn't. He never pulled rank. He was very kind, as a teacher, and really elicited the best from the students. As opposed to Peter Eisenmann, where it was an almost militaristic programme and entirely his own ideas, and you were there in his service, and it was like a religious calling . . . with Stirling it was not that at all, and I think he was a greater architect.'

In addition to the studios, there were the juries, when Jim gathered together a posse of architectural stars to look at the students' scheme at the end of each semester. By the later 1970s, at least, these were becoming more entertainment than useful events – entertainments, at least, for Jim, though the students did not always see it that way. It was Jim as people-player. Audrey Matlock remembers them vividly: 'He loved to get the biggest powerhouses on his jury . . . He'd get Peter Eisenmann and Michael Graves and Philip Johnson, or whoever . . . and he'd have a roomful of these people, and he'd sit back. He would never criticise his students' schemes in front of anyone. He was always, if anything, defensive, or supportive. But he knew these people probably as well as they knew themselves. He would know exactly what comment to make, or what conversation to start which would bring up a particular issue that would get someone fired up. And he'd just sit back there, this half smile on his face, and watch it happen. I remember once, a jury . . .

it was actually to mark my project, and John Colacola was there, and Peter Blake and Cesar Pelli. I've forgotten the rest, but it was a roomful of Who's Whos, as usual. My scheme was somewhat formalistic, and I remember Jim throwing all the right little comments in there till Peter Blake almost burst a blood vessel in his temples. The guy was screaming, he was so mad. There was this huge angry fight over my scheme. A lot of the times these conversations went completely outside of being useful to us. Jim loved them. It was all very deliberate. He'd ask exactly the right question. He knew how to push all the buttons. It was very mischievous, sometimes. I think he did it for fun. I've taught just a couple of years now, and these juries get very boring.'

The students knew all the stories about Jim in the 1960s, and were always hoping for something similar, but he did not oblige them. He was still spending a good deal of time with them, however, in the Old Heidelberg and elsewhere. Ulla Wilke remembers how 'he used to like his onion rings, three plates of onion rings. I'll never forget him sitting in the Old Heidelberg with a glass of wine and onion rings. It's something that sticks in my head. We had good times there. He loved talking about people. He liked – I wouldn't call it gossip – but he wanted to know what was going on.' But according to Audrey Matlock, 'He'd love it, but he never gave, though. He'd get a lot out of us. "What do you think of this? What do you think of that? How did you find Peter Eisenmann on the jury?" And then he'd sit there, and his eyes would twinkle. But he never bad-mouthed anybody or gossiped himself. He'd make jokes about people, but they weren't below the belt. He was careful about that. He was very cautious, actually.'

Matlock had worked for a time with Craig Hodgetts in Los Angeles before she came to Yale, and because of that struck up an immediate friendship with Jim. She had a white convertible, an English Triumph 3, 'like driving around in a soupcan with wheels'. She used to take Jim from the station to the School, and chauffeur him around a good deal. It amused Jim to be driven around by a pretty girl in an absurd open car much too small for him, drinking beer out of a can. 'He used me as a sort of ring-leader in the class. He'd have me gather up whoever wanted to go and get smashed after dinner. We would drink all night. Once, I think it was for a Hallowe'en party, Megan Walker, who was in our class, wanted to dress up as Jim. Because he wore the same clothes all the time, all you had to do was put on that blue shirt, and it was a done deal. And pad it out a bit. So we went over to Jim's, and he gave us a bunch of dirty clothes and blue shirts – maybe a pair of purple socks, because they were trademarks of his too. We wanted to prove true that he just had a suitcase full of these things, which he did, but they were all dirty. He'd been there for a while, and was about ready to go back home, or something, and take all his dirty laundry. I remember him thinking it was hilarious. Jim was always game. He thought everything was funny, and he was always happy to accommodate something like that.'

Jim never stayed in New Haven for weekends. If he was not away lecturing, he went down to New York. From the early 1970s, he usually stayed with Richard Meier and his English girlfriend Julia Bloomfield in Meier's apartment, a large duplex in an Art Deco building on East 72nd Street. Meier had knocked the floor through, and made a living room fifty feet by thirty, so that it seemed like a downtown loft, although it was on the Upper East Side. Meier was a friend of John Miller, and Julia Bloomfield had worked for both Douglas Stephen and the Smithsons in London.

After she and Meier split up, and Meier married in January 1978, Jim used to stay with Barbara Jakobson in her house at 167 East 74th Street: a brownstone house with curving stairs going down into a very large living room added on at the back in the 1950s, and redolent of that period. Barbara Jakobson has written of herself that 'it's by knowing what artists and architects are doing and being incredibly involved both intellectually and in a supportive way with their work that I derive pleasure in my own existence. So although I have never had the where-withal to be the kind of patron of architecture who could commission works on my own, I have always wanted to help artists and architects that I know to succeed.' She is sharp and kind, recognised Jim's quality at once, and became a friend for life. She had two lively pretty daughters of the same kind of age as his. He loved being with them, and felt happy and at home there. 'He would appear on Friday afternoon at the door, carrying a green plastic briefcase in which were all the things he needed for the weekend. We think that there was a pair of clean socks – we are not exactly sure. There may have been a change of shirt or there may not have been. He travelled light and never came in a suit jacket, or even owned one. He had a very baggy wonderful black sweater, and a raincoat, and that was it.'

Food, gossip and shopping were Jim's main preoccupations in New York. With Meier and Bloomfield he either ate at a restaurant on Park Avenue, or Julia Bloomfield would serve up meals in the dining room, at one end of the huge living area. 'I well remember the many many dinners with Jim. I used to make cottage pie that he loved so much, and he used to inhale practically the whole thing, and then two hours later he would need a vast sandwich before he went to bed. One was always preparing these huge amounts of food for Jim.' Barbara Jakobson found that 'Jim was a creature of habit. Like most great artists, you discover that their lives and their worlds depend upon certain anchors, and in New York Jim used to do the same things. We would usually have dinner on Friday night with an architect or someone that I would organise, or maybe we'd go to Rob Livesey's for dinner. On Saturday he always loved to go to SoHo, and round the galleries. A kind of Saturday ritual of the art world was to have lunch at a restaurant called Ballatto on East Houston Street. The patron of this restaurant was a wonderful man, the food was very good, it was very convivial, and everybody would go there for lunch. Then we would walk round SoHo, or Jim would leave us and go shopping.'

Jim loved shopping in New York. After his marriage to Mary Shand he bought clothes for her with a sure eye, especially at Yves St Laurent, 'very elegant, plain, simple clothes', as Julia Bloomfield remembers. 'Designer French clothes were much cheaper in New York than they were in France or England.' He bought from Hammacher Schlemmers on 57th Street, a firm which, very expensively, 'made normal everyday objects abnormal, because someone had thought up a different creative way of presenting them', from cigarette lighters and holders to soda-water siphons. He went to Bloomingdales and stocked up for his children. He bought lots of books. He bought Tiffany lamps.

Katrin Adam and Keith Godard had moved in 1972 into one floor of a converted warehouse at the Brooklyn end of Brooklyn Bridge, looking straight across the water to Manhattan. Jim often came there: he used to point out to the water and say 'I was conceived out there, you know.' He enjoyed being plied by them with what they called 'businessmen's mar-tinis – very cold, almost all gin, a bit of vermouth and an olive', and drank their Brandy Alexanders as though they were milk shakes. Kenneth Frampton, who was teaching at Columbia from 1972 to 1974, and then from 1977, saw a good deal of Jim, and remembers him 'drinking Brandy Alexanders one after another and saying "I rather like these: they taste just like ice-cream".'

Jim could drink amazing quantities of alcohol without it showing. On one occasion he drank in competition with Charles Gwathmey, at one of the Liveseys' dinners, which they often gave for Jim when he was in New York. 'Gwathmey came with Betty-Anne, his wife, and we were drinking a fair amount of alcohol, and Jim started on about "Whatever happened to your first wife? She looked so beautiful bicycling across Central Park. With that wonderful bottom." So then Gwathmey was trying to out drink Stirling, which just wasn't going to happen. In the end he lost, and had to excuse himself from the table and go and be violently ill.'

One of the main functions of all these luncheons and dinners for Jim was picking up the New York architectural gossip. As Barbara Jakobson puts it, 'Jim absolutely adored gossip. Loved it. Required it. Even though he pretended that he was totally above the politics of New York architecture, and in a way he was. He was not somebody who called Philip, ever. There was a Philip Johnson-Peter Eisenmann pudding that got stirred up every morning, with the six o'clock or seven o'clock phone call, in which the two of them would pretend that they pulled all the strings and controlled all the movements of the world. And when the Institute for Architecture and Urban Studies existed, and Peter was Director, there was a certain veracity to the idea that Peter controlled power, by virtue of the fact that he published *Skyline* and *Oppositions*. To the Institute's credit, I think it was immensely important during the years that it flourished. All these things that happened at the Institute, Jim wanted to know about, even though he didn't want to go to them, and he didn't care whether Peter and the Institute included him or not. I don't think he liked Peter, but that doesn't mean that he wasn't curious.'

Jim was always hoping, and usually failing, to get work in America. It is never easy for a foreign architect, especially one not resident in the country, to find work there, anymore than it is easy for an American architect to get work in Europe. Jim had established a powerful reputation among American architects, but architectural competitions with juries largely composed of or heavily influenced by architects, such as were common enough in England, were rare in America, and Jim had no contacts with the numerous regional elites which control American patronage. Campus architects, who had the ability to hand out university jobs, may have been unwilling to risk giving them to Jim because his reputation for designing buildings that ran into trouble was percolating across the Atlantic. He was always a little bitter that he never got a commission from Yale, in spite of all that he had contributed to it. The clutch of American commissions that came to him in 1979 arrived when his involvement with Yale was running down, and had little if anything to do with his presence there.

136

EIGHT

AFTER LEICESTER

The arrival of the Leicester Engineering Building was one of the major architectural events of post-war years. Among architects it became for a year or two the most talked-about new building in Britain, and possibly in the world. It was published in architectural magazines in Britain, France, Italy, Germany, America and Japan. It was discussed with excitement in architectural schools everywhere. In the non-specialist British press, it was given articles in the *Guardian*, the *Sunday Times Colour Supplement* and the *Evening Standard*. But it was above all among architects that it caused excitement. To David Gray, looking back, 'it was really wonderful to think that this was happening in this rather conservative country'. Leicester was 'a great shining light' to all his generation.

Leicester was completed towards the end of 1963. In the next ten years Jim and his office (now without Gowan) produced five major buildings or groups of buildings and a number of unexecuted projects. All were eagerly awaited, and became objects of pilgrimage for architects and architectural students from round the world. All the designs combined art and technology in the same kind of way as Leicester, but had a strong individuality. Each time architects wondered 'Will he be able to do it again?' and he always was able. It was an extraordinary story of creative ebullience.

There was a debit side. Jim's buildings of these years were much disliked by many people. Much went seriously wrong with them. Their defects were played down or ignored by his supporters, and publicised and derided by his enemies – or, too often, with good reason, by the people who occupied or lived in them. After 1969, with one minor exception growing out of an earlier commission, he got no new work other than abortive projects, for eleven years in Britain, and for eight years anywhere.

The partnership with Gowan broke up at the end of 1963. Stirling and Gowan had been chosen in December 1962 to be competitors for the

History Faculty Building at Cambridge, and won the commission in the spring of 1963, with a design substantially or entirely by Jim. On 23 December 1963, he sent a letter to the Financial Board of the University: 'I am writing to tell you that Mr Gowan and I are dividing the practice.' He took over the History Faculty Building, and Gowan was left with a sizeable old people's home in Putney, a commission which dated from 1960 but was still under construction.

The break-up caused much bitterness. Gowan still refuses to talk about it. As Eldred Evans remembers it, 'I think that Jim was the designer, basically, and always thought of himself as the main designer, and after a while Gowan got tired of it, and also wanted to design. When Jim did the History Faculty, Gowan did an alternative, which sent Jim into an absolute rage. I was shown Gowan's design and could understand the rage, because it was trying to do an entirely different architecture. It had none of the perfection of Leicester; it was more broken-up, corrupted form.'

In 1963 Gowan was offered the commission for a large new house in Hampstead, for the Schreiber family. Jim hated his designs for this, and did not want to be associated with them. This was the immediate cause of the break. The house has similarities with the Putney old people's home, and later designs by Gowan relate to this and to other, substantially brick, buildings built under the partnership, which probably owed more to Gowan than to Jim. It is an architecture of blocks and cubes, fragmented and bitten into rather than crystalline, and bears no resemblance to the Engineering Building; while Jim went on to produce, in quick succession, four remarkable buildings which develop clearly out of Leicester and, whatever their defects, have a brilliance which Gowan's buildings lack.

Gowan was bitter because he felt that Jim took too much of the credit, then and later, and bitter about money. Jim was a hard bargainer. Israel had come across this aspect of him when they were working out arrangements about splitting the fees for the Preston housing. Israel was tough in money matters, and, as David Gray puts it, 'it was a case of Greek meeting Greek.' Gowan still says that 'Jim would take the shirt off your back'. For a good time they were not on speaking terms. At a party not long after the break Gowan came into the room, saw that Jim was there, and walked straight out again. Some years later they met each other in the street in New York. They passed each other without saying a word, and then Jim turned his head and shouted 'I'm a father now too, you know.'

It was said at the time among architects that 'whoever of the two gets Wilford will succeed'. In the end it was Jim who got Wilford. He had been laid off when Leicester was coming to an end, because there was no longer enough work. Looking back, he thinks that: 'They wanted to clear the office out in order to split. But it wasn't made clear to me at the time. I think I was only away for six or eight months, and then I got a phone call from Jim saying, "We've split . . . Do you want to come back and work with me on the History Building?" So I of course said, "Yes."'

Jim became a showman and salesman for his own buildings. This came to him easily enough, for he was a showman by nature. Eldred Evans remembers how 'he was really up to date with every single thing that was being done, almost in the world, and he was also very interested in his own PR. He made sure that everything he did was published. He was very up-front with . . . "my latest design must be seen world-wide". I think he had friends in all the right places. That kind of international side of him remained throughout his life.'

Sandy Wilson had already experienced this aspect of Jim at Cambridge in the 1950s, when Jim had successfully put pressure on him to exhibit photographs of his Ham Common flats in the School of Architecture. Another means by which he propagated his work and acquired more contacts was by lecturing. In the 1960s he lectured at, among other places, Harvard, Columbia, Philadelphia, Berkeley and San Diego in America, and at Royaumont (near Paris), Copenhagen, Oslo, Trondheim, Bologna, Rome, Naples and Aachen in Europe. His lectures were always to architects or architectural students, and always took the same form: a down-to-earth account of the background to each project, the problems it presented, the solution adopted, and the building which this solution produced. There were no aesthetics, no theorising.

His presentation to potential clients was much in the same style. He talked about this in Bologna in 1966. 'In England, I find that, when making a presentation to the client, we must never talk about aesthetics and explanations should always be in terms of common sense, function and logic. If you mentioned the word "beauty" their hair might stand on end, and you could lose the commission. Perhaps this Philistine attitude is, in some ways, beneficial as it probably means that a design can never be too far removed from common sense and logic.'

But in fact Jim adopted the same approach when talking to architects in Bologna. Did he really believe that his buildings emerged automatically from correct analysis of the brief, like the solution to an algebraic problem: feed in the right questions, and out will pop the Leicester Engineering Building? Or did he secretly enjoy the combination of his matter-of-fact words and the extraordinary images which accompanied them on the screen?

By December 1966 Jim's History Faculty Building was well under way. It was started when he was with Eldred Evans and completed when he was with Mary Shand. The commission was awarded to Stirling and Gowan in April 1963. Three firms had been selected from an initial list of fifteen, and asked to submit designs. Stirling and Gowan's was chosen. Leslie Martin was on the relevant committee, and had produced the original list. The building resembled Leicester in using a vocabulary of engineering bricks, tiles, steel trusses and patent glazing. The concept of the plan is a simple one. Professor Geoffrey Elton, who was on the selection committee, admired it because it 'developed from a genuine (and accurate) conception of what the History Faculty is – a body of men, teachers and students, concentrating their lives upon their library'. An L-shaped main building, containing seven floors of student and staff lounges, seminar rooms and offices, is wrapped round a top-lit reading room. Around the outer edge of the reading room is a curved line of open stacks, on two levels looking into the reading room. The main building decreases in size as it goes upwards from the seminar rooms to the office floors, resulting in a profile stepped on the outside and ends, and vertical on the side of the reading room. On this side are glazed corridors, looking down into the reading room where its roof cuts across them. As at Leicester, the lifts and service stairs were in slender tiled towers linked to the main building, when necessary, by glazed bridges.

From the south-east the stepped glass roof of the reading room (through which can be seen the intricate web of its roof trusses) is silhouetted against the fragile encircling glass arms of the L. As one walks round to either side the brick silhouette of the end of the main building moves into the foreground, like a crisp red cut-out. At the back the reading room disappears, and one only sees the stepped glass wall of the main building, and the slender tiled turrets of lift and stairs silhouetted against it. But though the building changes as one moves round it, the dominant impression is of one clear delicate sparkling entity of enamel and crystal. Eldred Evans watched him design it. It was 'rather like designing jewellery. He used to draw really beautiful, small, three-dimensional drawings. That's how he designed . . . completely from the outside, and it was like watching a very large man doing a minute piece of jewellery.'

Jim's next commission came later in the same year. It was a direct invitation, without competition, to design student accommodation for St Andrews University. Jim moved on from the Leicester-Cambridge language and used prefabricated concrete units for the first time. He explained the reason to his audience at Bologna. 'There is no local material (not even bricks) or workmen (who have all come south). The problem was how to erect a battery of student residences as a continuous building process over a period of six or seven years. The only method which seemed to be possible was to design a kit of precast concrete elements to be manufactured elsewhere . . . The factory is in Edinburgh, about eighty miles south of St Andrews.'

A layman may feel sceptical about this argument, and wonder whether the main reason was that Jim wanted to see what he could do with precast concrete. Anyway, the result was another memorable design. The site was a fine one, the upper slope of a low line of hills running west from St Andrews, and looking down over dunes and golf-links to the sea and beyond to distant mountains. Jim designed what on plan looks like two four-fingered hands, placed with fingers wide apart side by side down the hillside. The fingers (only two were ever built) consist of piled-up rows of student rooms, each occupying a precast concrete box and running in steps down the hillside. They are tied together horizontally by a long glazed promenade running along the inside of each finger and meeting at communal rooms in the 'web' of the hand. From these a bridge leads to the crest of the hill and a bicycle path and footpath running along it into the town.

Each student room is angled so as to have a view of the sea from a window in the corner of its square. The jagged rhythm of angled and cut-away squares contrasts with the smooth glazed ribbon of the promenades threaded between them. The promenades clearly relate to the internal street which the Smithsons had planned, but never built, for the Golden Lane estate and Sheffield University, and which Ivor Smith and others

Jim Stirling's drawing of the St Andrews student residences

had made the dominant feature of the enormous Park Hill housing estate in Sheffield. But they were different in treatment and effect from the interminable low-ceilinged vistas and dour concrete which were so to depress the inhabitants of that estate. Although Jim always denied that it was intentional, they were styled like the promenade deck of a liner, but glazed: white, trimly detailed, opening out into recesses fitted with tables and long benches, and even with big round portholes, used internally to give light to the stairs which ran up and down from the promenade to give access to the rooms. It is tempting to see an echo of the promenade decks illustrated by Le Corbusier with approval in his *Vers une Architecture*.

The next commission came in 1965, and sadly came to nothing. The steel firm of Dorman Long commissioned Jim to design them a new headquarters, on a very grand scale. One of the provisos of this brief was that the building must advertise steel. So Jim and Michael Wilford worked out a main façade, fourteen storeys high and almost one thousand feet long, in which a heroic framework of huge steel beams, part angled, part vertical, was to be placed outside the building, with a smooth skin of continuous glass suspended behind it. It was 'high-tech' ten years before Foster and Rogers, but the commission collapsed with the nationalisation of the steel industry.

Another academic commission came in 1966, the designing of the new student residence for Queen's College, Oxford, which was to become known as the Florey Building. Jim was chosen for the commission after the college had interviewed at least four firms of architects, including the Smithsons. Jim used his Leicester-Cambridge mixture of brick, tiles and glass in a building which is as much a single shapely entity as the History Faculty Building, although the shape is different. The concept is that of a grandstand or amphitheatre, raised on concrete legs, and angled in a half octagon to look at the river view. The hollow river side is continuously glazed and contains stacked-up rooms. The outer sides face the city car park and are mainly faced with tiles, interrupted by thin strip windows that light the corridors. The profile of the river side is like that of the Dorman Long headquarters, sloped in the lower portion (and containing three storeys of undergraduate rooms) and vertical at the top (to contain two-storeyed studio rooms for graduates, with galleries at the back).

The building is based on a complex overlay of three grids, the second and third set at 45° and 22½° to the first. The plan is not symmetrical, but the geometry of the grids gives the building a strong sense of order. The sweep of the glazing, the meeting-up of different geometries and

142

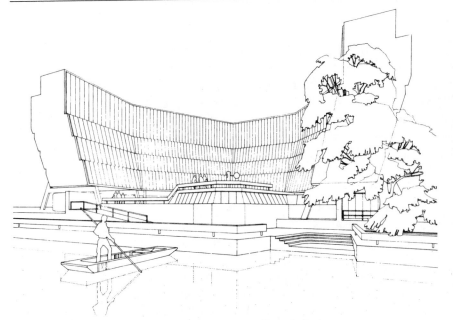

Florey Building, Queen's College, Oxford

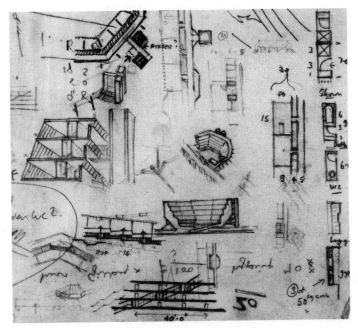

Sketch drawings for the Florey Building

143

materials as concrete stanchions merge into tiled walls, glazed staircases drop out of them or glazed bridges cross into them from the lift and staircase towers, the way the section of the building is shown in jagged cut-outs of tiles at its two ends, all merge to create a memorable and exotic object, a visitor from outer space, perhaps, which has alighted without warning among the trees on an Oxford river bank.

At the end of the 1960s the firm continued to experiment with prefabricated units, but increased its range to include prefabrication in GRP (glass-reinforced polyester). This was used in two projects, a big housing project at Runcorn New Town in Cheshire, and a Training School for Olivetti at Haslemere in Surrey. The Runcorn commission came in 1967, and that from Olivetti in 1969, but owing to the slow machinery of local government they were built at much the same time. At Runcorn the firm was chosen after interviews from a shortlist of three, put forward by David Gosling, the Deputy Chief Architect-Planner of the New Town. The Development Corporation was anxious to build an estate that would get it national acclaim, and wanted prefabrication in order to build quickly, so the choice of Stirling, on the strength of his now international reputation and work at St Andrews, was not surprising, although it may have helped that Fred Lloyd Roche, the Chief Architect, had been a student at the Regent Street Polytechnic when Jim was teaching there. The Olivetti commission reflected Jim's growing reputation in Japan, for it came on the recommendation of the Japanese architect Kenzo Tange, who had been employed by Olivetti. It was again not a surprising choice. Olivetti had a policy of employing leading designers, architects, graphic artists, artists and even poets, chosen internationally, to design or advertise its products, office furnishing, and buildings, and Jim's image was exactly what it wanted.

The different clients and nature of the two projects inevitably produced different results. At Runcorn Jim set Michael Wilford, and later Julian Harrap as job architect, the problem of using repetitive prefabricated elements to produce a twentieth-century equivalent of the squares and crescents of Bath. Long terraces of flats above maisonettes were arranged in a series of squares and one crescent – in fact two terraces put together in a shallow 'V'. All the terraces had the same design, a constantly repeated rhythm made up of raised streets or footways (as part of the brief), staircase towers and round windows, similar to those which Jim had used internally at St Andrews. The footways were lined with GRP panels in rectangles, of bright alternating colours. Panels of prefabricated concrete made up the rest.

The result (all demolished in the 1990s) may perhaps have had what

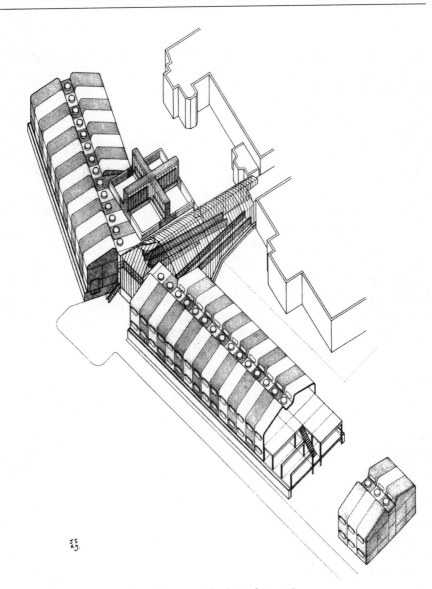

Olivetti Training School, Haslemere, Surrey

Kenneth Frampton called an 'ordered and elegant urbanity', but it aroused less international attention than the Olivetti Training School. This was visually and technologically more striking, and admirably achieved its purpose of advertising Olivetti as the firm of the future. Its plan was similar to that of Jim's building at St Andrews: two long wings

145

containing classrooms extending along corridors from a glazed concourse and a central assembly hall. The concourse continued as a wide glazed link between the new building and the Edwardian house which had been bought with the property, and which was converted by Edward Cullinan (on Jim's recommendation) as a residence for the trainees.

The resulting building was different from St Andrews, however, because it was expressed in the rounded forms suited to GRP or aluminium (both materials were considered) rather than the rectangular forms suited to precast concrete. Corners, profiles and windows are all rounded, and so is the dominant feature of the building, the cross-shaped superstructure of glass and plastic which rises above the assembly hall and from which portions can be mechanically lowered to divide the hall into four smaller spaces (to become known as 'Alhadeff's toy', from the enjoyment British Olivetti's managing director got in seeing it raised and lowered). Everything in the GRP portions of the building seems as a result to flow into everything else – roofs into walls, the superstructure into roofs – and the whole complex was to have been made gay by alternate panels being coloured lime green and mauve. The local planning authority jibbed, however (even though the building was almost completely screened by woods), and they ended up two sober shades of beige.

There are plenty of the trimmings which by now had become distinctive to Jim: tall ribbed radiators painted bright yellow and stretching from floor to roof in the glazed link, like pilasters; roof-lights in the corridors like rows of bubbles; a window-cleaning machine which straddles the roof of the link like a science-fiction insect. All this, combined with Edward Cullinan's quirky interiors in the old house (inspired by Victorian seaside piers and boathouses), encouraged Reyner Banham to describe the result as 'festive'.

Jim's buildings of this decade were so unlike anything else that critics had a field-day looking for sources. Silos, sewers, bunkers, rocket-launching pads, battleships, liners, greenhouses, seaside piers, viaducts and Martello towers were all called into service, as were St Elia, Lissitsky and Butterfield. Alvin Boyarsky, writing in *Architectural Design* in 1968, spliced a section of the rocket-launching pad at Cape Canaveral to its mirror image, and the result looked amazingly like the section of the History Faculty Building (Jim was at Cape Canaveral in 1966 and commented 'everything fantastic' on a postcard to Sandy Wilson). But Jim refused to be drawn, continued to give out his deadpan functional analyses, and sent a photograph of a detail of St Andrews to Charles Jencks, the architectural critic and historian, with 'Dear Charles, this is not a battleship' scribbled over it.

146

Jim's buildings of this period upset many people. They hated them because they were unfamiliar, or unlike anything they had seen before, or because they seemed brash and crude, or conflicted with their image of what was appropriate for Oxford or Cambridge or for an academic building or for a place to live in. The most learned and formidable of their critics was Nikolaus Pevsner. Pevsner could not bear Jim's architecture. 'Stirling is a rude man', he told Jim's friend Craig Hodgetts, 'and the buildings he designs are rude as well.' Of the Florey Building at Oxford he wrote: 'Some will adore it, and some detest it', and it was quite clear to which class he belonged. As an opponent he carried a lot of weight: learned, articulate, formidably well-informed, able to write and speak in a way that made architecture come alive for lay people as well as architects and architectural historians. As Slade Professor of Fine Art at Cambridge from 1945 to 1955 he lectured to packed houses, composed of dons and townspeople as well as students. Of the History Faculty Building he wrote:

> Here is the answer of a younger man. We must do away with beauty altogether. Don't be polite, be honest, even if it makes you brutal. . . . Here is anti-architecture. Here is an intelligent resourceful architect making it his business to design a building which fulfils all the functional demands and yet is actively ugly – not ugly in the vociferous way of the brutalists, but ugly more basically by avoiding anything that might attract . . . But never mind, it hits you, the architecture hits you, and that is what the façade – and the whole building is meant to do . . . The glazing is of an industrial kind, which is aesthetically as neutral as the glazing of a tomato-frame. The brick, where it appears, will never go mellow, let alone picturesque, and the glazing won't – so that is all right.

His gut reaction distorted his vision. By describing the lecture theatre at Leicester as being 'of exposed concrete; the rest is faced with blue engineering bricks', when the concrete is not exposed and the facing is of red tiles, he enabled Jim to write 'it is clear that when Professor Pevsner approaches a building which he THINKS he should not like, he closes his eyes'.

Pevsner was both a Modern Movement purist and a devotee of the English cult of the Picturesque. He rejected Jim on both counts. In the 1930s he had believed that Modern Movement architecture, as developed before 1914 and perfected in the 1920s, was something permanent.

'To me, what had been achieved in 1914 was the style of the century . . . it seemed folly to think that anybody would wish to abandon it.' It was 'a style of service, neutral, rational, functional, sensible'. In the later 1950s and 1960s he was still intellectually and emotionally committed to his earlier beliefs. He was deeply disturbed by the arrival of what he called the 'anti-pioneers', whose architecture was 'over-dramatic, aggressive and highly individual'. Jim was an anti-pioneer.

But Pevsner had also been converted to the Picturesque, to the extent of taking it on board as one of the forerunners of the Modern Movement. From 1942 to 1946 he had been joint editor of the *Architectural Review*; and he remained an important contributor. The *Review*, encouraged by its part-proprietor de Cronin Hastings, plugged the relevance of the Picturesque to contemporary architecture. Buildings should be composed with skilful irregularity to fit the landscape or town-scape, and to merge into it; walking through or round buildings should be as full of continued contrast and variety as walking through an eighteenth-century park; materials should be chosen so that they would weather and melt into their setting. But Jim's materials, as Pevsner put it, would 'never go mellow, let alone Picturesque'.

Pevsner's golden boys were the architects Powell and Moya, and the new building at Cambridge which met with his unqualified approval was their Cripps Building at St John's College. For him this was '*facile princeps*', 'a masterpiece by one of the best architectural partnerships in the country'. He admired it because, although unmistakably Modern, 'it shuns all excesses', and because of the skilful and sensitive way in which it was fitted to the river in one long zig-zag asymmetrical line. The Cripps Building and the History Faculty Building were almost exact contemporaries, and about as different from each other as it was possible to be.

Jim was consciously anti-Picturesque. His surfaces and materials were deliberately hard, bright, gleaming or crystalline. His buildings were designed to stand out, not to merge in – as, for that matter, was King's College Chapel, or Wren's Trinity College Library. He quite certainly had no desire to make them either ugly or brutal. Bruno Zevi, who wrote for Olivetti about Jim's buildings in 1973, was more perceptive than Pevsner. 'He likes to be called a humanist, it makes him happy. In fact he really deserves it.' Like all disciples of Colin Rowe, Jim saw himself as going back to the Renaissance. He and his circle disliked the Picturesque because it suggested to them architecture designed from the outside in, to make a pretty picture rather than generated by an inherent internal logic. Jim's favourite hate-adjective for buildings was 'wishy-washy', a metaphor drawn from the English watercolours which embodied the spirit of the Picturesque. His History Faculty Building was next door to Hugh Casson's group of Faculty Buildings, carefully composed and diversified on Picturesque principles. Casson – master-mind of the Festival of Britain, gentlemanly modernist, tireless purveyor of charming little water-colours – stood for everything in architecture that Jim disliked. He summed up his own philosophy with typical brevity when asked why he had designed the History Faculty Building in the way he had. He answered, 'To fuck Casson.' The remark went the round of Cambridge Senior Combination Rooms, and did Jim a good deal of harm.

Jim's divergence from mainstream Modernism upset some of the older Modern Movement architects. Even Leslie Martin was disconcerted when he first saw the design for the Leicester Engineering Building; it was not what he expected or wanted. But in rejecting the Picturesque Jim was rejecting the ruling aesthetic in England at that time, and upsetting the average cultivated Englishman, not just elderly architects. His buildings shocked them.

Jim's admirers also experienced a shock when they saw his buildings, but it was a shock of delight. There was an explosive originality about them that exhilarated their spirits. They were gay, witty, novel and daring. Craig Hodgetts said 'Holy Cow', upped sticks, left his wife and went off to Yale. To Leon Krier the Engineering Building 'seemed like something fantastic', and he left Stuttgart to work in Jim's office. Professor Watson at St Andrews 'felt like bursting into song'. David Gray in London found the buildings 'a great shining light'. The Leicester schoolchildren talked about the 'fairy palace'. Anyone who has had this kind of reaction or experience from Jim's buildings will understand, and be correspondingly amazed at talk of 'brutality' and 'ugliness'. It was straightforward aesthetic reaction on both sides; aesthetic delight on the one hand, aesthetic outrage on the other. When the buildings had faults the people who were delighted did their best to extenuate or ignore them, the people who were outraged were merciless in exposing them.

An admirer of Stirling might reverse Pevsner's comment on the History Faculty Building: not 'a building which fulfils all the functional demands, and yet is actively ugly', but 'a building which is actively beautiful, but does not fulfil all the functional demands'. Jim, in pre-oil-crisis days, argued that glass was flexible and cheap, but his gleaming surfaces of glass and tiles are there more for aesthetic reasons than practical ones. One does not need to be a specialist to look at the buildings and see that they are likely to have problems: problems of heat or cold, of sound, of privacy, of keeping out the weather. To obtain the required look of gleaming sleekness or crystalline sharpness, and to solve the problems which this look created, needed experience in the necessary technology, and money to pay for it.

Some time in the early 1960s the architect John Winter was driving north up the M1. He came on a car sitting in a lay-by with a flat tyre. Being a charitable man, he stopped to ask if he could help. Sitting in the car were Jim and Eldred Evans, quietly waiting for assistance. Neither had any idea how to change a tyre, and Winter changed it for them. Jim was not technologically minded. He was interested in technology mainly for the visual games which it enabled him to play. He left the solution of technical problems to his advisers, his subcontractors, and his office. At a certain level he lost interest. The kind of small details which infuriate the users when they go wrong too often did go wrong in his buildings. Considering such details had been one of Gowan's strengths, and it took Jim's office some time to acquire the experience needed to fill the gap left by his departure.

All the buildings were built under one or more of four constraints: lack of money, lack of time, lack of adequate contractors, and lack of technological expertise. They needed budgets which the University Grants Committee or whatever other body financed them was unable or unwilling to give. Sometimes, in order to qualify for a grant at all, they had to be built or designed in too much of a hurry. Jim was usually compelled to accept the lowest tender, and was landed as a result with contractors whom he would not have chosen, and who proved inadequate. The buildings required a level of technology which was not available at the time. Patent glazing, for instance, was designed for very simple repetitive situations in uninhabited glasshouses; Jim used it for complex situations in inhabited buildings. Jim was always being let down by his subcontractors, manufacturers and suppliers. It was because a subcontractor failed to deliver what had been promised that the tiles fell off at Cambridge, not because of any failure in design on the part of Jim or his office. With the benefit of hindsight the 'high-tech' architects who started off as disciples of Jim have developed the expertise and received the budgets to deal with problems which he too often was unable to solve.

In short, Jim set out to build buildings which, in the circumstances under which he was working, could not be built to satisfactory standards. The history of these years is an alternation of triumph and disaster: aesthetic triumphs and practical disasters. The story needs to be looked at in some detail, because Jim's career was based on the triumphs and never fully recovered from the disasters.

Leicester, in spite of its overall success, had problems which left the

Vice-Chancellor and University Grants Committee unhappy. The glazing of the tower leaked badly, especially to begin with. Edward Parkes admires and defends the building, but remembers how 'I was in my room in the tower, and my wife had come, because we were going on to some party. There was a heavy rainstorm, and the water was coming down the inside of the glass in absolute torrents. She'd always had a slightly romantic wish to have a house by a mountain stream, and she said, "Well, I know I asked for this, but I didn't know you would provide it in the Engineering Building."' The worst of the leaks was dealt with, but the glazing continued to present problems until the 1980s, when it was replaced by another firm with crushing and needless insensitivity.

Another defect arose from the fact that the skin of the tower was hung a little forward of the slabs. As a result, although the horizontal sound insulation between the rooms was excellent, the vertical was not. As Parkes put it, 'Although you could not hear anybody in the room next door, you could talk to someone four floors above without raising your voice.'

A third problem was explained by Jim in a letter to John Mills, the Director of Estate Management at Cambridge (he was urging him not to make the same mistake with the History Faculty Building). Leicester University, after work had started, asked the contractor to reverse the agreed and sensible order, and finish the workshops before the tower, so that the workshops could be completed before the end of the contract. This led to numerous complications, and 'at the end of the job the builders were able to present a claim for £60,000, largely based on the unforeseen factors which arose out of this change'.

The Cambridge commission was awarded to Stirling and Gowan in April 1963, a little before the completion of Leicester. They won it more on practical than aesthetic grounds. The members of the committee were impressed by the radial plan on which the reading room was organised, so that the whole room could be seen and supervised from the central desk. A book thief had been running wild in Cambridge libraries, so this system was attractive to them. They also liked the sensible, well-informed and down-to-earth approach of both partners. As John Mills puts it, 'When you asked questions, Stirling or Gowan seemed to have the answer. They fished out from their briefcases little sketches and said "Oh yes . . .", and they clearly had paid a great deal of attention. We were all impressed: no doubt about that.' They were indisputably better than the other two firms which were interviewed.

Before finalising their decision, the committee went to see the Leicester Engineering Building. They were impressed by the building, but taken aback by the Vice-Chancellor. At the lunch which he gave to the committee he announced: 'I think you should know, gentlemen, that we would never consider employing these architects again.' He retailed what had gone wrong. The members returned somewhat muted to Cambridge. But Leslie Martin rallied them by saying – or words to the same effect – 'here are two young architects, whose design for Leicester is accepted by the profession as outstanding. They may have made mistakes, but they will learn from them.'

The committee had another shock to absorb. John Mills informed them that the University Grants Committee was dead against Stirling and Gowan's being employed, for the same reasons as those of Leicester's Vice-Chancellor. It could not stop the University making its own choice, but had intimated that only the minimum grants could be expected. None the less the committee, by a small majority, recommended acceptance. By now the scheme had two committed backers, in the form of the two representatives of the History Faculty on the committee – Geoffrey Elton and Moses Finlay. They helped push the scheme through, although the chairman, Hugh Willink, was against it. They remained loyal backers of Jim throughout. Elton, in particular, was to become identified as the champion and defender of the building. This had its disadvantages, for he had an abrasive personality and had made many enemies.

John Mills was unhappy. The nature of the design suggested that it would benefit from air-conditioning, which the University Grants Committee in a more amenable mood would probably have financed, but there was now no chance of this. He hoped that the University would supplement the budget from its own funds, but it claimed to be already over-committed. He hoped that the tenders would come in too high, forcing either the UGC or the University to put up more money. But the Cambridge firm of Sindalls was short of work, and put in a suitably low tender. Jim's quantity surveyors, Monk and Dunstone, had written to him when the list of tenderers was first drawn up by the University: 'I feel I should inform you that we ourselves have had a most unsatisfactory relationship with Wm Sindall Limited. . . . The University, I think you will find, are including them because of local politics, in which case no doubt we may be forced to accept their instruction.' This is what happened. Sindalls was a respected local firm. It had put in the lowest tender, and was given the contract.

Jim started off with a contractor in whom he had no confidence, and saddled with three concessions made as a result of lack of time and money. The site allotted for the building included the garden of a house lived in by 85-year-old Mrs Lilley, whose family owned a long-established drapery business in Cambridge. Her relatives had assured the University that she would be willing to sell, and the site plans given to the competing firms in 1965 had been made on this assumption. In fact she refused. The University was faced by a dilemma: Jim's building would not fit on the site. Macpherson, the University Treasurer, pointed out that it would fit if rotated 90°. There was not much of an option. To get its UGC grant the tenders had to be in by a fixed date, and there was not time to redesign the building. The effect, in terms of extra heat gain, was significant because the great glass roof of the reading room now faced southeast, not north-east.

To cut the budget down to a level acceptable to the University Grants Committee, a number of economies were made, one of them undesirable, and one in the long term disastrous. The aluminium used in the glazing was not anodised, which meant that it was certain to corrode. The tiles on the towers were fixed to the concrete by a new process. At Leicester the traditional methods had been used, but at Cambridge the same subcontractor came to Stirling's firm with a new system. A new adhesive had been developed by the tiling industry. It was no longer necessary to go to the cost and trouble of making grooves in the surface of the concrete, or buying tiles with grooves in their rear surface. Smooth tiles, smooth concrete and the new adhesive would do the same job. The system was quicker and cheaper. It was accepted by Jim, as it was to be accepted by Yorke, Rosenberg and Mardell a little later for their extensive new buildings at Warwick University. It was a failure: the adhesive suffered from chemical degradation and twelve years or so after completion, at both Cambridge and Warwick, the tiles began to fall off.

It is scarcely surprising that with these beginnings the building experienced continual problems, both before and after completion. The relationship between architect and contractor was always bad. The contractor produced work of high quality for traditional crafts such as joinery and brickwork, but was not able to manage the subcontractors for the metal and glass, or to build to the very small tolerances which Jim had asked for – and which Sindalls had accepted. As John Mills puts it, 'With a very abusive Stirling chasing every detail, and a Sindalls director making sure that everything possible became an extra, progress was very slow.' The contract ran long over its delivery date. The University held back the last big payment due because the building was leaking so disastrously. After the final handover it continued to leak, even if not so badly. Sound insulation was bad, partly due to the fact that the separate lecture block, which had been planned for, had been scrapped, and lectures had to be given in the Stirling building.

The building was too hot in summer, and too cold in winter. Jim's friend, Michael Wickham, photographed it shortly before it was occupied. 'I can remember my assistant and I sweating, and taking all our clothes off, and walking about in our pants, because it was so hot in that building. And I said to Jim "All these books are going to fry and fall to pieces if you keep them like this." Jim said, "Oh, no, it'll be all right."'

Jim had been aware that there would be heat problems, exacerbated by the 90° rotation. He had devised a double-skin roof to the reading room, to act as what he called a heat cushion. Three extractor fans, looking like small space rockets and painted in different bright colours, were fixed at the top of the roof to suck out the air as it heated, and to replace it with cooler air drawn through louvres at the base of the building. The system was not a success: the louvres failed to live up to their performance specification and the fans made so much noise that they were said by the occupants to be unusable. Stirling and his office claimed that the library staff never learnt to use them properly. They ran at three speeds, and were only unacceptably noisy at the top speed, which was necessary only for short periods. At any rate they were little used, except on one occasion when the library was being televised. A member of the Sidgwick Site Committee, who intensely disliked the building, made recording impossible by turning the fans on at full speed; he said that the library should be televised under working conditions. He refused to turn them off, and Michael Wilford had to go up to the roof and remove their fuses in order to stop them running.

One can scarcely blame students for feeling resentful, as they froze or fried in the reading room, and looked through the windows at troops of Japanese or German architects, industriously photographing what the architectural press extolled as a masterpiece. The librarian hated the building. The students and other users complained. Stirling got all the blame. Gavin Stamp, who had recently finished reading history at Cambridge, wrote a long, sustained attack in the *Cambridge Review* in 1976. A Cambridge history don, Denis Brogan, wrote a short vituperative piece in the same periodical in 1978. Anti-History Faculty stories were related at High Tables and in Senior Combination Rooms throughout Cambridge. Sir John Plumb was one of the leading tellers of them. Plumb had a comfortable private income and lived in style like an eighteenth-century country gentleman. He was by nature antipathetic to the architecture of the History Faculty Building, and the fact that he and Geoffrey Elton hated each other added zest to his attacks.

The tiles began to fall off in 1980. For a time the University considered suing the architect and the subcontractor, and got as far as issuing a writ, but its legal advisers were against it because the period of guarantee had passed. In the mid-1980s the building was very nearly demolished. Its enemies lobbied, but it was saved by a few votes, thanks to a campaign mounted by two architect friends and admirers of Jim, one of whom was on the General Board of the University. At the cost of about £2 million defects were righted, and the building equipped with the double-glazing and other features which it should have had from the start.

At the University of St Andrews Jim had the advantage of working with the whole-hearted backing of Professor J. Steven Watson, the Principal, and Professor Lionel Butler, a medieval historian who was chairman of the project committee. Stirling's and Gowan's names as architects were put to the University Court by Watson on 1 January 1964. A previous memorandum suggesting them had been circulated to its members before the partnership was dissolved. Some members asked whether a Scottish architect could be appointed, and were reassured by being told that 'the Architects suggested are Scottish, although they practise in London'. Jim presented his sketch plans to the College Council and the University Court on 22 November 1964, and the Court 'agreed to express its appreciation of the Architects' most interesting design'.

£390,000 was allotted for New Residence No. 1 (soon to be named Andrew Melville Hall), which was to be erected as the first of Jim's four suggested residences. There was 'consternation' in the Council on 22 April 1966 when the tenders were announced. They varied between £553,144 and £496,000, and were way over the University Grants Committee's limit of £393,000, even when a permissible extra allowance for imported labour had been added on. The specifications were pared down, and on 15 August the University Grants Committee authorised a revised tender of £444,166, on condition, however, 'that subsequent residences on the site be so designed as to obviate the high cost implications of Residence No. 1'. This effectively ruled out the possibility of Jim's remaining three residences being built.

Andrew Melville Hall was first occupied in October 1968. It ran into trouble at once. The windows of the rooms leaked, and black tarry water poured down into them from the ceilings. There was dispute as to whether these faults were due to the contractor's negligence or (as the contractor inevitably contested) to faults in the design. The University backed its architect, and prepared to go to arbitration. The windows had not been adequately sealed. A report from the Building Research Station stated that 'the leakage of water was primarily due to the fact that the screeds had not been allowed to dry out before the roof was put on. They thus contained many times the tolerable water content. This was the fault of the contractor.' The committee reasonably felt that 'the Contractor could not now plead that he had been under pressure from the University to complete the work in haste. He had raised no such plea at the time.' On the other hand, some of the water penetration could be the result of interstitial condensation, possibly due to inadequate ventilation 'especially in periods of high atmospheric humidity' and 'no blame attached to the Contractor on this account'. In the end a compromise settlement was made before arbitration.

A further defect of the new building is made painfully obvious when one visits the building today. The effects on the promenades of the Residence's exposed site had probably been underestimated. Certainly there was no money for the double-glazing which they really needed. The original heating of the rooms, by a combination of off-peak underfloor heating and individual heaters in the rooms, was never adequate. There were constant complaints about it, and finally conventional gas-fired central heating was installed. The two long promenades, beautiful and enjoyable spaces in themselves, have suffered severely as a result, from the insertion of insensitive double-glazing and unsightly heating pipes running along the ceiling.

J.S. Watson and Lionel Butler never faltered in their support of Jim; Butler and his wife were to remain good friends for the rest of his life. His relations with the Queen's College, Oxford, ended less happily. They started well enough, a few months after he was given the St Andrews commission. On 7 July 1964 he was invited to Queen's to discuss the development possibilities of two sites for new student accommodation. Two or three other firms were also interviewed, but it was Stirling who was asked to design the building, on 4 August. Jim accepted, but said that he could not start work until at least February 1965. The original invitation had been for a site in Iffley Road, but in October the City of Oxford approached Queen's with the suggestion that it should build in St Clement's, across the river from Magdalen College and its Meadows. This area had been designated as 'suitable for University and College expansion' in the City Development Plan. Magdalen already had a new building in this area, and other Colleges were approached. In the end Queen's was the only one to build there. It was offered a good site, occupied by a boat yard and part of a city car park, looking across the river to Magdalen Tower, and closer to the main College buildings than the Iffley Road site. Jim was in favour of the change, but final negotiations with the City took some time, and it was not until 29 September 1966 that he presented small sketch designs to the Building Committee. They were found 'very acceptable'.

'Very acceptable' is, perhaps, a shade cooler than the 'most interesting' of St Andrews. Jim, like most architects, needed to work for an appreciative and enthusiastic client, and at Queen's he never had one. The new building was the brainchild of the President, Lord Florey, the distinguished pioneer of penicillin. He soon became ill, and died in February 1968. His successor, Robert Blake, was and is the most genial and delightful of men, but Jim's architecture was everything that he most disliked. The client for the day-to-day conduct of the building was the Bursar, A.A. Williams. Williams had been against any new building at all. He had encouraged Lazards, the College's financial consultants, to present a report explaining how the building of one would set the College on the path to bankruptcy. Not surprisingly, he and Jim never got on. Jim's warmest advocate on the selection committee was the Senior Tutor, Iain Macdonald, but his reasons were not architectural, according to John Prestwich, who was also on the committee: 'Iain Macdonald was a Scot, had a very strong personality, and was a great believer in the virtues of all Scots, particularly Glaswegians, providing that their name wasn't Campbell. He threw his very considerable weight in favour of Stirling.'

Prestwich himself was an enthusiast for contemporary architecture, but his preferred choice had been the firm of Ahrends Burton Koralek, who were soon to design a row of houses in Headington for the Prestwiches and others. He had put them forward with other architects (including some classicists) at an earlier set of interviews, but had failed to get a majority, and a fresh start had been made. (One of Prestwich's colleagues said he could not vote for a man with no turn-ups to his trousers.) Prestwich had not suggested Powell and Moya, because he thought that they already had too much work in Oxford; but he says today that he would have preferred a building strung out along the river bank, in the manner of the Cripps Building at St John's College, Cambridge.

On the other hand, his wife, Minna Prestwich, was a former colleague of Geoffrey Elton's, and had had enthusiastic reports on Jim from him. Inspired by these she was to ask him to design a new building for her own College, St Hilda's, in 1967. (Jim turned the offer down, because he had too much work, and the commission was given to the Smithsons.) Prestwich was happy enough to recognise Jim as a major architect, and accept him at Queen's, but he never really liked his design, and the relations of the two men suffered from a long and tedious dispute between them as to what materials should be used for the partition walls.

His summing up of the difference between Jim and the Smithsons is partial, but worth recording: the Smithsons seemed 'arty, pretentious, rhetorical' in conversation and appearance, but turned out to be sensible and efficient; Jim seemed a solid, laconic, down-to-earth Glaswegian, but turned out to be difficult and impractical.

The building history of the Florey Building makes depressing reading. It was one of those contracts where too much goes wrong, and there are failures of communication at all levels. The quantity surveyors' estimate came in well above what the College wanted to spend. Economies were made from which the building suffered, including replacement of bathrooms by showers, and the reduction in size of the student rooms from an average of 180 to 130 square feet. The rooms became uncomfortably small, especially those which had the columns of the concrete frame running through them. Another economy got rid of the blinds drawing up from the sill which were to have enabled occupants of the rooms to avoid feeling too exposed in their glass-fronted rooms. They were replaced by ordinary downward-drawing blinds, which were not so effective.

Although the contractor, W.E. Chivers and Sons, was chosen by negotiation not by competitive tender, it found a Stirling building as hard to construct as all British contractors at the time, and its relations with the architect were never good. Both contractor and subcontractors fell increasingly behind schedule. The College felt that the job architect was not sufficiently experienced and not tough enough to deal with them. Costs and delays were aggravated by problems with tiles and room-partitions for which Jim cannot reasonably be blamed. When the specifications were drawn up the tiled surface at the History Faculty Building showed no signs of failing, and the same patent system was adopted at Queen's. In 1969 the tiles started to fall off at other buildings where the system had been used, and there was no escaping the necessity to change over in mid-stream to traditional methods of fixing, which was inevitably more expensive.

Bad sound insulation between the rooms was to be the major cause of complaint in the finished building, and Jim has been much blamed for it. But the partitions were installed against his wishes and advice. He wanted 4-inch concrete block, plastered. Prestwich, who interested himself in technical details, said this would be inadequate, and pressed for patent lightweight plasterboard partitions. In January 1969 Jim unwillingly accepted the system which Prestwich recommended, but three months later the firm which made it announced that it was not able to install it. Jim pressed once more for block and continued to press for it. The Building Committee, at Prestwich's instigation, continued to object to it, and after a lot of toing and froing the Bursar informed Jim on 4 August 1969 that 'the Building Committee has agreed that we proceed with the installation of British Gypsum gyproc metal stud walls, to be fixed by J.H. Dry Construction Ltd.' This proved a great failure. Both the tile saga and the partition saga involved extra expense and delays, which had a knock-on effect on the other sections of the contract.

On 13 February 1969, Robert Blake had written the first of a series of angry letters to Jim, set off by the latter's estimate that the contract would run six months late. 'The news . . . came as a complete bombshell. The more I reflect upon it, the more scandalous it seems . . . If it really is true that a delay of this magnitude is probable, the Contractor seems on the face of things to have displayed deplorable incompetence . . . It is not simply that we would now lose two terms of possible occupancy, though this is in itself annoying enough. Much more serious, I have asked her Majesty the Queen Mother who is the Patroness of the College to open the new building some time in the Spring or early Summer of 1970 . . . It would be most embarrassing at this stage to change the date.'

In fact it was not until 11 May 1971 that the Queen Mother finally opened the building, and even then it was less than half occupied. By 16 February 1972 the Bursar was reporting that 'there is strong dissatisfaction amongst residents of the building with many of its features, principally the inadequacy of sound-insulation, the high running cost of the heating system, and the inconveniently restricted size of several rooms, especially those at the flanks of the building. Dissatisfaction last term reached the point of several residents of the building asking for permission to leave it and go into lodgings.' Relations between Jim and the Bursar were now of the worst. On 5 July, after trouble with the showers, the Bursar wrote 'in any event, we do not provide the occupants of the building with a manual of instructions indicating how they should adapt their way of life to the peculiar requirements of the building'. By 15 September, the contractors 'seem likely to take out a writ against the College in respect of liquidated damages'. On 19 February 1973 Jim was told that the College proposed to make a claim against him for damages for professional negligence. Jim replied on 23 February, 'after the years of effort spent on this building, I am amazed by your letter. That a claim for negligence could even be contemplated demonstrates in my view a lack of understanding of the facts relating to this contract.'

The newly arrived office secretary, Cathy Martin, was told that she was on no account to accept any document. 'I finished work at half-past five, the architects finished at six, and I said to them "Please don't accept anything." When I came in in the morning, lying on top of the typewriter was a parcel, all done up with red ribbon, and a seal on it. I was just semi-hysterical, and kept saying "Who accepted this?" The architects had packed it up that night and stuck it on my typewriter, just to give me a fright. Jim knew all about it.' But the writ was delivered in the end. It was the only one which the firm ever received, and liability was ultimately accepted, with 50 per cent being reluctantly paid by the insurance.

Jim's appointment as an architect for the Southgate housing estate at Runcorn was put to the Board of the Development Corporation in February 1967, when Jim and Queen's College were still in their honeymoon phase, and almost exactly a year before the Florey Building contract was signed with W.E. Chivers and Sons. His plans were approved in December 1968, and the first flats were occupied in the late summer of 1973. Plans for a second phase were finalised in 1974 and completed in 1978. The entire estate was demolished in the early 1990s, following on a decision made by the Development Corporation on 21 February 1989.

At the time of the demolition, Jim stated in an article in *Building Design* that instructions from the Corporation 'determined almost every aspect of the housing and were by far the largest contribution to the eventual appearance and environment of the estate'. Jane Martin is no friend to Jim or his architecture, but in her study *From Southgate to Hallwood Park* (1994) she agrees that 'the record largely bears him out'. The Corporation must carry most of the blame for the lamentable history of the estate. It was the Corporation which asked for high density, for walkways, for prefabrication, for a communal heating system, and for visually arresting architecture. It was the Corporation which had no qualms about providing flats and maisonettes, mostly without gardens, for families which would, almost without exception, have preferred houses with gardens. A different kind of architect from Jim might have questioned the brief, and the point of view. Jim was not that kind of architect. The Corporation presented him with a design problem which interested him – how to produce a coherent and striking whole out of precast units constantly repeated over a large area – and he and his office set themselves to find an answer for it.

The Corporation had to build a high-density estate in a hurry because it had done a deal with a commercial company, Grosvenor Estates Commercial Developments: the company were to build a big shopping centre for the infant New Town, and the Corporation guaranteed to provide the people to shop in it. The shopping centre was due to be opened in 1972, and high density and speed of building were considered essential for Southgate on the immediately adjacent site, so that enough potential shoppers would be in residence in time for the opening. Prefabrication was adopted because it was still optimistically believed to be quicker and possibly cheaper than traditional methods of construction. A further deal was done in May 1969, when Shell-Mex signed a contract to provide the entire estate, as well as the town centre and the hospital, with oil-fired central heating from a central boiler room and plant. The Ministry of Housing and Local Government were interested at the time in the possibility that such district heating schemes would work out more cost-effective than separate heating for each unit, and had persuaded Runcorn to try one out.

Both prefabrication and district-heating proved unfortunate choices. Derick Banwell, who was the General Manager of the Development Corporation at the time, thinks that the heating scheme, in particular, was 'probably our largest single mistake' and caused the downfall of Southgate. As happened too often throughout the country at that time, at Runcorn prefabrication (not helped along by strikes at the factory) turned out to be both slower and more expensive than building the estate in conventional load-bearing brick. In 1975 the massive world-wide increase in oil prices raised the cost of heating from 8p to 18p per therm.

There had been a short halcyon period immediately after Southgate began to be occupied in 1973 when the estate looked good and was filled with 'prosperous-looking handsome young families'. According to an architect with the Corporation at the time, Southgate was briefly considered rather a smart place in which to live. 'It attracted people we would now call "yuppies",' who found its architecture and flats satisfyingly trendy. But from November 1976, both rents and heating costs, which had been subsidised to begin with, in order to get the estate under way, had to be raised, heating costs by 40 per cent. The yuppies found homes with gardens to move into, new arrivals disliked the architecture, and had difficulty in paying the bills. The estate started a downward slide: quick turnover, difficulty in filling the flats, increasingly poor maintenance, and finally a situation in which more and more flats and maisonettes were either empty, or occupied by families on assistance, whose heating bills were paid for them. The estate was becoming a dump and a slum, and its demolition after 1989 was virtually unavoidable in terms of local politics and possibly of cost. After an intensive campaign of consultation and participation, a housing trust, Merseyside Improved Homes, replaced the 1,100 units of Southgate with the Hallwood Park Estate of 308 detached or semi-detached two-storey houses with pitched roofs, each with its own garden. They were the 1990s equivalent of the suburban houses in Liverpool in which Jim had been brought up, and from which he had escaped at the first opportunity.

One bizarre incident enlightened the last years of Southgate, and amused Jim. The round windows which were one of its dominant features had been adopted, Jim assured the Corporation, to provide maritime associations for the inhabitants, most of whom would be coming from Liverpool. In fact they were christened 'the washing machines' on the estate, and were much disliked by the conservative tenants, especially the bigger windows, which stretched from floor to ceiling. However, they had their uses, as was discovered by 36-year-old Mr Robert Dutch, married father of two young children, and employed as a driver and signwriter.

Mr Dutch exposed himself repeatedly at one of his round windows. He upset Nurse Elizabeth Dolman and fourteen others, who were being bussed to work. 'I noticed two portholes on the end of the row. There was a man standing in the window with his hand on his head, and the other outstretched, completely in the nude.' On another occasion Nurse Dolman saw Mr Dutch standing in front of the window with his arms and legs outstretched. 'He looked just like God,' she commented. A plain-clothes policewoman checked up on the story. 'He appeared, nude, waved at me and smiled.' Mr Dutch claimed that he was merely getting dressed, but was found guilty. The story was featured in the *Runcorn Daily News* in July 1981, under a big headline: 'Police Girl saw "God-like Pose" of Nude Man'.

It was the kind of story that made Jim laugh. In addition, he must have been intrigued by the fact that Mr Dutch, with arms outstretched in his round window, was duplicating the well-known Renaissance engraving of a naked man in a circle, with which Francesco di Giorgio and others demonstrated that proportional systems were based on the human figure. He sent the cutting to *Building Design* and suggested that it reproduce the report in its entirety. It did not do so.

'The natives are very friendly,' wrote Jim on the back of a postcard sent to his wife from Peru in 1969 or 1972: the postcard shows a pile of skulls and a skeleton dressed up as a monk in a Peruvian cemetery dating from the seventeenth century. He might have made the same comment about his experiences with British Olivetti. After so many excursions in which the natives had been far from friendly, it must have been balm to the spirit to embark on the Olivetti commission. Instead of being faced with people who reacted to his buildings with shock or horror, or swallowed them bravely to show that they could move with the times, instead of scraping and shrinking his designs to get them within meagre cost limits, he was working for clients who were delighted to have him, and who gave him as much money as he needed without demur. British Olivetti's charismatic general manager, Carlo Alhadeff, was a lavish patron, and believed that architecture was the mother of the arts. He once lined up his branch managers and exhorted them 'Architects are difficult people – but you must work with them.' He gave Jim his full support and became a good friend.

Jim came into the office one morning with a complete set of ⅟32 inch-to-the-foot drawings for the building. Barbara Littenberg, who had been his student at Yale, and was now in the office, is said to have helped him with these. He gave the drawings to Robin Nicholson, and said, 'Get on with it.' It was a young man's job. The team consisted of Nicholson, who had never built anything, David Weinberg, who had just left architecture school, and an assistant, who had not yet qualified. They had the help of a good engineer in Samuely's, Sven Rindl, and Jim always backed them up. He would come to site meetings and sit behind his team, never at the table, without saying a word. Nicholson thinks that this was because he had little idea of the details of what was going on, but the technique was effective. The contractors were terrified by the silent looming figure, and were always amenable.

The Olivetti contract at Haslemere ran over a year late, mainly because neither the plastic manufacturer nor the supplier of the lifting machinery for the assembly hall delivered on time, but no one blamed that on Jim. The rooms suffered, as too often was the case in his buildings, from bad acoustic separation. The commission, in spite of its striking dress, was really for little more than a school hall and two classroom blocks, but the image produced was what Olivetti wanted, and it celebrated accordingly. The training centre was opened on the evening of 21 June 1973. The opening was master-minded by David Moroni, Olivetti's head of publicity, who became a good friend of the Stirlings. Four hundred guests were brought down to Haslemere by a special train from Waterloo. British Rail used the occasion to launch a new type of carriage, and the special train served to unveil them. There were champagne and Vivaldi on the train, drinks on the lawn, a tour of the building, a concert, a dinner, speeches and fireworks. The food was brought over from Harry's Bar in Venice. The main feature of the concert was a 'Divertimento for Olivetti Machines, Chorus and Percussion', written for the occasion by Tristram Cary, in which live voices were combined with the sound of Olivetti typewriters computer-processed into electronic music. The whole event was lavishly produced and brilliantly organised to provide publicity for Olivetti.

163

It was a celebration for Jim, too, but his situation underneath all the glitter was a gloomy one – and that of British Olivetti by no means rosy. A business recession combined with Olivetti's failure to move early enough into the electronic market gave it a bad knock. The grand headquarters building, which Stirling and Wilford had designed for British Olivetti in 1971, had been put on hold, and was later cancelled. Apart from the second phase of Runcorn, Jim's office had no work on hand, and none in prospect.

NINE
MARRIAGE, HOME AND TRAVEL

In the mid-1960s Jim met up with and married Mary Shand. They had seen each other around, at parties and elsewhere, since the late 1950s. In the early 1960s Mary 'became interested in him and he became a bit interested in me, but I think he had other girlfriends at the time'. It was not until the spring of 1963 that they started to see each other regularly. Jim's affair with Eldred Evans had come to a friendly conclusion. As she puts it, 'I think we got interested in other people.' By now Jim was living in a flat in North London which Eldred Evans had found for him. During 1964 Mary moved into it. It was perhaps significant that this was the first time he had ever set up house with a girlfriend. They were married at Marylebone Registry Office on 4 October 1966. They had bought a house not far from the flat, and moved into it in 1967.

Mary Shand was the daughter of Sybil Sissons and John Ambrose Steel. Her mother had remarried soon after she was born, and Mary took the name of her stepfather, Philip Morton Shand, grew up in his stimulating but disturbing aura, and thought of him as her father. PMS, as he was always called, was gifted and impossible. He had three main interests, architecture, apples and wine. He wrote a classic book on wine, published in 1929; he was a cultivator of rare breeds of apple; he was a friend of Gropius and Aalto, worked during the 1930s on the *Architectural Review*, and was largely responsible for making it the main vehicle for publicising the continental Modern Movement in England. John Betjeman was on the *Review* with him, became a devoted friend, and in later life was always trying to find jobs for him. Shand was, as another colleague, J.M. Richards, put it, 'a difficult man, with a habit of taking irrational dislikes to people', and this, combined with three expensive divorces before his final marriage to Sybil Sissons, kept him in perpetual financial trouble, up till his death in 1960.

At the beginning of the war he had been working for the Admiralty in Bath, but had to leave. His wife was at the Admiralty too, and she stayed there and kept the family solvent while PMS remained at home, in a boiler suit and an Old Etonian tie, seething with ideas, reading omnivorously, corresponding round the world, and giving everyone else a hard time. 'He could be brilliant company, but he was also extremely difficult. I grew up in a house with constant terrible rows – especially at Christmas time. That seemed to raise the profile of the emotions. He was difficult in all sorts of ways. If we misbehaved, we used to get caned. We were always expected to be perfect. Still, we held our own, I think.

'My mother was amazing, when I think about it. Amazing energy. She completely accepted that she had to work to keep the family going. She thought he was a genius, you see, and geniuses had to be looked after.'

When war broke out the children had been evacuated with their school from London to Oxford, and joined their parents at weekends at the Oxford house of Paul Nash, the painter, and his wife. From there they moved to Bath, first to a flat, then to a house on Bathwick Hill, which Sybil Shand bought with money left to her by her mother. Elspeth, Mary's younger half-sister, was 'the house daughter, and I was the garden daughter. We had three gardens, two near the house and one at the top of the hill, which was the fruit and vegetable garden. When I wasn't doing my homework, I was usually up there. We didn't get much spare time.'

They spent much of their holidays with Edmund Dulac and Helen Beauclerk, in Dorset. Dulac is best known for his book illustrations, but he was a many-talented man, who made, for instance, all the furniture in his studio himself. Mary Stirling remembers him as 'a charming, delightful man, very erudite. He used to come and stay with us. He made our light-fitting over the dining-room table, which was an Aalto table. We grew up with Aalto, Aalto furniture in the dining room and the nursery.' John Betjeman was another regular visitor, and would embarrass Mary in later life by talking of his 'passion for sulky Mary Shand swinging her satchel as she walked reluctantly from school over the Bath pavements, lucky stones to have been trodden by her gym-shoes'. He taught her to look at buildings as they walked round Bath together: 'Don't look at the shopfronts, look above them.'

By the 1960s she was making a reputation for herself as a furniture designer. After happy and stimulating schooldays at Wycombe Abbey, she had spent a year at St Martin's School of Art, and 'hated it, and decided I wanted to do something more practical. My father had friends in Heal's, and I went there as a trainee for eighteen months, I think . . . and suddenly I realised that there was a thing called furniture design.' While at Heal's she went to evening classes in sculpture and engineering drawing at the Central School of Art. In 1952 she applied for the Royal

College of Art, was accepted, and spent three years studying under R.D. (Dick) Russell, who was Professor of Wood, Metal and Plastics there. Russell was one of two well-known brothers. The other brother, Gordon, designed and made furniture of high quality at Broadway in the Cotswolds as well as being head of the Council of Industrial Design. Dick Russell was also a gifted designer, with his own practice in London in addition to his professorship.

Mary Shand passed out with one of the two Firsts of her year. She got a job in the Architects Department of the London County Council, working in the Furniture Design and Display Unit. She was away for a year during her time there on a British Council Scholarship to Brazil. This led to a row with PMS, who had originally suggested Brazil but changed his mind and told her that she must go and study under his friend Max Bill in Ulm. Mary thought that Brazil sounded more exciting than Ulm, and refused to change her plans. Joseph Rykwert was brought in to persuade her, without success; he found her 'very shy and very determined'.

She began to meet architects when she was at Heal's. The Architectural Association was a few minutes' walk away, and her sister Elspeth was working as secretary to the Director, Michael Patrick, and was very popular with the students. Mary 'knew John Miller and that crowd, and liked them a lot'. While she worked there she lived in the top-floor flat of Leslie and Sadie Martin's house in Hampstead, and they became good friends. Leslie Martin was then the chief architect at the LCC, and Mary was under him when she moved there. More than half of the Design Unit had been trained as architects, 'so everyone knew the architects in other divisions'. Mary was introduced to Sam Stevens in one of the County Hall lifts; he explained Roman drainage to her from the first to the fifth floors, where she got out; he continued to explain it as the lift went out of sight and hearing. She got to know Bob Maxwell, and thinks that it was he or Sam Stevens who first introduced her to Jim, when she returned from Brazil in 1956.

In 1958 Dick Russell recruited her from the LCC to work in his firm, Russell, Hodgson and Leigh. Robin Wade, a talented Australian who had been at the Royal College with her and become a good friend, had gone there a little before. Mary stayed with the firm for eight years, and became an Associate. They were busy and creative years for her. With Dick Russell she designed a table for the Queen to give to President Eisenhower, the lecture desk for the big lecture room of the Royal Society of Arts, a Display Gallery for the Prints and Drawings Department at the British Museum, and what became known as the Coventry Chair, a stackable chair originally made for Coventry Cathedral, and subsequently much

167

used in other cathedrals. She did a good deal of work for hotels, museums, offices and hospitals. By the mid-1960s she was well set up, with a growing reputation, a Lambretta, and a tiny flat furnished with Aalto stools and table in Dunstable Mews, off Devonshire Street, 'behind the King Edward VII Hospital, where they brought out the corpses at the back entrance'. Her flat was the mews appendage of the house in Upper Wimpole Street where Elspeth was living with the successful barrister and newly-elected Tory MP Geoffrey Howe, whom she married in 1953. It featured in *House and Garden* in March 1965: '100 square feet: Mary Shand in W.1'. Jim's flat was in the same issue. By the time the articles came out, Mary had moved in with him.

Mary was and is serious, good-looking, determined, intelligent, sociable, loyal to her many friends, reliable and private. Robin Wade, who had come to the Royal College as a shy young Australian with few contacts in London, says that he was 'always a bit in awe of Mary; she had an aura of knowing people. She was a very good student, exceedingly conscientious, highly intelligent and a good and supportive friend'. But she was 'very quiet and difficult to get to know – a bit of an enigma'. John Betjeman told her that she would either marry a prince or go into a convent. As she comments, 'I suppose I did marry a prince, of sorts.'

It was not an obvious match. Jim had previously gone for more flamboyant girlfriends, and he was not Mary's physical type: 'I think he's the only really hefty fellow that I've been interested in.' Friends warned her that he would be 'a handful, and I realised that, but I thought that with my background I could cope'. She had already had experience of difficult men, starting with P. Morton Shand. Even so, she was far from feeling certain that the marriage would last.

It was his eyes that attracted her: 'that always attract me in a man. Grey-blue and powerful.' She was struck, too, by his choice of a car. 'Most of the boyfriends I'd had had flashy second-hand cars that always broke down. Jim had a very sensible, totally undistinguished Ford Prefect which worked, and that impressed me.' She saw, in fact, through his surface wildness and occasional moodiness to his core of seriousness and reliability; but perhaps the wildness appealed to her too.

Jim needed support, at home as well as in the office, and Mary provided the former just as Michael Wilford and Cathy Martin provided the latter. To act as a back-up to genius is not an easy role. Barbara Chase-Riboud had gone off to Paris because she could not face up to it. Mary had been brought up with it, accepted it and filled it for nearly thirty years, without ever becoming just an appendage to Jim.

It was a very private marriage. Only Elspeth and Geoffrey Howe came to the Registry Office; the four of them had a drink in a pub afterwards, and that was that. Mary told no one in her office that she was married until some time later. Robin Wade and others asked her 'Why didn't you tell us?' and 'she acted as though it were a mere nothing . . . Mary's a bit like that.' Jim was equally uncommunicative at work, and continued to address postcards to 'Mary Shand' into 1968.

Mary's description of him written to Lesley Borland, a friend in Australia, in August 1964, had scarcely been forthcoming: 'taciturn and moody, very ambitious . . . and I'm not sure you'll like him' (they were all about to spend a holiday on a boat together, and Mary was a little apprehensive, but in fact Lesley did like him, and the holiday was a success). In 1966 Jim was teaching and lecturing in America. Mary came out to join him for a few days, in May, but he was there on his own at the end of the year, after their marriage, and again at the beginning of 1967. He sent her postcards written in his usual laconic style but signed with a J inside or next to a heart, and occasional kisses. They had bought and were converting a terrace house a few minutes' walk from the flat, and Mary was pregnant. Jim sent enquiries and instructions, along with a little news.

From Raleigh, in North Carolina, where he was lecturing, he wrote in November: 'How are the avocadoes? And your teeth? Hope things are happening on the house. Raleigh real south everybody talks like babydoll, really KKK area. Thanks for your letter. Southern women beautiful but bitches, men very intimidated by them. Been to dinner at Philip Johnson, has been friendly. Have avoided the English so far J [J inside drawn heart].' On 27 November he wrote from New York: 'En route to Philadelphia. Get in touch with Ian Gow and find out what's happening in Camden, also – do working drawings or whatever is required of the kitchen, doesn't need to be same as specification. may be required by builders in 1 month. Have you had your teeth seen to? Doing what your supposed to vis the Doctors and hospitals etc. see you. J [drawing of a heart].' On 12 December he wrote from Indianapolis: 'Shall be back on Tuesday 20th about midday shall be back in flat at usual time. How is the book going – have you completed the first chapter? Have you been to see the car; did they put antifreeze in and wax body. Having dinner with Rudolph, Johnson and Co tomorrow. Are you doing your exercises otherwise won't get your shape back love J. shall be glad to be back XX.'

On 7 March he wrote from New Haven: '2 feet of snow on the ground – very cold siberian winter – Haven't been anywhere yet except TROY where I met C. Rowe and A. Boyarski. I think there should be cork tiles in the large front room, could you get bolt in kitchen – subcontractor to do this. KEEP FIT. Love J.' By 31 March he was in 'KANSAS CITY surrounded by prairy. this is the land of "In cold blood" T. Capote, which I've just finished reading. Apparently the "boys" (as they are affectionately referred to hereabouts) stayed in the hotel I'm in!! Keep fit – have you been to the dentist recently? seen "Blowup" twice in N.H. very good.'

Jim came back to England on 12 April. Their son Ben was born in the Middlesex Hospital on 25 April. Jim was over the moon. His mother was equally delighted with a grandson to carry on the Stirling name. It was a difficult birth, and she wrote Mary a sympathetic letter: 'I am so sorry, my dear, that you had such a strenuous time. These Stirlings are awkward at birth!' She begged her after leaving hospital, to 'be lazy and indulgent to yourself for a change'.

Mrs Stirling came a good deal to London up to the time of her death in 1974. Mary got on very well with her: 'I liked her a lot and I admired the way she had brought up her children with her husband away all the time. That was quite something for her generation. She was always very neatly dressed and immaculate. She was a good-looking woman, with thick white curly hair. Very Northern Irish accent, and very interested in her family in Armagh. Great talker, not much sense of humour, a bit fussy – that used to irritate Jim from time to time. But she was good and helpful and supportive in every possible way.' In spite of the occasional irritation there is no doubt of Jim's love for his mother; he saw her regularly and was deeply upset when she died.

Jim was back in America early in 1968. His mother was staying at the London house and he wrote from Kentucky to 'Mary/Ben/Mum. Tempture is 60°. down on the blue grass country – not blue at all . . . whats Bens next trick? Luv-luv-Jim.' By 19 February he was in New York, and wrote to Mary 'go to Toronto next week, back at end of month what's BEN up to? Did you get the bread basket cleaned and silver from Elizabeth? Luv Luv J [drawing of a heart].' In Toronto there was '6 ft of snow on the ground – very very cold. place is full of Scotsmen – should be back at end of next week. Love luv.'

Kate was born on 1 October 1968, and Sophie on 13 July 1970. Mary wrote to Lesley Borland from the Middlesex Hospital. 'This afternoon during visiting hours we had a celebration just outside on the landing of the hospital with Jenny, Phoebe, Jim and the kids all drinking champagne! As Jenny (the daily nanny) said it was like a midnight feast at school as I wasn't supposed to have kids up here.'

Outside the office and Jim's work as an architect Mary organised his life for him, and he subsided with gratitude into the role of a man who 'couldn't even boil an egg'. She looked after the house and the food, ran the dinner parties and Jim's clothes, hired the daily nanny (Jim refused to have a living-in one), and attended all the school activities which bored Jim. They already had many friends in common; she accepted the others and they became her friends as well. In their early days together they had one serious row, and she vowed never to have one again. She had been brought up to believe that creative men were difficult, and she accepted his awkward aspects and bore with them with equanimity.

She continued to work as a freelance designer, but it was not easy to do so. In 1967 Dick Russell became ill, and his firm broke up. Mary and Robin Wade set up in partnership, and opened a West End office in Crawford Street, but with him living in Richmond and Mary in North London, and Mary heavily committed at home, it proved unworkable, and they gave it up after about eighteen months. Mary started to teach part-time and designed furniture independently, including for Jim at St Andrews, the Florey Building, and the Tate Gallery; but her career now had to be combined with looking after Jim and the children.

In some ways Jim's home life was organised like his building projects; others did most of the work, but he was the creative orchestrator. At home or on holiday routines and rituals developed, originated by Jim or, more often, by Mary and welcomed by him. Characters were taken on board, and stayed for years. There was Mrs Bonfield, the Irish cleaning lady, whose pungent views on life and people made her a pleasure to talk to, lived with style and decision in a world of her own, and worked for the Stirlings for nearly thirty years. There was Mr Bush, who cooked and served the big dinners. There was Phoebe Mason, of the outstanding presence and forthright views, a nautical American friend of the whole family. There was a succession of cats, whom Jim loved. A framework of security developed, which was important to Jim and to the family as a whole.

Jim was much involved with the settings in which they lived. He had always been a buyer, although his first purchases were limited by lack of space and money. 'The first antique furniture I bought', he told Marina Gregotti in the 1980s, 'was when I was in Liverpool as a student. I bought a set of six early Victorian chairs, which I never brought down to London. I needed some chairs for my room, so I went out and paid £3 for six chairs, and when I think about it they were actually quite good.' Another early purchase was an ebonised chair in the style of Edward Godwin, probably bought for his room at Sam Stevens's. He started buying more seriously in the 1950s, when he moved into the office in Gloucester Place and the North London flat. At about this time he started collecting mementoes of the First World War, especially miniature china tanks. Bill Howell was making a similar Great War collection; unlike Jim's, it was to become a very large one. Gill Howell remembers with amusement that Bill would see Jim on the Portobello Road 'looking shifty', and the two men would pretend not to notice each other.

But the flat as shown in the article in *House and Garden* of March 1965 is much what one would expect of Jim at the time. It contained a cool uncluttered collection of contents: Aalto stools and tables, a Breuer chair, an Eames chair, two Mies chairs, Remploy shelving and two avocado plants. The walls were hung with a set of Paolozzi's 'Wittgenstein' lithographs; these arrived in 1965, and transformed the flat. The only object dating from before the twentieth century was a bow-fronted 'Hepplewhite' table; this was one of a pair which later turned out to be 1930s fakes, and Jim got rid of them.

Many of the same pieces of furniture appear in two photographs of the first-floor and ground-floor rooms at the new house, taken by Richard Einzig in 1970. But the nature of the mixture has been changed by a number of new arrivals: a Brion-Vega gramophone, for instance, bought for the house at Aram's stylish shop for modern furniture on the Fulham Road; a dining-room table designed by Mary Stirling and made for the house at the end of 1969; seven early nineteenth-century dining-room chairs; a bow-fronted Regency sideboard, this time genuine; a studded Chesterfield sofa of a type fashionable at the time among architects. The avocado trees had been left behind in Belsize Park and replaced by an aspidistra which is not yet in the photograph. The avocados, incidentally, both died early in 1992, a few months after Jim's own death.

The contents of the house, in contrast to the flat, now became increasingly eclectic, and the ratio of old to new steadily increased in favour of the former. By 16 September 1969, when Robert Harling came to the house for dinner, he commented in a thank-you letter to Jim and Mary: 'We loved all the things that you have done to, with and in the house. I do congratulate you – if I may – on all the courageous things you have done, and the mixture of Corb, Hope, Breuer, Eames and Chesterfield, a pleasure to the eyeballs.' As Harling realised, what was 'courageous' about the house was not the individual objects, any one of which could have been found in other architects' or collectors' houses in London at the time, but the mixture. Both Jim's treatment of the house and the mixture of objects in it were highly personal, and indicative of the way he and his architecture were moving.

The house was one of a row of moderate-sized speculative housing of about 1900. North London is full of such houses, but this particular terrace had an extra element of fantasy or perversity in its mixture of 'Queen Anne', Art Nouveau and vaguely Jacobean or Elizabethan motifs. The tone was set by the Art Nouveau stained glass and lively asymmetry of the entrance. The hall was spacious for a house of its size, enlivened and made entertaining by arched screens of elaborate fretwork, designed to support the knick-knacks of late Victorian housewives, and soon to support the knick-knacks of the Stirling family. The whole house was what Lutyens might have described as 'rather naughty'. A Modern Movement architect in the 1930s, or even the 1950s, would have found it beneath contempt, but it amused Jim, in a way that a panelled eighteenth-century house would not have amused him. He kept virtually all the original detail, painted the rooms white, and knocked them together. He put a dado on the first floor and in the dining room in the style of the house, and designed a Voyseyesque capital for the single column which now kept the first-floor ceiling from collapsing. On this floor the front and back rooms, the conservatory off the back room, and the staircase, were joined into one large space. This was not used as a living room. It was a room for entertaining, which the children got to call the 'No-No' room, because they were not allowed into it on their own.

Tom and Rosaleen Ellis came to dinner in March 1972, and Rosaleen wrote to thank on 30 March: 'We enjoyed it all very much indeed – the super meal and your vast elegant spaces – this place seemed appallingly cluttered when we returned.' In fact the spaces were already fuller than they had been in 1970, and were to continue to fill over succeeding years. Although Jim bought with a sure eye for quality, and became increasingly knowledgeable, he was never a collector in the sense that he bought objects to fill an art-historical gap or complete a sequence. He liked to say that he bought objects only because they suited his purpose; chairs for sitting on, a table for writing on, a cupboard in which to keep his slides. But in fact he could not stop buying, both for the house and for the office. He may not have been a collector but he was an insatiable acquirer, and, once he had started, bought far beyond what was necessary for practical purposes.

During the 1970s Colin Rowe was elaborating his idea of 'Collage City', the city which stimulated because of the collection and collision of disparate elements. Jim was creating a Collage House, in which the aim was stimulus rather than harmony. The tone was set by the big New York banner, of a hand pointing a pistol, which faced visitors as they came through the front door. Throughout the main spaces objects of many types and dates – Modern Movement chairs, Art Nouveau lamps, neo-classical furniture, Paolozzi prints, and much more to come – were contrasted to each other. Yet as the objects accumulated there was little sense of clutter, because Jim's eye was in control. The common factor was quality, and perhaps one should add to this what Jim called 'gutsiness'. Everything was full-blooded and there were no duds – or if there were, they quickly disappeared.

Jim was only interested in the main rooms of the house: the entrance hall, the library and dining room on the ground floor, and the big reception room on the first floor. In these rooms he had a clear idea of where each piece of furniture, each plant, each object, each ornament, should be positioned. When he came back from abroad, almost the first thing he would do was to tour the house. It made a deep impression on Mrs Bonfield, the cleaning lady. 'He would come into the kitchen, and have a sandwich or something. Then go round the house to see that everything was in place. If a matchbox was a few inches out he would put it back. If he found Mrs Stirling's bag or shoes lying around, he would throw them in the basket. He was a terror.'

The Stirlings were by no means wedded to their London house. From very early on they started looking at bigger houses, in the country, in Bath and in London. Jim enjoyed looking, but what he wanted was always beyond what he could afford, and they remained where they were.

Soon after the Stirlings moved in, they began to entertain on a·scale more lavish than was usual among architects. They gave regular formal dinner parties, usually for ten people, and a big drinks party at least once a year, usually on New Year's Eve. Jim's friends came to the dinners, and at first were startled because the occasions were so unlike the old gatherings around Sam Stevens's or Michael Wickham's kitchen tables, or in the bars and restaurants in Soho, Marylebone, New Haven and New York (though something like these continued in much more relaxed kitchen suppers given in addition to the grand dinners). Jim's reasons can only be guessed at. Establishing his image certainly played a part. Visiting architects of distinction were invited, so were clients, editors, journalists and historians. Perhaps there was an echo of Jim's feelings that Le Corbusier's villa at Garches needed to be 'occupied fully, and with grand personality individuals . . . by such as the Sitwells, with never less than half a dozen brilliant and permanent guests'. Perhaps there were memories of guest nights in army messes. And it certainly intrigued him to add contrasting people to the collage of contents, and to observe how they reacted with each other. Even when, as occasionally happened, there was a row between two or more of the guests, he was not entirely upset. His daughter Kate is perceptive about this: 'Dad always knew how to get together a group of people, and always used to enjoy seeing the relationships

Jim with Ben, Kate and Sophie

Mr Bush, a photograph
given to Sophie

Family lunch at
Le Beausset
with Marthe
Moreau

The Stirling family,
photographed by Robert Kahn
in the Vatican gardens

Jim and Mary in Cordoba in 1987

The Neue Staatsgalerie, Stuttgart,
1977-84, from the terrace

In the courtyard of the
Neue Staatsgalerie

The entrance hall and staircase,
Arthur M. Sackler Museum, Harvard University, 1978-84

The
Office.
Jim and
Michael
Wilford

With Cathy Martin and Jackie Simnet

Jim with models
of the Florey
Building and
Dorman Long
Headquarters,
outside the office
at 75 Gloucester
Place

In the
partners' room at
Gloucester Place

The Clore Building, Tate Gallery, London, 1980-86

Looking across the courtyard of the
Wissenschaftszentrum, Berlin, 1979-87.
The building on the right has since
been completed.

Jim being interviewed
in the courtyard

Model of the proposed library at Latina, Italy, 1983

The Cornell Center for the Performing Arts, Ithaca, USA, 1983-88

Headquarters for Braun AG, Melsungen, Germany, 1986-92. The pedestrian walkway

With Mary Stirling, receiving the Praemium Imperiale in Tokyo, 1991

Jim's hands, and
Jim at his desk,
(*below*) taken by
Marlies Hentrup

With Marlies
Hentrup
in the Museum
of Modern Art,
New York

The Bookshop in the Biennale Gardens, Venice, 1989-91

Number 1
Poultry, City
of London,
1986-98

The empty table. Jim's worktable at the office in Fitzroy Square,
photographed by him shortly before his death.

through these people. He used to pick his friends, and they were the people that surrounded him, and influenced him, and probably influenced his work, and then he would rotate them, and see how these different people would move together, and what they'd create together . . . you know, I think Dad was kind of a people player.'

Guests went up to the 'No-No' room on the first floor, and spent an hour or so sitting on Jim's neo-classical chairs, talking and drinking champagne. At some stage the three children appeared in their nightdresses and pyjamas, to say 'hello' to the guests. The party then went down to dinner, served in the back half of the ground-floor room on the table designed by Mary Stirling; Jim's library was in the other half. The table was dazzling with linen, silver and glass. The food was good, but always very much the same: a green soup, lamb or beef from the joint, bread-and-butter pudding or a lemon mousse, sometimes a suet pudding, salad with lashings of cheese; Jim's taste, in fact. The wine was superb. Mary Stirling knew about wine because Morton Shand was an expert, had written a good book on the subject, and had brought her up to appreciate it: Jim grew to love good wine, and quickly acquired his own expertise.

By way of the Howes Jim and Mary had discovered an inspired addition to the variety of the evenings. As Robert Harling wrote to Mary in 1969: 'Your cook-butler-footman-sommelier-receptionist was a great showpiece and aid.' This was Mr Bush, who for nine or ten years cooked and served the dinners. He is probably the only non-fictional gentleman's gentleman to have had a novel written about him, called, indeed, *Gentleman's Gentleman*, by Julian Fane. The novel was written shortly after his death, and published in 1981: it contains a good deal of straight biography, thinly disguised by changes of name.

Mr Bush came to work for a French friend who shared Fane's house, began to look after Fane as well, and stayed with him when the friend went back to France. His work for Fane was less than a full-time job, and by mutual agreement he went out to cook dinner for other people as well. He had much success, and the people who ate his dinners ranged from the Queen Mother downwards. For her he claimed to cook red-white-and-blue-tinted rice, but that may have been one of his many good stories. 'Cooking', Fane wrote, 'expressed the artistic part of his nature. He loved the challenge of it, and the drama, the thrills and the spills, and the implicit snobbery, and the competitive and boastful avenues it opened. He was greedy, he was neat-fingered, precise, inventive, intuitive, and presented food beautifully – presentation and the look of things counted for more with him than reality.' Family retainers who join in the conversation and are considered 'characters' can be a bore, but Mr Bush was

175

never boring. He was small, fat, red-faced, with a stomach spilling out over his trousers. He exuded good cheer and geniality – he camped up the part of butler with mockery and considerable skill. He chatted up the guests and flirted with Kate and Sophie. Sophie was his little sweetheart; he professed to be engaged to her, and brought her boxes of chocolates. Ben, on the other hand, he used to chase round the kitchen, brandishing a carving-knife in one hand, and a knife-sharpener in the other. He only cooked one menu for the Stirlings, but he cooked it very well. His problem was drink, and it grew worse over the years. He retired to relatives at Clacton-on-Sea in 1979, and died in 1980.

Mary Stirling sat at one end or in the centre of the dinner table, usually in an exquisite St Laurent or Nicole Farhi suit. The guests dressed up, though never in dinner jackets. Jim sat at the head of the table, and as Mary puts it 'his idea of dressing for dinner was to take off his tie and open his shirt neck'. His deep dislike for any kind of dress which could be described as formal dated back at least to his rebellion against the Montague Burton suits bought for him by his father when he was a teenager, and had been compounded by his pleasure at getting out of uniform at the end of the war. Moreover, he had composed his own image. The fact that it was in collision with the image presented by everyone else probably appealed to him.

Jim's almost invariable wear for many years consisted of a royal-blue poplin shirt, rough dark grey tweed jacket, grey flannel trousers, bright green or purple socks, and suede desert boots with high insteps. Sometimes he also wore a star-spotted tie, and if it were warm he dropped the coat. From the late 1970s, when travelling or going to the office, he carried a bright green plastic briefcase, first bought in Stuttgart and replaced over the years.

He moved into blue shirts in about 1965. Mary bought a royal-blue shirt at Austin Reed's for his birthday, because she remembered that PMS had had one, and Jim continued to buy them until Reed's ceased to stock them. He moved on to Henry Poole and Sons in Old Burlington Street. Pooles were already making the suits which, from the early 1980s, he wore for formal meetings with clients, but very seldom at other times. He had gone to them at Mary's suggestion, for Dick Russell had bought his suits there. The firm now made up royal-blue shirts for him in batches of a dozen or so, from a roll of cloth supplied by John Lewis and woven in a Japanese mill. The shirts had one pocket, always on the right instead of the conventional position on the left, probably because Jim's left hand was still partly disabled.

Jim designed himself just as much as he designed his buildings, and according to a similar method. Mary suggested possibilities, which he accepted or rejected, and on the whole it was she who did the buying. She bought most of his clothes in large batches; it simplified his life, and most of them had to be made up specially anyway, because he was outsize. She bought black cashmere V-necked sweaters from Simpson's until he had difficulty in getting them over his head. He then moved on to cardigans, bought in batches of eight through Simpson's, but supplied by Barries in Scotland. His dark grey jackets and trousers were first bought at Martin Green's in Marylebone High Street, and later in New Haven. His diamond-spotted woollen ties had been woven by an old lady in one of the Scottish islands, and supplied to Beale and Inman in Bond Street. These ties were fashionable in AA circles in the 1950s. Then the old lady died, and Jim moved on to plain black wool ties bought at Yale, and finally to spotted ties, bought in Burlington Arcade; the spots, like Jim, grew bigger over the years. All his clothes were expensively cleaned by Jeeves of Belgravia.

Jim's appearance was described in a letter, with accompanying drawing, which his daughter Sophie, aged 9, wrote to him for his birthday on 22 April 1980.

> Dear Daddy
> I am sure you know who the person is on the cover is,
> I mean it's obvious, its just like the person he is quite tall & his feet are
> a little big, so he has funny shoes. He has got about
> 12,000,00000,00000,00000,00000,00000,00000,00000, 00000,00000
> pairs of the same clothes, a blue shirt a pair of dark grey trousers with a
> matching top. And has a quadruple chin. Big eyes with a long nose
> > And its DADDY I knew you knew
> > Best wishes for your Brithda
> > Love Sophie

Jim's children meant a great deal to him. He took much more interest in Ben's school life than that of the girls, and seldom attended any of the latter's school functions, but out of school he spent as much time with them as he could. Michael Wilford was impressed by how 'he enjoyed the kids very much – loved the cats as well, I remember, always very fond of the cats. I suppose from the outside he was probably more of an ideal family man than I was. He always seemed to have the kids climbing over him. He would be very well entrenched. Often he used to make me feel quite guilty about the level of affection he exuded on the kids.'

Sophie remembers how 'when I was very young, I really felt the love

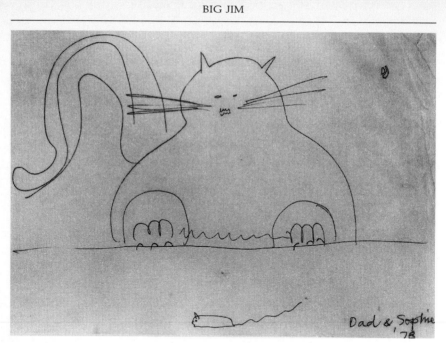

'Dad and Sophie', drawn by Jim for Sophie

Kate and blackbird's nest, drawn by Jim for Kate

Sophie's birthday card for Jim Stirling, 1984

of my father. I used to go and sit on his lap. Me and some friends, we used to go and sit on Dad's stomach and play and play . . . when I was very young.' But he was never demonstrative. As in many English families at the time, there was no hugging, kissing, or obvious physical affection. Kate thinks that 'he found it difficult to tell us that he loved us. He just took it for granted that we knew. I know he had a very close relationship with his mother, who was very like Sophie. I think I was six when she died. That's the only time I've ever seen Dad cry. I remember that. I was sitting on the edge of the kitchen table at home. I didn't know really what was going on.'

He was a strict father. For Ben, 'it was a serious thing when he used to sit down and talk to me.' Kate remembers that 'Dad was always hard on me, I think, on all of us. I think he knew all of our different personalities well enough to direct them correctly. He was blatantly critical of me in front of other people, which wasn't very nice. Sophie would always stand up to Dad, and that was her way, perhaps, of having attention from him. And my way was always just to give more of what that person wanted, because they were asking for something, and I thought they'd be pleased if they had it. In fact I think what he wanted me to do was to say "no" to him.'

Sophie went to day school, never left home, and had a stable childhood. 'I think me and Dad had quite a level of understanding. When I watched TV with him, we'd laugh at the same things. He teased me a lot. I didn't get upset by it, really, but I think my sister might have done. She might have taken it personally, but I knew it was more teasing.

'I think he had a very soft side. Because it was so real he couldn't show it as well as some people . . . you know, some people are very fake, they show it, but it's not very real. But for him it was so real, that it almost didn't seem like he had one. To some people. Not really to me, because I knew . . . but I think he was a bit worried about it.

'I suppose humour for me was the big thing with him. Like we laughed at things; we'd laugh a lot. I'd say we had lots of laughs, really. I suppose his actual physical shape made him much more lovable. When I was young I used to have all my bears on my bed. I had fourteen bears. I never had dolls. That's probably something to do with my father.'

At Mary's suggestion Jim used to take one of the children with him in rotation on outings at home and abroad. 'Saturday morning', according to Sophie, 'Dad would go to Wholefoods, just off Baker Street, to buy the meat. We used to have steak and salad every Saturday night. Dad bought the steak, and then he'd go to the vegetable shop and buy chicory, and then he'd make the salad later. Mum would go and do normal shopping, and I think she would take one of us, or two of us, and then Dad would take the other, and we'd take it in turns to go with Dad. First of all it would be buying food, which was the boring bit, and then we'd go and look round the antique shops . . . Camden Passage, up in Islington, or Portobello Road. We'd go and have a doughnut, or we'd have something to eat as well, and then we'd come back and have lunch. He used to buy me jewellery sometimes, and when I was younger that was obviously more interesting than looking at furniture. I've got a green jade bracelet that I wear. He picked that up in Camden Passage . . . and there's a ring I've got which is amethyst. I wear that all the time now.' Kate remembers these outings as 'an incredible experience that we had as children. Once every three weeks I would go with my father to either Portobello Road or what used to be a large antiques store, and became Hyper Hyper, in Kensington High Street. Or wander around the streets of Camden and pick things up. He had a very good eye, Dad. Mum in fact always used to say, if he'd been an art dealer, we would have been much richer. I used to be a little scared to go out with Dad because he was a very imposing figure, but this antique walking was interesting, and I always used to like going, because he always used to buy me a present. When we were kids, I remember he gave me this black ring once, which was a crocodile. He and I chose it together. And I remember losing it at school, when I was about sixteen. Actually, I was very upset.

'As children on Sunday we had to polish the furniture on the middle floor. The No-No room. We didn't enjoy it, but we didn't have a choice at that point. I was seven years old. He always polished the table tops, and we did the rest, because Dad couldn't get on his knees. He used to call us Slave Number One, Number Two, Number Three. Dad had this kind of wicked sense of humour. He thought it was funny. It is funny to think about now, but as a child, it's not nice.'

Jim's returns from his absences teaching in America are vividly remembered by all three children. 'He'd come back with this big green bag,' Sophie recollects, 'and other bags from Bloomingdales. Mum would get us up in the middle of the night, literally take us out of bed, and we'd all sit down on the couch on the first floor, and he'd give us out things, one by one, out of his bag. I remember a yellow top with blue collars, lots of brightly coloured things, stripy tights, knickerbockers . . . I had some purple ones, some red ones. They were quite colourful, quite American. He used to buy us toys as well, or new gadgets. I can't remember exactly what. When I was, I suppose, twelve or thirteen, I kind of rebelled against all that a bit. But up until then I really liked all the things he gave us. We were always really excited to know what we were going to get.' Ben remembers the thrill of being taken out to the airport to meet him.

The children went skiing with their mother in Scotland, from about 1978 to 1984. Jim came, but never skied. Sophie remembers him: 'We used to go for walks in quite deep snow, around the lakes. Dad used to wear a big coat, and a hat with a bobble on it, I think, and his brown boots, like Moon boots a bit. I remember there being ospreys' nests, big nests on the top of the trees. Dad and Mum used to talk about them. At home we used to have blackbirds in the garden, and he'd talk about them quite a lot. We weren't allowed to disturb the blackbird's nest.'

The most regular family holidays were in France. Since the early 1960s the Howes had been spending summer holidays in Normandy, on the Cherbourg peninsula – the Cotentin. The Stirlings, once they had children, began to come too. This lasted from 1969 until Jim's death and beyond. In the summer of 1969 they rented what Mary Stirling calls a 'Monsieur Hulot house', the Villa Pier-et-Hel, at Coutainville. From 1970 they rented a house from the Michels, a farming family who lived just outside Coutainville. They spent several happy holidays there, but the last ended in tragedy in August 1973. Monsieur and Madame Michel went out with some others to collect seaweed, and overloaded the boat. It overturned. They were wearing thigh boots and could not swim. Both of them were drowned.

Next year the Stirlings rented a house on the same peninsula, at Barfleur. It was in the garden of an older house, and had been built about 1900 by the then owner for his daughter. The Stirlings have rented the same house for a few weeks each summer ever since. Until 1996 it remained the epitome of French bourgeois taste and discomfort of about 1900, furniture, pictures, books and all. All the rooms were lined with pine-boarding. There was a shower, but no bathroom, and one outside chemical lavatory, outside the kitchen. Meals were usually eaten in the gravelled courtyard between the two houses. The upper rooms look out to sea, and to the great stone lighthouse built on the point in the early nineteenth century. It is a superb object, and Jim loved it. At night its rotating beams flash through the bedrooms.

Barfleur has a mixed community of fishermen and summer visitors, French, English, Italians and Belgians, who rent or own houses, and come every year. Church and houses, almost all built of granite, rise up on a spit between the harbour and the sea; the oldest date from the fifteenth or sixteenth centuries, and there are many eighteenth-century ones. For Kate, 'it was great, as kids. Dad used to fly in and out to Cherbourg on what he called the dragonfly plane – a very small bright yellow plane – and that was nice. It was nice to grow up with those different families that were there. All of us have this ongoing relationship with all those families, and I hope that I'll have children and go back to Barfleur, and they'll grow up with the children of all the others, and all that kind of stuff. It really is a second home, Barfleur.'

Geoffrey and Elspeth Howe and their children usually came out to Normandy too, and the families met up a good deal together. Elspeth Howe remembers how 'Jim would say "Right, that looks an interesting château", and we'd just drive straight up to it, with no regard for privacy or somebody's "No Entrance". It reminded me very much of my father, who used to say, "Well, that's an interesting apple. Go and pick it", from somebody's garden.'

From 1977 the family also went down to the South of France to stay with their friends the Burrells. According to Ben, 'We had this bizarre routine, which I suppose was the most economical way of doing it. We used to sit five of us in the Citroën, and drive over a two-day period from Barfleur to Toulon. And we always used to stay overnight at Villefranche-sur-Saône, with Marthe, who was a family friend. Or with Marthe's family. It was pretty stressful for Dad, I think, because he insisted on doing all the driving. He used to have a bottle of Evian spray, a sort of mist spray, that he'd spray on his face once in a while, and he always used to smoke disgusting cigars in the car, which gassed us all. Sophie always used to have to sit in the middle, which she hated. I remember him getting very annoyed by us screaming in the back, but I don't think that one can really blame us, if we'd been sitting in a car for six hours, or whatever.'

Jim never wrote letters to his family, but would send postcards to whoever was at home. If Mary was with him, she wrote most of the postcard, and Jim scrawled a few words at the bottom. In 1970 he and Mary wrote to Kate from Florence, where he was lecturing, on a postcard of a fresco in San Miniato, showing St Benedict welcoming King Totila: 'THE MAN ON HIS KNEES IS LIKE SIR GEOFFREY HOWE. CAN YOU FIND LADY ELSPETH?' (Geoffrey Howe had just been made Solicitor General and knighted.) In 1971 he wrote from Japan, over a fake Japanese signature, 'Just off to Kyoto. Tokio awfull city – worse than NY – super hotel – red carpet treatment all the way – Japanese food all the time – very sadistic of Japanese.' In 1974 he and Mary went on a tour of Baroque churches in Bohemia, with Jim's German publisher, Gerd Hatje, and his wife. Jim wrote for Ben, on a postcard of plaster cherubs at Ottobeuren, 'everybody here is naked and very white – sometimes pink'. In 1975 he was in India, and wrote to Ben: 'the two elephants look a bit like Mum and Dad at the swimming pool which we have in the hotel,' and for Sophie, on a postcard of a woman in a terrifying red mask for a Devil Dance in Nepal, 'She's gone quite red in the face – in fact she looks a bit like you when you are in a rage.' Kate was sent a postcard of an Indian miniature showing a woman at her toilette: 'I don't think she looks at herself in the mirror as much as you do.' In 1976 Jim was in Copenhagen with Mary. Kate got a postcard of the features of Hans Christian Andersen's Little Mermaid: 'I think she needs a good bathe – and her nails need cutting, and she's forgotten her bathing costume.' Ben's postcard was of the Amalienborg Palace, with the guard being changed before the big bronze or copper statue of King Frederick V on horseback: 'The man on the horse is green with cold.'

Jim and Mary went away a good deal without the children, sometimes on straightforward holidays, sometimes on outings connected with Jim's work. Mary went most years to America, when Jim was working there. For several years, starting in August 1970, Peter Blake, the American architectural critic, lent them a romantic flat overlooking the little harbour at Tellaro, near Lerici. They spent other good holidays, a little time later, with Carlo and Nora Alhadeff at their house at Strada-in-Chianti in Tuscany, along with Richard Meier and Julia Bloomfield. Carlo Alhadeff had left England in 1971 to manage Olivetti in America, and Meier had designed a prototype Olivetti service station for him.

Jim now acquired a lasting love for Italy. He grew attached to the informal piazzas, flights of steps, arcades, narrow streets and open spaces of small Italian towns. The Italian combination of sun, warmth, good food and drink, outdoor meals, café life, and plenty of buildings to see fitted him to perfection. Julia Bloomfield has vivid memories of him 'climbing up the steps in one of these hill towns, the light and dark of the steps, Jim in his outfit that never changed come winter or spring or summer, and this huge rear going up the steps to the light at the top'.

In June 1972, Mary went with Jim to Barcelona. Jim was lecturing there, along with Kenzo Tange, Frei Otto and Louis Kahn. This was one of Jim's earlier experiences of what he called the 'International Circus', the collection of architects of world reputation whose paths continually crossed each other at conferences, juries and symposia. Jim provided the English act. The entire circus congregated in Iran in 1974, in a hotel built for the occasion at Persepolis, wafted out there by the Shah's wife, who had trained as an architect. Buckminster Fuller, Tange, Aldo Van Eyck, Hans Hollein, Moshe Safdie, and others – along with Louis Kahn's widow, for Kahn had died earlier in the year. Mary came out with Jim to Persepolis, and they went on with a collection of architects to Isfahan and Shiraz, which they both loved. Jim sent M.J. Long and Sandy Wilson a postcard of the Masjid Shah Mosque: 'Isfahan and Shiraz are terrific . . . the Archi. congress was weird – good food, lousy stomach – hope to see you soon.' They spent a few days in Teheran, and bought Persian outfits for the children, which they wore in the neighbourhood festival later on that year.

In February 1975 they left for a three-week tour of India, where Jim was lecturing for the British Council. From Nepal Jim sent Alan Colquhoun a postcard of the Red Fort at Agra: 'Done Bombay (huge Victorian buildings), Ahmedabad, Madras (very hot), Baroda (very British Army), Delhi (very Liverpool School of Arch. sketch design circa 1938). Now in Nepal for 3 days hols – see Everest from the bedroom window. – I was much moved by 2 of Corbs buildings at Chandigarh, (should have gone to Chandigarh a long time ago). All the saluting is a bit much – makes me feel like a second lieutenant again?'

In Ahmedabad they stayed with Gautam and Gita Sarabhai, Jain textile millionaires and patrons of Le Corbusier. Mary vividly remembers Gautam Sarabhai's green eyes, and their traditional timber house built out over the river, and the bats flitting across the water and through the open windows of the house.

In January 1978 Jim and Mary went out to Helsinki, where Jim was being given the Aalto Prize. This was the first of Jim's official outings on which one of the children was brought along: in this case Ben, aged 9, in an Eton suit passed on for the occasion from the son of a friend. It was icy cold, and dark or twilight all the time. To Lesley Borland Mary described the view from the hotel window as 'like something from an Eisenstein film, shades of grey and the sea frozen solid'. The huge bronze medal, designed and made by Aalto, was presented by the President, and there was plenty of heavy drinking: 'They're rather dour when they're not drinking, but when they drink the Finns are marvellous.' In a letter written at the time Jim described how 'I went to Helsinki to collect the Aalto medal – saw Mrs Aalto etc. and tried to catch up on some of the booze that Aalto put away – but I'm afraid a feeble comparison.'

By 1978 Jim seemed trapped into obesity, and in spite of periodic attempts to lose weight was never able to escape from it. He had moved a long way from the slim officer of the 1940s, or even from the burly Lucky Jim of the later 1950s. In 1971, when he first came to the doctor who remained his GP for many years, he weighed 20.8 stone; after that there are almost no records, for his doctor's own weighing machine only recorded up to 20 stone, and Jim was always over the limit. The reasons can only be guessed at, but his enjoyment of good food and drink, and the continuous stress of his architectural life must both have played a part. He had a passion for cheese; guests were amazed by the huge chunks to which he helped himself at the Stirling dinner parties. He did a good deal of surreptitious eating away from Mary, round the corner from his office or in the doughnut café in Portobello Road with his children. His size became part of his image; so did the delicacy which so curiously combined and contrasted with it. Perhaps his most evocative feature was his hand. It seemed to epitomise the whole man: a bundle of sausages holding a pen or stubby pencil and drawing with rapidity, delicacy and skill.

TEN

BIG JIM AND STUTTGART

A much-reproduced drawing by Leon Krier shows Jim's bulky and powerful figure seated in the entrance lobby of the unexecuted Olivetti headquarters. He is sitting on one of his own chairs, looking across his own table, and apparently telling off his skinny young assistant, Brian Riches, who is standing across the room with one hand on a similar chair. At one side of the drawing a scrolled pier is surmounted by the spectacled head of Leon Krier, surveying the scene.

The drawing was reproduced in the *Architectural Review* in April 1974, again in an exhibition catalogue of Stirling's drawings held in the same year, and much more prominently in *James Stirling: Buildings and*

Jim, Brian Riches and Leon Krier in the projected Olivetti headquarters, Milton Keynes, drawn by Leon Krier

Projects 1950-74, published by Gerd Hatje in Stuttgart and Thames & Hudson in London in 1975. From the colour of its dust-jacket this is often referred to as the 'Black Book', to distinguish it from the 'White Book' of Stirling and Wilford's projects from 1975 to 1992, which was published in a similar format by the same publishers in 1994.

A good many threads converge on or depart from this drawing: Jim's architecture; his office style of draughtsmanship; the history and *raison d'être* of the Black Book; Krier's position in Jim's office and influence on Jim; Jim's taste in furniture; the changing nature of his house; and the establishment of Jim's own image as 'Big Jim'.

What became the Black Book had first been proposed by the German architectural publisher Gerd Hatje in 1969. He was producing a monograph on Paul Rudolph, which was published in 1970, and got in touch with Jim to suggest something similar, which he hoped to publish in 1971. Jim agreed, but the book moved slowly. Krier was put to work on it for a few months at the end of 1970, and after three years in Germany, during which little if any progress was made on the book, returned to England at the end of 1973 to work whole-time with Jim on getting it ready for publication in 1975.

Leon Krier (always Leo to his friends) was born in Luxembourg in 1946. As a very young man he saw a reproduction of Jim's 1954 design for a house in Woolton Park. He was intrigued because it resembled a house which he had designed during his army service for a friend, and wrote to Jim about it. Then he went to study architecture at Stuttgart University. In his first year he came across the Leicester Engineering Building in the special edition of Jim's architecture published by the Italian architectural magazine *Casa Bella* in June 1967. 'It seemed like something fantastic . . . And by that time I was so desperate at University that I thought "I will leave. I won't stay there for four years." So I did a brochure of my work, and I sent it to Jim. I rang him. I had never spoken English before. He said, "If you have done those drawings personally, you can work for me." That was enough for me, so I took my drawings and went to England.'

Krier's hero Le Corbusier had died in 1965, and 'I was looking for a second Le Corbusier'. He arrived in London in July 1968. He was a skinny, serious young man, speaking almost no English. His hair stood up straight round his head like a golliwog. His experiences with Jim were disconcerting. 'When I saw him first, I was very surprised to see him physically. I thought immediately "he looks like a pirate". I had never seen a creature like that. But when I came to his office I was terribly disappointed that an architect like that would work in such a miserable place, where there was no quality at all. The furniture was terrible. His own room had all this Aalto furniture, which I always found absolutely horrible.

'I was really looking for somebody to tell me what to do, who could tell you: "things are like this, and not like that" – which I couldn't find in Germany or anywhere. That's what I was looking for, but one didn't find that, because his system of designing was not to tell you at all what he wanted, but to let you work, and maybe then direct the design process. And in the beginning I didn't understand how this man works, because I was looking for somebody who would just make a sketch and say "Look . . . do this", and then one could develop, and it would be interesting. And it didn't work like that at all. It was a bit of a shock to me in the beginning.

'I think when I came there he must have been in a profound depression. That was my conclusion, because in the three years that I was there, I only saw him draw in the first two months. The only drawing I ever saw him do was of the canopy of the Cambridge Faculty, which was for publication. And very vague sketches for the Olivetti building, which I think was a year later. Very rough drawings, just a plan and . . . not architectural at all.

'I began to understand the man is not working the way he normally worked, because I stayed in the evenings to look at magazines, or go through the cupboards and the drawings of previous schemes; basically, to look at the archives. With each project, there were usually a bundle of drawings, small sketches, which were marvellous. They were marvellous little drawings, tiny little things, and they were very unusual and very characteristic. And a year later I found that he had thrown them all away. It was a tragedy. There were hundreds and hundreds of drawings, and he just threw them away. He had tiny little pencils with which he would do these doodles. Always doodling, doodling. And I didn't dare to take any, because I thought it was sacrosanct to keep things together. I wish I had taken at least one. I didn't dare.'

Krier had a preconception of how a great architect should work, and in what kind of office, and that was not how Jim worked, or what his office looked like. He never explained what he himself was doing, and he never told people in his office how to do something. If he liked what they did he accepted it; if he did not he rejected it; in cases in between he would hold his short stubby pencil in his short stubby fingers and work on the drawings, alter them, and get them to do them again, and so on, until he was satisfied.

But Krier may be right to surmise that at this period Jim was, if not depressed, at least going through a creatively dry period. Earlier projects

188

had always started off from his own tiny drawings, the drawings which Krier found in the cupboards, and which Eldred Evans had watched him produce for the History Faculty Building. In spite of what Krier says, Jim had produced such drawings for the Olivetti building. The best-known project on which Krier was engaged in Jim's office was the competition entry for a new Civic Centre at Derby, work on which started the year after Olivetti. Krier and Julian Harrap both worked on this, and both are agreed that Jim made no preliminary drawings. Instead Krier and Harrap were put to work to make conceptual drawings in rivalry so that, as Harrap expresses it, 'Leo says he did it. I think I did it.' But it was Krier whom Jim finally put in charge of developing the design beyond the conceptual state to presentation level.

The design is shaped like a horseshoe, enclosing a public piazza or place of assembly. In the inner edge of the horseshoe are a banqueting hall, an art gallery, and other accommodation, linked up to the early nineteenth-century town hall. The outer edge contains a curved shopping arcade, top-lit from a semi-circular glass roof. Behind the horseshoe a long row of lift-banks for cars links the centre to a ring road and shields it from it. Jim's input, as Harrap puts it, was 'a managing input, stimulating us, manipulating the design'. He made his final contribution in the last few days before the designs were sent in. Krier had designed the inside of his horseshoe stepped like an amphitheatre; Jim replaced most of the stepping with inclined patent glazing. Competitors had to decide what to do with the façade of the eighteenth-century Assembly Room, which had been burnt out before the competition. Krier had laid it out flat on the ground in the enclosed piazza. Jim tilted it up at 45°, and placed an outdoor proscenium beneath it. In these ways he, as Krier puts it, 'virtually signed the building in the last few days before it was finished'. The smooth sweep of the glazing, and the inclined front of the Assembly Rooms, are what most people remember about the design.

In fact Derby was important in the development of Jim's architecture for other reasons. It was his first major project in the centre of a city: all the others had been on suburban or green-belt sites, where they could create their own context. The Civic Centre was on the site of the Market Square, the historic heart of Derby. The area around it had been blown apart by one of the appalling ring roads, punctuated by huge roundabouts, which were in fashion in the 1960s. The Market Square had become, in effect, another roundabout, with a link to the ring road which burst through one side of the square. The competition design was an attempt to stitch the centre together again. The idea that this was something that an architect could do, and that new buildings could be creative in terms of context, and not just in themselves, was new to Jim, and he owed it to Krier, and possibly also to Harrap. Krier himself claims that this was his contribution to Jim's work, and not some kind of nudging him into classicism or post-modernism, as was to be much bruited in later years. When he was in Jim's office Krier was keen on Le Corbusier, not classicism.

Krier recollects that 'it was very pleasant to work for Jim, because I had a sort of special status, and we got on extremely well. I think it came about because I didn't speak very well English, so I didn't understand the office structure, so we had immediately a close relationship which was purely out of misunderstanding. Always, when I had a question, either he came to my table, or I went to him, which nobody else in the office was allowed to do. I remember Roy Cameron, who ran the site in Oxford, once shouted at me, "You know, you are not allowed in his office," and I couldn't care less. But this went on, and I got a special office to do competitions, and he came there and it was very nice, almost a collegial atmosphere; probably a relationship he had with students in America, but which he would never allow in the office. He talked, he would bring books, and I brought books ... but he talked about design very peripherally. He asked me always to do doodles, and then in the evening he would come and discuss a bit but there was no real direction. It was very very strange.'

Previous to the Derby competition, Leon worked for Jim on an ambitious competition entry for a huge new centre for Siemens AG, outside Munich: in effect a small town, with a projected daytime population of 13,000. This developed out of a project by Krier for a new University at Bielefeld: he had shown it to Jim who suggested using it as the basic idea for the Siemens competition.

Neither this nor the Derby entry had any success. The Derby entry was commended by the assessors as 'brilliantly conceived', but was ruled out because it did not keep to the brief. Krier worked for a few months on doing post-competition presentation drawings for Derby, and other drawings for the projected book. Then, at the end of 1970, he went to Germany for three years, with a view to the possibility of taking over a practice with his brother. It did not work out, and towards the end of 1973 he came back to London to work specifically on the Hatje book. Jim's old flat had been rented for a few years to Roy Cameron, when he was in Jim's office. In 1973 Cameron moved to Finland, and Krier and his wife Rita took the flat over from him. Krier worked partly at home, partly in the office. The office secretary Catherine Martin has memories of him at this period. 'Leo was there downstairs. Always cold; always complain-

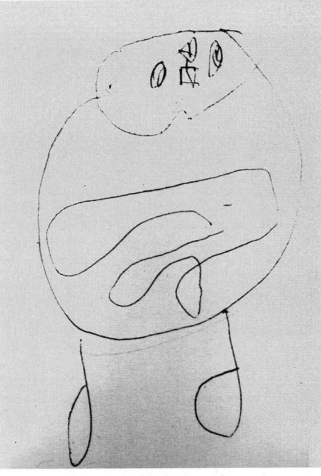

Drawing of Jim by Ben, aged 4

ing about being cold. He used to sit and draw with his coat, a liner under his coat, and his scarf on, and oh, he used to make me laugh. Everything was crazy. "Ah, is crazy, is crazy", you know. Everything was crazy, but he was very nice, Leo.'

In 1971 Jim had been commissioned by the University of St Andrews to design an Arts Centre as an extension to the Art Department, which was in an eighteenth-century house in the centre of the town. He worked on this with Julian Harrap, and produced one of his most attractive designs, fitted round the house and into the street in the manner of the Derby scheme, but on a much smaller scale. The finances collapsed, and it was never built. At the time Krier returned, there was

191

no work in the office apart from the second stage of Runcorn. This was large enough to keep a small office going, and in addition Jim had a yearly US$11,000 salary from Yale, and whatever he earned from lecturing. But he had plenty of time to spare, and the book assumed additional importance, as an advertisement to bring in more work. Jim turned all his skill and energy onto it. Leon Krier, when asked what Jim's influence on him was, says, 'Publishing, basically. He taught me how to publish. Publishing is very different from building, you need to produce special drawings, and very very special views. He was fantastic at editing.'

The Hatje Black Book was preceded in 1974 by *James Stirling*, the catalogue of a small exhibition of drawings held at the RIBA Drawing Collection between 24 April and 21 June in that year. This was a side-product and fore-runner of the Black Book, which was in full production at the time. It included a foreword by Reyner Banham, a useful bibliography and selection of quotations, and a charming drawing of Jim by Ben, aged 4.

The introduction to the Black Book was written as early as 1970 by John Jacobus, an American professor at Dartmouth University, who came into Jim's life to write it, and then went out of it again. It is, in fact, useful and interesting, but was heavily rewritten and edited by both Jim and Mary Stirling. It is preceded by a page of information headed 'Biography', 'Visits, Lectures', and 'Articles and Statements by James Stirling'. The dates in the first two sections have inevitably been repeated in later publications, but they are wildly inaccurate, especially for the earlier years – starting with Jim's year of birth. It would probably be a mistake to read more into this than that Jim was always slapdash about dates.

The Black Book and the RIBA catalogue are both remarkable pro-ductions. They are not perhaps hagiography, but very conscious, selec-tive, contrived image-making. As Krier sees it, 'Jim was fabricating an image which did not entirely correspond to what he was doing, and when I laid out the book for Hatje I encouraged him to work more consciously in that direction, to fabricate an image which I thought would be more interesting, because I was still very much enamoured with Le Corbusier as a master-planning genius, who has a total idea of everything.'

The Black Book was deliberately produced in the same format as the volumes of Le Corbusier's *Oeuvre Complète*. It is identical in size, and has a similar carefully contrived mixture of elements. It was making an implicit claim for Jim as a successor to Le Corbusier. In the 1950s Jim had described the *Oeuvre Complète* as a bible or source book for students and architects, to be 'utilised as catalogues, as had been previously the books of Alberti and Palladio in the Renaissance'. The Black Book was designed to fill the same role – and succeeded.

The atmosphere of the book is set by a combination of exquisitely composed black and white photographs, mostly by Richard Einzig, and equally exquisite plans, sections and axonometrics, drawn in spare precise line without shading. The drawing technique, down to the drawing of figures and trees, is inspired by Le Corbusier. As in an eighteenth-century pattern book, general drawings are supplemented by details, of metalwork or brickwork, and occasional diagrams, to show circulation or exposure to the sun. There are reproductions of models. Interiors are photographed either without people in them, or with a few carefully posed figures (Einzig's wife is a frequent feature) arranged with as much artistry as the figures in a drawing.

The impression given is of the clear logical progress of a master, moving on the base of accomplished early work to a series of master-pieces. That was a reasonable summary of Jim's career to date, but to make this impression with maximum force there was a good deal of redrawing or altogether new drawing. Jim would probably have been loath to admit it, but the Le Corbusier line-only technique had first been exploited in England by the Smithsons in the 1950s – in, for instance, their down-axonometric of their Sheffield University competition entry in 1953. Jim was then still in his Zipatone phase, producing clear attractive drawings, but embellished with much mechanically-precise Zipatone shading. He himself drew the first line-only axonometric to come out of the office. This was of the Leicester Engineering Building. Michael Wilford drew a similar axonometric of the History Faculty Building, and from Leicester on the style became the accepted one of the practice, though few if any of the later drawings are by Jim. The first of the 'worm's-eye' axonometrics, a type which was to become especially associated with Jim, was of the Florey Building, and was drawn (post-construction) by Leon Krier in about 1970.

A number of earlier drawings by Jim, especially for his Sheffield University entry, were redrawn by Leon Krier for the Black Book in this later style. They help to tie the earlier work into the later. Other drawings of the earlier projects were completely new, and also redrawn by Krier: a worm's-eye axonometric of the lobby, ramp, lift and staircase at Sheffield, for instance, and a general view of the hall in Jim's 1952 entry for Poole Technical College. Early drawings by Jim in the style of Frank Lloyd Wright were deliberately omitted; Krier found them 'horrible', and they conflicted with the Le Corbusier image. There are sadly few repro-ductions of Jim's 'marvellous small sketches' because they had almost all

193

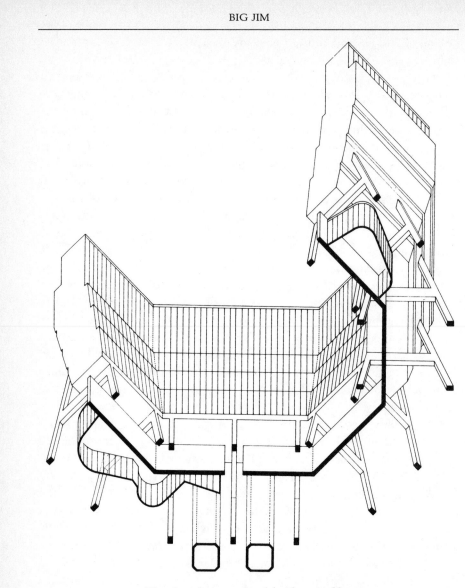

*Worm's-eye axonometric of the Florey Building,
Queen's College, Oxford, drawn by Leon Krier*

disappeared by 1974. The ones which are reproduced give some idea of
the quality of what had been lost: little drawings of the Woolton Park
house, a bird's-eye view of the Selwyn College scheme (over-enlarged for
the book), a sensitive bird's-eye view of the St Andrews scheme, with the
curve of the bay and the mountains in the distance. It remains a mystery
why the other drawings were thrown away. Was it deliberate or

194

accidental? Krier thinks that it was deliberate, and that Jim wanted his designs to survive and be shown only in a state of final perfection.

One curiosity is the little drawing by Jim reproduced in the introduction over the caption 'James Stirling. Sketch of a vernacular building near Aix-en-Provence, 1950'. It shows a square-walled enclosure with mono-pitch-roofed sheds around it, and six cypresses in the middle. The drawing is annotated 'Near Aix. Aug: 1950' in Jim's handwriting. Krier saw Jim draw it in 1974. Perhaps one should understand it as an explanatory sketch to show what Jim remembered seeing near Aix in 1950. If so, the image, given Jim's visual memory, can be taken as accurate, but in August 1950 he was touring market towns in Somerset. He may have seen the building at the same time as he was at Avignon in July 1949. One is left, however, with a sneaking suspicion that he saw it when he was in the South of France in 1955, and that he consciously or subconsciously adjusted the date, to show that he had been interested in vernacular buildings of this type several years before they became fashionable among architects.

The line-only drawings, especially the axonometrics, are in themselves beautiful objects. They have the purity of ideal Platonic form, existing outside time and space. Their value as icons was first exploited to its full extent by the *Architectural Review* in 1972. The worm's-eye view of the Florey Building is printed white-on-black on the cover of the November issue, which featured the Florey and the Derby designs. 'AR' is printed in red above it. It makes a sensational cover, presumably designed by Bill Slack, the *Review*'s Art Editor. The same axonometric reoccurs black-on-white, on the cover of the RIBA catalogue. The black dust-jacket of the Black Book is inspired by the *Architectural Review*'s cover; 'James Stirling' is printed in red, but the white-on-black image is of the History Faculty Building, not the Florey.

The drawings tell with especial strength and beauty in the catalogue, where they could be printed on average larger than in the Black Book, and in which there are no photographs to compete with them for attention. James Gowan wrote angrily to the RIBA to complain that several of the earlier drawings were by him, and were not acknowledged as such. Krier also had cause for complaint; the acknowledgement opposite the title page, 'To Leo Krier for his work on the drawings, catalogue and exhibition' would cause no one to realise that at least 60 per cent of the drawings had been actually drawn by Krier in the previous few years – indeed most of them in the previous few months. One could say, though, that Krier himself was caught up by the fascination of establishing Jim's image, to the extinction of everyone else's.

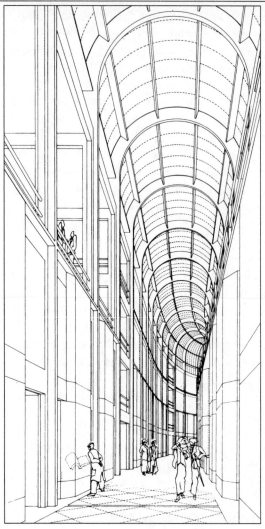

Derby Civic Centre competition.
The arcade, drawn by Leon Krier (James Stirling Foundation)

The Black Book established Jim's personal image, as well as the image of him as an architect. It set him on course to become an icon and the object of a personality cult, as 'Big Jim'. What remains in readers' minds from the book is not the self-effacing photograph of Jim on the back page, showing him in the 1950s, with his face partly obscured by his hand, but Krier's drawings of him bulking large in the setting of his buildings. Krier says that he originally did these 'because I liked to surprise him and please him', and that the inspiration came from Le

196

Corbusier's designs for the Palace of the Soviets: 'there are funny jokes in these drawings'. But the most of himself that Le Corbusier ever allowed into his publications on his buildings was in photographs of his car in front of them. To the best of my knowledge there is no other monograph on an architect's buildings, of any date, in which the architect himself is featured in this way.

Apart from Le Corbusier's drawings of the Palace of the Soviets one can also surmise the influence of Osbert Lancaster's illustrations of buildings with figures in his *Pillar to Post* and *Homes Sweet Homes*, especially the drawing of a Regency interior in *Homes Sweet Homes*; and possibly of Evelyn Waugh's drawing of Professor-Architect Otto Friedrich Silenus in *Decline and Fall*. All of these are line-only drawings, and have the same kind of wit as Krier's. There are in all seven drawings showing Jim in the Black Book. Of these the drawing of him in the Hope chair is the best-known, and is reproduced the largest. Another drawing shows Jim, Riches and Krier in another part of the Olivetti headquarters, along with more neo-classical furniture. Especially charming are two drawings of Runcorn, showing Jim, Mary and their son Ben walking across an empty square; Ben is trailing his toy dog behind him. Jim, Ben and dog reoccur, presumably, as a deliberate anachronism, in Krier's redrawing of the hall in the competition design for Poole, submitted by Jim in 1952. This is reproduced postage-stamp-size in the table of contents, and seems like a private joke between Krier and Jim. In general Krier seems deliberately to be increasing Jim's bulk to fit the chronological date of the designs; the Olivetti headquarters is the last in the sequence. Another private joke, or surreptitious piece of evidence, occurs in Krier's redrawing of the design for a 'core and crosswall house' of 1951; the car in the garage is a model of the 1970s.

By seating Jim in his own chair at his own table in the drawing of the Olivetti headquarters Krier, presumably with Jim's approval, was making a statement about the way in which Jim's taste was developing. The furniture was designed by Thomas Hope in the early nineteenth century, and is a notable example of his idiosyncratic neo-classical style. Jim had become interested in Hope because he had a new appreciation of the monumental, and was about to develop this in his own architecture. The Hope chairs, with their statuesque simplicity and swooping curves, were like individual monuments designed for Regency drawing rooms. Krier's drawing suggested that they were also the perfect accompaniment to Jim's monumental presence. But although it is tempting to connect Jim's changing physique with a change in his taste and architecture, monumentality can be found in the work of other, skinnier, architects in the 1960s; in Louis Kahn's glorious thunder of arches and drums at his Indian Institute of Management, for instance, or in the splendidly remorseless rhythm of Denys Lasdun's Institutes of Law and Education at the University of London.

The pendulum of taste was on a return swing. Jim's way of reacting was, as always, individual. In 1984 he was to write that he liked Hope's chairs because 'they are extreme, outrageous, over the top, eccentric, and much more gutsy than anything French Empire. There's absolutely no feeling of restraint or lack of confidence. But they aren't huge in scale either.' On other occasions he cited them as examples of the fact that monumentality was a matter of presence, rather than of size.

The endlessly repeating terraces of Runcorn suggested a monumentality in the manner of Lasdun's University of London ranges, but even more extended. However impressive, they were an overpowering way of housing modest Lancashire and Cheshire families. Jim did not pursue that line. Over the next fifteen years or more he and his office exploited the monumental in more appropriate contexts and in a different way – relatively modest in scale, never repetitive, highly idiosyncratic and collaged together with elements reminiscent of his earlier buildings. Jim's Modern Movement background was to make it virtually impossible for him to make direct quotations from the historic styles but he was able to go much further in the way of historic allusion than was possible for Kahn or Lasdun.

In 1975 Jim was invited to take part in a competition for a new art gallery in Dusseldorf. This was open to any German-based firm of architects, and in addition a shortlist of non-German competitors were invited to compete, and, unlike German competitors, were paid for doing so. Runcorn was at the stage when Jim had little involvement in it, and he had finished work on the Hatje Black Book, which had been published in Germany and England at the beginning of the year: its publication in Germany may have helped to get him the Dusseldorf invitation. Jim could give the competition all his time, during the several months before the entries had to be submitted.

He worked on it in the office with a team of three: Russell Bevington, Robert Livesey and Crispin Osborne. Crispin Osborne had been in the office for several years. Bevington had been a student at the Royal College, under John Miller, had done some work for him after graduating, and then been sent by him to see Jim, who took him on specifically to work on Dusseldorf; he has stayed in the firm ever since. Livesey had been a Prix de Rome student from America for two years, with a sabbatical year in which he had come to Gloucester Place to show

Jim his work, and ask if there was a job. There was not, but at the end of his second year he got a telegram from Jim inviting him to come and work on Dusseldorf. He was to go on to work with Jim at Yale. He and his English wife became members of Jim's circle of friends. Bevington describes him in those days as 'very lively – a fantastic character, and he would test Jim and challenge Jim and throw ideas at Jim, and I think Jim enjoyed that. Crispin was very methodical, very thorough, full of good ideas and good at resolving ideas that Jim had.

'Jim made a site visit, and there's a classic sketch made on the back of an airline ticket coming back, of his thoughts about the project. Which we then laid onto the site, his sketch idea. And as was so often the case with Jim, he'd got it right in one, the whole thing fitted, the brief fell into the diagram he'd drawn, and it worked beautifully . . . And the nice thing about working on the project was that Jim himself, because Runcorn was on site and all the design work was out of the way, and being run by another team in the office, was able to devote an incredible amount of time to the project. He would sit downstairs with us in the basement at Gloucester Place, at a drawing board of his own in the room, and work beside us or sit beside us at our boards.

'Jim's input was amazing. In those days we would always draw everything in pencil – large pencil drawings – as underlays before we laid a clean sheet of paper over them and then did the final tracing perfect image for submission. We would spend hours and hours just making minor, minor adjustments with Jim on those drawings. Long days – seven days a week most of the time through that period. The thing was really singing, actually. It was a fantastic project so a fantastic experience for me. Jim was convinced we were going to win.'

The Dusseldorf scheme carries on the development of Jim's architecture which had started with the design for Derby Civic Centre. It is fitted carefully into the centre of a city, its mass is broken up by the retention of existing buildings, and it is responsive to the existing street plan. But in plan it is quite different. In Jim's usual manner, it is divided into four distinct elements: an open entrance pavilion in a forecourt above car parking; a glazed hall or concourse running in a rippling wall of glass along the forecourt; a lesser gallery, planned in concentric circles above an auditorium, to one side; and the big rectangular block of the main galleries, on the first floor around a circular courtyard.

The entrance pavilion acts as a marker for the gallery. It is monumental but not large, the architectural equivalent of a Hope chair. The street in front of the museum is cranked. The main gallery building follows the line of the eastern end of the street onto which the terrace abuts. The pavilion aligns with its western end, and is an overall set-off grid on the forecourt, and terminates the vista down the street from the west. It has great impact. It acts as the setting-off place for three routes: steps down into the car park; revolving doors into the concourse of the gallery; and a pedestrian route or street, open to the public, leading from the pavilion into the circular court and on to join up with the streets on the other side of the gallery. It supplies a natural route for people walking through the city.

The starting-off point for Jim's design for Dusseldorf is Le Corbusier's Maison du Salut in Paris – which, in 1954, he had admired so much for its 'very clever town planning', and for being 'in motion, in contrast to Garches, which is static'. At the Maison de Salut an entrance pavilion set back from the street leads by way of a bridge into a circular hall, and on into the main building. Jim's Dusseldorf has a similar sequence, but the route leads into the rest of the city, as well as into the building, and the circular hall has become an open court. Jim may have been thinking here of two eighteenth-century open spaces in Germany, the circular Koenigsplatz at Cassel and the Friedrichsplatz in Berlin. On his sketches he calls the court a 'public square'. But he also thought of it, on his own admission, as the central rotunda of Schinkel's Altes Museum in Berlin, with the roof removed.

The structure at Dusseldorf would have been of clad concrete, as in most of Jim's buildings. But the cladding shown is not of brick or tile, but of large slabs of stone – reconstituted stone laid in courses of different widths. Openings have segmental arches, and the pavilion is supported on arcades of piers and segmental arches. The historical references are no longer to Russian constructivism or nineteenth-century English functionalism; they are to the marble-on-brick of Late Gothic and Early Renaissance buildings in Italy, to German neo-classicism, perhaps to the paintings of Chirico and Italian stripped-classical buildings of the 1930s. Four cypresses, rising out of the circular court, repeat the eight cypresses in Jim's so-called 1950 drawing of vernacular building near Aix, published in the Hatje Black Book a few months before the competition.

The scheme is a pleasure to study, in its richness and inventiveness, in its contrast between solid and delicate, intricate and simple, new and old. It relates to Collage City, to Hope furniture, to the eclecticism of Jim's house. It has threads going back and forth into his career. One can see why Russell Bevington thought that 'the thing was really singing', and why Jim was convinced that they had a winner. He was wrong, however; the scheme was not even placed. The main reason seems to have been that the museum director and staff hated – as museum people always do – the curved walls in the side gallery.

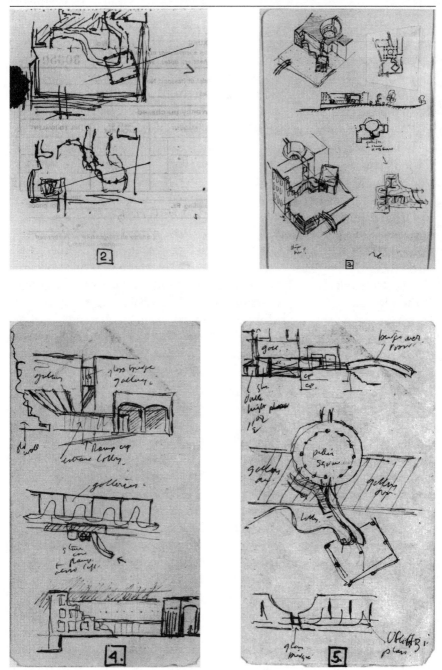

Sketch designs for the Dusseldorf Art Gallery competition

201

A competition entry for a new development in Cologne, entered, again by invitation, later in the year, was equally unsuccessful. Projects for developments in Berlin, Qatar, Florence, Nairobi, Marburg and Rotterdam in 1976 and 1977 were all abortive. At the beginning of 1977 Jim, along with a number of other architects, was invited by the mayor of Rome to replan a section of the famous Nolli plan of Rome published in 1748. This was only a publicity exercise for the mayor, a *jeu d'esprit*, but Jim and his office had a good deal of fun with it. He paid homage both to Collage City and to himself. The area was replanned by ingeniously fitting into it almost all his past projects, built and unbuilt. The main vista led from the baroque palace on the perimeter of the section to a statue of Jim leaning against a column, replacing one of Garibaldi which had been erected on the site in the nineteenth century. It was a blown-up version of the birthday cake which his office had made for his ostensible fiftieth birthday in the previous year.

In the summer of 1977 Stirling and Wilford was one of the firms invited to compete for an extension to the Staatsgalerie in Stuttgart. The invitation came shortly before Jim left to teach in America. He put Russell Bevington on to working on it, along with Ulli Schaad, a young Swiss architect who had been working on Runcorn, and on the Florence and Marburg projects. They were the two best designers in the office. Jim had not seen the site, but looked at the detailed site plans, and went off to America, saying 'Let's do a Phase 2 Dusseldorf'. Schaad and Bevington worked in his absence, and found that the basic elements of the Dusseldorf scheme fitted naturally and sensibly onto the Stuttgart site: the main gallery round a circular court, the glazed concourse, the terrace over the car parking, the public route through the building by way of the court and terrace. There were inevitable differences. The site was longer and narrower, and there was a considerable difference in level between back and front. The terrace was too narrow for a pavilion. 'The scheme fell into place very quickly, within two or three days,' according to Bevington. Jim returned, and got down with his team to work out the details and get the project ready for submission. The main problem was how to take the public route down and through the building. It was achieved by means of a semi-circular ramp, looking through arched openings into the circular space, which became a sculpture court. The same language of coursed stone facing and arched openings was used as at Dusseldorf; the concourse had a similar glazed wall in contrast to the solidity of the stone.

The Stirling and Wilford entry was sent in to Stuttgart at the end of the summer. Runcorn had been finished, and the office had no work.

Most of the staff went off on holiday, knowing that in all probability they would be laid off when they came back. Then the news came through that Stirling and Wilford had won. The jury of eighteen had chosen their entry unanimously, only a few days after submission.

The members of staff on holiday were hastily recalled, and new staff were taken on. The ground-breaking ceremony took place in September 1979, the topping-out ceremony on 12 February 1982, and the new building was opened in March 1984. It was immediately recognised throughout the world as a masterpiece. In the first seven months it had nearly a million visitors. The Staatsgalerie moved from 56th to 2nd place in the league table of attendance figures for German museums. Jim never became a national figure in England, but in Stuttgart he seemed known to everyone. People constantly came up to him on the streets, to congratulate him, to ask for his autograph, or just to greet him. The mayor of Stuttgart (the son of Field-Marshal Rommel) acclaimed the Neue Staatsgalerie as the best post-war building in the city. Rover used it with great success to sell their cars in Gemany; their advertisement featured car and building together, with the caption, 'Britischer auto, Britischer architekt'.

To begin with, however, German architects gave the design a rough passage. At what became a heated public meeting held in Stuttgart to discuss the design, the Stuttgart architect Gunter Benesch went up to Jim and seized him by the lapels; it seemed for a moment as though they would come to blows. Benesch had come third in the competition for the Staatsgalerie, and first in an abortive competition held in 1974 for a cultural centre including a new Staatsgalerie on a different site. There was a flavour of sour grapes in his resentment, or, as Jim put it, 'understandably, perhaps, he was a little put out'. But there were also basic stylistic divergences. The Stuttgart approach to town planning was still a Corbusian one, of isolated buildings set in parkland: the important post-war buildings there had been arranged in this way around the big public garden across Konrad-Adenauer-strasse from the museum, in accordance with a development plan made in the 1960s. All or most of the competition entries had followed this approach, and the Stirling and Wilford solution of fitting the building to the old street pattern and incorporating existing buildings was a heretical one, in terms of contemporary German architecture and planning.

But there was a more emotionally charged reaction on top of this. It was expressed as well by Frei Otto, the Stuttgart architect-engineer, and a more distinguished man than Benesch. It became the subject of architectural gossip, and was picked up by the *Sunday Times*. This reported that 'the German engineer Frei Otto once showed a student audience a slide of Stirling's design for a new civic art gallery in Stuttgart alongside a photograph of Auschwitz. "These are the same things", he told them.' Otto immediately denied this, but it is likely that he had made some kind of comparison between Stirling's Stuttgart and the Nazi buildings of the 1930s. Stirling's design seemed monumental and covertly neo-classical. For many German architects neo-classicism stood for Nazism, and anti-monumental Modern Movement architecture stood for German liberal socialism before and after Hitler. The coved cornices at Stuttgart were not only similar to the cornices of Egyptian temples, but to cornices in buildings designed by Albert Speer and others. Otto had written in a private letter to Stirling on 20 July 1979 (which Stirling never answered), 'Since the war an opposition against monumental and formal architecture has built up in West Germany, and I am surely one of its leaders . . . It might be quite useful to reflect upon the reasons why many Germans who, like myself, went through the cruelties of the last war and the double-faced German history of architecture cannot master their feelings now in a cool manner, but react angrily.' Angry reactions ceased, however, as a result of the great architectural and popular success of the Gallery, and today Otto plays down his opposition to it in those early years.

During and after construction the building ran into comparatively few problems, compared to the traumas which had beset Jim's British buildings in the 1960s. Partly this was due to the nature of a building so much less heavily glazed than the earlier ones, and a good deal more conservative in its technology. But it was due at least as much to sympathetic and supportive clients, and to the high quality of the German building industry. According to Michael Wilford: 'Working with German contractors as opposed to English ones was Paradise. The German contractors are far more efficient. They're better organised. They maintain better control over the quality of construction and over the general cleanliness and tidiness and safety of the site. But I believe that it's part of a much more general attitude to building and architecture, in Germany particularly, but also in many countries on the Continent. I think people expect to invest money in building because they realise that the return in terms of maintenance is justified or compensated through the life of the building. I think building workers are better trained in Germany, and they're paid better, so that the industry generally enjoys a status that it doesn't in this country. In England, the building industry was used as a kind of economic regulator, so that the more skilled tradesmen got sick and tired of the ebb and flow of fortunes, and left the industry. And then, when there was a boom, you got all the cowboys coming in.' Mary Stirling was impressed at Stuttgart by seeing the German building workers in their white overalls, playing classical music on their portable radios. It was not at all like a British building site.

The building process at that time was organised in different ways in Germany and Britain. The system of general contractors did not exist there: the architect acted as, in effect, general contractor, hired and supervised all the subcontractors, and even acted as quantity surveyor. In this role an architect was called the *Bauleiter*, and German architects had specialised training to fill it. 'It was clear to us that we didn't have the right kind of experience to perform those particular tasks', according to Wilford. 'The Land of Baden-Wurtemburg – who had set up the competition and paid for the building – had their own Building Department, and they seconded key staff members to act as *Bauleiter*, as the building supervisors.'

The design work on the project was all done in London, but once construction started Jim opened an office in Stuttgart, and recruited German staff for it. It was run by Tommy Tafel, and later by Siegfried Wernik. Jim came over regularly for meetings. The clients for the project were effectively a group of three: Professor Peter Baer, the Director of the Gallery, Dr von Holst, his assistant, and Herr Herbert Fecker, who was the Chief Architect of the Finance Ministry of the Land. Jim and his office had an excellent relationship with all of them. Jim became especially good friends of Herbert Fecker and his wife, Marianne. Fecker enormously admired Jim's architecture and his design for Stuttgart, and fought for the necessary finance for its realisation. A very notional sum had originally been set aside for the new building, and the first estimate came in at around twice that amount. Some cuts were made, but none of them was disastrous, and the Landes parliament authorised a larger budget. There were none of the problems resulting from under-funding which plagued so many of Jim's other buildings.

Jim acquired a reputation in England for being difficult and touchy, but Fecker never found him so. He realised that Fecker was on his side. As Fecker says, 'It was a very successful personal relationship from the beginning, because we always talked about architecture, and not about money ... He was a serious person, he always wanted to know the background, there was hardly any situation in which he was scratching the surface. He was immensely human and very open-minded. I think that surprised many people in Germany, because Jim was always sold by the press as a star, but as soon as one worked with Jim, he was not at all arrogant, not at all unapproachable or inaccessible, even for little things.

He was esteemed very highly, but even with the lower hierarchies he made clear that he was working in a partnership relationship. He would explain why things had to be done as they were. He wasn't arrogant, just deciding and saying "Well, it has to be like this". No "star allure", as we would say in German.'

After his official meetings at the Finance Ministry or the Building Department, Jim often used to have dinner with the Feckers. Herr Fecker was a connoisseur of wine, and Frau Fecker had a reputation as a cook. Jim was her favourite guest, and the person for whom she most liked to cook. 'I tried in the beginning to go through the full scope of German cooking, to present to him as much as possible. He liked German noodles, spaetzle. He always used to say "Gribbensmalz. I like Gribbensmalz", meaning Griebenschmalz. It's basically lard, from either a goose or a pig, the leftover from bacon, with little pieces of apple and onion, and you have it on very dark bread. It's a very typical German dish, but a very heavy dish as well.' Jim used to bring jars of it home, and Mary would put them at the back of the fridge and hope that he would forget about them.

They remember him 'one evening, leaning backwards and resting a glass of wine on his belly, saying "that's as good as a table"', and on other occasions playing table-tennis with their son Jurg. The Feckers happened to be in London, visiting the Stirlings, when Jurg had his eighteenth birthday, 'so Jim, when he heard this, went down and found a bottle which was eighteen years old, and gave it as a present to him'. Herr Fecker was touched when Jim came to his retirement party in 1988 and made a speech in which he said, 'Since you, Mr Fecker, are now a pensioner, and we have a less official relationship, we can say "Jim" and "Herbert" to each other.' In German terms, this was a very personal thing to say.

The Neue Staatsgalerie is simple in concept, yet filled with complexities. Its basic organisation is easily grasped: externally the round court in its drum, the terrace raised above the motorway, and the descending path that links them together; internally the entrance hall looking through its curving glazed wall to the terrace, and the ramped ascent up to the galleries around the sculpture court. But there are all kinds of different themes which play and interact with each other. There is a language of ramps and steps; a language of curves and drums; a language of boldly patterned stone facing contrasted in weight and colour with the metal frames over the entrance and the fat metal tubes of the rails; a language of natural growth, in the creeper that crowns the drum and cascades down the walls of the sculpture court. There is a language of movement. It is a building without façades. The façade at the upper level is of the library building, in effect a separate entity, with an elegant neo-Le Corbusier façade nicely in scale with the street. The main gallery is concealed behind it. The other frontage on the roaring traffic artery of Konrad-Adenauer-strasse climbs and recedes in a series of levels and slopes. The building is in motion, as Jim described the Maison de Salut, and is designed to be walked through rather than looked at from some fixed external viewpoint.

When Jim surprised the Japanese modernists by setting 'a house for Karl Friedrich Schinkel' as a competition project in Japan in 1979, he wrote 'It is shocking to realise how very limited the language of contemporary architecture has become ... Now is perhaps the time to acknowledge our continuity and remember our cultural background ... This must be more important than any attempt at outright historical revivalism.' The Neue Staatsgalerie in Stuttgart, and to a lesser extent his earlier Dusseldorf competition design, were essays in enlarging 'the language of contemporary architecture'. But for Jim, as for most architects of his generation who came from a committed Modernist background, 'outright historical revivalism' was impossible. The Neue Staatsgalerie alludes to, or draws ideas from, historic buildings, rather than repeating or even rephrasing their language. There is a constant dialogue or collision between modernism and tradition. Both traditional and 'modern' motifs are given an often ironic twist that brings them into the 1970s. The great central space, for instance, is inspired by a neo-classical rotunda but is opened to the sky; 'modern' steel and glass is unashamedly used as an ornament, in the shape of the canopies that are fixed to the monumental striped-stone walls. Jim wrote that he was attracted to Schinkel because his houses, in particular, were products of an epoch of transition, between classicism and romanticism, and 'we also are in transition'. He liked those competition entries which showed 'a delightful ambiguity ... neither ancient nor modern; primitive nor technological; chaotic nor systematic; too vigorous nor too picturesque'. He liked them, in fact, because they reflected what he had been doing at Stuttgart.

The topping-out ceremony, when the main structure of a building has been completed, is a bigger event in Germany than in England. A wreath is suspended from the crane, or from a pole above the building, the building is blessed, speeches are made, the head tradesman, dressed in traditional costume, toasts the building in champagne and tosses the glass across his shoulder, and a great feast is given, for workmen, designers and clients. At Stuttgart this *Richtfest*, as it is termed, took place on 12 February 1982, and was held in the central court. The main speech-giver stood on the rim of the drum and addressed the assembly below.

The building existed only in its concrete shell, before any of the cladding, glazing or metalwork had been added. It was extraordinarily impressive. Jim spoke at the *Richtfest*, and also, around this period, took tours round the building and explained how it worked through a megaphone. Many of Jim's architect contemporaries still express a wistful regret that the gallery was not left in essence at this stage, without the stone veneer and the trimmings. Even Herbert Fecker said, 'Well, it is so beautiful, we should just give it some white paint and leave it as sculpture.' He was not serious (or perhaps semi-serious), but Jim reacted violently. He said that if he did not get his stone facing he would never come to Stuttgart again. In a lecture which he gave in 1984 he made clear how important the complexities were to him. He explained, 'I'd like to think our work is not simple and that within a design, for every act there is a counter-act. We hope the Staatsgalerie is monumental, because that is a tradition for public buildings, but we also hope it is informal and populist.' The stone facing contributed to the monumentality; 'colourful elements' such as the metal canopies, the tube parapets and handrails, and the air-intake funnels 'counteract the possible appearance of a monumental stone quarry'. Jim, along with everyone else, was in the long run delighted that, as one of the savings, the stone paving originally intended for the entrance hall was replaced by bright green studded rubber (to go with Jim's briefcase, one might say). It 'reminds us that museums today are also places of popular entertainment'. He concludes his analysis by saying, 'And for the painstaking, there is more ambiguity and innuendo to be discovered.'

This kind of language is rather different from his deadpan functional analyses of his earlier buildings. He recognised this. In the speech which he made at the topping-out, he referred to his earlier 'pleading . . . that our design solutions result – hey presto! – from a study of the context and a logical interpretation of a building's functions'. He admitted that there was also 'the question of presence and personality, of formalism and style, in our work. The fact that our designs sometimes come in series has led me recently to believe that formal aspects may be stronger than I had thought.'

'If you mentioned the word "beauty" their hair might stand on end,' Jim had said in 1966. His expositions, although admitting more complexities, were still a long way from that. But he was now pleased when others said more than he wanted, or was able, to say himself. He finished his 1984 lecture by quoting from what Emilio Ambasz had written in the *Architectural Review* of December 1984. He called it 'a most beautifully perceptive article', and since it has his rare imprimatur it is worth quoting the passages which he read out:

> As to his other works, parody plays in the Neue Staatsgalerie a defensive role. It doesn't criticise either the Post-Modern, the High-Tech, or the Neo-Classical modes but is, rather, self-critical of his own use of these devices . . . But one could also suspect that Stirling is a Romantic who uses architectural parody to disguise his passionate love for architecture.
>
> However, these episodes of architectural parody rapidly recede into the background when, in awe, we call to the fore the powerful earthy sounds which seem to emanate from the marble chords composing the circular courtyard. The ramp can be perceived as crescendo, the wall openings as basso continuo, and the open sky as a chorus. But they cannot, by themselves, explain the powerful telluric sound which pervades this chamber as if it were coming from a gigantic mountain horn. To walk inside is to enter into a magical domain where architecture is condensed to its essentials: the courtyard is a processional stage set where the spirit of architecture promenades its hieratic presence.
>
> Not unlike Cameron – who draped a most princely garment on provincial St Petersburg's imperial dreams – it has again taken a British architect . . . to sing with a marble voice the legitimate cravings of the German soul for a secular chamber where to celebrate a Te Deum in quiet grandeur. In this courtyard dwell together the spirits of Biedermeier and Schinkel; if ever a present-day culture were to declare that its longings have found permanent embodiment, Germany would have to point to this courtyard . . . In providing a monumental frame for ineffable rituals, this courtyard stands as metaphor for the spirit of the building, and so doing, raises it to be the exalted level of memorable architecture.

The opening took place in March 1984. It was one of the highlights of Jim's career, a lavish and festive occasion attended by all the office, by Jim's family, and by several hundred people, including many of his friends. Charles Jencks, whom Jim both appreciated and made fun of, was there with a telescopic camera. Jim teased him by describing it as male jewellery or a penis substitute. He was happy and contented, well-primed with drink, and full of good spirits. He said to John Tuomey,

'Something's wrong. They like it.' As Cathy Martin remembers, 'It was just so crowded, it was incredible. Towards the end we were all there in the entrance hall, and we joined up, linking arms, and we were dancing with one foot forward and kicking one leg out, and going back kicking one leg out, and it was all reflected in the bevelled green and glass window. That was really funny, because it's the only time I've ever seen Jim lift his legs energetically in all the years I've worked for him. But we had to push him out of the building; we were all going for dinner, and he just couldn't get to the entrance. So we formed a chain gang behind him, and we pushed him out in the end, like a big snake. It was a wonderfully happy time.'

ELEVEN

AFTER STUTTGART

The Neue Staatsgalerie was the most impressive and convincing expression of that dissatisfaction with the limitations of Modernism which was being felt by architects all round the world in the 1970s and 1980s. Apart from the minority which practised a straightforward classicism, most of those who now set out to enrich their architectural language did so in ways similar to those exploited by Jim: by allusion, by collage, by collision, by parody. The results were extremely varied, but they had enough in common to be convincingly grouped together as 'Post-Modern' by Charles Jencks, who became the apostle of Post-Modernism. His *The Language of Post-Modern Architecture*, first published in 1977, was to go into frequent enlarged editions. Jim used to make fun of Jencks as 'Charlie Junk', but he enjoyed arguing with him and once commented 'whatever Charlie has to say is interesting'. But he hated all labels, very much disliked the architecture of many of the Post-Modernists, and objected to being called a Post-Modernist himself. In the sense now given to the term, however, that is what he had become.

Contemporary architecture split into two main groups, the Post-Moderns and what Charles Jencks called the Late-Moderns, the architects who remained faithful to the language and approaches of the Modern Movement, even if they set out to develop or perfect it. The most successful expression of this Late-Modernism was what became known as 'High-Tech', and in England was especially associated with Richard Rogers and Norman Foster: an architecture of steel, glass and boldly expressed structure, carried out with extraordinary technical virtuosity, in the case of Foster, and with a kind of gay romanticism in the case of Richard Rogers, who used externally exposed services, escalators, lifts and walkways to give the Pompidou Centre in Paris and the Lloyds Building in London something of the same exotic quality that Stirling had given his buildings of the 1960s. Foster and Rogers were Jim's friends and had been to some extent his disciples, but now, as it must have seemed to them, they kept to the high road and he took the low road. Modernists

211

regarded Post-Modernism as a betrayal. But even so they had to admit that Stuttgart was a masterpiece.

In contrast to the lean mid-1970s, no less than five commissions came to Stirling and Wilford in 1979, four of which were built. The resulting designs all showed the same kind of exploration that Jim and his office had inaugurated to such sensational effect at Stuttgart. Its successors were awaited with eagerness, and on the whole greeted with disappointment. The explanation lies partly in the history of each project, which was, for various reasons, far more troubled than at Stuttgart; partly, perhaps, in the nature of what Stirling and Wilford were doing. One needs to look at the buildings together rather than individually. Individually none is completely successful, but as a group there is a richness, a variety, a wit and a willingness to experiment about them that makes them fascinating to study. As Professor Randall was to put it at Cornell: 'There was no house style. Jim and Michael's approach to building was to understand the client's problem and try to solve it in a creative way. You couldn't be sure of what one of their buildings was going to look like.'

Of the five commissions that arrived in 1979, three were in America, one in England and one in Germany: the School of Architecture at Rice University, Texas; the Chemistry Building at Columbia; the Arthur M. Sackler Museum at Harvard; the Clore Gallery at the Tate in London; and the Wissenschaftszentrum (WZB) in Berlin. The Chemistry Building was an impressive design, but fell through at working-drawing stage, when a new bursar decided that there was no need for a new building at all. The other four were built. Construction only started at Stuttgart towards the end of 1979, and the great *réclame* that was to follow on its completion was still in the future; but the news of the winning of the competition must have boosted the firm's image, and helped to bring in new commissions.

The job at Rice came through Michael Wilford, who had been teaching there since 1978 as Visiting Critic and Tutor, and was to become Visiting Professor in 1980. Of the four commissions, it impinged on Jim least, after the design stage, and was to cause him least grief. Jim, as always, made an input, but the project was run by Wilford and he was much involved in the design. The building had its problems, including what was to become a familiar tussle over Jim's decorative scheme for the interior. A member of the Faculty Building Committee hated what he described as Jim's 'cheap lingerie colours', but was over-ruled. In the first long vacation after the building was completed he had them painted over with a light grey. The students were so annoyed that they spent a weekend painting Jim's colours in again; but the light grey won in the end. The exterior design, too, suffered from cut-backs. But the basic architectural concept survived, and the end result, deliberately unassuming and in the same idiom as the rest of the campus, is a pleasant and civilised building. It is said that when Philip Johnson was visiting Rice and looked for it, he could not find it, because it was so like everything else.

In contrast to relative uneventfulness at Rice, the Sackler Museum presents what one is tempted to call a typical Jim story: comic and tragic, mixed success and failure, not enough money, too many rows; and an imbroglio in University politics, with which Jim was not well qualified to deal.

The story started off, as far as Jim was concerned, with an ideal client. Seymour Slive was the Director of the Fogg Museum at Harvard, and had been largely instrumental in launching the project for an extension to the museum on a site across the road. A selection committee was set up, about seventy architectural practices were considered, and members of the committee toured the buildings of a shortlist, and talked to the architects. Slive was on the road on and off for a year. He came to England in February 1979, met Jim and Michael Wilford, visited most of their buildings, and talked, directly or by telephone, to a number of relevant people. He went on to Stuttgart, and talked to the Director of the Staatsgalerie. He wrote to Jim on 2 March seeking reassurance on a number of points: 'high-cost over-run at Leicester, Cambridge and Oxford', 'leakage and acoustical problems in some buildings, and technical problems of an ever-graver nature elsewhere, as at Queens'. 'We know', he added, 'that one can commute from Gloucester Place to Quincy Street, but how much commuting would you yourself do? How much of your time would we get? Will your current project with Stuttgart, and possibly the one at Columbia, leave much time for us?'

The letter ends: 'It goes without saying that we are certain that there are excellent responses to the above questions.' Jim and Michael Wilford came over to be interviewed at Harvard in March, and their appointment as architects was ratified in May. Slive had been captivated by Jim's buildings, and the two men had immediately taken to each other. Jim always had difficulty with East Coast academics, but Seymour Slive came from a different mould. He was the tubby, rumpled, effervescent son of a Russian American fur merchant in Chicago. He had a continuously good relationship with Jim. 'I loved his sense of humour. It was a dry sense of humour, and it was wonderful. I loved everything about Jim, including the colour of his socks, and his shirt, and his tie.' He had come to one of Jim and Mary's kitchen suppers, and loved that too. Later he was to be invited to one of the big dinners and could not understand Jim's reasons for giving them.

As an architect he found Jim resourceful, flexible and understanding. 'I knew we were on a short budget, but I saw that Jim could build by just ordering stuff from a catalogue, and get great architecture out of it.' He loved Jim's attitude to design, and quotes as an example his reaction when asked why one handrail on the big staircase was completely different from the other: 'Why not?' He was delighted with a story told by Philip Parsons, who was involved with the construction from the Harvard end: 'There was some detail where we had to make a change, and we couldn't resolve it before he had to go on the plane, so he said, "Oh Philip, just do whatever you want, so long as it's not in good taste."' Two telegrams, sent in June 1980, give the flavour of the project-history and the relationship of the two men: 'Tad informs me that half design fee will not be received until mid July which is no good for paying this month's salaries. Please help. Jim.' 'Help is en route. Check was mailed today. St Bernard Slive.'

The initial design was largely worked out while Jim was teaching at Yale in 1980. Ulli Schaad came out from London to work with him, and was given a desk in Cesar Pelli's office; the design owes a good deal to him. He was intrigued to find that Jim changed at New Haven. He became boisterous, larger than life, and a little looser and freer than in London. There was a lot of socialising and 'Jim was the king'.

Slive was delighted with the resulting design. Unfortunately for Jim, as with all projects in American universities there were two clients, the University and the Department, and the University was ultimately in control. The situation can be illustrated by a visual image. It is a sweltering August day in 1980. The President of Harvard, Derek Bok, is worried about the proposed green-and-pink-striped brick of the new museum façade, and Jim and Slive have gone to talk to him and the Vice-President. The two rotund, rumpled, sweaty figures sit on one side of the room, Jim with his usual green briefcase and purple socks. Facing them are two elegant, perfectly-groomed men in Brooks Brothers three-piece suits. When they leave, Jim says to Slive: 'You know, I still don't know which one was Bok and which one was the Vice-President.'

In fact, Jim got what he wanted at this meeting. Suzannah Fabing, the assistant director of the Fogg at the time, and as committed as Slive to Jim, reckons that Bok 'took one look at Jim's socks, and the whole rest of the outfit, and decided that he was going to be lucky to get away with pink and green brick, so he went along with it with very little fuss'. The green brick was later given up for purely technical reasons; it was decided that it would not stand up to a Massachusetts winter.

But Bok and the Harvard administration in general felt no enthusiasm for Jim's design, or for the whole museum project. When Slive originally presented the scheme to the President and Fellows, who form the governing body of Harvard, one of them said: 'Looks like a chicken coop to me,' and Bok said 'Well, Seymour, if you want it I guess it'll be all right.' It was a period of galloping inflation, and the University had its own considerable financial problems, and its own fund-raising programme. Slive and his team had to raise all the money for the new building and its endowment themselves, and were discouraged from approaching Harvard alumni. Arthur M. Sackler, publisher, medical researcher and millionaire, who gave ten million dollars and after whom the building was to be named, had no connections with Harvard. Even so, an adverse financial report about the adequacy of the endowment led to President Bok cancelling the project in February 1982. Slive and Fabing fought back and, by raising more money and a great deal of adverse publicity for Harvard, put so much pressure on Bok that he allowed the project to go forward again. It had been an unpleasant business, causing resentment on all sides. Slive resigned in 1982; Suzannah Fabing was effectively forced to resign at much the same time. The construction of the new building commenced in contentious circumstances; as Philip Parsons puts it: 'I think buildings don't work out well if you don't have a good relationship, because every decision is made in an ugly spirit.' There were problems with the Boston firm which was appointed as executive architect, problems with the contractors, problems with the flooring and the HVAC system. Money was very tight (the unit cost was one quarter that of the Neue Staatsgalerie). Jim became fed up and resentful, and did not come to Harvard as often as he should have done. The job was finished off by Bob Dye, who came out from the office to live at Harvard until the museum was completed in October 1985. It was launched with a ball at which Suzannah Fabing wore a hat shaped like the new building, and Jim wore a dinner jacket.

What finally emerged after all the trauma was not especially well received. The *Wall Street Journal* called it 'a plain little building with a pedestrian exterior and a problematic entrance façade'. There was, perhaps, some disappointment that Stirling the wild man had not produced something a little more outrageous than this low-key, low-budget, mildly eccentric building. There was certainly no desire to shock: the building was carefully contrived to fit into a very random assortment of neighbours in brick or concrete, including Le Corbusier's concrete Carpenter Center, and Memorial Hall, a large Ruskinian essay in polychromatic brick, much more violent than the Sackler Museum (Jim liked it).

The plan is a neat and simple one. It is L-shaped. The long stroke of the L is divided into two by a spine in which the staircase rises in one long straight flight to the galleries at the top of the building. There are three storeys of galleries on one side of the staircase, and five storeys of offices on the other; each floor of offices is served by a long corridor looking through openings into the staircase, so the staircase is not claustrophobic, in spite of its tunnel plan. The stairs rise out of a rather elegant hall, not large, but very high, with four slender concrete piers rising up through it. The hall is white, the staircase is divided into deep horizontal stripes coloured alternately violet and buff, into which part of the museum's collection of sculptural reliefs is set: a Greek statue in the top gallery, seen through a glass door, terminates the vista up the staircase.

Hall, staircase and galleries are enjoyable and inventive spaces. The controversial elements of the museum were on the exterior. The galleries were on the side of the service yard; it was the offices, wrapped around the outside of the L, which looked, reasonably enough, onto the streets and the view. These façades were treated in stripes, two stripes to a floor, carried in a curve round the angle of the L. The stripes were of the same depth as the stripes on the staircase, and in the end were coloured in alternate dark-grey and brown bricks, instead of green and pink ones. The windows were set irregularly into the stripes, following on the arrangement of the offices which they lit. One of the reasons for the stripes was to overlap the random fenestration and unify the façades. Because of them, and the streamlined corner, the building was compared to a 'peanut-butter and jelly sandwich', 'a parking garage', and 'a 1930s housing project'. There are certainly echoes of 1930s Expressionist buildings: there was one within a few hundred yards of Gloucester Place, the striped and streamlined Mount Royal apartment block on Oxford Street. The Sackler stripes fall short of what Jim had hoped for, a single smooth gleaming skin of hard bricks precisely jointed: the quality of bricks that could be afforded, the quality of the bricklaying, and the need for expansion joints all worked against this.

Jim planned one big gesture, but was not allowed to make it. The Sackler was to have been joined to the main museum by a connecting bridge which would also have been a gallery. It would have been striped in the same way as the façades, and lit by an enormous round window, like a Cyclops eye, in the centre of the span. It would have increased the impact of the whole building, served as an entrance gateway to Harvard, and have been a splendid object. But local residents disliked it, and campaigned against it, and the University was not especially enthusiastic about either the design or the cost. The bridge was never built. The two

216

columns which would have supported one end now frame the entrance like pylons (and also act as air-intake ducts). The great square window above the entrance marks where the tunnel would have started. In fact, even without the tunnel, the elements combine to form an entrance façade that is monumental in miniature, and Jim was always aware that this would be so.

In 1985 Jim must have washed his hands with relief of the Sackler Gallery, but by then he was in the thick of an English commission that was to cause him at least as much stress and irritation, and to increase his English reputation for being prickly and pig-headed – or, if one looks at it from another angle, for tenacious ability to stand his ground. On looking back it seems an unnecessary story.

Towards the end of 1979 Stirling and Wilford had been appointed, after interview, to work on a staged development plan for the expansion of the Tate Gallery. Then, in December of that year, an anonymous donor offered five million pounds for a new gallery to contain the Tate's Turner Collection. The donor soon turned out to be Vivien Duffield, the daughter of the property developer Charles Clore. What became known as the Clore Gallery, in his memory, was made the first stage of the proposed development, and Stirling and Wilford were appointed the architects. It was a radical and exciting enrichment of the original brief, but it had its disadvantages. The Tate has a curious double identity, as a gallery of Modern Art and a gallery of historical British painting. Jim liked Turner well enough, but he had no especially close sympathy with him, or with the British school of painting in general. Nor, as it was to turn out, was there to be much rapport between him and the curators of the British and Turner collections.

The initial designs were shown to Vivien Duffield and the Tate Trustees in the early months of 1981 – in Jim's absence in hospital, undergoing a major operation for peritonitis. On 25 February the Director, Alan Bowness, wrote to Michael Wilford, conveying the Trustees' regrets for Jim's illness: 'I was, however, asked to convey their welcome to the designs, which in general are regarded as a most imaginative and successful response to our brief'. They had one or two reservations, leading to minor changes in the designs, which were finally approved on 25 March.

The design was based on the strategy typical of Stirling and Wilford's post-Dusseldorf work. Old buildings were kept, the new buildings were fitted in with them; features of the old buildings generated elements in the new, but these were deployed in such a way as to give the new building a strong individual identity. Fitting in with the neighbours had by now become a standard policy for architects of new buildings anxious to get planning permission in a conservation-minded decade. But Jim, unlike most architects, was able to fit in creatively. He may even have welcomed the need as providing a starting-off point for his designs.

At the Tate he kept the building that became known as the 'Lodge', a red-brick late nineteenth-century building on the corner of the site. The building was not listed, and its retention was not asked for in the brief. Keeping it gave Jim his design strategy. The new building is L-shaped, and links one corner of the main Tate with the Lodge. It mediates between the ashlar stonework and monumental classicism of the Tate and the modest red-brick and bay windows of the Lodge. The mediating elements are a stone parapet and cornice duplicating those of the Tate, and a stone grid enclosing squares, which is carried across all the main façades, but filled in three different ways. In the wing attached to the Tate, the squares are filled with buff-coloured rendering, distinct from the colour of the stone but not all that different from it. In the end by the Lodge the squares are filled, to either side of a diagonal, with rendering on the side towards the Tate, and red brick on the side towards the red-brick Lodge. This end is broken up by two bay windows, one small and one large; the corner of the building is cut away to insert the large one, and the windows echo the bay windows of the Lodge. The Lodge-element penetrates to the wing by the Tate in the form of another bay window, and a long wooden pergola stained red to match with the brickwork.

Between the rendered section and the half-brick section is the entrance to the new gallery. Here the squares are filled flush with the same stone as the frame, so that the frame and filling merge together to form a simple cut-stone façade dramatically cut into by the great glass-filled opening of the entrance, to which punctuation is added by the little semi-circular window above it and the brilliant green of the revolving doors: these are reflected in the pool set symmetrically in front of the entrance. Pool and surrounding garden were designed by Janet Jack, formerly Janet Kaye, Jim's friend of the 1950s, who was now practising as a landscape architect.

The different elements of the façades reflect the different activities going on behind them: the main galleries behind the long arm of the L, the reserve galleries and reading room in the end by the Lodge, the big hall behind the entrance. But the end result is an abstract composition in colour and geometry. Jim coloured the final elevations himself as he liked doing, and like many of the office drawings they are independent works of art.

The entrance hall behind its glass-and-emerald wall is one of Stirling's most ingenious spaces, its comparatively small size disguised by carefully calculated extensions, by a narrow slot up to a glazed roof above the staircase, and through various openings into the galleries, bookshops and other areas. The main galleries are on the first floor, approached by the staircase in the entrance hall. As at Stuttgart and the Sackler these galleries are divided into separate rooms, and Jim's design personality is more subdued in them than in the exterior and circulation spaces.

The job architect was Russell Bevington, both a good designer and good at calming troubled waters; he was to make himself much liked. Jim and he had to deal with three bodies, who did not necessarily agree, even among themselves: the Property Services Agency, which owned the buildings and the site, as an agency of the government, and was strictly speaking the client; the Trustees, who had appointed Stirling and Wilford in the first place; and the Gallery staff. The Trustees were a mixed bag of artists and art-interested worthies, and always included one architect. Up to 1981 this was Sandy Wilson, who was probably responsible for bringing in Jim in the first place; he was succeeded by Richard Rogers. The chairman from 1980 was Lord Hutchinson, succeeded by Richard Rogers in 1984. Peter Palumbo was a Trustee from 1978 to 1985. Jim established a good relationship with Hutchinson; Rogers was already a friend and admirer, and Palumbo soon became one. But the project was effectively run from early in 1982 by a Building Sub-Committee, made up of a mixture of Trustees and Gallery staff. The Trustees were represented by Hutchinson, Rogers and Palumbo, the staff members included Alan Bowness, Martin Butlin, who was the Curator of Historic British Paintings, Robin Hamlyn, one of his assistant curators, and Alexander Dunluce, the Head of Conservation; the Drawings Conservation Department for the whole Tate was to be in the new building. The curator of the Turner Collection and Clore Gallery was not appointed until August 1984, by which time the building was well under way, and most of the design decisions had been taken; even when appointed he did not sit on the Buildings Sub-Committee. The delay was for reasons outside Bowness's control but was likely to lead to trouble, as indeed it did.

Committee meetings could be turbulent. Robin Hamlyn had trained as an architect, which perhaps should have brought him and Jim together, but in fact they disliked each other. Alan Bowness, as Michael Wilford puts it, was 'a very democratic administrator, and felt that everybody should have their say'. He was always ready – perhaps too ready – to suggest that decisions should be reconsidered, if sufficient pressure was put on him. He liked Jim, and admired him as an architect, but 'Let's not

219

be mealy-mouthed about it, he was very difficult. He just did not have the graces, which in a way one expects from a leading architect, of being persuasive with clients. He was always very brusque and honest, and could be quite petulant and difficult if he was not getting his own way. He had a childish streak, really. There were one or two occasions where I think some of the trustees thought he was behaving in an inappropriate manner. He was a passionate person, Jim.' Bowness and Palumbo did not get on, and Palumbo expresses a different point of view: 'The curators treated Jim outrageously. But far from the Director intervening, and telling them to shut up, which in my opinion he should have done, he said nothing.'

The new building suffered serious delays due to water penetration, which held back its completion by at least a year. The contractor and sub-contractor finally accepted responsibility for this, and the architects cannot be blamed, though inevitably they were. Where relations between architects and clients ran into trouble was over the colour of the galleries.

It was decided in August 1985 that the galleries would be lined with fabric, rather than painted. A sizeable mock-up of gallery space was erected in a warehouse belonging to the Tate in Acton, a selection of Turners was taken over there, and the effect of various colours of fabrics as background to them was tried out. After a good deal of discussion the Building Sub-Committee divided more or less into two groups, made up of modernists and art historians. The modernists wanted a beige, or as it was described 'light oatmeal' colour; the art historians wanted a darker red or green. The argument for the dark colours are that they were the accepted background of Turner's time; for the light colours that pictures were now more widely spaced than in the nineteenth century and that this would make intervening dark colour overpowering. The historians had already given an opinion that the final choice should be made in consultation with the Clore curator, who still did not exist.

At a Building Sub-Committee meeting held on 16 May 1984, 'after discussion and experiment' it was agreed that a cotton and linen fabric in a natural light warm oatmeal colour would be used throughout the painting galleries. 'This solution was proposed by Mr Stirling and warmly welcomed by Lord Hutchinson, Mr Rogers and the Director. Martin Butlin and Robin Hamlyn accepted the decision, but wished to record their firm disagreement, as they preferred the stronger red and green colours, which in their opinion were far more sympathetic and appropriate for Turner's paintings.'

Butlin and Hamlyn could scarcely refuse to accept a decision backed by the Director, the Chairman of the Trustees, and the architect. But they resented it intensely. They were in a minority, but they were also the relevant curators; moreover, Butlin was the world expert on Turner. In August 1984 the post of curator of the Clore Gallery was finally filled. Andrew Wilton, the new curator, disliked the oatmeal at least as much as Butlin. The anti-oatmealers lobbied Bowness to reconsider the colours of the main galleries, and to agree to darker colours in the Watercolour and Reserve galleries. At a Building Sub-Committee meeting held in May 1985, 'it was decided to look again at the colour of the fabric for gallery walls'. In the end a slightly different oatmeal was chosen for the main gallery walls, but the historians got their darker colours in the other galleries: what Jim called 'strawberry-mousse' in the Reserve gallery and 'excrement' in the Watercolour gallery.

One of the maxims by which Jim ran his life and his practice was that a decision, once taken, was taken, and attempts, successful or not, to go into reverse always infuriated him. The unhappy result of the colour war in the galleries was that relations between architect and curators deteriorated everywhere. Robin Hamlyn, who was responsible for day-to-day relations in the new building, gave Russell Bevington a tough time, and Jim, acting through Bevington or in letters to Bowness, dug his heels in on all matters of dispute. In particular, other colour-battles were fought throughout the building. To go into all of them would be wearisome, but it is worth looking at two, in one of which Jim was surely unreasonable, and in the other surely in the right.

The window mullions of the paper conservation studio had been shown on the original elevations painted a vivid green. Dunluce, the Head of Conservation, said the green would disturb the colour values of the room for the restorers. Jim reluctantly agreed, in September 1984, to the mullions being painted white on the inside, but the exterior was left green on trial. Conservation found this external green was still distracting, and in September 1986 it was determined to paint the exterior white as well. Jim compromised with black, but complained that 'this tendency to resolve every situation specifically without regard to the whole is that which produces the ad hoc tattiness for which some UK museums and institutions are rightly regarded (internationally) with dismay'. Hamlyn retorted that green was impossible for the practical purposes of the studio and 'had it been retained our Conservation department would have been rightly regarded with dismay – both nationally and internationally'. Jim sent an angry reply: 'I would prefer the public (and press) not to believe it was my first choice.' The windows in question faced onto a small courtyard at the back.

The battle of the arch was a more crucial affair. The entrance arch to the galleries is from a balcony cantilevered out over the lower half of the entrance hall: the arch is lined in concentric bands of pink, green and mauve, and because of the cantilever seems to hang shimmering above a void. It is highly effective but the historians claimed that it distorted the colour values of visitors passing through to look at Turner. In any case they hated Jim's idiosyncratic taste in colours. Battle engaged, with Bowness unhappily in the middle between curators and architects.

In February 1985 Bowness assured Jim that he had a free hand in the entrance hall (or words to that effect). In May he was happy about the colours of the archway. In October he found them 'quite unsatisfactory in a space which introduces the public to Turner's work . . . I should therefore like you to arrange for the archway to be repainted.' Jim made no such arrangement, and the matter was not decided until a meeting of the Building Sub-Committee on 16 October 1986. Jim contested that 'to eliminate the bright colours would be a loss to the gallery and to its visitors'. Bowness stated that 'his own view was that Mr Stirling was right in exercising his taste over the exterior of the building and entrance spaces and he did not think that visitors would be visually upset. Some Tate staff, however, felt that bright colours presented an unacceptable approach to the subdued galleries and the works by Turner.' Butlin and Wilton expressed strong opposition. 'Mr Wilton stated that, as Curator of the new gallery, the colours were antagonistic to the Turners. What, he asked, was the main concern – the building or the Turners?' The Sub-Committee then processed through the arch into the galleries.

Two painters and a sculptor had recently come onto the Sub-Committee: Patrick Heron, John Golding and Anthony Caro. The artists turned out to be as enthusiastic for Jim's arch as the art historians were against it. 'Mr Heron said that morning had been his first sight of the new building. He had at first been startled but now was all for the colours: they were an extraordinary architectural device. Moving through the painted arch was like going through a rainbow or spectrum into a subdued biscuit-coloured space. The colours would not affect the way he looked at the Turners.' Golding 'found the whole very exciting. The building is wonderful and he found no need for change.' Caro backed up the other two, but diplomatically suggested 'that the colours should be left for a year, and then reviewed'. This suggestion was adopted by the Sub-Committee, perhaps with relief.

The Clore was opened by the Queen on 1 April 1987. Oatmeal, strawberry-mousse and excrement all vanished before a redecoration of the galleries under a new Director and the supervision of Michael Wilford and Partners in 1995. Jim's colours are still on the arch.

To move from Stirling and Wilford's post-Stuttgart English and

American buildings to the Wissenschaftszentrum in Berlin is to move to a different world. The building had its problems and its crises, but these did not affect the quality of the final result, or the relations between the client and the architects, or the architects and the contractors. In contrast to the exterior of the Clore, which is ingenious but perhaps a little contrived, it is the gayest and most relaxed of the immediate post-Stuttgart buildings.

The Wissenschaftszentrum (WZB) came to Stirling and Wilford by

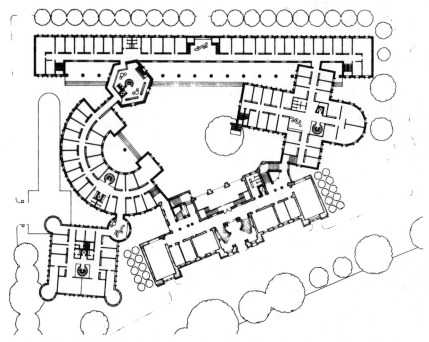

The plan of the Wissenschaftszentrum (WZB), Berlin (James Stirling Foundation)

way of a limited competition in 1979. It was a building for an institute of sociological research, funded by the government, and its main constituent was a great many small offices. Professor Dierkes, the Director, once asked Jim why he had designed the building to look as it did. 'We were standing somewhere on the roof, and he pointed at one of the standard high-rise buildings and said, "Do you want to do your research in an up-ended shoebox?"' The building was an attempt to escape from the slab or tower office formula, and the way out had already been suggested by the Stirling and Wilford Nolli Plan contribution and Colin Rowe's Collage City.

223

Jim came into the office fresh from a holiday at Barfleur, brandishing a little book on the different architectural styles and saying 'We'll have one of each.' The office was set to work to link and 'juggle' (in Jim's phrase) five different building types around a central courtyard: an amphitheatre, a keep (not yet built), an octagonal tower, a cruciform church (Jim called it a basilica), and an existing *c.* 1900 classical building which had survived the war. Then Jim went home for Christmas, and came back saying 'I've done the elevations.' As John Tuomey, who was in the office, expresses it, 'He had put pyjamas on the whole scheme.'

The different elements resemble their different building types in plan and outline, not in detail. The main feature of the façades is their windows and their colouring. Most of the windows have deep projecting stone frames, like upside-down Us designed so that from the inside occupants have the feeling of being in a traditional thick-walled building. The buildings are coloured in alternate bands of blue and pink rendering, one band to each storey. The colours are soft, inspired by those of rendered classical buildings in Copenhagen, Helsinki and St Petersburg. The plastering is slightly irregular: 'The plasterers wouldn't stop working accurately and consistently, so we had to bring in two old restorers from the Charlottenburg Palace, who taught them how not to be so perfect.' Jim had moved a long way from the diamond-cut precision of Leicester and Cambridge.

Each building was intended to house a separate department. The main entrance is through the old building, the library is in the tower. On their inner sides, each building has its own terrace looking onto the grassed central court. Dierkes liked the design because the buildings were 'open to the inside and light, but a fortress to the outside. Don't forget, at that time Social Science came under severe pressure from politicians, so I wanted a fortress.'

The terrace in front of the long block is backed by a loggia, or, as Jim called it, a stoa, the first of three that he was to design. It was inspired by Italian loggias, and was one of the first fruits of Jim's visits to Italy at this period. But the detailing was Jim's own: base, column, capital, but bearing no relationship to a classical order. The 'capital' is made of steel, and supports a glass and steel roof. Each column is hollow, to take rainwater and 'tuned like an organ pipe, so that in really depressing wet weather the rainwater makes a metaphysical sound rather like Japanese music'. Jim was evoking the accidentally musical pipes at Leicester, twenty years on.

There was no urban weave into which to fit; the area had been largely flattened during the war. New buildings had been designed as free-standing individual essays, in the Modern Movement manner: they included Mies van der Rohe's National Gallery and Hans Scharoun's Philharmonic Hall, each doing their own distinguished but quite different act a hundred yards or so apart. Jim said to Dierkes, 'Well, we have an architectural zoo round here, and we have added maybe a zebra or so.'

The design was highly controversial in Germany when it was first published, and up to the completion. The building was unexpected and quite unlike anything else; it stimulated violent attack and equally violent defence. For Frank Gehry, 'I just love that building. I love the colour. He did just the right thing. It shows you that one building can be bigger than it is by what it does, if it's thoughtful. He doesn't trash Mies. He doesn't trash Scharoun. He doesn't snub his nose at Berlin. He takes it head on, and makes a building that takes a horrible piece of urbanism and pulls it together. Every time I go there, I always chuckle and think how wonderful it is that it's there.'

That the WZB was built at all was due to the determination of Professor Dierkes. The Zentrum was his brainchild, and he fought for it, and for adequate money to build it properly, with determination, resourcefulness, if necessary cunning, and a buccaneering spirit that must have endeared him to Jim. When the relevant Ministry, long after the building had been designed, initiated a move to put it into the existing back premises of the 1900 building, he persuaded the local government works department to demolish these overnight, and blandly explained to the Minister: 'What can I do if the State of Berlin cannot co-ordinate on two levels of government?' He also believed that matters of design, including choice of colour, should be left to the architect. He only jibbed once, at Jim's suggestion of a pink neon logo over the entrance in the 1900 building, as a kind of infiltration of the new building through the old. 'I told him, we are neither a supermarket nor a pub, nor part of the red-light district.'

'When the building had finally reached its topping-out ceremony, and the Minister of the time was making a suitable congratulatory speech, Jim whispered into my ear – I will never forget it – "You know, Professor Dierkes, I remember the time when there were only two people in the world believing that this would ever come about."' The two men got on well together. 'We were always very formal. It was "Professor Dierkes" and "Professor Stirling". But we were very congenial minds. We loved to sit in the pub, have a good meal, have good wine. Simply, I liked him as a person. I liked his sense of humour and it was just great to work with him. I liked his creativity, and ability to listen, and to feel his way into an institution like ours.' After Jim's death, Dierkes came to the memorial meeting at the Royal Academy, although he had recently had a near-fatal accident, and was on crutches with one leg in calipers: 'It was just immensely important to me to be there.'

The WZB was designed in London in 1979 and two more years were spent developing the competition design. Then progress came to a halt while Professor Dierkes fought his battles, and it was not until 1984 that construction started. The Stuttgart office was then on the verge of closing, as the Staatsgalerie came to completion, but once the WZB became real again Siegfried (Sigi) Wernik, who had been running the Stuttgart office, moved it to Berlin. Walter Nägeli, who had been in the London office since 1979, came to Berlin to join him. Stuttgart had been built through the collaboration of two offices, with, roughly speaking, basic design taking place in London and being developed and construction drawings made in Stuttgart. But the construction of the WZB was completely run from Berlin. Although Jim came over on regular visits to make his input, the detailing owes much to Wernik and Nägeli.

The Performing Arts Center at Cornell University was opened in the same year as the WZB building. It had been projected in 1979, as a centre for dance, music and theatre, to be run by the Department of Performing Arts. The commission had come to Stirling and Wilford in 1982, by way of interview. Their name had originally been suggested by Gerry Wells, who was in the School of Architecture at Cornell and was a friend of Jim's. ('I'm sorry I got you into it. This University is the world's worst client' he was to write in 1987.) According to Don Randall, the Professor of Music, who was on the selection committee and involved with the Center through design and construction: 'It was clear in everybody's view that Jim was one of the great talents of his day, extraordinarily important and imaginative. There was no "house style". Jim and Michael's approach to building was to understand the client's problem and try to solve it in a creative way. You couldn't be sure of what one of their buildings was going to look like, because it would be made to order for your particular purposes, which I thought was a great virtue.'

The Center represents the extreme limit in Jim's move away from Modernism. It is the result of his increasing knowledge and love of Italy. In 1982 he was fresh from a stint at the American Academy in Rome, and the Center is unavowedly and unashamedly an evocation of Italian architecture and Italian hill towns. It evokes by way of massing and plan, never by detail. But there, quite plain to see, is a campanile (the lift tower), a baptistery (the information kiosk), the silhouette of two basilicas (the auditorium, and the studios), and a loggia, all piled up together on the edge of a gorge.

226

One could ask, why should the Performing Arts Center at an East Coast American university look like an Italian hill town? To which Jim might have given the same answer as he gave to the question about the different baluster rails at the Sackler: 'Why not?' One could think of reasons, though. The central feature of the Cornell campus is a clock tower clearly inspired by a campanile: it looked down the long central vista of the campus to the site of the Performing Arts Center; one Italian note evokes another. The Performing Arts Center is separated from the main campus by the deep gash of the Cascadilla Gorge, and runs along the side of it. If one blinkers out the houses and shops to either side, one is not so far removed from the ideal Italian landscape and hilltop buildings of Poussin's *Woman and the Snake*. But the Center is perhaps more evocative of a stage-set Italian town than a real one. Suitable for a Performing Arts Center, perhaps. Less suitably, in the circumstances, like a stage-set it had to be run up on the cheap.

Work on the Center started according to the usual system at Gloucester Place. Jim dumped a fat brief onto the desk of his assistant Robert Kahn and had him melt it down into a clip of explanatory A4 sheets. Kahn had been one of Jim's students at Yale, and had recently entered the office. He was much younger than Jim but, like Keith Godard and Craig Hodgetts, became a close friend. Together with Michael Wilford he produced a number of alternatives to show how the requirements of the brief could be answered. 'There was one that worked really well. It was just a series of rectangles that organised the site: one long bar piece, and then three boxes, and my idea was that you walk into the bar piece, which was a building, and from there, you entered all three of these other buildings. Jim took out this big fat pencil that he used to draw with, and he took the bar, and just drew some dashes and turned it into a loggia, and then drew arrows to show that those buildings were going to have directions, one of them to the street, one of them to the gorge, and one of them neutral, with a tower. Within a matter of ten minutes that became the entire building.'

There followed a period of visits to Ithaca by Jim and Michael, or by Michael on his own, to work out the design in detail. 'We'd have all the client and consultant team together', according to Michael Wilford, 'made up of really dedicated people. There was the Professor of Music, Don Randall; there was the chief architect from the campus planning office; there was a young stage-set designer; there was a technician, part of the department. We would have these two- or three-day sessions, beating through the design. Ithaca is a fairly bleak place; it's a small town, interesting town, but places to dine in are somewhat limited, and we would often find ourselves in a Chinese restaurant. There was what was called the project bar. Because all these places are unlicensed, Don Randall used to have a large cardboard box in the boot of his car, full of whisky, brandy, gin and that kind of thing, and we would take this into the restaurant.' Randall vividly remembers 'these great day-long marathons, and at ten o'clock at night we would adjourn to the local Chinese restaurant and put the project bar in the middle of the table. We'd get to work, and Jim would still be talking about the project.' According to Wilford, 'At the end of the meal you would get your fortune cookie, and we used to delight in opening them. There would always be one which would describe the current crisis, or an individual who was propagating the current crisis. I kept about six of them, which were wonderful. It was possible, by placing the quotes in context, for people who knew Cornell to identify the individuals. There was one, I remember, which said "Beware of him who speaks with forked tongue". When I gave a lecture on the building at Cornell, I interspersed the talk with quotes from the fortune cookies at various critical stages.' Colin Rowe was on the faculty at Cornell, though not involved with the building, and 'was much amused by this'.

Jim was into stripes, and as originally designed the Center, or the greater part of it, was to have been faced with alternate stripes of red brick and grey stone – the same stone as on an adjacent building. President Rhodes of Cornell (English by birth, but long resident in America) disliked brick, and disliked the colour contrast. At his insistence, the brick and stone were replaced by two much less contrasting types of grey marble, quarried in Vermont.

The preparatory months seem, in retrospect, something of a honeymoon period, in which architects, academics and specialists worked hard and happily together. The cost consultants reckoned the design was not significantly over budget. The building went out to tender in the summer of 1985. 'Let's hope that the 17th of July brings no unpleasant surprises,' Hal Craft, of the Facilities and Business Operations Division, which was to build the Center, wrote to Jim. It did. The budget limit was approximately $12.5 million; the lowest tender was a little under $5 million over this. Pandemonium ensued.

The huge excess is a little mysterious. There was a similar excess in the bids for a new apartment block, being built by the University at the same time, but with different architects and different cost consultants. Stuart Donnell, of Hanscomb Consultants, the cost consultants employed for the Center, is convinced that, by negotiating with the contractors and subcontractors, and possibly bringing in new ones from outside the area, the excess could have been substantially reduced. It is not a claim that can be tested, since his firm was promptly fired after the high bids came in.

Over the next few years a complex and frustrating situation developed, as the various interests concerned struggled or negotiated with each other. There were the future users of the building, concerned about getting a building with an attractive public image that also answered their practical requirements. There was the President, who disliked the design, and a considerable element among the University trustees and administration which was unenthusiastic about the whole project of a Performing Arts Center. There was the Facilities and Business Operations Division, which set about making cuts, too many of which reduced levels of performance in the Center below what was acceptable. There was the College of Arts and Sciences (of which the Performing Arts Center was to form part), which fought with success to get many elements taken out by Facilities and Business Operations put back as far as was possible – at greater cost and to less effect than if they had been left in in the first place. There was Stirling and Wilford, concerned with an end-product with which their practice would want to be associated. There was Wank Adams Slavin, the New York firm of architects which oversaw the project from the American end, and which at one stage was given more control of it by the University than Stirling and Wilford found acceptable. At the end of the day the Center cost very much the same as if the excess costs had been accepted in the first place, but it had suffered in both visual and practical terms. One of the visual losses was the replacement of substantial areas originally to have been faced with marble by rendered surfaces, which added to the stage-set effect. 'The project', according to Jane Pedersen, in the financial department of the College, 'is still used round here as an example of how we should not do things.'

It was the kind of situation in which Jim got fed up. As Robert Kahn puts it, 'The more we came to loggerheads, the more Jim would become stubborn and not want to give in, and I think there were many instances where he might have done things in a different way had he enjoyed the client more, or felt that they respected him more.' In fact, he largely opted out of the construction stage, and it was Michael Wilford, and Robert Dye, who worked on the Center with him, who came regularly to Ithaca, saw it through to completion, and earned the admiration of all those who supported the Center. The building was finally completed in 1988. The loggia was carved with the names of the donors, who had put up 90 per cent of the cost, in lettering designed by Jim's old friend Keith Godard. The big window of the main dance studio looked down on the main street, and passers-by could enjoy the view of dancing girls, as Jim had envisaged with pleasure. With all the faults which arose, for the most part, out of its troubled history, and whatever reservations one may feel about the design, the Center is still the outstanding building on the campus. Jim and Michael Wilford came out for the opening, and all was sweetness and light. Jim made a speech in which he related how he had listened to an elderly couple, gazing at the Center. One said to the other: 'I think it's some kind of Italian rip-off.' 'Which', said Jim, 'I take to be some kind of compliment.'

Two of the biggest disappointments in Jim's career came at the end of 1984 and the beginning of 1986. At the end of October 1984 he heard, by way of a telephone call at four in the morning from Barbara Jakobson in New York, that he had not been chosen to design the Getty Center in Los Angeles. Fifteen months later he heard that Venturi, Rauch and Scott Brown's design had won the competition for the National Gallery extension in London. In both cases Stirling, Wilford and Associates were the runners-up.

There was no competition for the Getty; the architects were chosen by an exhaustive process of visiting architects' buildings and offices all round the world, and interviewing the architects. The list was finally whittled down to four, and then to Richard Meier and Stirling, Wilford. A contributory cause to the decision was worry about confiding so huge a commission in Los Angeles to a practice based in London, even if, as would have been the case, it opened an office in Los Angeles. Jim, when he heard of the decision, said, 'They'll get another washing-machine.'

The National Gallery award was the result of a limited competition. It followed on an abortive competition for a new building that was to have been financed by a commercial element. This became unnecessary when the three Sainsbury brothers offered to pay for the new wing. The site was a superb one, looking over Trafalgar Square and balancing Gibbs's St Martin's in the Fields at the opposite end of Wilkins's National Gallery. Jim's solution was less tricky than Venturi's, and, unlike it, incorporated no Wilkins details. A monumental stone pavilion, capped by a coved cornice similar to the ones at Stuttgart, was placed in the square in front of the bigger and simpler block containing the actual gallery. Following Jim's theme of the 'monumentally informal', it was cut and scooped out to allow for great glass windows lighting the entrance hall, and the information and other rooms above it, and the glass-screened entrance into the building. The post-competition drawings, coloured by Jim and Russell Bevington, are amongst the most beautiful to come out of the office. It was a close-drawn contest. The gallery staff and Lord Rothschild, the chairman of the Trustees, preferred the Stirling, Wilford design; the Sainsbury brothers preferred Venturi, Rauch and Scott Brown. So did Isaiah Berlin, who was on the selection committee and knew all the stories retailed in Oxford against the Florey building. Jim, on learning of the result, sent Venturi a telegram: 'Congratulations, best wishes, and bloody good luck. You'll need it.' In 1991 the *Evening Standard* asked him to name three post-war London buildings that 'will stand the test of time', and three that 'will not'. Jim listed the National Gallery extension among the three that would not.

These two defeats were preceded and followed by two lesser, but still considerable, disappointments. In 1983 the commission to design a library building for Mussolini's new town of Latina produced one of the firm's most attractive designs, but was a casualty of local politics; a left-wing mayor commissioned it, a right-wing mayor threw it out. In 1986 the commission, won in a limited competition, to design a gallery for the Thyssen collection of paintings at Baron von Thyssen's villa overlooking Lake Lugano, fell a victim to the Baron's new Spanish wife, who deflected the collection to Madrid. The Baron, before this happened, caused a mild stir at Fitzroy Square, as related by Catherine Martin. 'I remember Baron von Thyssen-Bornemisza coming with his bodyguard. He was left out with us, to have his tea or coffee, while Baron von Thyssen went with three or four others into the partners' room. This guy had a gun inside his jacket. The Baron had five bodyguards, all American, ex-FBI, and they had five-hour or seven-hour shifts. After the meeting they all left, and they were standing at the corner of Fitzroy Square, waiting for a taxi, and it was very comical; in the middle was Baron von Thyssen, and round him were all these men, all hunched together, as if somebody was going to attack them in the middle of Fitzroy Square.'

In 1984 Stirling, Wilford were asked to convert one wing of the nineteenth-century warehouses at Albert Dock in Liverpool as galleries for the Tate in the North. For Jim to convert one of the buildings he most admired in his home town was an attractive commission, and he did a sympathetic low-key job, making the minimum of changes to the building, but producing a series of excellent galleries and a small but ingenious entrance hall.

Stirling, Wilford by now had a major reputation as designers of art galleries. In 1987 they were invited to convert the eighteenth-century Palazzo Citterio in Milan as an extension to the neighbouring Brera Art Gallery. Jim had suffered from the collapse of the Latina library project, and was wary of taking on work in Italy. He asked Thomas Muirhead, who was living in Florence at the time, to look into the background.

231

Muirhead was a friend and ex-colleague of Colin Rowe's, and had acted as go-between between Stirling, Wilford and the Italian firm which had collaborated with them on their Florence entry. The dominant force behind the request from Milan turned out to be Signora Rina Brion, a formidable matriarch and widow of the industrialist whose firm were major manufacturers of Italian electronic goods, and had an international reputation for good design; Jim's own gramophone was one of its products. The family had been patrons of the architect Carlo Scarpa, who had died in 1978, and were on the look-out for another big name.

The Palazzo Citterio has the typical courtyard plan of an Italian town palace. In post-war years a banal, inappropriate but useful upper storey had been added around the courtyard. When Jim was brought into this by Signora Brion he immediately commented that it should be roofed over, to shut out the top floor. This covered-in court became the central feature of the Stirling, Wilford design. Its evolution is typical of Jim's particular genius. Muirhead, following the usual system in the office, had presented a clip of varying possibilities. One was a 'wine-glass' solution, a central column supporting an inverted glass cone, down which rainwater drained through the column; another had a glazed roof and central lantern without a column. Jim elided the two designs, and produced a slender stone column, soaring up into a lantern, which was hung from the metal framework which the column supported. It was a combination as unconventional as it was striking. Its effect can only be judged from the beautiful drawing by Toby Lewis, one of the design team; the commission proved as elusive as other Italian projects, and although never officially cancelled it is still unbuilt.

In 1986 another commission came to the firm, and was to be completed (in its first phase) just before Jim died. Herr Braun, the head of a very large, family-owned pharmaceutical company in Germany, contacted the Berlin office to ask if Stirling, Wilford would consider entering a limited competition for a large new factory complex to be built at Melsungen, near Kassel. Walter Nägeli, who was running the office, rang Jim in London to see if he was interested in the firm's entering it. Jim was doubtful, because they had no experience of factory design, but in the end he agreed to the Berlin office competing. The competition entry was drawn up in Berlin, but Nägeli went over to London several times to show it to Jim and Michael, and to discuss it. Jim, still not enthusiastic, guessed that it would be placed third; in fact, it was placed second, and in the end the winner was paid off, and the commission was given to Stirling, Wilford.

Jim and Michael now agreed that a four-way partnership should be

232

Proposal for roofing the courtyard of the Palazzo Citterio (Pinacoteca di Brera), Milan

formed, between Jim and Michael in London, and Walter Nägeli and Sigi Wernik in Berlin. The plan was that the design would be developed to working-drawing stage and the contract supervised from Berlin, in consultation with London; and that in Berlin Nägeli would be the design partner and Wernik the organising partner. A contract was drawn up with the four names at the bottom of it, waiting for signature.

But Wernik fell out with Nägeli and dropped out of the arrangement shortly before it was signed. Jim and Michael had reservations about Nägeli's competence to run a contract on his own, and in the end the two German names were crossed out and only Jim and Michael signed. Nägeli continued to lead the German team, but as an employee of Stirling, Wilford. It was a big job, and he had to take on a sizeable number of extra people. Because of his recognised role in the design and responsibility in running the office, a formula was worked out: the building should be described as 'by James Stirling, Michael Wilford and Associates, in association with Walter Nägeli'.

Jim devised this rather odd formula (since Nägeli was an employee) after he had been angered by a short piece which appeared in the *Architects' Journal* of 8 August 1991: 'While Germany is working for unification James Stirling has allowed his Berlin office to secede, and to independently design a new headquarters factory for medical specialist B. Braun.' Nägeli and his Berlin colleague Renzo Vallebuona were quoted as saying 'Our design has a very different identity to the work coming out of Stirling's London office' and Nägeli still further angered Jim by suggesting to him a 'Brief description' for future issue to the press in which the project would be described as 'designed by Walter Nägeli, Renzo Vallebuona and a team of architects in the Berlin office of James Stirling, Michael Wilford and Associates'.

Jim was always a stickler for legal accuracy. Any work which came out of a Stirling, Wilford and Associates office was the work of Stirling, Wilford and Associates, a description which applied to the firm as an entity, not to the individuals in its name. From his point of view, allowing 'in association with Walter Nägeli' to be added to the description was an altogether unusual concession. But Nägeli, sore from having been dropped from the contract, and conscious of how much he had contributed to the design, wanted more. An unhappy situation arose, which split the German office into factions, and led, after Jim's death, to Nägeli lecturing on the building as his, without once mentioning Jim's name, and to a legal battle as to the ownership of drawings, which was lost by Nägeli.

The legal niceties are of less interest to a biographer than the question of what Jim contributed to the grand, forceful and very large complex of buildings that was publicly opened in May 1992. Nägeli was

234

not someone who, like Krier or Kahn or so many others, had come to Jim's office because he had fallen in love with his buildings. He had come almost by chance, at the suggestion of Ulli Schaad. Because he was a clever young man and a good designer he was quickly promoted from translating German documents into English, and vice versa, to work on the Performing Arts Center at Cornell and the Wissenschaftszentrum building in Berlin, and ended up as the architect in charge of the latter.

Nägeli had no sympathy with Post-Modernism. He disliked both the Performing Arts Center and the WZB, although he later came to appreciate the merits of the latter. On the other hand, he admired Jim's earlier buildings. He knew that Braun wanted a recognisable Stirling design, but although Braun admired Stuttgart and wanted something like it, his own preference was to go back to early Stirling (and to Louis Kahn) for inspiration and ideas. By 1986 Jim was ready for a change, and he undoubtedly accepted Nägeli's approach (as did Braun), perhaps especially because what was involved was a factory building on a green-field site.

The building evolved a good deal in execution, partly because of changes imposed by the client, but its relationship to early Stirling is still much in evidence; in some ways it got closer, because as an economy the stone cladding originally designed for the walkway was dropped. The basic concept is that of the unexecuted design of 1971 for the Olivetti headquarters: a long spine, with the office and recreational elements on one side, looking onto a park-like landscape and a lake, and the workshop and utilitarian elements on the other. Melsungen is more complex than the Olivetti scheme, but the basic principles are the same. There are other early-Stirling echoes but there is much variety and novelty (though none, or almost none, of Stuttgart's historic references, and in the end no cladding): a curving office wing supported on cone-like piloti, for instance, and a dramatic raised walkway in front of the spine wall, supported on a criss-cross of struts in a changing, curving rhythm caused by the change in the level of the ground beneath them. One is reminded of the subtly changing curve of the façade before the entrance hall at Stuttgart.

Michael Wilford was certainly in close contact with Braun over the development and running of the project; but the outstanding question is, to what extent did Jim in his customary role of manipulator and orchestrator direct or mould the ideas which undoubtedly poured forth from Nägeli and his team? Nägeli claims that almost no changes were made in London, or by Jim when he came to Berlin: all he will admit is the addition of a multi-storey car park behind the wall, suggested by Michael Wilford, and the serpentine curve of the waterfall in the lake, suggested by Jim. Jim undoubtedly felt, and felt strongly, that he had contributed more than that; there are members of the Berlin office who agree with him and remember, for instance, how Nägeli's sketches for the competition only took convincing shape after discussion in London with Jim. The issues have been so darkened by controversy and the death of Jim that perhaps only an exhaustive analysis of the surviving drawings will give an answer. But what one can say with confidence is that if the buildings had not been designed under the umbrella of Stirling, Wilford, they would have looked very different.

Two other projects of these years were built in the end, but only after Jim's death. The commission, which came at the very end of 1985, to design a new office building at what became No. 1 Poultry, in the centre of the City of London, had to negotiate two Public Inquiries and other planning hurdles. The commission in 1987 to design a big Music Academy on the adjacent site to the Neue Staatsgalerie ran into problems of finance, and it was not until 1996 that the completed building finally lifted its great round tower on the skyline of Stuttgart.

The Poultry commission came from Peter Palumbo. Palumbo was the son of a property developer of Italian extraction who had made a fortune in the 1930s out of development in London, and built up a considerable portfolio of London properties. The son appeared at first sight a rich, amiable, polo-playing ex-Etonian socialite. He was all that, but he was also a dedicated patron of contemporary art and architecture. When passions were running at their highest, at the time of the Public Inquiry over No. 1 Poultry, those who opposed it conceived of Palumbo as a sinister figure, a Mafia-type operator under the Etonian veneer, unscrupulously wheeling and dealing and snaring supporters with champagne and smoked salmon, and free trips to the Farnsworth House, the Mies van der Rohe masterpiece owned by him in America. It was an unfair picture, because, although Palumbo certainly used every resource available to him to get his project through, it did not allow for his genuine idealism in wanting to build an architectural masterpiece in the City: it was a dream which he pursued with unflagging dedication for over thirty years.

He had an engaging capacity for hero-worship. In the 1960s his hero was Mies van der Rohe. In 1972 he was to buy one of Mies's best-known buildings, the Farnsworth House near Chicago, as an American residence for himself, and later to add a house by Frank Lloyd Wright and Le Corbusier's Maisons Jaoul to his collection. In 1962 he approached Mies to design a scheme for the site he and his father were assembling near the Mansion House in the City of London. In 1967 Mies finally came to

London to present a design for a tower block looking onto a new square, adjacent to the side façade of the Mansion House. This was exhibited, and then put in for planning permission in 1969, the year in which Mies died. Permission was approved subject to the Palumbos obtaining possession of the whole site: 13 freeholds and 348 leasehold interests were involved. It took until 1981 to acquire these, by when a new planning application was needed. In the 1980s both tower and square, which had sailed through the initial planning process in the 1960s, were widely felt to be out of scale and out of place in this particular location, besides involving the destruction of a number of listed buildings. Set against this was the feeling that Mies was one of the two greatest architects of the Modern Movement, and that to have a building by him in London, even posthumously, was worth fighting for. The design was rejected. Palumbo appealed, and it went to Public Inquiry in May 1984. Palumbo assembled an impressive array of support from contemporary architects, and from Sir John Summerson, the doyen of English architectural historians. None the less, the Inspector's report, when it appeared a year later, recommended rejection. The report was accepted by the Minister for the Environment of the day, Patrick Jenkin, and he refused permission on 22 May 1985. However, he accompanied his refusal with a statement that 'he did not rule out redevelopment of this site if there were acceptable proposals for replacing the existing buildings. He does not consider that the buildings are of such over-riding importance that their preservation should outweigh all other considerations.' This left the way open for another scheme.

Jim had given evidence in support of the Mies van der Rohe scheme. On 5 May 1984, Palumbo sent him a bottle of champagne, in celebration of the completion of Stuttgart, of Jim's birthday, and possibly of his evidence. 'Champagne', he wrote in the accompanying letter, 'as we know, is the wine of celebration. I can think of no more appropriate way in which to salute your triumph or your birthday, than by offering you this bottle, which should drink reasonably well. It comes to you with congratulations, deep admiration and all my very best wishes.' A live Stirling was taking the place of a dead Mies. When the Mansion House Square scheme was turned down, Palumbo, encouraged by recommendations from John Summerson and Sandy Wilson, asked Stirling to prepare another one. On 16 July 1985 he wrote to him from America:

> There is no point denying that the demise of Mansion House Square was a disappointment and a setback; but when one door closes another very often opens, and this will be such an

occasion. I want you to know how thrilled I am that you have agreed to undertake the feasibility studies for the site at Number One Poultry, and I could not be happier or more delighted that we shall be working together. It will be a rewarding and formidable partnership, and I know that you will give me a truly great modern building appropriate to the importance of the site and the needs of the City of London as we approach the Millennium.

The idea of a tower and a new square was given up. The new building was to be relatively low and fitted to the existing street pattern, in the wedge-shaped site where Queen Victoria Street, a new street cut through the City in the 1880s, met the ancient street of Poultry, the continuation of Cheapside. The site included the Mappin and Webb building, a major Victorian Gothic building on the apex of the wedge, and a number of smaller buildings which formed as a whole one of the best surviving groups of Victorian commercial architecture in the City. But for an architect it was a site to be dreamed of: prominent and adjacent to the Mansion House, the Bank of England, the Royal Exchange, Lutyens's Midland Bank, Hawksmoor's St Mary Woolnoth and Wren's St Stephen Walbrook (to which Palumbo had earlier donated an altar sculpted by Henry Moore). For Jim the opportunity to design a building in such company was irresistible, and it was not difficult for him to accept Patrick Jenkin's judgement that the nine listed buildings on the site were replaceable.

Jim presented Palumbo with his first 'doodles' in September 1985. On 13 September Palumbo wrote to him from the Farnsworth House:

> This is just a short note to say how thrilled I was to see the 'doodles' on Tuesday evening. I haven't stopped since – hence the delay in writing to you. I realise that there is a long way to go before the final design takes shape, but there is no doubt in my mind that the building will be a masterpiece by any standards. I am so excited about the prospect that I am finding it difficult to concentrate upon anything else!

There was indeed a long way to go: the design was developed within six months, but this was followed by lengthy consultations with the City planning department, submission to the Royal Fine Art Commission, and tireless lobbying for support from architects, the media, City worthies, and anyone else who had influence and might give support, including the

Engineering Building, Leicester University 1959-63.
The base of the tower and the workshop block.

The Florey Building, Queen's College, Oxford, 1966-71

(*Facing page*) History Faculty Building, Cambridge, 1964-67

Jim in the sculpture
court at the Neue
Staatsgalerie, Stuttgart,
taken by Charles Jencks

Jim on holiday in
Italy in 1982, taken
by Robert Kahn

(*Facing page*)
Jim on the concourse
at the Olivetti
Training School,
Haslemere, taken by
Charles Jencks

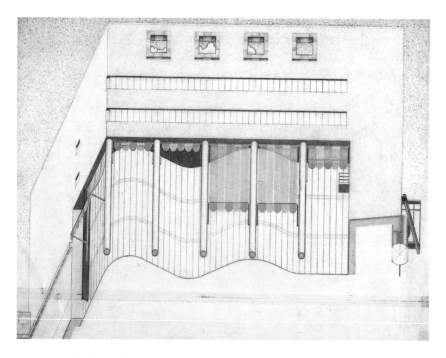

The Library Building, Neue Staatsgalerie, Stuttgart

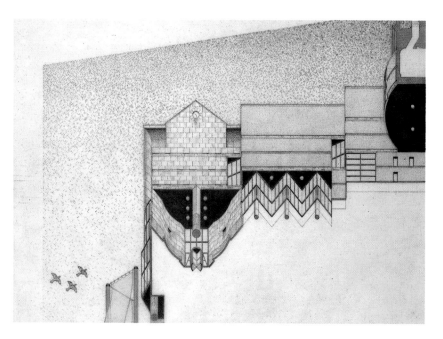

Competition design for the National Gallery extension, London 1986

The Entrance Hall, Neue Staatsgalerie, Stuttgart

Number 1 Poultry, City of London

Prince of Wales, who was a polo-playing friend of Palumbo's. 'We went to see him twice', according to Palumbo, 'and on the second occasion, as we were going downstairs at Kensington Palace, he said from the top of the stairs, "well, goodbye; you can rest assured that this is one scheme I shan't be saying anything about."' So they did not take it too well when he denigrated it as a '1930s wireless set' in a speech delivered some months later.

At the same time as Palumbo was lobbying there was rival campaigning by the very considerable body of opinion which opposed the project, mainly because of the destruction of listed buildings which it involved. Feelings were running high on both sides by the time the design went to Public Inquiry on 17 May 1988. Lined up for Palumbo were the President of the RIBA, the architectural critics and historians John Summerson and Charles Jencks, and many eminent architects including Philip Johnson, Richard Rogers, Norman Foster and Sandy Wilson. Lined up against it were the whole conservation lobby, including English Heritage, Save Britain's Heritage (a small but extremely effective pressure group, which to some extent master-minded the opposition), and the City of London, which had been persuaded to oppose the design by its Historic Buildings Division. Jim attended much of the Inquiry, and gave evidence. He found this extremely stressful, but proved an excellent witness, and more than held his own in cross-examination.

On 12 December 1987 Palumbo had written to Charles Jencks: 'Being as objective as I can in the circumstances, the building promises to be one of incredible invention, sophistication, monumentality and elegance.' One might perhaps question the 'elegance', but the design deserved the praise that Palumbo gave it. It is remarkable. It is also as far removed as one could conceive from Mies's Mansion House Square tower. This, however sophisticated and exquisitely detailed, was one of the 'up-ended shoeboxes' which had sprung up round the world from Mies's seed, and which Jim had already reacted against in his Wissenschaftszentrum building in Berlin. He used two devices to give variety to his building: rustication and a counterpoint between angles and curves. The rustication related partly to the rusticated façade of St Mary Woolnoth, but even more to the heroic rustication that covers almost the entire façade of Lutyens's Midland Bank. At No. 1 Poultry it is made up of stripes of different coloured stone and alternated, as Lutyens would never have alternated it, with great expanses of continuous glazing.

The counterpoint is complex and enjoyable to analyse. The two long façades, to Poultry and Queen Victoria Street, are twins, each divided horizontally into three sections, and vertically into five. The three middle sections of the upper two layers are modelled in alternating rhythms of angled, curved, angled and curved, angled, curved; the angled sections are entirely glazed, the curved section mainly wall. At roof level the two central curved sections on either façade are joined to form a drum, enclosing an open court between a roof-top restaurant and a roof-top garden. This drum gives the illusion of dropping down into the lower storeys; in fact it goes no lower than the roof, but it reappears in the form of a much smaller circular rotunda at ground- and first-floor level. Great trapezoidal openings cut into the rustication give access from the street on either side to this central rotunda, and the rotunda is linked to the roof-level drum by a triangular light-well.

At the apex of the wedge, where the two roads join, there is another, somewhat different play of angled and curved: a tall round-headed arch at ground level (contrasting with the trapezoidal openings round the corner); an angled window wall above it (carrying on the alternation of the two long façades), and above that a circular tower, which breaks free from the main building. The entrance arch is joined to the first floor of the rotunda by one of Jim's long *Scala Regia* staircases. The top level of the tower has projecting balconies protruding like horns or handles to either side, and was designed to act as a viewing platform. Tower and balconies were reminiscent of the rostral columns, with the beaks of ships protruded from them towards the top of the columns, which were set up to celebrate naval victories in Roman times, and revived to adorn neo-classical buildings. When Sandy Wilson pointed this out Jim said that he did not know what a rostral column was but he must have known of the rostral columns in front of the Bourse in St Petersburg, even if he did not know their origin. The device was, at any rate, apposite. No. 1 Poultry was only going to get built as the result of hard-won victory in the Public Inquiry.

The immediate prototype of the counterpoint between angles and curves is somewhat unexpected. In 1978 Jim and Richard Meier had been invited by Sheldon Solo, a New York property developer, to present separate schemes for a row of houses on East 67th Street. In the end neither design was used. Jim, working in New Haven with Robert Livesey, had produced an ingenious plan of interlocking large and small units, lit by large bay windows, alternately angled and rounded. The ground floor was rusticated. Between the big windows were smaller windows set back in trapezoidal (more or less) openings.

Basically, however, what Jim was playing was a sophisticated Baroque game. It was a game played in the grand manner, in keeping with its neighbours. It was Jim's equivalent of what Lutyens called the 'High

Game', and had played with brio in his Midland Bank across the road. It was a façade game. The curved and angled windows of the New York house related to their plan, but the façades at No. 1 Poultry bore little necessary relationship to its plan, or to the main practical function of the building, which was to provide five floors of unencumbered lettable office space. But the building had more than a practical function, and Jim recognised and celebrated this.

A somewhat ridiculous situation arose at the Public Inquiry. The 'high-tech' architects lined up to support Jim, because they were his friends, had been his disciples, or wanted to give witness for new building as opposed to conservation. But most of them did not very much like the design, as was revealed in conversations at the time, or is obvious if one reads between the lines of, for instance, Norman Foster's letter of support. The conservationists who opposed the design were often more sympathetic to it than its supporters, but they could not accept the destruction of the nine listed buildings.

The Inspector sent his report to the Ministry in December 1988. It concluded that the building 'might be a masterpiece' and recommended that planning permission be given. The Minister, Nicholas Ridley, accepted the recommendation and announced his acceptance on 9 June 1989. SAVE and others fought a long rearguard action, first appealing to the House of Lords, and then opposing the closure of Bucklersbury, the little street which crossed the site. Palumbo did not win final clearance until after Jim's death, and under Laurence Bain, who had been job architect from the beginning, the building was only completed in the spring of 1998. When the scaffolding was taken down what Jim and his office had achieved was revealed. However much one may regret the destruction of the listed buildings, there was probably no other contemporary firm which could have fitted a building onto this difficult site with such a combination of skill, consideration for neighbours, and panache.

TWELVE

THE OFFICE

Visitors were amazed by the small size and lack of pretension, not to say seediness, of Jim's office at 75 Gloucester Place, in which all the firm's buildings were designed between 1963 and 1986. Americans, in particular, used to offices of up to several hundred people, cool and glossy on the upper floor or floors of some prestigious skyscraper, were taken aback, sometimes horrified and sometimes a little envious when they found the great Jim Stirling in such a place. One could say that it was more like a workshop or an atelier than an office; or one could just say that it was a tip.

The office was in a late eighteenth-century terrace house, in a long street running north from Portman Square, on the ground floor and basement under a dentist. There was no lobby or waiting room. Visitors came into the front room, and the first thing that they saw, as described by Ulla Wilke, was a very large mirror 'and under the mirror there was a sideboard, and on that there was a kettle. The kettle was always on, and the steam of the kettle had cracked the mirror, so there was a big crack right across that mirror. The sideboard was always in an incredible mess, so the first thing clients would see was washed and unwashed cups, and old coffee and coffee-filters. It was terrible, I mean, how unprofessional, but it had great atmosphere.'

The two secretaries, Catherine (Cathy) Martin and Jackie Simnet, sat in the front room, along with two or three of the architects. 'Everyone walked in,' according to the former, 'looked at the mirror, and immediately the men would fix their tie, or something . . . it was an automatic reaction, it was very human. Also, Jim had this photograph, taken on holiday, a pair of topless women, one on either side of him. He thought it was marvellous, because he was so fat his chest almost had breasts as well. He had it blown up and put on the mirror. It was taken, I think, on holiday somewhere in the South of France. Lots of little things were often stuck on the mirror, but Jim put this particular photograph there himself. Everybody laughed about it, but the comical thing about it was, any

242

client who came in would look at the mirror, look at the picture, and then look at Jackie and I. It was so funny, and it often broke the ice, you know, because we would say "No, it's not us, it's not us".'

Catherine Martin came in December 1972 to be interviewed for the job of secretary. She was twenty-three and had come down to London from Glasgow earlier in the year. She had no idea that Jim had been born in Glasgow, or that his family was Scottish by origin, and he did not tell her. 'Both Jim and Michael interviewed me. I remember thinking Jim was very nervous. He kept twiddling a pen between his fingers, and Michael just sat grinning at me. I remember saying that my brother was an architect, and Jim said to me, "Oh well, he probably knows me," and I indignantly said, "No, he certainly doesn't know you." And when I went home and told my brother, of course he knew him. I knew nothing about the office, or any of his work at all.' She was offered the job, came in January, and stayed twelve and a half years. In about 1979 she was made an Associate: 'Oh dear, I had to apologise about that, because when they called me and said to me they'd like to make me an Associate, I went into hysterical laughter. It didn't mean anything, as such. Yes, it was a compliment in that they trusted me, and that was their way of saying thank you, I suppose. They were very nice about it, and the next day I went in and apologised for laughing so much.'

She was responsible for the petty cash and the wages, kept the books and did all the typing, until Jackie came in 1978 to look after the German correspondence. 'Cathy was a kind of mother figure, which she hated,' according to Russell Bevington. One of the young foreign architects, whose English was limited, was too shy to go to Marks and Spencer's to buy underclothes, so she went for him. She was everybody's friend and confidante. But above all she looked after Jim. She ran his correspondence. Sometimes he dictated letters, but more often he scrawled a few lines at the bottom of an incoming letter, and she typed them out. These laconic letters became known as 'Jimspeak' in the office. She shopped for him, went on errands for him and Mary, paid the nanny's wages, and brought down a haggis from Glasgow for him. She bought his lunch for him. Russell Bevington remembers that 'for a long time he was on a lunchtime diet. He was always on a diet, Jim. Catherine would provide his lunch for him. Which he'd eat. Then he'd say he was popping out for a newspaper. I can remember one day I said to Catherine "Where the hell's Jim?" "Oh, he's popped out to get a paper." "Well, OK, I'll pop out and get a sandwich." I used to go to a sandwich bar on Paddington Street, to get their fantastic toasted cheese and ham sandwiches. So I went in there, and there was Jim sitting there, with a plateful of toasted sandwiches. He was having his diet lunch in the office, and going out for his paper and having his real lunch somewhere else. He would never say anything like "Don't tell Catherine". He thought those things were a great joke. And she probably knew anyway.

'When we were doing Dusseldorf, I used to bring corned beef and tomato sandwiches which I would leave by my board. I came back one day to my board, where Jim had been sitting, working on the plans, to find that he'd eaten my sandwiches. If there was food around, he would eat it.'

Jim was putting on weight all during the 1970s, in spite of the diet. 'There was a classic occasion', according to Catherine Martin, 'when he'd to go off to a meeting in a hurry, and he went to the toilet just before, and he burst his trousers. The button came off, and he came upstairs in a real flap. He used to panic sometimes something awful, Jim. I had to sew the button on. He was standing there, and I was level with his waistband, and he was huge. I thought, "Oh, I'm in a real position of power here, now. I've got the needle and everything else." We were all teasing him, and saying, "You'd better watch it, Jim. Cathy's round a very sensitive area here." He thought that was quite funny.

'People always knew my mood . . . if Jim had made me angry, by the speed at which I typed. The angrier I got, the more efficient I became. The architects did very well to put up with the noise of clicking typewriters all day long. It's very difficult to concentrate. Walkmans had just come out, and all the architects had their Walkmans on. Jackie and I used to resent it sometimes, and we used to ask, "Can we put a Walkman on?" and Jim would say, "Well, just for a short while." It was just impossible, because I would put the Walkman on, and Jim never picked the phone up to speak to you; he always called for you, always, and if I had the Walkman on I couldn't hear him, and he would get very cross that I wasn't responding. On the whole he was quite placid, but if he got angry, woe betide anyone in his path.'

There were up to three architects working in the front room, and Jim and Michael were in the back one. For a time an extra room was rented nearby, and then, in about 1974, the basement was taken over. When Catherine Martin came there were seven people in the office, including herself and Jim and Michael. From the late 1970s it varied around fifteen, in addition to the half dozen or so in the Stuttgart office from 1979.

'The cool place to be was in the basement', according to Robert Livesey. It was there that the Dusseldorf, Cologne and Stuttgart competition entries were hatched. Cathy Martin says that the main basement was known as the 'sweat-pit': 'They never opened the windows, and the air was awful. Between the smell of bodies that were working . . . and most of the people in the office smoked. They were doing Dusseldorf and Cologne, and they worked long long hours. It just used to smell, so it became known as the Sweat Pit. Jim very rarely left his room to go and look at any work, but once the Sweat Pit started, when Russell, Werner Kreiss and John Corrigan got together down in that room in the basement, Jim would spend the day there, down with them. I think he really liked being in their company, and with their banter they had a good time together.

'We called the seat Russell had the Throne. The dentist who was above the office was renovating his premises. He threw out his big chairs, somebody took one and Russell took the other, so he used to have it at his desk. It was at the time when Jim had acquired a desk that Geoffrey Howe didn't want, Geoffrey Howe's old dining-table, a mahogany Regency-style table. Russell had this table bang in the middle of the floor, and he had this huge chair that the dentist had thrown out repaired. It's very much like a throne, big high back, with all sorts of scrollwork around, and pillars.' The 'Howe table' became part of the office legend, but in fact it had nothing to do with the Howes, and how the legend started remains mysterious. It was a reproduction table which Jim had bought himself, specifically for the office.

The front room on the ground floor was the social centre. 'Everybody passed through that room to get coffee, or to get Catherine to do something. The Xerox machine was in that room.' Coffee was kept brewing all morning, and it was there that Catherine and Jackie served up tea or coffee every afternoon. 'We used to ring round and say "tea's ready", and they'd all come up. It was how the downstairs met the upstairs, so to speak. Sometimes Jim would appear in the doorway, wondering what was happening', but tea and coffee were always brought to him in his own room. Sometimes he came into the front room at lunch time and 'they would sit there talking about all sorts of things. I used to love these times when they would sit and talk like that. I was just about ten feet away, or six feet away, and I would learn a lot.' But on the whole Jim talked very little in the office, except about the job in hand. According to Michael Wilford, who saw most of him, because they shared a room: 'Inside the premises, he was always very strict, and somehow cold and focused. He made few jokes in the office. Well, it's curious, actually. I don't quite know why that should be. He felt that somehow the office was a serious business. It was quite extraordinary, how just leaving those premises . . . if you were ever away for a night somewhere with Jim, staying in a hotel, you would have dinner together.

And that was always a totally different experience. In fact, if ever I wanted to discuss difficulties I had about projects, my status in the office, or all those kinds of things, I would always say "Let's just go and have a drink", or "Let's go and have dinner together".'

Jim would sometimes join the others for out-of-office drinking in the pub round the corner. The office also ran a football team, jointly with Ove Arup Associates, and played matches in Regent's Park against Ahrends Burton Koralek and other firms of architects. Jim only once took part, in 1973. He played goalkeeper.

Almost everyone who was in the office then has happy memories of Gloucester Place days: 'It was a bit like a family.' 'There was a fantastic crowd of people.' 'It was a fabulous wonderful time.' It was also a very cosmopolitan crowd, 'like the League of Nations', as Catherine Martin puts it. At one time or another there were American, German, Swiss, Japanese, Irish and Italian architects working there. They came drawn by the glamour of Jim's reputation, but also by the interest and independence of the work which they were given to do, and by the extraordinary experience of working with Jim.

Modern buildings are complicated to design and build, and getting more complicated all the time. In any architect's office the design of each project is almost invariably the product of a team. Only in small practices taking on few commissions can the designs emanate from one man, in the way that perhaps the general public imagine: the creative genius giving birth to masterpieces.

In those larger practices which operate under the flag of a prestigious name, the role of the 'big man' can vary enormously. He can be a charismatic front man who charms potential clients, gets commissions and leaves the designing to others. He can have the power of quickly absorbing a brief and producing a striking concept to answer it, but leave it to his office to turn this into a building. He can be an extinct volcano, out of which once erupted a memorable building or buildings, from which his office have evolved a recognisable formula, which can be endlessly repeated.

Jim came into none of these categories. Except on the occasions when he established an immediate personal rapport with a potential client he was not good at selling himself or the practice, and hated being taken away from the work of design to do so. He never ossified. He remained creative up till the time of his death. But he provided the original concept less and less. His importance in the design process was enormous for other reasons. His genius lay in taking on board ideas from other people, and adapting and transforming them.

In the early days, as Michael Wilford puts it, 'Jim would sketch and establish the direction, the basic concept – *parti* is the expression he used – and then others would embellish, and he would edit the ideas in support of the basic concept.' People working in the office were allowed a great deal of initiative but at this period this was mainly employed on detailing and working drawings. For a young architect, being put to make a set of working drawings could be daunting but also exciting. 'Jim would never tell you what to do. He knew what he wanted, what he expected, but he would never tell you how to achieve that. You'd see what he'd done, you'd know what was missing, and then you would actually fill in the gaps, to make a complete set of working drawings, or whatever. You had to work it out for yourself, so as well as working on these amazing buildings, one was also learning to be very self-reliant and organised.'

From Derby Civic Centre onwards, Jim provided the *parti*, the basic concept, less and less often. Instead a way of designing very distinctive of the office was evolved. The team working on a project supplied alternatives, which Jim selected, edited, altered, and added to. The design process was carefully programmed, stage by state. At each stage Jim was completely open-minded and would take on board any suggestion which appealed to him, but once he had made a choice that was that, and he would move on to the next stage. The standard process is described by Ulla Wilke, who worked on many projects from 1980 onwards. 'Jim would put a brief on our desks, whoever was working on the scheme. Then there was quite a strict process, that was understood by everybody at the time, and it went like this. First of all we would draw the areas required in the brief in squares at 1 to 500 scale, so we had a representation in graphic form of the sizes in the brief. Very very pragmatic. Then he would say "Well, if you spread the whole of the programme on the site, how many layers would there be? One storey? Two storeys? If you covered half the site, how fat would that pancake be? If you did a tower, how tall would that tower be?" Then he would say, "Well, do us a clip", and that meant staple a few A4 pages together. They must never be bigger than A4 because he hated big pieces of paper. So we did clips, and the clips were the courtyard scheme, the tower scheme, the pancake scheme, the doughnut scheme – we always had names for them – to try out the programme on the site, without preconception. Then he started to form certain opinions, as to whether he liked the tower scheme better than the doughnut scheme, or vice versa. Then he would make certain critical moves on the chessboard, in terms of continuation, and give it input, and that's when five or six clips of various prototype schemes were put together in maybe two schemes, and then we kept on working on two schemes for a while, and then that got narrowed down to one scheme.

'His input was in the form of taking the A4 photocopied clip and putting an A4 sheet of tracing paper on top of it and doodling, and we would get these doodles back on the drawing board. He would then start a process of combining, eliminating, adding, in what we called a redlining way. He drew with a red pen on an overlay on the top of our drawings. He took them as the skeleton, the framework, which doesn't mean to say that he couldn't with three or four lines change the scheme completely. Yes, it was based on our framework, but that gave him, with his masterly skills, an amazing range of possibilities, which he explored. He did that in plan and section, and also in axo. We never built models during design, so a part of the clip would always be in axo. He would then shift masses around in three-dimensional form, on the axo; always tiny, tiny small drawings. Then we would get the overlay back, and he would say "Try that." He was always very open to sensible pragmatic changes. If you said, "Well, Jim, the ramp just doesn't fit here," he would say, "Oh, how does the ramp fit?" and then he took that on board. I think the people who worked on the schemes had a great deal of influence; their handwriting always shows through. But it's still a James Stirling scheme.'

According to Russell Bevington, 'We did a lot of projects together, and they were always just fantastic. He had this intuitive sense about so many things. We would table sketches and he would just turn through them. Some things that had been laboured over and maybe taken a couple of days would just get turned aside, and absolutely no comment. That was that, it was gone. Then he would either alight on something or not. There would be a brief discussion about how we might progress, develop it. I think in some cases he would pick on things or put things together that one felt were a bit strange. But over time and in the development of things, one would realise how clever some of those combinations were. He would see things beyond what was immediately apparent to us, on some of the simplest of sketchings.

'He would start doing things often that, God knows where they came from, but just enrich the thing. An instance is the entrance glazing at Stuttgart – a curious, tipping plane of glass that starts vertical, ends up pitched. What generated that, I've no idea. He just drew it. When he drew it initially in plan we all read it as being vertical, which looks rather dumb, but once you've inclined one end of it, and therefore it's twisting across its length, it becomes an extraordinarily interesting thing.'

Everyone who was involved in the office describes the excitement and at times the pain of working with Jim. They were 'feeding his fire'. Sometimes he would take on board ideas without altering them.

Sometimes he would reject them outright. Sometimes he would accept them and 'with some magical manipulation make them his own'. He never talked much, and never explained. Often they did not understand what he was doing; they would mutter angrily, 'He's ruining my scheme.' In other cases he accepted what was offered so readily that they could feel that the end result was theirs, not his. But 'he let us flow fast and freely – but he was steering.' They were designing for him, in an office dominated by him. In another setting something quite different would have emerged.

There was a good deal of variation in Jim's involvement in schemes. The Dusseldorf competition entry started off from a sketch design by him. For Stuttgart there was an initial sketch but there was a direction to Bevington and Schaad, 'Let's try Dusseldorf Mark 2', which effectively generated the design, and from then on Jim was closely involved at every stage. In some projects, especially some of the later ones, Jim's involvement was very much less. An example of the way in which he could creatively transform the work of a design team is the competition entry for the Business and Administrative Centre at Florence. Jim did no initial sketch. Russell Bevington relates how he, Ulrich Schaad and John Tuomey were set to do three separate projects: 'I can remember we had a pin-up of the three projects that we produced or the various projects we produced between us and I had basically done a rectilinear scheme, a square, which contained the whole of the project. Ulli Schaad had done a four-tower scheme, a little bit post-Siemens, which contained the whole of the project, and John Tuomey had done a fairly sophisticated slab-block which contained the whole of the project. Jim just went through them all with us, didn't say much but came in the next morning with a drawing, a sketch, which incorporated all three of those ideas. And you can see in the final project that it's a square and a set of four towers and within the square there is the remnants of the slab-block which was one of the administration buildings and the slab-block at the south of the square which was the judicial building. Once that diagram was laid down that became the scheme.'

The drawings that came out of Stirling's office are quite unlike those produced by other English practices at the time. As a collection they are as beautiful as any English architectural drawings since such drawings made their first appearance in the late fifteenth and early sixteenth centuries. They are full of variety. There are the concept sketches or 'doodles' with their nervous living hand-drawing line; the axonometrics taken both from below or above, sometimes showing the whole building, sometimes pulling out some part of it in order to make a point of detail;

the plans and sections, beautiful in their economy and precision; the perspective views, many in the tradition of the line-only drawings initiated by Leon Krier, others developing different techniques, a shaded one, or a pointillist one of dotted lines, but almost always drawn with wit and elegance. Jim once said that he did not consider these drawings to be works of art in themselves, but few people who went to the office in Fitzroy Square, where they hung and still hang framed on the walls, or to the various exhibitions where they were on show, would agree with him. Yet they are not just pretty drawings, or exercises in advertisement; they relate closely to, and are explanatory of, the nature of the building. Computer drawing was never allowed in the office in Jim's lifetime.

Only the concept drawings (and by no means all of those) were drawn by Jim. After the History Faculty Building he stopped working at

Drawing by Jim for a proposed terrace of houses in New York

a drawing board in the office, except at the time of the competition entry for Dusseldorf. The drawings are by members of his office, or in some early projects by people who came in from outside to help out, among others early ones by David Gray; Leon Krier's seminal contribution; Michael Wilford's exquisitely spare detail drawings; Russ Bevington's worm's-eye axonometrics of Dusseldorf and of many other projects (in fact not accurate axonometrics, but ones carefully adjusted for visual effect); witty perspective views by Toby Lewis and Richard Portchmouth.

Jim would often edit these drawings, especially by directing that lines or details which he thought unnecessary be taken out. He always said that he designed the drawings just as much as he designed the buildings, and for this reason he had no hesitation in signing them even if he had not drawn a line of them. This could be upsetting for those who

250

Drawing by Richard Portchmouth showing the proposed extension
to the National Gallery, London

had done the actual work. His main personal contribution as a draughtsman was a curious one: he coloured many of the drawings himself, in whole or part. He coloured up older drawings for publication, especially of the Staatsgalerie and the Clore. He coloured parts of the post-competition drawings of the National Gallery. He used a very slow technique. Each drawing was painstakingly covered with literally thousands of small notes of colour, applied with a crayon. Some of the resulting drawings are extraordinarily beautiful objects, virtually abstract symphonies in line and colour.

Jim sometimes worked at colouring in the office, sometimes at home or on holiday. Many of the National Gallery drawings were coloured while he was on holiday with Mary and the children in Cornwall, accompanied by much cursing and swearing at himself for being such a fool as to start on such a time-consuming job. But at times, in the office especially, he seemed to find the colouring therapeutic.

He coloured more existing older drawings for the Bologna exhibition in 1990 and the Venice exhibition in 1991. It is hard to forgive some of these later essays, for they destroyed the particular spare quality of the original drawings. Leon Krier was quite rightly infuriated to find that Jim had coloured many of his drawings for the Black Book and elsewhere. Among others the wonderful worm's-eye axonometric of the Florey Building, and the famous drawing of Jim and his Hope furniture were, in effect, ruined in this way. There may have been an element of jealousy or mischief in what Jim did.

It is curious that Jim drew so comparatively little, when he could draw so beautifully. When he wanted to he could make quick, witty sketches, often with a few sensitive lines, for family or friends, or inspired by a particular occasion. When Ulla Wilke left the office, for instance, he drew and coloured a plate of fried eggs as a present for her. But this happened comparatively seldom. He never drew other people's buildings. When he looked at buildings on holiday or on tour and was interested by them, he photographed rather than sketched them. He never drew imaginary buildings. Like many people he would doodle nervously and quite elaborately during a meeting, but in general he drew for a purpose rather than for pleasure.

There were whole swathes of the practice that did not especially interest Jim, and in which he liked to be involved as little as possible. The office had to be kept running, bills paid, and an eye kept on the finance. Contracts had to be drawn up, and agreed to, a working relationship established with the contractor, and contractual problems dealt with. Working drawings had to be prepared and checked. Jim was only interested if these involved a change in the design, which needed to be discussed. But, as Russell Bevington puts it, 'the design is one thing; making it work as a set of construction, making it buildable, water-tight and the rest, is another.' In all these exceedingly important aspects, Michael Wilford played the main and essential role. In his own words, 'In the early years, my role was that of enabler. I made the building happen. Jim never had an interest in detail, that is, in minutiae. I organised the staff and dealt with contractors on a day-to-day basis.' All this work was extremely time-absorbing, but Wilford never ceased to be involved in design matters too, and became more so in the last years of the practice. 'There was the design side and there was the technical managerial side. But over the years that distinction became progressively blurred, to the extent that in the last ten years it was almost impossible to draw a line between the two. I have maintained an involvement in the managerial and financial side of the practice but have also been fundamentally involved in design.'

Wilford also found himself increasingly involved in the getting of work. 'Jim never sold himself to clients. On the contrary, he always undersold himself. This worked to the detriment of our practice, particularly in the United States, where we were frequently outclassed at interviews by American architects. Architect selection committees often expected more than Jim could or would deliver in words. In the last ten years or so, we attended interviews together and I had to do the selling.' Michael Wilford comes across as a likeable, reasonable and very competent man; in terms both of getting work and getting buildings built, this was and is a useful image.

Jim's personal relationship with Michael Wilford was never as tense as his relationship with James Gowan. He relied on him and trusted him, but, as Wilford honestly and candidly admits, they were friendly but never friends. Jim was always opaque, but the opacity could be especially frustrating for his partner, who sat in the same room with him for so many years. 'He wouldn't level with you somehow. There was always the sense that he was withholding something. Maybe it wasn't conscious, maybe it was part of his personality, but it was frustrating. I know, now, from my own experience of running the practice, that there are times when a lot of things are churning through your mind. I felt that he wouldn't share those with me.'

Jim's relations with the people in his office varied a good deal. He could be mean to those whom he did not like, and there were others whose quality he appreciated, but with whom he was never close. But there was always an inner ring in the office, of those with whom he got on especially well, and who were especially devoted to him. To those who were not in it, this circle or court of Jim's could seem sycophantic. Perhaps some members on the edge of it were, but there is no denying the genuine devotion which the real inner ring felt for Jim, and which comes across movingly when one talks to them. They teased him, imitated him, made jokes about him and loved him. The feeling that you were one of his people and that he trusted you was of enormous importance to them.

Jim was a sphinx, who kept his own secrets; a magician, who could transform a design with a few strokes of his pencil; a king surrounded by a court; an *enfant terrible* who was indulged and enjoyed; for some a father figure, to be looked up to or reacted against. But he entirely dominated the office.

In 1986 the office needed more space and moved to 8 Fitzroy Square, off the top of Tottenham Court Road. A lease was taken of the whole house in one of the two ranges of the square designed by Robert Adam. It was a much handsomer house than the one in Gloucester Place. It had high, well-proportioned rooms, and a spacious stone staircase. There were five floors. The partners' room was on the first floor, in the front half of what had been the double drawing room when it was a private house. It had three tall sash windows running from floor to ceiling and was separated from the back room by double doors, which were often left open. Cathy Martin and Jackie Simnet moved into the back room.

The numbers in the office rose and fell; at the peak there were thirty-seven. This was still not a large number, but inevitably something of the family atmosphere went. There was no longer communal tea in the afternoon. Jim's overweight, and the fact that his knees were now troubling him, made him reluctant to move from the first floor. Instead of his going from drawing board to drawing board, playing with his stubby pencil on the drawings, designs were more often discussed round the big table in the partners' room. And he was increasingly out of the office.

None the less the new office had great style and individuality. It was a pleasure to visit, because of its sense of spaciousness combined with intense creative activity, all taking place against an evocative background of contents, with Jim's massive figure ambling amiably at the centre of it, while recorded music played from his favourite operas. His purchase of furniture and objects had begun to percolate into Gloucester Place in the office's last years there. Some of the more handsome drawings were beginning to be framed and hung up. Both these developments went much further in Fitzroy Square. There was fine early nineteenth-century furniture in the partners' room, and other pieces percolated into other parts of the office, and mixed with practical modern chairs and tables. There were models of the firm's buildings everywhere. The walls of the first-floor room were entirely lined with framed drawings, and the staircase with framed posters, caricatures of Jim, and other personal items. Among them was a signed photograph of Le Corbusier, dated by him after his death, for it was in fact a forgery by Leon Krier.

Over all, but in the partners' room especially, was an overlay expressive of Jim's jackdaw instincts. The inventory of his belongings in the office, made after his death, runs to over 4 pages and 127 entries, many of them multiple, as well as 14 entries for furniture. Among them were 2 marble obelisks; 1 green-mauve glass cactus; 18 assorted eggs, of marble or china; 5 cigarette lighters; 15 paperweights; 4 fossils; 1 set of building bricks; 2 bronze sphinxes and 3 brass pigs.

THIRTEEN

JIM REGNANT

In the 1980s Jim was probably the best-known architect in the world –
among architects, that is, for like the vast majority of the profession, he
remained comparatively little known to the general public. His buildings
were constantly visited, Stuttgart was added to his masterpieces of the
1960s, and if some of the buildings that came after Stuttgart disappointed
some and puzzled others, what he was doing and where he was going was
widely discussed and argued about by architects all over the world. He
frequently lectured on his work, at architectural conferences or to schools
of architecture, always to packed audiences, and turned down far more
invitations than he accepted. There were exhibitions of his work in New
York, Bologna, Berlin and Japan and in 1986, he, Richard Rogers and
Norman Foster were given a very large joint exhibition at the Royal
Academy: pieces of the original to-scale mock-ups for the Neue
Staatsgalerie were set together in a collage and filled the central rotunda
there (they were bought after the exhibition by Charles and Maggie
Jencks, and re-erected as a garden feature in Scotland).

A big monograph was published by Rizzoli in New York in 1984,
with an introductory essay by Colin Rowe, and there were numerous
smaller publications discussing and illustrating aspects of his work. An
hour-long film on him, made by Michael Blackwood, was shown on
English and German television in 1987. He was awarded the RIBA
Queen's Gold Medal in 1980, the American Pritzker Prize in 1981, the
Thomas Jefferson Medal in 1986, the German Hugo Haring Prize in
1988, and the Japanese Praemium Imperiale Award in 1990. The Gold
Medal, the Pritzker Prize and the Praemium Imperiale Award were the
three most prestigious architectural awards of their respective countries.
The Gold Medal just conferred honour and glory, but the other two had
very substantial financial awards attached.

Jim and Mary were in New York when the Pritzker Prize was
announced. They had come over with Ben, in celebration of Ben's getting
into Westminster and Jim's getting over an operation. Jim was wanted for

a press conference, but he had a meeting in London, and the only way in which the conference could be fitted in was by his returning on Concorde, so he, Mary and Ben were all sent back on it together. Jim and Mary returned for the presentation in Washington, in the great columned interior of the old Pensions Office, 'with candles in every alcove and everyone dressed up to the nines' as Mary remembers. The prize is given by Mr Pritzker himself, and takes the form of a cheque and a Henry Moore figure. When the moment came for the actual presentation it was found that this had been left in New York.

Jim remained a foremost member of the 'International Circus', one of the dozen or so architects whose paths intersected as they travelled the world lecturing, attending conferences, sitting on juries for architectural competitions, opening exhibitions and receiving their own prizes. His performance on juries was always impressive: he had the gift of quickly sizing up, and clearly expressing, the merits and demerits of a scheme; he could carry his colleagues, and the one which he preferred usually won the competition. These competitions could involve a certain amount of teaming up outside the jury sessions. Phyllis Lambert, the founder and head of the Canadian Center for Architecture in Montreal, has agreeable memories of 'sort of plotting' with Jim to make sure that the, in their opinion, right candidate won the competition for the Mississauga Town Hall in Canada and the Brooklyn Museum in New York: 'We used to meet for breakfast in the courtyard and discuss strategy . . . it was always fun working with him, because you had somebody who was coherent about ideas.'

Jim was on the jury for the competition for the new Arts Centre in Nîmes, next to the Maison Carrée, held in 1984. Mary went out to Nîmes with him. He had declined to enter the competition, because too many members of the office were away on holiday at the relevant time. His competition notes survive. Competitors had to decide whether or not to keep the façade of the burnt-out neo-classical theatre on the site. Jim's final list was made up of Norman Foster, Frank Gehry, Jean Nouvel and Cesar Pelli. Jim thought that '*None* are good enough', that 'the pro-gramme may be too large for the site', and that the 'theatre façade *should be kept*'. He placed Foster first and Nouvel second, but even for Foster he noted 'boring/banal building', 'finish is good but concept not so', '1st prize only if changes'. In the end Foster won. Jim talked his entry through with him, and Foster made changes and remembers him with gratitude as 'very human behind the gruff bear image', 'constructive and helpful . . . I was surprised at his generosity on this occasion'.

Jim finally gave up teaching at Yale in 1984, because his practice had too much work. In 1977 he had accepted a less time-demanding and very well-paid Professorship teaching the Master Class at the Dusseldorf Kunstakademie, and he kept it on until he reached retiring age in 1989. In 1982 he spent some months as Architect-in-Residence at the American Academy in Rome; and from 1984 to 1986 he taught a class for a few weeks each year at the School of Architecture in Venice. One way and another, he was much the most international of English architects, even though he resolutely refused to learn more than a word or two of any foreign language.

Jim went less regularly to New York once he gave up teaching at Yale, but he still visited it, to lecture, or on the way to or from other parts of America, and retained his fondness for it. When his expenses were paid he usually stayed at the Gotham Hotel, but he did the round of his friends, especially Katrin Adam, Keith Godard, Barbara Jakobson, Kenneth Frampton and Robert Kahn. He was now much in Germany, in Stuttgart, Dusseldorf and Berlin, and was always happy there, because he was so much admired and appreciated and because he enjoyed dis-covering German neo-classical architecture, especially that of Schinkel.

Jim's time at Dusseldorf is described by Vefik Soyeren and Elisabeth Farkashazi, who were his students there, and by Marlies Hentrup, who was first his student and later his colleague. The Master Class was for qualified architects, many of whom were also in practice. Students stayed until their project was finished, which could be up to seven or eight years. They worked under four visiting architects, who each came for a day every few weeks. Jim usually flew in from London just for the day. He carried books (and sometimes a pot of Griebenschmalz) in a plastic carrier bag, and everything else in his green briefcase. On occasions when he was staying one or more nights there would be a little more in the carrier bag. He worked with intense concentration all through the day, without taking lunch. But metaphors to do with food, with cake, fried eggs, ice-cream, bananas or doughnuts, had a way of coming into his conversation or his drawings.

His teaching methods were similar to those at Yale, with some differences, due perhaps to language problems and to his development as an architect. On the whole students chose their own projects. Schemes had to be developed logically, stage by stage, starting with a *parti* and ending with a buildable design. Jim was never interested in anything fantastic or visionary. Any style was acceptable, as long as it was well done; there was no one right solution. He was open-minded and clear-minded. He urged his students not to get stuck with their first solution, but to try out alternatives, even if they ended up by returning to their first one. He liked it if they did not take themselves or their projects too seriously. He thought it a good thing if buildings were funny and made one smile.

Jim's German was virtually limited to 'Guten Morgen'. His students were internationally selected and had to have some English, but there were inevitable language problems. As a result Jim relied very much on drawing as a method of communication. As Marlies Hentrup puts it, 'He produced sketch after sketch on a fat paper roll as on an assembly line,' and although he never directed students what to do this proliferation of ideas could make it difficult for them to work out their own solutions. The language barrier, Jim's spaced-out visits and his own nature could also make him seem unapproachable. Soyeren found that it took three or four bleak years before he could establish a friendly personal relationship. Once the barrier was penetrated, however, the students had the same kind of feeling as the members of Jim's office. They became his people, and he backed them loyally, in the School and outside, and in their subsequent careers. He was generous, too, with both time and money. He went on regular architectural outings with them, and if these were combined with a lecture assignment would give up his honorarium in return for free accommodation for the students.

Jim's fame as an architect was consolidated by his appearance and his personality. He was the most distinctive, memorable and easily recognised of international architects. Thousands of architects and architectural students around the world knew about Big Jim, had stories to tell about him, and could imitate or caricature him. His office made an iced cake in his image for his supposed 60th birthday in 1986, and a snowman in his image outside the office in Fitzroy Square in 1991. This image and personality to go with it, which he had perfected in the 1970s, remained virtually unchanged: the blue (or in the last few years green) shirt, the crumpled grey trousers, the purple or green socks, the bright green or blue briefcase, the single carrier bag for his luggage when he travelled, the laconic speech, the gruff voice, the dry wit, the inordinate appetite for food and gossip and amazing capacity for drink when he relaxed in sympathetic company, all this draped on the massive frame: the 'monumentally informal' could be applied to Jim's person in the 1980s, as well as to his architecture. In the 1960s he had tended when photographed to hold one hand in such a way as to conceal his incipient double chin. By the end of the 1970s he accepted his size with apparent unselfconsciousness, or deliberate promotion, in countless photographs taken by family, friends, or professionals. One of the most memorable appeared on the cover of the *Sunday Times* magazine in August 1980. The paper had run a feature in which selected architects and other designers built their own sandcastle. Jim was photographed, massively triumphant, in his blue shirt, with the blue shorts and floppy hat which he habitually wore on the beach, as he appeared to be. In fact the photograph was taken in the studio, and the sandcastle had been built in advance by Paul Keogh from the office.

Jim was often approached by friends or colleagues past and present for references. When he was ready to give one he early on adopted a consistent policy. He asked the applicants to write their own references, which he then sent off as his, often all but unchanged, occasionally with a sentence or two added, very rarely with something taken out. The references, which are all in his files, make entertaining reading. It is intriguing to see how shamelessly (but in terms of self-interest, sensibly) people were prepared to praise themselves. When Bob Maxwell applied to be Dean of Architecture at Princeton, Jim was too late to send in a reference, but telephoned instead; whatever he said must have helped Maxwell to get the job.

He got a stream of letters with requests for help, information, invitations to give lectures, attend dinners or write articles, and so on. He turned down most of the invitations, usually scrawling a few words at the bottom of the letter: 'Regrets, I have no desire to talk about the Florey Building'; 'Regrets, I'm unable to help in your dissertation', 'Regrets, I have stopped doing talks for the time being', and so on, which Catherine Martin then typed out. He was often abrupt, but only very occasionally rude. To a request from two teachers and twelve students from Barcelona to visit his office and be shown some of his latest work, he answered on 20 March 1989: 'Regret we are not Madame Tussauds or a jolly Tourist Agency. We are private architects and want to remain private.' He was more often helpful, or at least entertaining. On 22 April 1981, in answer to Kirk Train of Mississippi, who had asked for help in seeing some of his buildings, he wrote 'in no way is it possible for me to let you have a letter – it would in many cases get you thrown out. All the building owners hate architects as they have been trampled to death. Best to pretend to be a student, child, Olivetti salesman.' On 20 January 1990 he was asked, at some length, 'Is there a secret path to this life of ours? . . . I must gain a logical answer to this question before I truly embark upon my future career within the Hotel and Catering Industry . . . Have a nice life, with my warmest affection.' Jim just answered, 'Have a nice life yourself, and best wishes in the Hotel/Catering Industry.'

Jim's gift for a quick brief reaction made him popular for questionnaires. He enjoyed answering them, and his answers are characteristic. 'Do you feel that you owe a debt to Krier?' 'He was a good draughtsman.'

'Is your present partner Michael Wilford, more similar or complementary to you?' 'Complementary; he's younger and slimmer.' 'Do you feel that you are a more European or Anglo-Saxon architect?' 'Scots.' 'Which of your projects would you put first?' 'The last.' 'Can you be attributed with the philosophy "Let me have fun"? i.e. can one say that you too have fun crazily, madly, and enormously?' 'I wish I did.' 'What do you think of Prince Charles?' 'Well, I wouldn't go skiing with him.'

Prince Charles had made three much publicised attacks on con-temporary architects and architecture in a speech at Hampton Court on 30 May 1984, a speech at the Mansion House in December 1987, and a television programme broadcast on 28 October 1988. In the programme he had referred to Jim's design for No. 1 Poultry as resembling 'an old 1930s wireless'. 'I rather took that as a compliment,' Jim commented, 'because 1930s wireless sets are really rather beautiful objects – I have the privilege of owning two of them myself.' But the comment, and the quip about skiing (the Prince and some friends had skied down a slope known to be dangerous, and one of them had been killed), were both made some time after the event. The architectural profession reacted to the Prince's remarks with absurdly exaggerated outrage, none more so than Jim. At the time of the broadcast he had drafted a letter resigning his Queen's Gold Medal in protest; fortunately a sensible letter from Peter Palumbo had stopped him from doing so. In 1989 he refused an appeal for donations from the North London Rescue Commando by writing 'Regrets, due to the bad-mouthing of HRH we do not have commissions and moneys to spare'.

In June 1989, when asked for copies of articles on the Clore, Jim replied 'Regrets, we are not able to help as we always throw away press cuttings as rubbish.' In October he wrote to a student, 'Regrets, I've long ago given up having reactions or thinking about press articles on our buildings.' Such comments were far from the truth. Jim was exceedingly sensitive to criticism: every adverse article evoked furious letters of protest, and all the articles remain on the office files. In 1991 an adverse article on the Clore produced a letter to Nicholas Serota, Alan Bowness's successor, and a soothing reply: 'I am sorry you were hurt, but both you and the building are robust enough to shrug off this light-weight article.' Jim answered, 'I don't give a fart in regard to my personal robustness. My *only* concern is in regard to possible clients who may read this disparaging stuff in the press – which could – and I think does affect our practice adversely.' On one occasion Alan Powers, a most amiable and inoffensive architectural writer and historian, was startled when Jim came up to him at a party and said that he was going to punch him in the face. It turned out that he thought Powers was Gavin Stamp, who had been a baiter of Jim since History Faculty days. Jim and Stamp in fact never met.

Jim, as he admitted in answers to questionnaires, was always worried that the office would run out of work, as it so nearly had done before the winning of the Stuttgart competition in 1977. In the 1980s, against the triumphant completion of Stuttgart had to be set the failure to win the Getty and the National Gallery extension, the collapse of the Latina library and Thyssen Gallery commissions, and the controversy and Public Inquiry involving No. 1 Poultry. After the WZB building the factory complex at Melsungen was the only big European project which was to be built during Jim's lifetime; commissions for a huge transport exchange at Bilbao (1985), for the Music Academy at Stuttgart (1987) and for the Milan gallery (1985) were all unfinalised, and Jim knew from bitter experience how often commissions failed to become solid. The building histories of the Sackler, the Clore and the Performing Arts Center had all been troubled. The controversies over the colours at the Clore had surfaced in the press, as had the decision to demolish Runcorn in 1989, and the threat of a lawsuit and near demolition at the History Faculty Buildings in 1983 and 1985. This kind of publicity, and the gossip that went with it, probably did more harm to the practice than anything that the Prince of Wales said. It kept alive Jim's English reputation as an architect whose buildings were likely to run into trouble. The Clore, the Tate Liverpool, No. 1 Poultry and a joint office and residential development in Carlton Gardens were the firm's only four commissions in Britain in the 1980s, and it was far from certain whether the last two would ever be built. Jim felt with some bitterness that he was not sufficiently valued in his own country, and would never accept or admit how much the problems of his earlier buildings had to do with this.

The exhibition at the Royal Academy in 1986 canonised Stirling, Foster and Rogers as the three big names in contemporary English architecture. Jim was the senior, and was given the central position in the exhibition. He was nine years older than Rogers, and eleven years older than Foster. They were to some extent his disciples, and he had passed on to them their first important job. But he was conscious that they both had bigger offices and more work than he had. They had profited from his mistakes. Rogers was to be knighted in 1990, Foster in 1991, Jim not till 1992, just before his death.

Jim had always had an awkward relationship with architects who could be considered rivals, even when he liked them and admired their work. He kept up a semi-playful rivalry with Foster and Rogers. One of the features of the Royal Academy was a projected bridge across the

Thames designed by Rogers. This was shown in the form of a large model crossing a long shallow sheet of water, which ran down the centre of the main gallery where Rogers's work was on show. Jim put up a member of his office to emptying a bag of goldfish into this pool. It was a tease that ended in disaster, since the goldfish were absorbed into the recycling machinery and cut to pieces.

Jim's friend John Miller recollects a conversation between Jim and Foster, which left Jim far from happy. Both were summering in houses in the South of France. The Stirlings went to lunch with the Fosters, and something like the following dialogue took place at lunch:

Jim: 'Do you take this house every year?'

Foster: 'Well, I own it, actually.'

Jim: 'I suppose one has to decide between a house in the country in France or in England.'

Foster: 'Well, I have one in England as well, actually.'

Jim: 'I would find commuting to and fro at weekends too much of a bore.'

Foster: 'Well, I travel up and down in my helicopter.'

Jim gives up discomfited.

But when Jim was asked by the *Evening Standard* in August 1991 to name three post-war buildings in London that 'will stand the test of time' he named Foster's Sackler Galleries at the Royal Academy, and Richard Rogers's Lloyds Building in the City, along with Ron Herron's 'Imagination' building in Store Street: 'The sheer exuberance I feel in them is similar to being in a great (light-filled) classical interior.' He had already written to Foster on 12 June: 'I was at the Sackler last night and this is just a note to say how elegant and good I think your galleries are, – and a very clever solution. I'm very pleased – particularly in the current climate – i.e. Paternoster. V. *big* congratulations, best wishes, Jim.' Such a letter from Jim was a great rarity.

Honours, prizes, exhibitions, international reputation, travelling the world, lecturing to packed audiences, were all very well, but what Jim wanted to do was to build. He was not building enough, what he did build was usually built with too little money, the search for more building work was exhausting and full of disappointment, and he was always worried that he would cease to build at all, as had so nearly happened before the Stuttgart competition was won in 1977. His life was full of tension, and the 1980s were at least as bad in this respect as the 1970s. His compulsive eating was due, in part at least, to this. So was his prickliness about the press and about any kind of criticism.

The stress of his life and his overweight made him a constant worry to his doctors, accentuated by the fact that he disliked going to see them, hated the idea of hospital, and seldom did what he was told he ought to do. As his GP puts it, 'He was never rude, but he was an obstinate pig-headed chap.' This led to disaster at the beginning of 1981. He delayed taking action when he was in pain, and ended up with a burst appendix and peritonitis. He was operated on in the Middlesex Hospital in London, as a National Health patient, and nearly died. He was back at work by the spring, but when he was on holiday in the South of France that summer his stomach ruptured at the end of the appendix scar. It was a Saturday night; with great difficulty Mary got hold of the local doctor, who 'calmly put Jim's intestines back in place' and possibly saved his life. He was taken to a hospital near Toulon and then flown back for another operation and further treatment in the Middlesex Hospital. While he was recuperating he had further complications from a trapped nerve, resulting from lying with his great weight on one arm.

He was left with a considerable antipathy to the Middlesex Hospital, which he held responsible, perhaps unfairly, for his trapped nerve. The staff had had their problems with him. He came into hospital with an ancient mackintosh, and insisted on wearing it instead of his dressing-gown. The nurses hated it, as a health hazard, and a disgraceful object. Russell Bevington's wife, who was a matron at the hospital, was deputed to reason with him, but to no avail. He seemed to cling to it as a symbolic link with the outside world.

Renewed efforts were made to get Jim to lose weight, but only for a short time towards the end of the 1980s with any success; he managed to lose as much as three and a half stones, but all too soon put it on again. Quite apart from any question of stress, he loved drinking and good food too much. He continued to travel the world and amaze his friends and hosts by his gargantuan capacities. His figure suffered, but on the other hand these trips abroad, working or on holiday, or a bit of both, were amongst his happiest times.

He loved the semi-outdoor Italian life in cafés and restaurants, and Italian towns, especially Rome, Bologna, and above all Venice. When he was teaching in Venice, the School of Architecture put him up in a little sixteenth-century house in a piazzetta near the Palazzo Mocenigo. Francesco Dal Co, the Head of the School, called it the House of the Cats, because of the extended family of Venetian cats which congregated in the yard behind it. Mary came out for each visit, along with one of the children in rotation, and they spent happy times wandering, and eating and drinking in Harry's Bar and elsewhere. Francesco Dal Co became a new friend, and introduced Jim to the Palladian scholar Manfredo Tafuri.

Jim, Tafuri and Dal Co spent hours together in cafés, Tafuri sketching to illustrate points about Palladio for Jim, in his quick, vivid, nervous calligraphy, and Jim drawing on top of Tafuri's sketches. Tafuri thought Jim the greatest living architect.

His period at the American School at Rome was another good time. He was given his own apartment. Frank Stella was the visiting artist in that year, and had the apartment below him. Mary and the children came out some of the time to stay there, and went on expeditions with him. Robert Kahn, who had been Jim's student at Yale and gone on to win the Rome Prize, had already spent a year at the American Academy. When Jim was offered the position of architect-in-residence he agreed to come on condition that Kahn stayed on another few months, basically to look after him 'not in a spoiled way', as Kahn puts it, 'but because, for all his boisterousness, he is a very shy man, and likes to be taken care of'. 'So Jim came to Rome, and for whatever time he was there . . . which was off and on, like two or three weeks at a time . . . we just spent all of our time together. We went all over Rome, we took a lot of day trips, and we planned one very long trip North, with the Fellows. Because he was the Resident, he was supposed to give a lecture and plan a trip, so basically, I planned the trip, and Mary came on it too.

'What was really interesting for me was that I came quickly to realise that his knowledge of history was very peculiar. He had an incredible eye for looking at something that nobody else wanted to look at, odd buildings that he would know about that no one else would know about, or that he would see and love, and there were buildings that every art historian, and probably every first-year architecture student knew, that he'd never even heard of.

'He took a lot of pictures, with that little tiny camera in his giant hands; I always remember that. I think he just adored being in Rome. I think that is the happiest I've ever known him. Sometimes Mary and the kids were there, and sometimes they were not there; it would depend when he came. There's a Christmas pageant at the Academy every year, done for the children. The background was painted by Frank Stella and Jim dressed up as Father Christmas, beard and all, and Mark Strand, who became the Poet Laureate of the United States, dressed up as Mother Christmas.'

Jim always enjoyed going to Ireland, and got on especially well with the members of the large Irish contingent which passed through the Stirling, Wilford office, both in London and Germany, and returned to Ireland to start their own practices and look after Jim when he came over. His Irish lectures were always packed, and accompanied by much genial drinking in Dublin bars, and the visit which he, John Tuomey and others made in 1981, to see the buildings by Lutyens on the island of Lambay, has acquired a legendary quality.

Lambay is only three miles from the mainland and thirteen miles from the centre of Dublin, but visits to it seemed like explorers' expeditions, owing to the erratic communications and the nature of Lord Revelstoke, the son of Lutyens's clients, who lived on the island like a hermit, alone with an elderly housekeeper, a bottle of whiskey, a wireless set by which he communicated to the mainland through the nearest lighthouse, and his memories of Lutyens, whom he always referred to as 'Uncle Ned'.

The Revelstoke boat was out of order, and the efficient modern launch with its own kitchen hired to take the party over proved to be a battered boat equipped with a single gas ring, on which Billy Hatch, the owner, heated up kippers. The propeller fouled up, the boat was becalmed, and while someone dived under it to see what could be done Billy Hatch set an alarm clock and announced that if it went off before the propeller was freed, the tide would have gone out and the boat would be stuck on a sand bank. Jim got in a state because he had a plane to catch, en route to Washington to collect the Pritzker Prize.

All ended happily, however. They got to the island, Jim hit it off with Lord Revelstoke, and was intrigued and amused by him, as he darted to and fro, showing off the buildings and Lutyens's drawings: 'Look at this, Sir James. Yes, Sir James. You're quite right, Sir James. Uncle Ned always said the same, Sir James.' He loved the architecture, which he felt had just the right combination of the serious and the off-beat. But when Philip Johnson expressed a wish to go to Lambay too, Jim told him that he would never survive the journey.

Geoffrey Howe was Foreign Secretary from 1983 to 1989, and had Chevening House and 1 Carlton Gardens as his official residences in the country and London. A big joint birthday party was given for Jim and Ben at Carlton Gardens in May 1984, and the Stirlings regularly went to Elspeth and Geoffrey at Chevening for lunch on Christmas Day and on other occasions. They were still spending family holidays every summer in France, at Barfleur and down further south, either with their friends Santa and Timothy Burrell, or in a rented house of their own, often close to one rented by Geoffrey and Elspeth Howe. Santa Burrell had been Santa Raymond, Jim's sailing friend in the late 1950s. She had three children, Tabitha, Jemima and Joshua; Tabitha was Jim's god-daughter. Santa and her au pair girl, Janine Murray, were the two women in the photograph of Jim on the beach, which he stuck up on the mirror in his office.

The Burrell property contained four houses, one of which would be occupied by the Stirlings. There was a swimming pool in which, as Santa remembers, 'the six children would play silly games for ages, and then Jim would say, "It's my turn. All out." Everybody would have to get out, and would moan and groan. Jim would spend ten minutes swimming very slowly up and down, with everybody glowering at him.' He swam, and read a lot, and sunbathed, turning pink but never brown; he signed himself 'Pink Jim' in the visitors' book. The Burrell children remember how his yell 'BEN!!! KATE!!! SOPHIE!!!' would echo round the property. 'He was a bit of a tyrant, that's for sure. He was incredibly tough, on Kate and Sophie particularly. But he was lovely, he really was. He was amazingly generous to us. He used to give Joshua a hundred francs, for carrying his luggage and things like that. He gave us little figures from a pottery shop near where we lived, which looked just like him. They were of penguins with big noses. Their noses were just like his nose, and he signed them for us.

'He liked to play games. He was always good for a laugh. We had long tables with plastic tablecloths on them. We'd all sit around the table and pull up the tablecloth, and then pour water on it. The water would trickle down, and end up on someone's lap. Jim thought that was absolutely hysterical. It wasn't competitive, it was just to make some poor person soaking wet. They would be sitting there happily eating away, and suddenly the water would come running down the tablecloth into their lap.'

There was a lot of eating at restaurants, often with the Howes or other friends holidaying or living in the neighbourhood, and of genial boozing by Jim and Timothy Burrell. Once the two of them raced back down the winding road from the restaurant to the house, Timothy in his BMW and Jim in his Citroën. Jim overshot the turning to the house, had to reverse into a side lane, and found the back wheels of his car hanging over a cliff. The children in the back of the car were panicking. 'Jim was completely calm, because it was a front-wheel drive, and he got back somehow.'

Their own home life went on to much the same pattern. In the late 1970s Jim began to buy Victorian furniture, as well as earlier pieces. Martin Levy, who worked in his family firm, H. Blairman, in Mount Street, has good memories of him both as a buyer and as a man. 'He used to drive his big black BMW into Mount Street, put two wheels on the pavement, and cross the road to our shop. He made pretty instant decisions with things that we showed him. He either liked something, or didn't like it. There were some strange criteria. Tables that he bought for the office had to have wooden tops, because he didn't like leather tops when it came to using them at the office. He used to put his hands on things and shake them, and if they were too shaky, that wasn't any good either. And when it came to working out whether things were going to fit or not, he used to measure down the table with his hands and say, "Well, I'll go and see if it fits and give you a call." And he used to call within an hour, when he got back to his office. He didn't like chairs with castors; that was another non-possibility.

'He was very positive. It was just straight in. You could never persuade him to buy anything – bar once. I can remember showing him a pair of hall chairs – very strong, very simple design, but very architectural and geometric. I knew they were things that he would like, or ought to like. I didn't get very much reaction when he came in. Anyway, I said to him, "Really, I think these are things you'll quite like." So he said, "Okay, I'll take them." He took them back to the office, and sent us a cheque. He put a note on the cheque, saying "Thank you very much for persuading me."

'The things that we had back from him were interesting as well. There was an E.W. Pugin writing table that he had for a short while. It was a little too elegant, in the sense that it was satinwood, with white and gold paint on it, and it didn't quite fit into the severity of the rooms. So that came back to us, and went to the National Gallery of Victoria, in Australia. We sold a pair of Aalto chairs for him – one of those ended up in the V & A, and I'm not sure that the other didn't also. I remember another piece which he bought, a large side cabinet attributed to Owen Jones, and thought to be made by Jackson and Graham. It was in the main room for many years, and was only ousted when he bought a piece that was slightly better in scale for the room. So that came back, and is now in the Metropolitan in New York. It's interesting how things which he acquired visually have moved into interesting subsequent homes.

'I don't think he had the instincts of a furniture historian. He was quite knowledgeable, he had all the standard works, and I wouldn't in any way diminish the intellectual interest he had in furniture, but first and foremost he was a visual collector. He was not a collector of the type that appeared to be doing an ego trip. It was simply that he enjoyed being surrounded by things; they looked completely at home. There was nothing that was just there to fill a corner. Everything was used. I remember he had a small neo-classical cabinet with columns just inside the dining room, which was full of all his slides. Things weren't placed in a conventional way. The big room was a mixture – neo-classical and modern furniture, a big Gothic sideboard that was nothing in particular, a hi-fi from the flat, that he didn't upgrade, and a bronze bust of himself. It was a wonderful mixture of things, and a nice house to go and have a whisky in the evening, on your way home.'

The big dinners were still taking place, and Jim was still being a people player. Robert Kahn remembers that, 'If Colin Rowe was in Town, Jim would invite Ken Frampton, and then he'd look over at me after some wine, and he'd wink and say, "Let's talk about Frank Lloyd Wright," because he knew that one of them hated Frank Lloyd Wright, and the other one loved him. He'd actually get them in fights; he'd get them going.'

One evening Alberto Sartoris, by now a very old man, came to dinner. Jim had met him in Rome. Jim told him how much his book *Encyclopedie de l'Architecture Nouvelle* had meant to him. Sartoris said, 'Please don't flatter an old man,' so Jim produced the book, to show how he had valued it so much that he had had it bound in white fur fabric, by now very dirty. Sartoris stared at the curious object in amazement.

Robert Kahn had come on from Rome to work in Jim's office, and was often invited for Saturday suppers. 'It was always the same routine. I would buy smoked salmon in a package, and three bottles of Margaux, a very good one; we both liked it. I would go over to the house, and of course Jim would be angry with everybody, as he always was round his house; you know, sort of being curmudgeonly. Then we'd go into the kitchen, and he would get his phenomenally beautiful martini shaker and we'd have, I think, quite frankly, three or four martinis. Then we'd sit down, and Mary would cook a steak . . . it was always exactly the same meal. Mary would cook the steak, and Jim would start to eat, and then she would start the next steak, so that no one ever ate the meal at the same time, because she could only cook one steak at a time. We would go through I think all three of those bottles of wine, and then one night I remember there was some catfood, and Jim and I started to bet Sophie that she wouldn't eat the catfood, because we were pretty drunk. So we opened the can up and she kept raising the stakes. I wanted to let her out of it, but Jim just wouldn't let up, and so finally we got the stakes up to about ten pounds, I think, and she actually put this catfood in her mouth. I start to hand her the money, and he goes "Uh Uh, she has to swallow it". . . this is her own father. I was photographing the whole thing; it's all documented. He made her swallow it, just a little bit, and then he gave her the money.'

Jim loved his cats. The family's cat history had started in the early 1970s with a black and white moggie cat called Tom. Then, towards the end of the 1970s, they acquired a Russian Blue kitten. Jim's publisher

Gerd Hatje, who was house-sitting for the Stirlings that summer, named it Ruskin. According to Ben, 'It was lovely, a really friendly fantastic character, but after about two months it got run over in the street. Dad cried then, I remember. We all did.' Jim buried it in the garden, and its grave was marked with one of the big stones which the Stirlings used to collect on a beach in Normandy and bring back to London. In April 1984, Mary gave Jim and Ben Russian Blues on their birthdays, Tom for Jim and Jerry for Ben. Tom died before Jim, and was buried in the garden by all the family, in one of Jim's blue shirts. Jerry lived on until 1997.

Robert Kahn was intrigued that, 'Here was this big gruff man, and he loved those two little cats of his; he just adored those little cats. He'd tend to like anything that was exaggerated, either as being too small or too big, or too long. He liked either things that were low and flat, or tall and thin. I remember that if you went to a hotel, you always had to steal for him those tiny little thin hotel pencils. For a birthday of his, when I went over to visit once after I stopped working for him, I bought him I think a thousand thin little grey pencils that said JS on them. And he loved these. It was either that, or the one that he used to teach with, which was this metal thing which was very short and fat. Like everything with him, it was always anything but what was the right proportion. It was always his odd way of looking at things. It was quite full of dichotomies.'

Jim seldom gave praise at home, and often found fault, especially when there were guests there. He told off all his children and could be putting down and sometimes downright rude to Mary. All this could be upsetting to his friends, or even to casual visitors to the house. It did not alienate his family; they were confident of his love and knew what fun he could also be. Mary Stirling cannot see what the fuss was about. She knew Jim; he was not always like that; it was just an act that he put on; she did not take it seriously.

He used to lose his temper with Sophie and her friend Jessica, at Saturday suppers in the kitchen, because they could not stop giggling together. 'We'd get sent out of the room. That's the time when he used to get really angry. He used to call us the giggling idiots.' When Kate was a teenager he was always telling her off for wearing her skirts too short and for her appearance generally. 'He used constantly to tell me to put more clothes on. So I used to smuggle clothes out of the house and change outside. That's kind of natural, I suppose, in a father. I was a very obvious-looking person, far too obvious, I think, for Dad. I had dyed blonde hair, all that kind of stuff. He didn't like that.' Kate rebelled against him in some ways, but 'if he ever asked me to do anything I'd do it for him'. Looking back, she thinks that 'when he was critical about my appearance I don't think for a minute that he did that just to be nasty. I think he did that for a reason, and that was to toughen us up for the world, which is a big bad world, etc.'

Like many men who had been wild in their youth he disliked it when his daughters started to go out in the evening, and fought a rearguard action to stop them doing it. Sophie has vivid memories of running in rebellion out of the house, and her father jumping in his car to pursue her, and the sound of the car engine as it revved up behind her. She shot off down a side-street and took refuge in the house of a friend.

Jim still found it difficult to show or express affection. He was very close to Sophie, and they both had strong feelings for each other, but in later years Sophie sometimes found being on her own with him painful. 'I'd have the TV on or something. I just couldn't handle sitting talking to him, because it would just be too uncomfortable. It was just too intense.' Kate remembers a conversation that she and Jim and her friend Belinda had, when they were staying in the South of France. 'We had this conversation about family, her and I and Dad. I was saying that there had never been any physical contact in our family, obvious kissing or hugging, or whatever. I was commenting that this had probably influenced me in my relationships with my male partners, and Dad found this very interesting, and was very interested to hear what we both said. . . . I didn't really miss it, because I didn't know it. I don't think it's really scarred me, or anything like that. I think Dad felt bad about it, though.'

Tension could accentuate his less likeable characteristics. He became eager for flattery and attention. Walter Nägeli describes Jim's visits to the Berlin office. 'He was very much a person who always wanted to be the centre of attraction. He came once or twice to Berlin to have a party. If there was a conversation and no one cared about him which occasionally happened, then he felt left out, and started making fun noises, and making faces, just to draw attention.' Nägeli was recollecting after he and Jim had fallen out, but Mary was at one of the parties and confirms the description; she was surprised, because it seemed so unlike him.

It was not difficult for those who did not know Jim well to dislike him. He made no effort with people who were not on his wavelength. To them he could seem unforgivably rude, although he did not mean to be so. It was hard to make contact with him unless one shared his interests, and these were very limited. As a young man he had read quite widely, but in his middle years he read comparatively little outside his subject, except for occasional biographies; shortly before he died he began to read poetry again, and went back to Auden who had been a favourite in his youth. He had almost stopped listening to jazz, but he liked classical

270

Jim in outline in his chair

music, especially opera. On weekends he would spend hours lying full length on the Chesterfield sofa in the 'No-No' room, listening to music.

When drunk, frustrated or bored, he could misbehave and seem a 'coarse brute', as someone who suffered from this put it. But people who had to deal with him were often surprised and touched to find what gentleness there was in him. Marthe Moreau, an old friend of the Shand family with whom they usually spent a night on the way to the South of France, vividly remembers the tenderness and courtesy with which he treated her 80-year-old mother. Bob Maxwell's wife Celia Scott made a bust of him (not at his suggestion) and was apprehensive about sittings. 'I had always been terrified of him, but he was not terrifying at all.' He came to her for eight two-hour sittings, and sat peaceably listening to opera, or to Celia's architectural gossip, without comment or criticism about what she was doing. The bust is an excellent likeness, with all of Jim's monumental presence. It was cast in bronze, and installed in the big room. Jim liked it, and liked polishing things; he used to polish it himself.

To Robert Kahn it seemed that 'Jim really had multiple per-sonalities. To me at a personal level he was just the most giving person, one of the most giving people I have ever known. He took care of me, I think as his way of paying me back for taking care of him, but I also found him extremely funny, charming, warm, oddly enough I know women that have described him as being sexy ... all these kinds of things, because of his personality, his charm. But I think his myopia working on a project ... there was a price for that, and the price was sometimes his personal relations with people. He could be very hard on his family, and very short with them, which I used to find distressing, to be quite honest, and he could be almost the same with people he didn't care for. People would come up, very enthusiastic to meet him and all that, and he would almost slap them off, not in a cruel way, but just have nothing to do with them. So there was that incredibly warm, charming, friendly, generous side when you were part of that little circle, and then there was another part of him that was quite short with people, and irritable, and not always as kind as he could be. In the office he had this remarkable ability to focus, to just concentrate on the subject in hand. He was irritated if something got in his way, and he was never distracted. It was just so myopic. But one pays a price for that sometimes.'

For Martin Levy, 'I think he knew himself very well; he knew what he wanted. He was no one's fool. I think he was very kind and generous; or certainly, he always was to me. I think it would be fair to say there was a sort of shyness about him, and a modesty about him, which was extremely endearing. It really was only in the few years before he died, as

I became a little older and knew him a little better, that I really began to enjoy the conversations that we had, and feel more comfortable and more confident. As a younger person, encouraging though he was to students (and I used to often see students up there in the evening, you know, working and so on), he did take getting to know. He was quite difficult to get through to. You would sometimes make a comment about something which, in one's naïveté, you perhaps felt was appropriate, and get very little response, and therefore not be quite sure what he was thinking. But as time went by I found him far more responsive, and far more direct, and far more conversational.

'If you have to sum it up in essence, he was one of the nicest people. It's a silly word in a way, but he was just a delight to deal with, because he was passionate.'

FOURTEEN

THE BROKEN CHAPTER

On 9 July 1986, Mr Gutman, of 46 Craven Walk, N.16, was working from a ladder on the side of the flyover which takes the Westway across Edgware Road. A bright green briefcase fell out of the sky and dropped at the feet of his ladder. He descended, examined its contents, ascertained that it belonged to J.F. Stirling, of 75 Gloucester Place, and returned it to that address. Michael Wilford confirmed receipt on 10 July: 'We thank you very much for returning it to us, and we will be in touch.'

On 9 June Jim had written to the President of the RIBA accepting, on his and Mary's behalf, an invitation to the Gold Medal presentation on 8 July. 'I have a German architectural colleague staying with me', he added, 'and I would be very grateful if she could be invited. Her name is Marlies Hentrup.'

Marlies Hentrup was in Jim's Master Class at the Dusseldorf Kunst-akademie. She had come over to London with a group of his students, on a tour of buildings in England which she had helped to organise. Jim gave a party for them at 8 Fitzroy Square, into which the office was about to move, and the students spent the night sleeping on the floor there. On 9 July they set off with Jim for a tour of buildings in the West Country. Jim drove separately with Marlies, and it was on the way out of London that the briefcase incident occurred. Jim suggested, on his return, that the back window had been left open, and that the briefcase had been sucked off the back seat; or that the briefcase had been left by mistake on the top of the car, when they got into it, and had been dislodged on the flyover. He later told Catherine Martin that Marlies Hentrup had thrown it out of the window, but she denies this. The incident was a little mysterious; but the briefcase dropping from the sky does seem like a messenger announcing that something new was happening in Jim's life.

Marlies Hentrup was twenty-five years younger than Jim. She was, and is, small, dark, pretty, outgoing and vivacious, with an infectious giggle. She had first met Jim when he gave his inaugural lecture at the Kunstakademie in 1977; she was not yet a student herself, but she was introduced to him before the lecture. She had been in England in 1975, had seen and admired the History Faculty Building, and bought the Black Book. At that time she was studying for her diploma in architecture at Aachen. She went on to get the equivalent of an English postgraduate degree at Dusseldorf; at first she was studying under another professor, but in 1980 Jim encouraged her to become one of his students. Dusseldorf was a part-time course, and she was also working as an architect in Aachen. She was married and had two sons, aged six and seventeen in 1986.

In 1981 Marlies became Jim's 'tutor', the term given in Germany to the student who organises the professor's schedule, generally looks after him, and if necessary meets him at the airport or station. In 1986, shortly after the English visit, she joined the staff at the Kunstakademie, and worked with Jim as his assistant teacher there, until he retired as professor in 1989. 'I think he was always very interested in me, or attracted to me. I think we both got attracted about architecture, and because we had such a lot of common interests. We liked talking to each other about everything. He was interested in my architecture and my sensibility about architecture, and that is how our relationship started. I wasn't only the pretty face. I think it took a long time until we fell in love, and I have the feeling that we knew each other very well before this happened.'

He had started an affair with Marlies just before she came to England in 1986. Jim was always extremely susceptible to women, and never made any attempt to disguise his feelings; Cathy Martin thinks that he enjoyed playing the part of a dirty old man. He could be a bottom-pincher and foot-rubber; he said to Dorothy Girouard 'You look as though you're very passionate' (she was so startled that she spilled her glass of red wine over the tablecloth), and no doubt he made similar remarks to others. He loved gossipy and teasing conversations with pretty women and with his daughters' friends or his friends' daughters. He sometimes came down from New Haven to New York with a student in tow and his relationship to them was a subject of surmise among his New York friends. There were rumours of affairs; but he told his daughter Kate that up till 1986 he had been faithful to Mary. Certainly Mary had never had any feeling that their marriage was threatened. Marlies Hentrup was different, although at first Mary did not appreciate it. She had realised immediately that the two were having an affair, but she did not take it too seriously. Morton Shand had been an incessant womaniser, but his marriage had survived; it was a pattern that she was used to.

According to Cathy Martin, 'it was just before we moved from

Gloucester Place to Fitzroy Square that I realised the affair was serious. Before that he used to come back from Dusseldorf saying that there was this beautiful woman . . . and "you see, the trouble is, the man's around". We just used to pooh-pooh it, because Jim was always going on about women . . . It was comical watching him; when a beautiful woman was around, he was like a wee boy. He was always shifting, and he'd be fiddling with his hands a little; almost awkward. It was quite endearing to see. So he always talked about Marlies, and then she came over. Well, she is a beautiful-looking woman and I thought she was very nice. They went off places together, and then it dawned on me, and I was quite shaken. But Jim just laughed, and said, "It's all right, Cathy; don't worry about it", you know, saying it wasn't serious between him and Marlies. But I think it got too serious for Jim to control.'

From 1986 until his death Jim travelled round Europe and the world with Marlies, sometimes on student outings from Dusseldorf organised by her, sometimes accompanying him on lecturing or business trips, or to conferences, sometimes straightforwardly on holiday. They went together on student outings to different places in Germany, and to Vienna, Copenhagen, Brussels, Bruges, Ghent, Istanbul and Bursa. Marlies went just with Jim to Chicago, Indianapolis, Los Angeles, and twice to New York, to Brussels, Portugal, Madeira, Prague, Barcelona, Finland and Scotland, twice to Sicily and Japan, at least twice to the South of France, three times to Paris, and many times to Italy, especially to Venice. They spent summer holidays with Marlies's young son Till in a rented house at Serreta in Liguria; Jim loved the relaxed informality of this unfashionable seaside town, its neighbours Imperia and Porto Maurizio, and the little medieval towns in the Ligurian hills. He inevitably saw much of Marlies in Dusseldorf and elsewhere in Germany, and twice visited Stirling, Wilford's building at Melsungen with her. She drove round the South of England with him in the summer of 1987, and came many times to London, sometimes on her own, sometimes with Till.

Jim's odyssey round the world with Marlies usually involved visiting buildings. They saw a great many together, new and old, from the Greek Doric temples of Sicily and the mosques of Istanbul to buildings by Jim's younger contemporaries. Echoes of what they saw are to be seen in Jim's work. He was attracted by the soft colours and slightly irregular plaster-work of the Thorwaldsen museum and other neo-classical buildings in Copenhagen, and when he came back from the visit changed the specifications for the Wissenschaftszentrum in Berlin accordingly. The huge fat columns of Sinan's Blue Mosque in Istanbul seem to relate to the even fatter pseudo-columns, cut away at the bottom to provide information desks, in his competition design for the Bibliothèque Nationale in Paris. He loved these fat Turkish columns, which echoed his own proportions; Marlies photographed him standing against one of them, one of the countless photographs of them separately or together, which record their relationship.

Looking at the photographs, reading what they wrote to or about each other, talking to Marlies or to people who saw them together, leaves one in no doubt. They were very much in love. This was not just a physical relationship, although this side of it was obvious. It was based on affinity and shared interests. Marlies was a passionate admirer of Jim's buildings, and perceptive about architecture generally; looking at buildings together and talking about them was an important part of their relationship. She teased Jim and made him laugh. If he was in a bad mood she could laugh him out of it. They were obviously happy and relaxed together. At times Marlies could be emotional and demanding; she could seem a bit of a princess, but Jim did not necessarily dislike that.

With Jim, who for so long had put the bulk of his energy and his emotional force into architecture, it was as though some kind of barrier had been broken. He was sixty-two in 1986, had nearly died five years before, and may have thought that he did not have all that much time. He was ready to let himself go in a big romance, and being Jim he let himself go zestfully and at times outrageously. The relationship brought him times of great happiness. It may have made him less lonely and more accessible. But it also brought problems, and conflicts of love and loyalty, with which he was unable to cope.

Marlies's feelings about Jim, and her memories and impressions of him, come across when she talks about him: 'What was so nice about him, he never said "I'm so important". He never name-dropped. He did not behave like a star . . . I didn't feel his age, because he was so young in his spirit and open-minded, and interested about everything. He wanted to stay young, perhaps.

'He really liked good design, good things . . . he was interested in them, and touching them all the time, to get a feeling . . . I think everything he loved he was touching.

'He disliked people with principles, and said "they are very dangerous people, they don't have an open mind". He was very shy . . . He sometimes played the fool, when people took photographs of him especially. I think he was hiding behind this.

'He was not a very talkative person. When I met him first he wasn't used to talking intimately. He sometimes said that I should remind him to talk to me, because he forgot about talking to people. I realised that he was a very lonely person, emotionally. Then he started to talk about important relationships he had had in his life. I think he opened up . . . I think he was a bit worried that he couldn't show his emotions or that people saw him as a very cool person, which was not true. I think he was afraid his children never saw that he was a warm person, or that he was tender. For me, I got such a lot of warmth from him, I never got from any other person.

'I think I was able to show him new aspects in his life and about life, and that somehow I brought him back to life.

'. . . We honoured each other. I honoured him as a person, his work, and I think he also honoured me a lot as a person, with my work, with my ideas. It was a big friendship, and it was a companionship, it was somehow everything. It was not only love but it was very trustful. We had a very happy, a very intimate and also a very erotic relationship. And also I would say a spiritual relationship. There was a spiritual attraction or connection. Somehow it didn't matter that we didn't live together or didn't see each other. In our spirits we always were together. Well, but we tried to be together as much as possible.'

The affair became increasingly important in Jim's life. He never made a proper will, but on 15 January 1988, he wrote an 'Act of Will' in Marlies's favour, witnessed by Catherine Martin (two witnesses would have been needed to make this legally valid). He left her all 'my framed drawings, prints and photographs that are in the office'. He made it clear that these drawings did not include any of his own architectural drawings, with the exception of 'the coloured drawing by JS of the Manhattan houses'. In fact the architectural drawings belonged to the practice and were not Jim's to give away without Michael Wilford's agreement; Michael was upset that Jim did not ask him at the time, and this was the one part of the deed of gift which was not honoured after Jim's death.

In 1989 in a long, passionate and moving love-letter written to Marlies from Tokyo, he said how much he wanted to live with her permanently. He repeated this early in 1991 in a letter to his and Douglas Stephen's friend Colin Glennie, written after he and Marlies had been staying with him near Siena, for New Year's Eve. 'I wish my luck with Marlies could be made permanent . . . We send you some pics – part of our collection of photographs of our good times together in exotic places – our substitute for a proper life together.'

The obstacles to a proper life together were serious. It would involve the break-up of their marriages, their homes, and probably their work. Till was at school in Germany, and Marlies knew that if she came to

England she had in German law no chance of getting custody of him without his father's agreement, even if it seemed acceptable to uproot him from Germany; it was not until the end of Jim's and her relationship that a possible arrangement was worked out. Jim had little free money of his own with which to buy a house, or a flat of what he considered acceptable quality. And if they became married was there a chance that, as Marlies puts it, "love would go away"? Catherine Martin is down to earth about this. 'Marlies was beautiful, and he did love her. He cared about her and everything else, but I think they were in Cloud Cuckoo Land. They went to the most wonderful places, had the most wonderful times, but it was irresponsible, you know, no responsibilities with it, and that helped to make the love beautiful.' For this reason she thought that they should try living together, to see how it worked out.

Catherine's affection for Jim and loyalty as a secretary meant that she was much involved in the relationship. It was she who bought the tickets, booked rooms in hotels. It was she who found flats and houses for them to look at, when they finally decided to do so in 1991. It was she whom Jim sent out to do his Christmas shopping for Marlies. 'Jim would say to me "I want a handbag. Go out and buy a handbag. It's got to be black". "I want to buy her a suit, but it's got to be black . . . cashmere." I would go off shopping with a list for Marlies. And I loved it; it was great fun. I bought them all, wrapped them all. Jim did buy her jewellery, right enough. He chose that himself. But quite often he'd come back with jewellery and call me in, and say "put that round your neck", or "put that on your finger", and I'd have to parade up and down like a little mannequin for him to decide if he liked it or not.'

There was a time in the early days of the affair when Jim pretended not to know who Marlies was when she telephoned him at the office, and instructed Cathy to make double entries in his diary: ostensible engagements in longhand, real engagements in shorthand. Catherine felt she had to let Michael know what was happening. He and Jim had a talk and Michael said that Jim's life was his own affair, 'as long as it didn't compromise me, or affect the partnership'. In the last few years the affair was taken for granted in the office. As Michael Wilford puts it, 'I think the office reacted with amusement to the affair, not horror or outrage. I suppose in a way one saw it as an extension of his character – his some- what outrageous and unconventional character. I think he enjoyed flouting convention.' A room upstairs, where Jim used to shut himself away for long telephone conversations with Marlies, became known as the 'love-nest'.

Marlies came often to the office, and was brought to office parties by

Jim. Once they hid Marlies behind a door in the partners' room when she arrived, and when Jim, who had been out of his room, came upstairs, Catherine said ' "We've just had a phone call from Marlies in Dusseldorf. Plane's cancelled. She can't come." They had planned things for that evening, and Jim's face . . . he was like a little boy, you'd stolen his chocolate. Then he walked into his room, and of course Marlies was behind the door. The door was closed, and then he came out shaking his fist at me. He was quite good fun like that.'

When Jim and Marlies went together to look at a house for sale in Islington, and ran into a friend of Jim's, he came back to tell Cathy about it, roaring with laughter. As she puts it, 'most people having an affair would have been quite upset, thinking "Oh dear, we've got a problem", but not him. He just thought it was a joke.' It was incidents like these that used to make her imagine him making a film of himself; 'he was an imaginary cameraman, and Jim Stirling was the star, wooing this woman, and it was all like a fairy tale, and he almost started to live it.'

To Elisabeth Farkashazi, the only other woman in the Dusseldorf group and a good friend of both Jim and Marlies, it seemed 'Kismet', an inevitable coming together of two people who 'understood each other without talking'. She had watched the slow development of the relationship with sympathy, and encouraged Jim when he confided in her his worries as to whether a relationship with so big a difference in age could last. She felt that Jim was escaping from an English way of life which did not suit him. 'He didn't like stiff and strict things . . . What he wanted to do was to live the rest of his life with Marlies.'

But for Jim it was not simple. He had times of doubt and despondency, which perhaps he revealed more to English friends, to Cathy Martin and Ulla Wilke in particular, than to Marlies and friends in Germany. The possible break-up of his marriage was not something that he took lightly. To Cathy 'he kept saying "What shall I do? What shall I do?" Every time we had drinks in the office, and Jim had a couple of drinks, it would all start. "Cathy, come over here", and he'd start talking about it. It was on his mind, and he said three or four times that on at least one occasion he had tried to break it off, and that Marlies wouldn't have it. Which is why I always swore he would never live with her. He'd say "What would you do?" He always said that, and I'd say "You know what I'd do, Jim. I'd break it off. It's just crazy, the way you're living".' But Marlies denies that Jim ever tried to break it off, 'though we often talked about our doubts and difficulties'.

All this time the rhythm of previous years was continuing. Jim was still living at home, still travelling and holidaying with Mary and his family; they were still having happy times together. Amongst other outings he went with Mary to receive his award of the Jefferson Prize in Virginia in 1986, and to open a Mackintosh exhibition and receive an honorary doctorate in Glasgow in 1990. It gave him great pleasure to be honoured in the city of his birth, and he was delighted that Elizabeth Schwartzkopf, whom he admired, was amongst those given a doctorate with him. He and Mary went together to see Sophie in Los Angeles in 1991, and Kate in New York. He went with her and Sophie to judge a competition at Cordoba in 1987, and to collect the Praemium Imperiale Prize in Japan in 1990. The yearly holidays at Barfleur and in the South of France continued. For a long time the children knew nothing about Marlies.

Jim's relationship with Marlies could be difficult for his friends, most of whom had great affection for Mary. He was not sensitive about this. He appeared surprised and somewhat put out when John and Su Miller refused to talk to him about Marlies, let alone lend him their cottage in Cornwall for a weekend with her. Others accepted the situation. Jim took Marlies to dinner with Ed and Margot Jones, and with Ulla Wilke and Laurence Bain in London, and to lunch with the Wickhams; Douglas and Sandy Stephen lent them their house in the South of France. Marlies became friendly with all of them, perhaps especially with Ulla Wilke; they could talk together in German, which could be a relief for Marlies in London. In Venice she became good friends with Francesco Dal Co and his wife, and she and Jim went down with them to stay at the Villa Malaparte at Capri and worked there on the Venice competition design. Francesco thought that they should get married: 'it is better to have two people unhappy than four people unhappy.'

The relationship gradually began to be talked about, first by Jim's friends, then by other architects, as Jim travelled with Marlies more and more openly, and she was looked after as his 'partner' at lectures and conferences abroad.

In 1987 and 1990 Jim collaborated on two building projects with Hentrup Heyers, the practice which Marlies had started in Aachen in association with Norbert Heyers, at the same time as she was working part-time in Dusseldorf. The first of these was for a redevelopment around the Kaiserbad in Aachen, the second for a new building on the Lido for the Venice Film Festival. Jim took time off from his own office's work, with Michael Wilford's agreement: 'He said that he was acting as a consultant; all the work would be done in Germany, etc. etc., so I acknowledged that and I didn't raise any objection.' As in office schemes, the design team drew up options which were presented to Jim for his input, in this case either on his visits to Aachen, or when drawings were taken or faxed over to him in London.

The Kaiserbad commission developed out of Marlies's thesis project at Dusseldorf, for a scheme centring round the ancient mineral spring at Aachen, which Charlemagne had used. The head of the City Development Department saw and liked it, and asked her to develop it as a solid commission, in association with an architect of more experience. Jim offered to collaborate, and Norbert Heyers joined with Marlies to set up an office in Aachen. By 1989 the scheme had reached foundation level, when there was a change of local government in Aachen, and it was cancelled. The Venice project was the result of a similar collaboration, but was a competition entry, for ten invited architects, not a commission; it was won by the Spanish architect Rafael Moneo.

The two schemes are of quite different character. The Kaiserbad scheme is a pleasing exercise in the manner of the WZB in Berlin and of Collage City: three small separate buildings (one of them enclosing the thermal spring) loosely grouped round a square. The Venice design is for a single building, almost completely transparent on its public sides, where a zig-zag screen of glass sheltered under a great projecting roof terrace looks towards the sea and the nearby hotel and casino. A ramped entrance is designed to show off the arriving stars and VIPs to the crowds on the adjacent piazzale. On the roof terrace 'up to 3,000 people can congregate and mingle informally, against the spectacular backdrop of the Adriatic'. A long canopy at the back of the terrace rises up and down like a wave and adds a note of frivolity to the design.

The differences between the two projects reflect a change in the character of the work being done in the Stirling, Wilford office in the intervening four years. Frank Gehry sees this as Jim 'trying to reinvent himself as a Modernist'. The designs were all for extensively glazed buildings, with no obvious historical references, except to earlier buildings of the Modern Movement. The only one of these projects to be built during Jim's lifetime, and one of the best known and successful of his buildings, is the little bookshop for the Electa publishing company in the Biennale Gardens at Venice.

The project originated with Francesco Dal Co in 1989. The 1991 Biennale was to centre round two events, the 68th International Venice Film Festival and the 5th International Exhibition of Architecture. Francesco Dal Co was organising the latter. Besides having brought Jim to Venice to teach there, and co-operating with Thomas Muirhead on the exhibition of Jim's drawings in Bologna, he had been involved for many years with Electa, the biggest architectural publishing company in Italy. As Muirhead puts it, 'Francesco eventually synthesised his involvement in Electa, his involvement in Venice, his involvement with the Venice Architecture Biennale, his involvement with Jim, his involvement with me, and who knows how many other involvements into a single operation which enabled him to invite Stirling to design the new Bookshop. This was a high-risk operation conducted against formidable odds in the minefield of Italian politics, and had the intention of bringing off a commercial coup for Electa whilst simultaneously making the new building – Stirling's first for some considerable time – the centrepiece of the 1992 Biennale.'

For Jim the project turned out to be almost pure joy, all the way through; even the crises were enjoyable, or only marginally involved Jim. It was technically a project of Stirling Wilford's, but in fact Jim did it on his own in collaboration with Muirhead, an Italian architect, G.B. Cuman, of Building Project Studio, and Cuman's colleague Giovanne Leone. Jim did not ask for a fee. It was almost a holiday job, small, manageable, enjoyable, and involving regular visits to his beloved Venice.

It was perhaps less enjoyable for Muirhead, who was responsible for the drawings, for liaising with the Italians, and generally for overseeing the project. Moreover 'Stirling was the most uncommunicative man I have ever known, and any form of interchange with him was largely a matter of trying to guess what he was thinking'. The design process took the familiar path: dozens of little sketch designs by Jim or Muirhead, then alternatives drawn up more formally by Muirhead and edited, altered and ultimately transformed by Jim.

The Biennale Gardens are at one end of the Grand Canal, beyond the Arsenal and a little out of the centre. They consist of what is, in effect, a grove of trees, with the pavilions of the various nations involved in the Biennale scattered around the grove. The site for the bookshop, in the middle of the grove, was chosen when Jim was in Venice with Mary in the summer of 1989. The idea of a pavilion in a park was present from the start. Two alternatives were considered, one rectangular, one octagonal, like a baptistery. Jim at one time favoured the octagon; Muirhead produced and preferred a thin rectangle, entered centrally in the middle of one long side; one advantage of this, as Jim recognised, was that it could be fitted into the existing trees.

Jim then took the rectangular version and transformed it. He moved the entrance to one of the thin ends, and rounded the other end, and the metaphor of a boat immediately emerged. He raised the roof in the centre, to provide a clerestory, and the metaphor of a church emerged as well, along with, as Muirhead puts it (paraphrasing Jim), the 'intelligent and sensual idea' of 'the bright clear light of a Venetian summer, filtering down through overhanging branches, through the clerestory overhead, and throwing the shadows of dancing leaves onto the pages of an open book'.

The building became Jim's 'bookship-boatshop' or 'bookshop-boatship'. It was as though it had floated off the Canal and landed among the trees. A round turret at one end, sporting the Electa logo, was like the funnel of a tug, or a miniature tanker; but the pipes which projected all round the flat surrounding roof suggested abortive oars of a Venetian galley. The deep overhanging roof suggested the high deep-eaved thatched roofs of agricultural buildings in the Veneto. Apart from the entry-end, which was white-plastered, like a cut-out silhouette of a church, the bookshop was all of steel and glass, with the roof boarded internally under the steel, and externally sheathed in copper – a last-minute suggestion by Cuman, which Jim welcomed. The plan of the paving round the shop was an enlarged version of the plan of the shop, but in reverse, with the curved end in front of the building. The end result was a beautiful little building, deceptively simple, full of sophistication and resonances. It recalls Jim's comment on a building by Philippe Starck which he saw in Tokyo in 1990: 'simple, elegant and humorous – how many new buildings make you smile?'

Once the main lines of the building had been decided on in 1990, Jim largely left the realisation and detailing to Muirhead and the Italians. There were various hang-ups and problems, and it was not until March 1991 that work began on the foundations. There were only six months in which to build it. Just before work started Jim had come out to Venice, met the construction team, listened to the problems and given one instruction: 'don't make it too perfect'. This relaxed everyone, according to Muirhead, 'and we set to work to achieve a simultaneously sophisticated and handmade effect'. He believes that Jim would have developed this concept still further, if he had lived: Humane-Tech perhaps, rather than High-Tech.

The steel framework of the building was made and erected in workshops on the mainland, and then carried by barge in sections to Venice and the Gardens. Jim must have got great pleasure from photographs of sections of his building, and their sunburnt semi-naked attendants, floating past the façade of Palladio's San Giorgio Maggiore. But when Jim came out, a week before the opening, it seemed impossible that it could be finished; two days before the opening there was still no floor; the carpenters were a tough lot from the mountains, and Jim bet the foreman a bottle of whisky that he would not get the floor ready on time. He lost his bet; and the building was finally finished a few minutes before the opening.

Jim's 'boatshop bookship', drawn by Jim for Till

Jim was happy and relaxed on his Venice visits at this time. Sometimes he came with Marlies, sometimes on his own. Francesco Dal Co was married to a beautiful young American architect, Gretchen, and she and Jim got on very well together. She remembers one game that he played with her and others. 'When you would travel with him, or sit down and have lunch, or start to drink . . . he would put his hands out and say "OK, with one movement of your hands, one movement without stopping, you have to design the building" (and he would choose the building) "in air". He had these incredible hands; they were like paws. You could tell him any building in the world, because it was a game that was like a challenge. He was fantastic. He could design any building, just with a movement in the air with his hands, and it was absolutely recognisable. That's really extraordinary, because it's one thing to be able to do it with a pencil. He would do it just sitting at a table with his hands.

'He loved drinking Bloody Marys. I remember him sitting at Harry's Dolce, which is on the Giudecca, laughing about some game he was making up again, and drinking a giant Bloody Mary. We would have normal Bloody Marys, and he would order this giant one, and I think they had a giant glass only for him. I think he had drunk two of them, and he had his back to the water, and I remember him laughing, laughing, laughing, laughing, and all of us pulling his chair, because his chair was falling, and he was about to land in the water.'

The 1991 Biennale was Jim's Biennale. To Gretchen Dal Co it seemed that 'he was like a king'. Architects from all over the world, famous and less famous, were there. Most of his London office came, and his Stuttgart office hired a bus and drove down to Venice to be there too. A group of his Dusseldorf students were there. Marlies came, and so did her elder son, Karsten. Many of his friends were there, Barbara Jakobson, Kenneth Frampton and Douglas and Sandy Stephen among them. His drawings were on show in the main room of the British Pavilion. His bookshop was a success, he knew it was a success, everyone liked it and was talking about it. He and Marlies were obviously lovers, and everyone was talking about that too. Douglas Stephen, watching them from behind, said that they seemed to be walking one foot above the ground. Most of the people there had been unaware of the relationship. As Barbara Jakobson puts it, 'There was a lot of buzz buzz buzz . . . that was when the big buzz started.'

There were numerous parties and events, official, private, and spontaneous: a party at the Villa Malcontenta, a dinner party in the Dal Cos' apartment, dancing in the Piazza San Marco, the official opening of the bookshop on the morning of 7 September, followed by a lunch at Harry's on the Giudecca in Jim's honour, a Beaux Arts Ball in the Biennale Gardens that evening, and the official opening of the International Exhibition of Architecture the next morning. Jim never wore a jacket in Venice, just his inevitable shirt, which by now had changed from blue to green; and the Dal Cos and others had teased him about what he would wear for these official events. '"Jim, what are you going to do? You have to buy a coat. You have to wear a jacket, you know, because it's so formal." So he started laughing, and he said "well, I have a surprise for you". And in front of all the photographers who were around at the inauguration, he pulled out of a bag a green hat, exactly the same colour as his shirt.' It was in his green shirt and hat, and his flapping spotted tie, that he made a speech, while the head of the Carabinieri in Venice, in splendid uniform and helmet, stood by him like a bodyguard.

All through the Biennale Jim showed a preference for being with his friends and 'his people'. He spent much of the Dal Cos' party in the kitchen with Marlies and Karsten, discussing his and Marlies's relationship. After the inauguration of the bookshop the important invited guests were to be ferried over to the Giudecca for the lunch. Manuel Schupp had come down with the Stuttgart contingent, and remembers how 'there was this luxurious big boat waiting, and about half of the office were around Jim, and there was this man, checking who was important, etc. etc., and who could get on the boat for this luxurious lunch party. And when we were accompanying Jim to the boat, he suddenly said "well, you all join me". And he said "they all belong to me", and waved us into the boat. So we had this wonderful luncheon over there . . . some of us were obviously dressed much more simply than the other people, as people from the office didn't expect to be invited to such a formal thing.

I think it caused slight irritation, but it was a very nice gesture from Jim.'

Thomas Muirhead recalls thinking, as the boat went across, that if it sank the cream of world architecture would be lost.

The Beaux Arts Ball that evening was a glamorous affair. Gretchen Dal Co describes it. 'They had a big dance, a big ball in front of the bookshop at night, in the garden. It was packed with people: I mean, all of the garden was packed with people, because there was also the Cinema Biennale. Everybody wanted to come to this party. As the students of the School of Architecture had come, as well, they didn't have invitations, so they waited until two or three o'clock in the morning, and then they all came in. Jim was really famous at the School of Architecture, because he had come here in Venice to teach, and he was also so famous as an architect, that the students were just dying to see him. So they came in. And at some point they danced what in Italian is called a Giratondo, which is like when you do Ring a Ring of Roses. Everyone holds hands, you know. And Jim was in the middle, in his green shirt, and all the students, even the youngest of them, the first, second and third year, were dancing around him holding hands. He was in the middle, laughing and dancing, like the King. Like a Shakespearean king. And that was really beautiful.'

In a questionnaire from France, which Jim answered that October, one of the questions was 'Since you began working as an architect, what changes have you undergone?' He answered 'Full circle – more than once.' Perhaps a spiral would be a better metaphor: a series of circles, or near circles, related to each other, but different. By 1991 Jim was clearly moving out of the phase which had started with Dusseldorf and Stuttgart, and returning to something more like his work of the 1960s – but by no means entirely like it. Frank Gehry's phrase 'recreating himself as a Modernist' seems to relate to what was happening, even if Jim might not have put it like that.

Jim had told Marlies that it was refreshing working with Hentrup Heyers, because their reactions were less predictable than those from his own office; he had gone off on his own with Thomas Muirhead to design the bookshop; he had said to Gretchen Dal Co, not seriously, but perhaps semi-seriously, 'I'll come to Venice, and we'll open a little office.' Michael Wilford talks of Jim's 'gradual withdrawing from the day-to-day activities of the office'. He seemed to be withdrawing himself in order to make a fresh start.

In the golden glow of the Biennale it may have seemed that Jim was on the threshold of a new decade of achievement: a new architecture and perhaps a new life. In fact the next nine months were to contain much uncertainty and distress, and to end in his death. However youthfully he was behaving, he was 67 years old, dangerously overweight, and leading an exhausting life. For some time a weakening had appeared in his stomach lining, and an operation was needed to deal with it, unless Jim was to have another rupture. Jim hated hospitals, and kept putting this off; he ought anyway to lose weight before undergoing an operation, and although he had lost a substantial amount in 1990, he had put it on again. His architecture was moving, but he was still, to judge from his output, not certain where it was moving to; the bookshop was a beautiful building, but it was only a pavilion, and the firm's bigger, still-unbuilt projects at Singapore, in Tokyo and elsewhere, interesting though they were in their suggestion of a possible 'humane-tech' style, did not have the epoch-making quality of Leicester and Stuttgart. He was spending too much time away from his work. At the end of the year he was deeply upset by the sudden death of Douglas Stephen. Above all his personal life was still full of unresolved problems.

Mary was hurt and angered by the Biennale, by being shut out of enjoyment of Jim's triumph herself, and by having what should naturally have been her place so publicly occupied by Marlies. Kate had come back from eight weeks in the South of France. 'I hadn't been home for a long time and I was very happy and very healthy and in great spirits. I walked into the house, and my mother was sitting at the kitchen table, and she told me "Your father's here, and he's been having this affair for X amount of years", and she was really upset that Marlies had gone to the Venice Biennale, and she hadn't. Which I think was totally correct.' Up till that moment Kate had been unaware of the affair, and Ben and Sophie still knew nothing about it.

The rest of the year passed in a low key. Jim and Marlies were still planning a future together and looking for a house or flat, but there was always a gap between what Jim wanted and the money available to buy it. Marlies came to London, and she and Jim went shopping together for a possible new home in Portobello Road and Camden Passage. She was with him when he lectured in Paris in early December, and in Helsinki in February. Jim took her to Glasgow and elsewhere in Scotland at the New Year.

In January Jim took a big step; he asked his three children individually to the office, and told them about Marlies. In fact, Kate knew about her already and Ben had at least a suspicion. He told each of them in a slightly different way, and they had different reactions. He told Ben about the relationship and that he did not know what was going to

288

happen. Ben 'didn't get heated, but I was definitely very negative about it, and very anti'. To Kate, her father 'said that he'd been having an affair with this woman, and he was thinking of living with her, and this, that and the other, and what did I think of it? He wasn't just telling us, he was asking our opinion, because he didn't know what to do. I just said to him "I can't answer that for you. I'll support you in whatever your decision is". I felt bad because of my mum, at that point, but what can I do? I don't want Dad to be unhappy. He has to make his own decision. But he really was so lost . . . What I think about the situation is that it was all well and good for Dad to have this woman who was X amount of years younger than he was, glamorous, bit of excitement, but my dad could not live without my mother.' Sophie was taken by surprise, and 'just said "I'm not going to live in the house, if you're going to move . . . I want to go with you". I don't know if I really meant that, but I just said it anyway. I remember when Dad told me he kept going on about how he didn't want to be thought of as a cold fish. He meant the fact that he wasn't showing us emotion, me, Ben and Kate.' All three children were moved that he had told them, and that he seemed to ask their advice. Kate 'thought that he was taking my opinion seriously, for the first time. And our relationship really changed.'

Jim wanted all three children to meet Marlies after their talk with him. A planned meeting with Ben never took place, but Kate and Sophie went out to a meal with her and Jim. The occasion was not unfriendly, but, as was only to be expected, not at all relaxed. In order that they could all get to know each other better she and Jim booked a small house near Grasse for some of the summer, and hoped that his children would come and stay there, to get to know Marlies and her sons, as well as staying in the house which had been rented near Uzes for the usual family holiday.

In March Marlies and Till came over to England, and stayed a night with Cathy Martin, along with Jim. Cathy's husband had moved to a new job the previous autumn; Cathy had left the office, and gone to live near Brighton. Cathy agreed to keep a look-out at the property section of the *Financial Times* for them but she did not find Jim cheerful. 'We had dinner together, the five of us. Till went to bed early. Marlies went to bed, Ian went to bed, and Jim and I just sat talking, and he got more and more doleful. He was very, very sad that night. I said "Oh, for goodness sake, there is an easy answer to this. Why are you killing yourself?" Even in the morning, when they were leaving, Marlies had come downstairs; she was looking for her handbag, and Jim was standing at the bottom of the stairs, all ready to go, and he said, out of her hearing, "What am I going to do? I don't know what to do. What am I going to do?" That was the last time

I saw him, to speak to, and I said "You know what I think, Jim. Chuck it. Just chuck it". That's the words I used to always use. And that was it; off they went.

'He always said "I do love Mary. I respect Mary", and then I used to get really wild with him and say "Well, why the Dickens are you putting everyone through this? Why don't you just do what you feel?" But for some reason, and I don't know what it was, he didn't break it off.'

Jim and Marlies were together for much of April and May. From 19 to 27 April they were in Sicily, partly on holiday and partly for Jim to give a lecture; they went to the baroque city of Noto, where Jim was distressed at the recent earthquake damage, and sent a postcard to Francesco Dal Co, asking what could be done about it. Early in May they went to Melsungen, to take slides to be shown in Japan later that month, at a symposium on world architecture at Nara. There they found a selection of the architectural circus, including Meier, Correa, Kurokawa, Hollein, Foster, Portzamparc and Jencks. There was an exhibition of the bookshop and cinema designs, and a film of Jim's work; he lectured on Melsungen and sat on a jury. Marlies felt that he had 'too many balls in the air and was over stressed'.

From Japan they went on to Los Angeles, where Jim was lecturing. Frank Gehry gave a dinner for them, and found Jim 'like a child' with Marlies. 'He seemed very happy with her. She seemed very adoring, and I know now that she truly loved him.' Dinner was in a restaurant and Julia Bloomfield, who was there, remembers how Jim was delighted with a little model train which went round and round the outside wall, as part of the decor.

They also met up with Jim's good friend Craig Hodgetts. Jim was delighted to visit the Library which Hodgetts had recently designed on the UCLA campus. 'He was really excited and running around, and that made me feel good.' Hodgetts had 'vaguely heard' about Marlies, but had not met her before. He found himself 'very comfortable' with Jim and her. 'We went for a long drive; we had a nice breakfast at the Gardner Hotel. Jim had been sleeping in the sun the day before, so he'd gotten himself really bad sunburn, and Marlies was putting lotion on his shoulders. I was a little bit shocked; because I didn't know about Marlies. But he made me feel quite comfortable, and I was simply trying to be discreet. They had a really genuinely good time together. That's what was very clear. This was something that had a lot to do with pleasure, and it had a lot to do with adventure. There was a kind of spontaneity about Jim that I hadn't seen. Usually with Jim it was almost as though he was always playing a role, always putting a twist on things, and being the entertainer in a group. With Marlies, he seemed not to have that so much. So we just had a very fine time.'

At the end of May, after his return, Jim and Marlies went out from the 26th to the 29th for the opening of the Braun factory at Melsungen. It was an on-the-surface celebratory but in fact awkward occasion, owing to Jim and Michael Wilford's difficult relationship with Walter Nägeli; they were worried that he would stand up and claim the design as his. Marlies says that she had never seen him so tense.

A possibility now arose of a commission to design a University library in Kentucky. The office was in need of work and Jim, although he was exhausted, flew out on 6 June with Michael for an, as it turned out, abortive interview, which exhausted him still more. He was back in London on 9 June. It is scarcely surprising that his stomach weakness now developed into a hernia. He consulted his doctor about this, and was told that he should have an operation as soon as possible. He hated the idea, and could not bring himself to make a firm date. He did cancel two trips that he was due to make, to Naples with Marlies to receive an architectural award, and to Arc-et-Senans in Franch-Comte to open an exhibition of his work. Instead he spent the weekend of 12-14 June with Marlies in Dusseldorf.

On Saturday 13 June, while Jim was in Germany, it was announced that he had been given a knighthood. The announcement came as no surprise to him, because he had been approached about it some time before, in the usual fashion. He was a little embarrassed at seeming to be taken into the Establishment, to which he had never felt that he belonged. There was never any doubt of his accepting the offer, but he followed a pattern not uncommon in these situations; when it was made he asked Michael if a knighthood would help the practice, and when Michael said that it would, used this as a reason to accept. He and Mary, with Ben and Sophie, had dinner together and went to the opera at Glyndebourne, to celebrate in advance of the announcement.

He came into the office on Monday morning to receive congratulations, and a certain amount of teasing, from colleagues and friends. The telephone rang incessantly. Laurence Bain went out from the office to buy a toy sword, for a fake dubbing; Andrew Birds, who had left the office to set up in independent practice with Richard Portchmouth and Mike Russum, drew a caricature showing an enormous Jim being knighted by a midget Prince of Wales.

By the time Bain had returned Jim was no longer there, and he never saw the caricature. He had been attacked by acute internal pain, had gone to the doctor and then home to his bed. Mary found him there when she came back from her office. He should have gone straight into hospital, but the pain got less bad, and he put off going in till the next morning. When Sophie came home later that afternoon, she was told by her mother 'Oh, Dad's not very well; you'd better go and see him.' She went up to the bedroom, and Jim started to play the fool, writhing and making faces to pretend he was in enormous agony. It was a way he had, to disguise the fact that he was in some discomfort.

During the night Jim's pain got much worse, and he was taken by ambulance to the Hospital of St John and St Elizabeth in St John's Wood. Mary was told that he must be operated on in the morning. Mary was there when he had his pre-med, and rang after the operation to be told that all had gone well, but that he had not yet come round. She went out to lunch with Douglas Stephen's widow Sandy Boyle. She rang again after lunch, and was told that he had been removed down the road to the Intensive Therapy Unit of the Wellington Hospital nearby; there was no such unit at the Hospital of St John and St Elizabeth. She went straight round to the Wellington.

What should not have been a hazardous operation had gone badly wrong. Evidence later showed that during attempted intubation in the operating theatre Jim had inhaled the contents of his stomach. A second intubation was made with success, and a naso-gastric tube inserted. The operation followed without event, but when he was coming round he pulled out his tube. Refitting this when the patient is semi-conscious is a job for an anaesthetist, but his anaesthetist had left the hospital, and repeated attempts to contact him on his mobile phone were unsuccessful. Jim was without a tube from 13.00 to 14.40. In this period his chest was X-rayed, and his lungs were shown to be suffering from acute congestion.

For reasons unconnected with Jim another anaesthetist came into the hospital at 14.40 and was at once asked for his help. He refitted the tube, but realised that Jim was in serious danger, and arranged for him to be taken immediately to the nearby Wellington Hospital (there were to be legal proceedings after Jim's death and the case was settled out of court in November 1996).

Marlies had talked to Jim several times on the telephone on Monday, and had been ringing through the day on Tuesday, without contacting anyone who could tell her what was happening. At 5 o'clock she learnt that Jim had been moved to the Wellington. She talked to Cathy Martin's successor, Lisa Groom, who contacted Mary. Mary said that it would not be right to stop her coming to London. It was a public holiday in Germany; she had difficulty in finding a flight, and her son had to drive her to Brussels to catch a plane. Ulla Wilke's husband Laurence Bain met her and drove her to her hotel; Kate and Sophie picked her up there, and took her to the hospital. Jim was conscious, but his throat was full of tubes, and he could not speak. He tried to make jokes, with his hands and eyebrows, to give the impression that he was all right.

On the first day in the Wellington Jim was able to write some notes to Mary. He held Mary and the children by their hands. 'He held out his hand', Ben says, 'for us to put our hand in, and then clutched it, really strong . . . I'd never had that experience before.' On Thursday he had to be sedated and by Friday he was in a coma. A two-bed room was made available to the family at the hospital, and they spent the nights there.

Marlies had to go back to Aachen at the weekend, but was back on Monday; she spent the night at the hospital, and for the rest of the week stayed with Sandy Boyle, and was at the hospital daily. All this time there were evening conferences with the doctors. Michael Wilford had flown back from Singapore on Friday, and was constantly at the hospital. The Howes, Jim's sister Oonagh, Russ Bevington, Cathy Martin and others were coming in to see Jim. When Oonagh spoke to him he twitched, as though he recognised her voice.

It was a nightmare time for all of them. On Wednesday Jim was dialysed, as a last resort; he showed signs of improvement, and Sophie went home for the night. Mary, Kate and Ben stayed at the hospital. At two in the morning they were told that he was dying, and went down to his bedside. Sophie was called from home and arrived just in time. Marlies and Michael were also telephoned, but did not come until after he had died. The family stood round the bed. Ben remembers how he watched the heart monitor. 'It didn't stop suddenly, it just faded away.'

EPILOGUE

Jim was cut off when still at the height of his powers, and his sudden and unnecessary death sent waves of shock to friends and architects around the world. Many of them, along with his daughter Kate, spoke movingly at the meetings held in tribute to him, at the Royal Academy in London on 2 November and at the Guggenheim Museum in New York on 19 November. Three friends – Arata Isosaki, Manfredo Tafuri and Barbara Chase-Riboud – wrote poems about him. Special issues were published by the *Architectural Review* in December 1992, by the New York magazine *ANY* in September/October 1993, and elsewhere.

Inevitably he left much that was incomplete. A number of buildings designed during his lifetime were completed, and even started, after his death. The Irvine Science Library in California was completed in 1994, the Temasek Polytechnic in Singapore in 1995, the Music School in Stuttgart in 1996, No. 1 Poultry in 1998. The London office block in Carlton Gardens, designed in 1988, was only given the go-ahead in 1997.

The Irvine Library had been taken out of the hands of Stirling, Wilford and built under a local firm of architects, but the other buildings have been carried out in sympathy with his ideas by his office, since 1993 renamed Michael Wilford and Partners (incorporating James Stirling, Michael Wilford and Associates). Russell Bevington and Laurence Bain are the partners. All designs necessarily need amplification, and often changes, in the course of the contract, and these have, of course, been made without Jim, although as far as possible in his spirit. There remains the burning and unanswerable question: how would Jim's architecture, always so full of inventiveness and surprises, have developed if he had lived?

At the end of a biography one feels under some kind of compulsion to look back and sum up. What was Jim's status, as an architect and a man? What was his influence? I find it hard to do this except in personal terms. Jim's status comes from his having designed some extraordinary and wonderful buildings. I have always found them so, I find them so still, and I hope the biography has put across some of their quality to readers. One of the rewards of writing it has been the need to revisit them, or sometimes to visit them for the first time. I have driven through a bleak Cambridge day and come with a shock of surprise and delight on the History Faculty Building, glowing and gleaming in the rain and fulfilling to perfection Jim's ambition in all his buildings – to raise the spirits. I have sat writing a letter on the terrace at Stuttgart when overwhelmed by personal problems, and been, to some degree, sustained and comforted by the heroic quality of the architecture around me.

What was Jim's influence? I am tempted to draw an analogy between him and the eighteenth-century architect Nicholas Hawksmoor, with a side look at Hawksmoor's contemporary James Gibbs. Gibbs's buildings are always civilised and agreeable. They followed certain formulas, and as a result were easy to copy, and were copied, often very pleasantly, by architects and builders all over the English-speaking world. Hawksmoor's buildings were sometimes strange and not always successful, but they can catch and haunt the imagination in a way that Gibbs's buildings never can. They are highly personal and there is, virtually speaking, no school of Hawksmoor. Jim was closer to Hawksmoor than to Gibbs, though perhaps one should add that unlike Hawksmoor he needed a colleague or an office to 'feed his fire'.

I admire Jim because he was true to himself and his friends, was not personally self-seeking and did not compromise. But these are not the reasons for his extraordinary attraction, both as a man and an architect. It is hard to define this. I think of his description of *Strelitzia reginae*, when asked in 1991 to name his favourite plant: 'I admire this plant because it is asymmetrical, over the top, aggressive, brightly coloured and ambiguous (is it a bird, is it a flower?).' I think of what I was told by a former member of his office: 'Jim didn't like things that were too tidy, that flowed too sweetly.' I think of the couplet in Isosaki's poem: 'that inescapable craziness at the very heart of your spirit is what attracted me'. I think of Jim saying to Seymour Slive 'Why not?', and of Audrey Matlock's comment 'Jim was always game'.

Jim came to the Modern Movement when its pioneering days were over, and when many of its supporters believed that the solutions had been worked out for all time, and that all that was left to do was to apply them. His whole nature revolted against this kind of acceptance. He spent his life pushing forward; he was never satisfied; he was never in a rut. His dislike of 'good taste' was in a similar vein. Good taste implies working within accepted standards and doing, as a result, nothing that is uncomfortable. Jim liked giving people a jolt, in everyday life as well as

295

in his buildings. He was always game to try something new. He wasn't afraid of going to extremes.

But although his buildings could be extreme they were never overbearing. He was never a bully in his architecture, and only very occasionally in personal relations. He was a considerate and surprisingly gentle man. I remember when my wife and I spent the day in Bayeux, and returned to Barfleur in the evening. Jim was meeting us at the nearest station. We spent too long in a café, and missed the train. We went off for a walk, to pass the time, and somehow managed to miss the next train. We arrived on the third train. There had been no way of reaching Jim, who had been sitting for an hour or two in his big car, listening to opera on tape. He wasn't in a rage. He teased us gently, and that was all. We were surprised and touched. But Jim was full of surprises, at every level. He kept one guessing. He keeps one guessing still.

A NOTE ON THE SOURCES

The main sources for the biography have been interviews with friends, family and associates of Jim Stirling, and the office files of his architectural practice, supplemented by the personal archives in the possession of the family.

I. Interviews The majority of these are recorded on tape, but for some I only took notes. Their nature varies from long, in-depth interviews, to brief (but often interesting) conversations, some held by telephone. Transcripts of all the tapes have been typed out, and transcripts and notes add up to a detailed and very interesting body of information, memories and comments, only a small proportion of which I could make use of.

I have talked to (and in a few cases corresponded with) the following people, and to all of them I must express my grateful thanks for their help:

Jane Abdy, Katryn Adam, Noel Annan, Dick Archer, Laurence Bain, Arthur Baker, Mary Banham, Robin Bell, Isaiah Berlin, Russell Bevington, Peter Bicknell, Michael Blackwood, Julia Bloomfield, Phil Bobrow, Derek Bok, Mrs Bonfield, Alan Bowness, Charles Brewer, George Buchanan, Jemima Burrell, Michael Carmady, Peter Carolin, Barbara Chase-Riboud, Geoffrey Chester, Cristoffa Ciaionne (Owtram), Alan Colquhoun, Magda Cordell, Edward Cullinan, Joe Dawson, Judy Di Maio, Gretchen Dal Co, Professor Dierkes, Stuart Donnell, Marcel Echenique, Geoffrey Elton, Eldred Evans, Suzannah Fabing, Elizabeth Farkashazi, Herbert Fecker, Marianne Fecker, Norman Foster, Kenneth Frampton, June Furlong, Frank Gehry, Dorothy Girouard, Keith Godard, Alexander Gorlin, David Gray, Ilse Gray, Marina Gregotti, Vittorio Gregotti, Charles Gwathmey, Robert Harling, Eric Hardy, Julian Harrap, Jonathan Harris, Barbara Hayes, George Hayes, Karsten Hentrup, Marlies Hentrup, Malcolm Higgs, Craig Hodgetts, Patrick Hodgkinson,

Elspeth Howe, Geoffrey Howe, Gill Howell, Ada-Louise Huxtable, Janet Jack (Kaye), Barbara Jakobson, Charles Jencks, Philip Johnson, Ed Jones, Margot Jones, Robert Kahn, Anne Kerr, Fred Koetter, Leon Krier, Bruce Levitt, Martin Levy, Kenneth Lewis, Robert Livesey, M.J. Long, Sandra Lousada, Angus MacPherson, Cynthia Manners, Keith Manners, Paul Manousso, Catherine Martin, Phoebe Mason, Audrey Matlock, Robert Matyas, Celia Maxwell, Robert Maxwell, Richard Meier, George Melly, John Miller, Su Miller, John Mills, Marthe Moreau, David Moroni, Thomas Muirhead, Walter Nägeli, Evelyn Newby (Hogge), Frank Newby, Robin Nicholson, Eilis O'Donnell, Frei Otto, George Palin, Oonagh Palin, Peter Palumbo, Edward Parkes, Philip Parsons, Jan Pederson, Cesar Pelli, Barton Phelps, Jim Polshek, Alan Powers, John Prestwich, Cedric Price, David Queensberry, Santa Raymond, Brian Richards, Jacquelin Robertson, G.K. Robinson, Richard Rogers, Colin Rowe, Paul Rudolph, Joseph Rykwert, Ulli Schaad, Manuel Schupp, Vincent Scully, Seymour Slive, Vefik Soyeren, Robert Stern, Ben Stirling, Kate Stirling, Mary Stirling, Sophie Stirling, Quinlan Terry, Stanley Tigerman, John Tuomey, Drexel Turner, Renzo Vallebuona, Robin Wade, Siegfried Wernik, Michael Wickham, Michael Wilford, Ulla Wilke, Colin St John Wilson, John Winter, Mike Wormfield.

II. Office archive This major archive belongs to the James Stirling Foundation, and is referred to as Foundation Archive in the notes. Its main elements are:

1. The drawings
2. Photographs
3. Correspondence etc. files, especially Project and Personal files.

Project files: a very large collection, covering most projects in great detail, but only starting with the History Faculty Building, Cambridge (little in the way of archives, other than the drawings, survive for earlier buildings and projects, including the Leicester Engineering Building). It adds up to a formidable collection; there are, for instance, 82 boxes of files for the Clore Gallery alone. To make my research manageable, I drew almost entirely on the small run of the client-correspondence files in each group, supplemented by minutes of relevant meetings, often filed with the correspondence.

Personal files: these contain Jim's office correspondence and a great deal of miscellaneous material not tied to individual projects. The contents are seldom 'personal' in the normal sense, and include much routine correspondence of little interest, but scattered amongst this is biographical material of great interest. There are thirty boxes, starting in December 1977 and a more haphazard, miscellaneous Preliminary Box, covering material for 1976-7.

Miscellaneous files: among these I made use of files covering Jim's time at Yale, his work on the Manhattan planning project, and his work on the 'Black Book'.

III. Family archive Access to this was given to me by Mary Stirling. It includes letters, postcards, and a large collection of photographs, mainly arranged chronologically. Photographs reproduced from this collection are credited to 'James Stirling Estate', except for those taken by Mary Stirling herself, which are credited to her.

CHAPTER NOTES

Chapter 1. Young Jim

p.1   The story of Jim's conception was told by him to many
        friends, and by his mother to Colin Rowe, who related it at
        the memorial meeting held in New York in 1992 (see note
        on p.22). A copy of his birth certificate is in the Family
        Archive.
        Information about the earlier Stirlings derives from census,
        marriage and birth records held in the Registry House,
        Edinburgh.

p.2   Information about Joseph Stirling and the Frazer family from
        Oonagh Palin.

p.4   'Fascinated by beautiful drawings.' Article by Philip Purser,
        Telegraph Magazine August 1981 (typescript Personal File
        V) and by Deyan Sudjic, 'Stirling Revalued', *Sunday Times*,
        22 January 1984, both based on interviews.
        The photograph of Joseph Stirling in the garden belongs to
        Oonagh Palin.

p.5   Jim and Liverpool. For example, his letter to Raymond
        Andrews, 17 February 1978 (Foundation Archive, Personal
        File I), about the 'insipid mess' that had been made of
        Liverpool. On 4 March 1991 (Personal File XXVII) he
        declined the offer of an hon. Litt.D. from Liverpool.

p.6   I am most grateful to A.G. (Alan) Finch for information
        about Quarry Bank School and Bailey, and for
        communicating his list of distinguished ex-pupils of the
        school, his own memoir of Bailey, and other material. Jim
        Stirling's brother-in-law, George Palin, who was at the
        school shortly after him, also supplied memories, and Brian
        Bagnall, who was his contemporary, confirmed his nickname
        of 'Blimey'.

p.11   The bird-watching diary is in the Family Archive.
p.17   'Last girl in China.' Recollected by George Hayes.

Chapter 2. Jim in the Army

I have discovered too little about Jim Stirling's army career. The War Office records can provide only the barest outlines (letter from Ministry of Defence to Mary Stirling, 27 January 1995); the archive and museum of the Parachute Regiment in Aldershot can find no material. This lack must be in part due to the fact that his period of active service was so short, and so many of his contemporaries were killed or have died; nevertheless, people who served with him must still be living, perhaps unaware of his subsequent career, but I have failed to find them. Much of what information I have gathered came from Oonagh Palin.

p.18   Group photographs of Jim at Perth and Mons in the Family Archive.
        Colin Rowe's memories given at the memorial meeting held in New York on 19 November 1992, at the Guggenheim Museum, and expanded for publication in 'A Tribute to James Stirling', special issue of *ANY* (*Architecture New York*), September/October 1993.
p.19   Officers' Mess memories. Told to Philip Purser (see note on Chapter 1 p.5), and to Mary Stirling.
p.20   Glasgow and Mackintosh memories related by Jim in his speech at the opening of the Mackintosh exhibition in Glasgow in 1990 (text kindly sent to me by Alison Brown).
p.21   A Hulton Library Group photograph of parachutists at a briefing includes Jim. It seems not to have been published. It was probably taken in the winter of 1943–4 for an article on the Paratroops which appeared in *Picture Post* on 18 March 1944; according to a later article, 'The First Man to Land in France' (*Picture Post*, 24 June 1944), 'many of the pictures were stopped by the censor'.
p.22   The poems survive in typescript in the Family Archive.
p.23   Disability Pension. Information from a letter to Jim from the Department of Health and Social Security, 21 October 1987, confirming the continuation of the pension (Family Archive).
        Budden Statement. Copy in Family Archive. Jim referred to it in a letter to Kate Macintosh, refusing to join her anti-

nuclear Architects for Peace group, 26 February 1982. Foundation Archive, Personal File V.

p.24 Jim at Harewood. He told this story several times, e.g. in an interview with Jane Hardy 'Work in Progress', *She* magazine December 1984. Text in Personal File X.

Jim's time at Albany Barracks is documented by the inscription in two of his books.

p.25 Information about Jim's early affair from Barbara Hayes, and from Marlies Hentrup, to whom he talked about it in later years.

Chapter 3. Jim at Architecture School

The group photograph, reproduced in the first signature, was sent to Jim by a contemporary in the School, Richard S. Westmacott. He had no explanation for Jim's isolation.

p.27 'Back to 1946'. From notes for lecture (*c.* 1957) on 'Influence of Corb on me now and when a student', folded into the Black Notebook (Family Archive).

p.30 Liverpool School of Architecture. I have derived much information from the illustrated *Prospectus of the Liverpool School of Architecture 1941-2*, communicated by George Hayes. Jim's student portfolio in the Foundation Archive contains an incomplete selection of student projects and some early post-college designs.

p.32 Polish School. Jim to Tadeusz Barucki, 2 February 1983. Foundation Archive, Personal File VII.

p.33 'Embracing the orders.' Bernard Wilson to Jim, 5 December 1983, and Jim's response, 14 December 1983. Personal File VIII.

Jim on Beaux Arts influence. See his talk for Beaux Arts Week, Architectural Association, reported in *Architectural Design* November/December 1978; Royal Gold Medal Address, *RIBA Journal*, September 1980, pp.36, 38. His reference to Budden on quality in paper given at RIBA on 23 February 1985, *RIBA Journal*, May 1965. I owe the last two references to Charlotte Ellis.

p.36 'Modern architecture was to become the norm.' From *c.* 1957 lecture notes (see note on p.31).

Jim's library. Early purchases identified by Jim's inscription in them (he stopped writing his name in later years) or by

Charles Wilson and Medici Gallery labels. A few bills also survive in the Family Archive.

p.37   List of books. Jim to Peter Brown, 19 November 1984. Personal File X.

Jim in Bath. Postcard given to the author by Robin Bell.

p.38   'Stiff Art Nouveau designs.' Lecture given at Cambridge, 25 May 1980. Typescript of text in Personal File III.

p.39   Colin Rowe on early days. In a letter to John Jacobus, quoted in RIBA Drawings Collection *James Stirling* (1974) p.4.

p.41   Letter from New York. Given to the author by Robin Bell.

p.45   Memories of New York. 'Retrospective Statement' by Jim in *The Independent Group* (see reference for Chapter 4.)

p.47   Postcards given by Robin Bell to the author.

p.48   Thesis. Designs and accompanying text (the latter in box marked 'Lecture Notes') in the Foundation Archive.

Chapter 4. London in the 50s

For everything to do with the Independent Group, I have drawn heavily on the admirable *The Independent Group: Postwar Britain and the Aesthetics of Plenty* (Cambridge, Massachusetts, 1990), ed. David Robbins, published in conjunction with an exhibition in America and England. This includes, among much else, 'retrospective statements' by members of the group, and a reproduction of the catalogue for the 1956 exhibition 'This is Tomorrow'.

The standard monograph on Brutalism is Reyner Banham, *The New Brutalism* (Architectural Press, London, 1966).

p.58   Architects and the Picturesque. For example, letter by Alan Colquhoun reacting to article by Pevsner, *Architectural Review*, July 1954.

Chapter 5. Jim comes to London

p.68   Alison Smithson's collar. Bob Maxwell remember this being tied by Douglas Stephen, not by Jim.

p.75   The Rymans notebook. In the Family Archive and referred to elsewhere in the notes as Black Notebook.

p.80   The 'Paris Corbfinder' is in the Family Archive.

p.82   Postcards communicated by Colin St John Wilson.

p.85	For This is Tomorrow, see *The Independent Group* (note, Chapter 4).
p.86	For Lyons Israel Ellis, see *Lyons Israel Ellis Gray: Buildings and Projects 1932-83* (ed. by Alan Forsyth and David Gray, Architectural Association, London, 1988), with interesting contributions by David Gray, James Gowan, Alan Colquhoun, Jim Stirling, John Miller, Frank Newby and others, portions of which I have quoted.
p.87	'Jim would visit our house'. From the letter of condolence written by John Ellis to Mary Stirling (Family Archive).
p.90	'Notes for a lecture'. In the Black Notebook (see note on Chapter 3, p.27).

Chapter 6. The Leicester Explosion

p.96	'Huge though it was'. Obituary, Michael Wickham, *The Times*, 2 January 1996. Photograph of 'Poppet' in the Family Archive. I am grateful to Ed Jones for impressions of Douglas Stephen.
p.104	Colin Rowe, 'The Blenheim of the Welfare State', *The Cambridge Review*, 31 October 1959, reprinted in Colin Rowe, *As I Was Saying: recollections and miscellaneous essays* (ed. A. Caragonice, MIT Press, Cambridge, Massachusetts, 1996) I, pp.143-52.
p.105	'College members walking' . . . James Stirling, 'An architect's approach to architecture', *RIBA Journal*, May 1965.
p.106	Engineering Building, University of Leicester. None of the firm's office files survive for Leicester. In addition to my own interviews, I have made use of John McKean's comprehensive monograph *Leicester University Engineering Building* (Phaidon, London, 1994). McKean had the benefit of conversations with James Gowan.

Chapter 7. American Interludes

A loose file captioned 'James Stirling – Yale University File' in the Stirling Foundation Archive contains correspondence with Yale School of Art and Architecture and other American schools, together with pay cheques and documents re tax and social security. Another file, captioned 'James Stirling – New York File' contains correspondence with the New York City Planning Commission, bank statements, hotel bills, etc.

p.113   Edward Reynold's AA design is reproduced in McKean, op. cit., p.29.

p.114   Mary Quant on PVC, from *Quant by Quant* (Pan Books, London, 1967), p.139.

p.119   Postcards communicated by Colin St John Wilson.

p.128   Bird's-eye view. This view was not published in the report, and I have not been able to trace it.

Chapter 8. After Leicester

p.138   Letter to Financial Board. Foundation Archive, File CAM 38, Box 115.

p.139   Bologna. 'Anti Structure', talk given at Bologna University, November 1966. Text published in *James Stirling* (catalogue, RIBA Heinz Gallery Exhibition, 1974), pp.37-54.

p.140   History Faculty Building. In the Foundation Archive I have used especially File CAM 38, Box 115 (Correspondence with University Estates Management and Financial Board) and File CAM 32, Box 113 (Correspondence with Monk and Dunstone, Quantity Surveyors). I have also worked through the 'History Building File' kept by the Librarian of the History Faculty Building, which contains press cuttings, correspondence, and much material about the problems of the building as experienced by the Librarians and users.
Geoffrey Elton. His appreciation of the building comes from his letter about it to Minna Prestwich, St Hilda's College Oxford, 30 June 1967. I am grateful to Miss M. Clewlow, the College Archivist, for sending me a photocopy of the letter and other information.

p.146   Cape Canaveral. Alvin Boyarsky 'Stirling "Dimonstrationi".' *Architectural Design*, October 1968, p.455. The note to Charles Jencks reproduced in the Black Book, p.104.

p.147   Hodgetts and Pevsner. Related in Hodgett's perceptive 'Inside James Stirling', *Design Quarterly*, No.100 (Minneapolis 1976). Pevsner on History Faculty Building. *Buildings of England: Cambridgeshire* (Penguin, 2nd ed. 1970), p.217. On Leicester Engineering Building, 'The Anti-pioneers', *The Listener*, 5 January 1967, and Jim's letter of correction, 12 January 1967. Pevsner's remarks on the Modern Movement are from the same article. Pevsner on the Cripps Building, *Cambridgeshire*, p.156.

p.148   Zevi on Stirling. Article in the British *Olivetti* magazine, July/August, 1973, communicated by David Moroni.

p.149   Jim on Casson. The remark was related to me by several people, including Peter Bicknell, who heard him make it.

p.151   Letter to John Mills, 18 October 1965. Foundation Archive, File CAM 38, Box 115.

p.152   Monk and Dunstone on Sindall's. K.W. Monk to Jim Stirling, 23 April 1964. Foundation Archive, File CAM 32, Box 113.

p.154   Gavin Stamp article 'Stirling's Worth. The History Faculty Building', *Cambridge Review*, 30 January 1976.

p.155   University of St Andrews. Account drawn from University Court Minutes and correspondence, minutes etc. in the Andrew Melville Hall file (Professor J.S. Watson, Principal), University Archives.

p.157   Minna Prestwich and Geoffrey Elton. See note on Chapter 8, p.140. Her letter to Jim Stirling is in the Florey Building client file.

p.158   Florey Building. Client and other correspondence and Building Committee minutes are in Foundation Archive Files FBO 25 and 26, Box 99.

p.160   Runcorn. My account owes much to Jane Martin's book.

p.162   Mr Dutch. The cutting and Jim's letter about it are in Stirling Foundation Archive Personal File V.

          'The natives are friendly.' Postcard in Family Archive.

p.163   Olivetti, Haslemere. Client correspondence etc., in Stirling Foundation Archive, File BOH 10, Box 66. Monk and Dunstone correspondence Files BOH 2 and 5, Box 64. Polyplan (Plastic consultant) correspondence, File BOH 11, Box 74. I am grateful to Mr and Mrs David Maroni for talking to me and showing me his collection of cuttings and other material relating to the opening.

Chapter 9. Marriage, Home and Travel

Postcards and letters quoted in this chapter are in the Family Archive, in original or copy, unless otherwise stated. Much information was supplied by Mary Stirling.

p.165   Richards on Shand. J.M.Richards *Memoirs of an Unjust Fella* (London 1980) p.123.

p.166   John Betjeman on Mary Shand. From a letter to Bruce Shand, 30 December 1974, *John Betjeman: Letters* (ed. Candida Lycett-Green), vol 2 (Methuen, London, 1995), p.487, with a footnote on Mary Shand's father.

p.171   'The first antique furniture.' Interview and article by Marina Gregotti, 'In omaggio a James Stirling', supplement *Elle Decor*, October 1992. I am grateful to her for a tape of the full interview.

p.175   Mr Bush. I am grateful to Julian Fane for permission to quote from *Gentleman's Gentleman* and for further information about Mr Bush.

p.176   Shirts. There is a protracted correspondence about shirts with Henry Poole and Sons in Foundation Archive Personal File XIII.

p.184   Isfahan and Agra postcards communicated by Colin St John Wilson and Alan Colquhoun.

p.185   Jim on Aalto Medal. Letter to Jane Drew, February 24 1978, Personal File I.

Chapter 10. Big Jim and Stuttgart

p.187   The Black Book. The long and sometimes painful gestation of this, and the enormous pains which Jim finally took over its make-up and layout, are fully documented in the Foundation Archive file marked 'Correspondence with Verlag Gerd Hatje', kept in a box marked 'Books'. An early letter from Hatje, written to Jim on 11 December 1969, and hoping for publication in 'Fall, 1970', is in the 'James Stirling – Yale University' File (see note on Chapter 7).

p.192   Jim on *Oeuvre Complète*. In his *c.* 1957 lecture; see note on Chapter 3, p.40.

p.195   James Gowan complains. Information from John Harris.

p.198   Jim on Thomas Hope. Talking to Deyan Sudjic, 'Stirling Revalued', *Sunday Times*, 22 January 1984.

p.204   Letters from Frei Otto (20 July 1979 and 18 February 1982) and extract from the *Sunday Times* (25 October 1981) are in Personal File V.

p.208   Lecture on Neue Staatsgalerie. Typescript in Personal File XI.

p.209   Charles Jencks was in fact not at the actual opening, but there shortly before or after it.

Chapter 11. After Stuttgart

p.213   Sackler Museum. Client correspondence, telegrams etc., filed in Stirling Foundation Archive, File Fogg 14, Box 255.

p.217   Clore Gallery. Voluminous client correspondence, Building Sub-Committee minutes, etc. filed in Stirling Foundation Archive, Files C 86-88, 90, Box 138.

p.222   Articles on Clore. A bound volume of press cuttings on the Clore was given by Alan Bowness to Jim Stirling, and is now in the Family Archive.

p.226   Performing Arts Center, Cornell University. Client correspondence is in Stirling Foundation Archive, File Cornell 9, Box 92.

p.230   Jim's speech, Cornell opening. Given 10 April 1988. Copy of text in Stirling Foundation Archive, Personal File XXIX.

p.231   Telegram to Venturi, 25 January 1986. Foundation Archive, Personal File XIII.
Evening Standard. Letter from Jim, 15 August 1991. Foundation Archive, Personal File XXVIII.

p.232   Melsungen. My account is based on conversations with Walter Nägeli, Michael Wilford, Renzo Vallebuona and Siegfried Wernik, and letters to Michael Wilford from Wernik and Robert Niess. Letters from Jim to Nägeli following on the *Architects' Journal* piece are in Foundation Archive, Personal File XXVIII.

p.237   Palumbo to Stirling, 5 May 1984, and 16 July 1985. Foundation Archive, Personal File IX and XII.

p.241   Public Inquiry. Jim especially liked Sandy Wilson's evidence, which he got published in the architectural magazines *Zodiac* (Italy) and *A.U.* (Japan).

Chapter 12. The Office

p.245   'The Howe table.' Corrected information from Mary Stirling.

p.254   Inventory. Typescript copy in Family Archive.

Chapter 13. Jim Regnant

p.256 Pritzker presentation. The ceremony, and the lack of the figure, described in an article by Sarah Booth Conroy, probably from the *Washington Post*, filed in the Family Archive.

    Nîmes competition. Jim's notes, etc., filed in Foundation Archive, Personal File X.

p.257 Dusseldorf. See *Kunstakademie Dusseldorf: Architekturclasse James Stirling* (Berlin 1987), with introduction by Kristin Feireiss and Hans-Peter Schwarz, with contributions, in German and English, by James Stirling and Marlies Hentrup. An evocative album of photographs, presented by Jim's students on his retirement, is in the Foundation Archive.

p.259 Answers to letters all in Foundation Archive, Personal Files. Answers to questionnaires in the Personal Files, e.g. *Archi et Colonni* August 1984 ('having fun'), Personal File X; on skiing with Prince of Wales, letter to Papadakis 13 September 1989, Personal File XXII.

p.260 Prince of Wales. Jim on wireless sets, quoted in *New York Times* article, 4 March 1991, filed in Personal File XXVII. Letter from Palumbo, 28 October 1988, Personal File XIX. Letter to Rescue Commando, 15 November 1989, Personal File XXIII.

    Jim and Press. Letters from Jim, 13 June 1989, Personal File XXI; 18 October 1989, Personal File XXII; Letter from Serota, 2 July 1991, Personal File XXVIII.

p.262 *Evening Standard* questionnaire. Letter from Jim, 15 August 1991. Personal File XXVIII.

    Jim to Foster, 12 June 1991, Personal File XXVIII.

Chapter 14. The Broken Chapter

p.274 Marlies Hentrup visit. Wilford letter and Jim's letter to RIBA both in Foundation Archive, Personal File XIV.

p.276 Travels with Marlies Hentrup. Mostly documented by correspondence, bills, tickets etc. in Personal Files.

p.278 Copy of Act of Will, Jim's letter from Japan and photocopy of his letter to Glennie shown to me by Marlies Hentrup.

p.283 Thomas Muirhead quotes from his 'Bookshop in the Biennale Gardens, Venice', *L'Industria delle Costrzioni*,

Rome, November 1994. See also *Padiglione del libro Electa della Biennale di Venezia*, ed. Francesco Dal Co, Electa, Milan, 1991.

p. 287   Questionnaire from France filed in Personal File XXIX.

Addenda

I am grateful to those who wrote in with corrections or suggestions after the publication of the hardback.

p.62   Audley End picnic. According to Mary Stevens no such picnic took place, but nonetheless 'there *is* a basis of fact to this story'. The incident, involving neither Colquhoun nor Audley End, occurred on the way back from a visit to Bradfield in Berkshire with Sam Stevens's then lodger, Allen Svoboda. All three left the car for a stroll; Sam got talking to Allen and the two men then got into the car and drove off without Mary. 'Far from sitting quietly on a rug, I rushed after them yelling and waving. They drove a couple of hundred yards before spotting me in the rear mirror.'

p.112   Sources for Leicester. Robin Nicholson writes about 'a further critical source for the glass cascade, which Jim talked about when we went as students with him to Leicester in 1965 – that was, I think, a silk weaving loft called York House in central Manchester.'

p.149   'To fuck Casson'. Neville Conder remembers Stirling saying this in reference to his Selwyn College design. 'On reflection I see that he may have made the remark to different people in relationship to *both* buildings.'

p.158   Acoustic problems of Florey Building. Robin Nicholson writes 'the real acoustic flaw was that the sound went through one room's louvres, round the end of the partition wall and through the next-door louvre, by-passing any sound-proofing in the walls.'

p.260   Jim and Powers. My memory was at fault here. The story was certainly told to me by someone but not, according to him, by or about Alan Powers.

Owing to a last-minute change from integrated text and pictures to signatures, all the page references in the notes were incorrect in the hardback, and have now been corrected.

A MINIMAL BIBLIOGRAPHY

I have not written an architectural monograph and cannot hope to do more than whet readers' appetites by giving them a taste of some of Jim's buildings and projects. A full bibliography of books and articles would be enormous, but the three standard general works are:

James Stirling: Buildings and Projects 1950-74 (Introduction by John Jacobus). Thames and Hudson, London, 1975.

James Stirling, Michael Wilford and Associates: Buildings and Projects 1975-92 (Introduction by Robert Maxwell. Essays by Thomas Muirhead and Michael Wilford). Thames and Hudson, London, 1994.

Both titles were published simultaneously in German by Gerd Hatje, Stuttgart.

James Stirling: Buildings and Projects (Introduction by Colin Rowe). Rizzoli, New York, 1984, with a comprehensive bibliography.

INDEX

AA *see* Architectural Association
Aachen, Germany: Kaiserbad scheme
  281–2
Aalto, Alvar 165, 166, 184; furniture
  172, 166, 188, 267
Aalto Prize 184
Adam, Katrin 126, 130, 135, 257
Adams, Robert 85
Ahrends Burton Koralek 157, 246
Aix-en-Provence, France 195, 200
Albers, Josef 53
Alhadeff, Carlo 146, 163, 183
Alhadeff, Nora 183
Alloway, Lawrence 56
Ambasz, Emilio 208–9
Archigram (broadsheet) 93
Architects' Journal 102, 234
Architects' Year Book 84
Architectural Association (AA),
  London 30, 40, 60, 71, 72, 75, 92,
  100, 113, 167, 177
Architectural Design 58, 146
Architectural Review xiii, 31, 51, 58,
  81, 82–3, 148, 165, 186, 195,
  208–9, 294
Arendt, Hannah: *The Human
  Condition* 62

Bacon, Francis 59
Baer, Peter 205
Bailey, Richard Fitzroy 6–7, 13
Bain, Laurence 241, 281, 291, 293,
  294

Bakema, Brit 96
Baker, Arthur 128
Banham, Mary (*née* Mullett) 51, 52,
  53, 54, 55, 56, 61, 66, 68, 93, 111
Banham, Peter Reyner 51–2, 53, 56,
  58, 59, 60, 66, 67, 70, 74, 82, 91,
  93, 146, 192
Banwell, Derick 161
Barcelona (1972) 183–4
Barfleur, France 181–2, 265, 281
Bath 37–8
Beauclerk, Helen 166
Beaux Arts, Ecole des 29–30
Bell, Robin xv, 13, 14–15, 16, 17, 37,
  40, 46
Benesch, Gunter 203
Berlin: Altes Museum 200;
  Wissenschaftszentrum 212, *223*,
  223–6, 235, 276
Berlin, Isaiah 231
Betjeman, John 165, 166, 168
beton brut 58–9
Beveridge, D. A. 13
Bevington, Russell 198, 200, 202,
  219, 221, 230, 243, 245, 248, 249,
  250, 252, 293, 294
Bill, Max 167
Birds, Andrew 291
Black, Robin 64
'Black Book' (*James Stirling: Buildings
  and Projects 1950–74*) 186–7, 190,
  192–7, 198, 200
Blackwood, Michael 255

Blake, Peter 133, 183
Blake, Robert 157, 159
Bloomfield, Julia 134, 135, 183, 290
Bok, Derek 214–15
Bonfield, Mrs (cleaning lady) 171, 174
Borland, Lesley 169, 170, 184
Bowness, Alan 217, 219–20, 222, 260
Boyarsky, Alvin 146, 169
Boyle, Sandy (Stephen) 98, 281, 286, 292, 293
Braun, Herr 232, 235
Bravington, Miss: Dancing School 14
Brewer, Charles 117, 118
Brion, Signora Rina 232
British Birds (magazine) 8
Brogan, Denis 154
Brown, Neave 60, 74, 87
Brunswick Park School, Camberwell 105
'Brutalism' 58–9
Buchanan, George 118, 123
Budden, Lionel 23, 30–2, 33, 38, 40, 49
Building Design 160, 162
Burrells, the 182, 265–6
Bush, Mr (cook) 171, 175–6
Butler, Professor Lionel 155, 156
Butlin, Martin 219, 220–1

Cambridge Review 104–5, 154
Cambridge University: Churchill College 102–5, 103; Cripps Building, St John's College 148, 157; History Faculty Building xiv, 137–8, 139, 140, 146, 147, 149, 151–5, 158, 193, 195, 295; Selwyn College scheme 105–6, 112, 194; University Centre 96
Cameron, Roy 190
Campbell, Robert ('Bobby') 6, 13
Campbell, Will 2, 6
Carlisle, Clarice and Molly 14, 15–16
Caro, Anthony 222

Carrere and Hastings 30
Carter, Peter 51–2, 67, 85
Cary, Tristram: 'Divertimento for Olivetti Machines, Chorus and Percussion' 163
Casa Bella (magazine) 187
Casson, Hugh 149
Cattaneo, Cesare 38, 47
Chamberlin, Powell and Bon 104
Charles, Prince of Wales 239, 260, 261
Charreau, Pierre: Maison de Verre 112
Chase-Riboud, Barbara 99, 120–2, 168, 294
Cheeseman, Georgina 99
Chicago 124; Johnson Wax Building 79, 83, 113, 124
Chivers (W. E.) and Sons 158
CIAM (Congrès Internationaux d'Architecture Moderne) 84
Clore, Charles 217
Clore Gallery, Tate 212, 217–22, 260, 261
Colacola, John 133
Colquhoun, Alan 51, 58, 59, 60, 62, 72, 73, 74, 82, 87, 100, 113, 184
Columbia University: Chemistry Building 212
Connel Ward and Lucas 80
Conran, Terence 95
Constructivism 73–4, 77, 112
Cordell, Frank 52, 53, 59
Cordell, Magda xvi, 52–3, 55, 59, 66–7, 68, 93
Cordingley, Alan 39, 60, 74, 75
Cornell University: Performing Arts Center 226–30, 235
Correa, Charles 290
Corrigan, John 245
Courtauld Institute, London 60, 61
Coventry Chair, the 167–8
Craft, Hal 228
Crosby, Theo 58

Cubitt (James) and Partners 64, 88
Cullinan, Edward ('Ted') 94, 146
Cuman, G. B. 283, 284
Cunningham, Allen 123

Dal Co, Francesco 263–4, 281,
    282–3, 286, 290
Dal Co, Gretchen xvi, 286, 287
Dannatt, Trevor 84
Dawson, 'Dippy' (schoolmaster) 7
Deakin, John 59
Dent, Margaret 65–6, 97, 98
Derby Civic Centre competition
    189–90, *196*, 199
Diamond, John 64
Dierkes, Professor 223, 225–6
Dolman, Elizabeth 162
Domus (magazine) 114, 126
Donnell, Stuart 228
Dorman Long 142
Drake, Paul 113
Dray sisters 14, 15
Drexler, Arthur 130
Duffield, Vivienne 217
Dulac, Edmund 166
Dunluce, Alexander 219, 221
Düsseldorf Art Gallery competition
    198–200, *201*; Kunstakademie
    257–8
Dutch, Robert 162
Dye, Robert 215, 229

Eames, Charles 71, 172
Eden, W. A. 37, 47
Einzig, Richard 172
Eisenhower, President Dwight D. 167
Eisenmann, Peter 132, 133, 136
Electa (publishers) 282, 283
Elizabeth II, Queen 93, 167, 222
Elizabeth, the Queen Mother 159,
    175
Ellis, John 87
Ellis, Peter 38, 112
Ellis, Rosaleen 173

Ellis, Tom 86, 87, 88, 173
Ellwood, Craig 124
Elton, Professor Geoffrey 140, 152,
    154, 157
English Heritage 239
Ernst, Max 36
Evans, Eldred 96, 99–102, 107, 111,
    112, 122–3, 124, 125, 138, 139,
    140, 150, 165
Evans, Kit 94, 95, 99
Evans, Marsha 95
Evans, Merlin 101–2
Evans, Tommy 14, 16–17
Evening Standard 65, 231, 262

Fabing, Suzannah 214, 215
Fane, Julian: *Gentleman's Gentleman*
    175
Farkashazi, Elisabeth 257, 280
Fecker, Herbert xvi, 205–6, 208
Fecker, Jurg 206
Fecker, Marianne 205, 206
Finlay, Moses 152
Florey, Lord 157
Foster, Sir Norman xiv, 100, 118,
    122, 123, 124, 211, 239, 241, 261,
    262, 290; Royal Academy
    exhibition 255, 261; Nîmes Arts
    Centre 256; Sackler Galleries,
    Royal Academy 262
Frampton, Kenneth 60, 62, 72, 73,
    74, 94, 120, 128, 135, 145, 257,
    268, 286
Frazer, Henry 3
Fuller, Richard Buckminster 79, 98,
    184

Gale, Adie 94
Gehry, Frank 225, 256, 282, 287,
    290
Gibbs, James 295
Girouard, Dorothy xiv, 275
Glasgow 1–2, 20, 281
Glennie, Colin 60, 278

Godard, Keith 126, 130, 135, 227, 229, 257
Goldfinger, Erno 94
Golding, John 222
Gollins, Melville and Ward 75
Gordon, Max 99
Gorlin, Alexander 131, 132
Gosling, David 144
Gowan, James xvi, 86, 88–9, 137–8, 150, 195; in partnership with JS 89–91, 98, 102–15, 151
Graves, Michael 132
Gray, David 60, 62–3, 87, 88, 89, 93, 94, 95, 137, 138, 149, 250
Gray, Ilse 62, 93
Great Orme 10
Gregotti, Marina 171
Groom, Lisa 292
Gropius, Walter 28, 31, 36, 40, 46, 165
Grosvenor Estates Commercial Developments 160
GRP (glass-reinforced polyester) 144, 146
Guggenheim, Peggy 55
Gwathmey, Betty-Anne 135
Gwathmey, Charles 123, 135–6

Hackney: Bentham Road estate 58
Ham Common, London: flats 89–91, 102
Hamilton, Richard 53, 57, 59, 85, 113–14
Hamilton, Terry 53
Hamlyn, Robin 219, 220, 221
Hanscomb Consultants 228
Hardwick Hall, Derbyshire 20
Hardy, Eric 8, 11, 17, 23; *The Birds of the Liverpool Area* 8, 9, 15
Harewood House, Yorkshire 23–4
Harling, Robert 172, 175
Harrap, Julian 107, 144, 189, 190, 191
Harvard University: Arthur M.

Sackler Museum xvii, 212, 213–17
Hatch, Billy 265
Hatje, Gerd 183, 187, 269
Hawksmoor, Nicholas 58, 295
Hayes, Barbara (*née* Bennett) 20–1, 24–5, 35, 40, 96, 121
Hayes, George 14–15, 16, 18, 19, 20, 24–5, 34, 35, 38, 40, 48, 96, 121
Helsinki (1978) 184
Henderson, Nigel 57
Hentrup, Karsten 275, 286
Hentrup, Marlies 257, 258, 274–80, 281–2, 285, 286, 287, 288–91, 292–3
Hentrup, Till 275, 276, 278–9, *285*, 289
Hentrup Heyers 281
Heron, Patrick 222
Herron, Ron: 'Imagination' building, Store Street, London 262
Heyers, Norbert 281, 282
Higgs, Malcolm 99, 107
Hodgetts, Craig 114, 126–7, 128, 129, 133, 147, 149, 227, 290
Hodgkinson, Patrick 60, 62, 74
Hogge, Evelyn *see* Newby, Evelyn
Holford, William 48
Hollein, Hans 184, 290
Holst, Dr von 205
Holzbauer, Wilhelm 122–3
Hope, Thomas; furniture xvii, 198
House and Garden 93, 168, 172
Howe, Elspeth (*née* Shand) 166, 167, 168, 169, 175, 181, 182, 265, 293
Howe, Geoffrey 168, 169, 175, 181, 182–3, 245, 265, 293
Howell, Bill 58, 67, 84, 96, 172; Howell, Killick and Partridge 104
Howell, Gill 96, 172
Hunstanton, Norfolk: school 54
Hutchinson, Lord 219, 220

ICA *see* Institute of Contemporary Arts

Independent Group 56–7, 58, 59–60, 66, 72, 85

India (1975) 184

Indian Institute of Management 198

Institute of Contemporary Arts (ICA) 55–7, 59, 66, 70, 71; *Parallel of Life and Art* (exhibition) 57; *Tomorrow's Furniture* (exhibition) 66

Iran (1974) 184

Ireland 264–5

Irvine Science Library, California 294

Isosaki, Arata 294, 295

Italy 182, 183; *see also* Rome; Venice

Jack, Janet (*née* Kaye) 71, 74, 96–9, 100, 104, 119, 218

Jacobus, John 192

Jakobson, Barbara 134, 135, 136, 230, 257, 286

Jefferson Prize 255, 281

Jencks, Charles 146, 209, 239, 255, 290; *The Language of Post-Modern Architecture* 211

Jencks, Margaret 255

Jenkin, Patrick 237

Jenkins, Roy 7

J.H. Dry Construction Ltd 159

Johnson, Philip 99, 116, 119, 120, 124, 132, 136, 169, 213, 239, 265; Seagram Building 124

Jones, Ed 98, 281

Jones, Margot 281

Kahn, Louis 99, 119, 120, 124, 183, 184, 198; Yale Art Gallery 117; Yale Center for British Art 118

Kahn, Robert 131, 227, 229, 257, 264, 268, 269, 272

Kaye, Janet *see* Jack, Janet

Keogh, Paul 259

Kerr, Anne 34–5, 39

Kidd, Bill 18

Killick, John 96, 104

Koetter, Fred 131

Kreiss, Werner 245

Krier, Leon 149, 187–9, 190–2, 193, 195, 196–7, 250, 252, 254, 259; Derby Civic Centre competition 196; Florey Building *194*; Olivetti headquarters and JS *186*, 197

Krier, Rita 190

Kurokawa, Kisho 290

Lambay, island of 265

Lambert, Phyllis 256

Lancaster, Osbert: *Homes Sweet Homes* 197

Lasdun, Denys 198

Latina, Italy: Library competition 231

Le Corbusier (Charles-Edouard Jeanneret) 26, 28–9, 31, 36, 37, 39, 69–70, 73, 79, 92, 187, 192, 193; Carpenter Center and Memorial Hall, Harvard 215; Maison Cook 80, 81; Maison du Salut (Cité de Refuge) 81, 200; Maisons Jaoul, Neuilly 80, 82, 83, 90, 236; Notre-Dame-du-Haut, Ronchamp 82, 83, 85; Palace of the Soviets 197; Pavillon Suisse, Paris 47, 81; *Towards a New Architecture* 31, 37, 46; Unité, Marseilles 48, 58, 82; Villa Savoie, Poissy 72, 79, 81; Villa Stein, Garches 70, 76, 79, 80, 81, 82, 174; *When the Cathedrals Were White* 45

Leicester, University of: Engineering Building xiv, 92, 106–15, *109*, 137, 147, 149, 150–2, 153, 187, 193

Lennon, John 7

Leone, Giovanne 283

Levy, Martin 266, 272–3

Lewis, Toby 250

Lilley, Mrs 152–3

Lindsay, Mayor 128

Littenberg, Barbara 163

Liverpool 4–5, 34; Cook Street 38, 112; Gilmour Hall, Students' Union 30, 32; Oriel Chambers 38, 112; Quarry Bank Secondary Day School 6–7, 12–13; Queen Victoria statue 49; School of Architecture 23, 27, 30–3, 34, 37–40, 47–8, 60, 64; School of Art 7, 13, 14, 32–3, 38; Tate Gallery 231, 261; Watson's Motor Show Room 13

Livesey, Robert 135, 198–9, 240, 244

London 50–1; Alton estate, Roehampton 58; Bentham Road estate, Hackney 58; Brunswick Park School, Camberwell 105; Carlton Gardens development 261, 294; Devonshire House 30; Doctors' Restaurant 74; French House Pub 59, 60, 62, 66, 71, 93, 98; Ham Common flats 89–91, 102; 'Imagination' building, Store Street 262; Institutes of Law and Education 198; Lloyds Building 211; Mansion House Square scheme 236–8; Midland Bank (Lutyens) 238, 239, 240–1; National Gallery extension (proposed) 230–1, 251, 251; No. 1 Poultry xiv, 236–41, 260, 294; Peckham Comprehensive School 88; Peter Jones's 30; Putney Old People's Home 138; St John's Smith Square 37; St Mary Woolnoth 238, 239; St Stephen Walbrook 238; School of Town Planning and Regional Research 64; Tate Clore Gallery 212, 217–22, 260

London County Council (LCC): Architects' Department 50, 52, 58, 60, 96, 167; Planning Department 64, 67

Long, M. J. 116–17, 126, 128, 129–30, 184

Los Angeles: Getty Center 230

Lousada, Sandra 74–5

Lowrie, Joyce 60

Lubetkin, Berthold 36

Lutyens, Sir 173, 240–1, 265; Midland Bank 238, 239, 240–1

Lyons Israel Ellis 64, 86–9, 93, 102

Macdonald, Iain 157

McHale, John 45, 53, 56, 57, 85, 93

Mackintosh, Charles Rennie 20, 38, 79

Manners, Cynthia (née Blackburn, formerly Wickham) 93–5, 97, 100, 281

Manners, Keith 87, 93, 95, 101, 102

Manousso, Luke 89, 90

Manousso, Paul 23, 60, 72, 73–4, 77, 89

Martin, Catherine xvii, 159–60, 168, 190–1, 210, 231, 242–6, 254, 259, 274–6, 278–80, 289, 293

Martin, Jane: From Southgate to Hallwood Park 160

Martin, Sir Leslie 92, 103–4, 105, 106, 140, 149, 152, 167

Martin, Sadie 167

Mason, Phoebe 170, 171

Matlock, Audrey 132, 133–4, 295

Matthews, Richard 85

Maxwell, Margaret 39, 51

Maxwell, Robert ('Bob') 37, 39, 47–8, 51, 52, 59, 60, 64, 72, 75, 167, 259, 272

Maybrook Properties 89

Meier, Richard 134, 183, 230, 240, 290

Melly, Andrée 65, 70

Melly, George 64–5, 70

Melnikov, Konstaintin 77, 112

Melsungen 261

Melsungen, Germany: factory 232–6, 276, 290, 291

Mendelsohn, Erich 31, 47–8

Merseyside Improved Homes 161–2
Merseyside Naturalists' Association 8, 9
Mies van der Rohe, Ludwig 28, 36, 48, 79, 120, 236–7; Barcelona Pavilion 28, 79; chairs 172; Farnsworth House 236; National Gallery, Berlin 225; Seagram Building 79, 124
Milan: Palazzo Citterio (unbuilt) 231–2, *233*
Miller, John 40, 60, 87, 94, 122, 123, 167, 198, 262
Miller, Su (*formerly* Rogers) 100, 122, 123–4
Mills, John 151, 152, 153
Modern Movement 27–30, 31, 36, 37, 49, 60, 79, 147–8, 211, 295
Moneo, Rafael 282
Monk and Dunstone 152
Montreal 46; Canadian Centre for Architecture 256
Moore, Charles 125, 126, 127, 131
Moore, Henry 56, 238, 256
Moreau, Marthe 272
Moretti, Gaetano 73
Moroni, David 163
Moscow: Pravda building 112; Workers' Clubhouse 77
Muirhead, Thomas 114, 231–2, 282–3, 284, 287
Mulligan, Mick 64, 65, 70
Murray, Janine 265
Museum of Modern Art: *Three Buildings* (exhibition) 131

Nägeli, Walter 226, 232–5, 236, 270, 291
Nash, Paul 166
National Gallery: Sainsbury Wing 230–1, 251, *251*
'New Brutalism' 54, 91
'New Empiricism', Swedish 31, 58
New York xv, 40–6; Lever Building

79; Redevelopment Study 127–30; Seagram Building 79, 124
Newby, Evelyn (*née* Hogge) 55, 68–71, 72, 82–3, 89
Newby, Frank 59, 85, 87, 106, 113, 114, 115
Nicholson, Ben 56, 104
Nicholson, Robin 163
Nîmes, France: Arts Centre 256
Nimmo, Derek 7
Nouvel, Jean 256

O'Connor and Kilham 40, 56
Olivetti: Headquarters, Milton Keynes (unexecuted) 186, *186*, 235; Training School, Haslemere 144, *145*, 145–6, 162–4
Osborne, Crispin 198, 199
Otto, Frei 183, 203–4
Ove Arup Associates 246
Owtram, Christopher (Dennis) 18, 23, 38, 39, 48, 77–9, 113
Oxford University: Florey Building (Queen's College) xiii, xiv, 142–4, *143*, 147, 156–60, 193, *194*, 195, 252; St Hilda's 157

Palin, George 34
Palin, Oonagh (*née* Stirling) 2, 3, 4, 5, 21, 34, 293
Palumbo, Peter 219, 220, 236–9, 241, 260
Paolozzi, Eduardo 54, 57, 59, 89, 97, 174; 'Wittgenstein' lithographs 172
Parker, Alec 14, 16, 37, 40, 46
Parker, Pat 14, 16, 40, 46
Parkes, Edward 106, 107, 108, 109, 111, 115, 151
Parsons, Philip 214, 215
Patrick, Michael 167
Peckham, London: comprehensive school 88
Pedersen, Jane 229
Pei, I. M. 99

Pelli, Cesar 131, 133, 214, 256
Penrose, Roland 55, 56
Pevsner, Nikolaus 126, 147–8, 149
Picasso, Pablo 56, 73
Picturesque, the 58, 148–9
Pine, Michael 85
Plumb, Sir John 154
Poole (Henry) and Sons (tailors) 176
Poole Technical College competition 75, 193, 197
Pop Art 57–8, 59, 85, 113–14
Portchmouth, Richard 250, 291; National Gallery extension 251
Portzamparc, Christian de 290
Post-Modernism 211, 212
Pot, Paul 70–1
Powell and Moya 89, 148, 157
Powers, Alan 260–1
Prestwich, Minna 157
Prestwich, John 157–9
Price, Cedric 59, 94
Pritzker Prize 255–6
Puffin Island 10

Quant, Mary 114
Quarry Bank Secondary Day School, Liverpool 6–7, 12–13
Queensberry, David 16

Randall, Professor Don 212, 226, 227, 228
Raymond, Santa 96
Read, Herbert 55, 56
Reilly, Sir Charles 30, 31, 33, 40, 64
Renzio, Toni del 59
Revelstoke, Lord 265
Reynolds, Edward 59, 113
Rhodes, President of Cornell University 228, 229
RIBA see Royal Institute of British Architects
Riboud, Marc 121
Rice University, Texas: School of Architecture 212–13

Richards, Brian 27
Richards, J. M. 165
Riches, Brian 186, 195
Ridley, Nicholas 241
Rindl, Sven 163
Rizzoli: monograph on JS (1984) 255
Robertson, Jacquelin ('Jack') 116, 127, 129
Robinson, Gerald Kirby ('Gerry') 7–12, 14, 15
Roche, Fred Lloyd 144
Rogers, Bill 7
Rogers, Richard 100–1, 122, 123, 124, 211, 219, 220, 262, 239, 255, 261; Lloyds Building 211, 262; Pompidou Center 211
Rogers, Su see Miller, Su
Rome: American School 264; Nolli Plan (unexecuted) 202, 223
Ronchamp, France: Notre-Dame-du-Haut 82, 83, 85
Rothschild, Lord 231
Rowe, Colin xvi, 18–19, 23, 38–40, 46, 47, 48, 49, 58, 60, 73, 104–5, 111, 112, 114, 169, 173, 228, 255, 268; 'Collage City' 173, 223
Rowe, David 73
Royal Academy: exhibition (1986) 261; Sackler Galleries 262
Royal Institute of British Architects (RIBA): JS exhibition catalogue 192, 195; Queen's Gold Medal xiv, 255, 274
Rudolph, Paul xvi, 116–17, 118, 119, 124–6, 169, 187; Married Students' Housing Yale 117
Runcorn, Lancashire: Southgate housing estate 144–5, 160–2, 192, 197, 198, 261
Russell, Gordon 167
Russell, Richard D. ('Dick') 167, 171, 176; Russell, Hodson and Leigh 167, 171
Russum, Michael 291

Rykwert, Joseph 60, 167

Saarinen, Eero 117, 126
Sackler, Arthur M. 215
Sackler Museum *see* Harvard
Safdie, Moshe 184
St Andrew's University: Arts Centre
  (unbuilt) 191; student residences
  140–2, *141*, 146, 149, 155–6, 194
St Bees Head 8–9, 10–12
Sarabhai, Gautam and Gita 184
Sartoris, Alberto 268; *Encyclopédie de
  l'Architecture* 37, 268
Save Britain's Heritage 239
Scarpa, Carlo 232
Schaad, Ulrich ('Ulli') 214, 235, 249
Scharoun, Hans: Philharmonic Hall,
  Berlin 225
Schinkel, Karl Friedrich 207; Altes
  Museum, Berlin 200
Schupp, Manuel 286–7
Schwartzkopf, Elizabeth 281
Scott, Celia 272
Scott, Gilbert 105
Scully, Vincent 117
Serota, Nicholas 260
Shand, Elspeth *see* Howe, Elspeth
Shand, Philip 165–6, 167, 175, 176,
  275
Shand, Sybil 165–6
Sharpley, Anne 65
Sheffield: Park Hill housing estate
  142; University competition 75–7,
  76, 193
Sheppard, Robson and Partners 104
Shore, Peter 7
Siemens AG competition 190
Simmonds, Jack 7, 13
Simnet, Jackie 242, 243, 245, 254
Sindall (William) Ltd 152, 153
Singapore: Temasek Polytechnic 294
Slack, Bill 195
Slive, Seymour 213–15
Smith, Ivor 141

Smithson, Alison 53, 54–5, *see also*
  Smithsons, the
Smithson, Peter xvi, 53, 54, 55, 73,
  79, 86, 117, *see also* Smithsons, the
Smithsons, the 57, 59, 60, 67–8, 75,
  84, 134, 141, 157, 158, 193
Solo, Sheldon 240
Soriana, Rafael 124
Soyeren, Vefik xvi, 257
Spazio (magazine) 73
Stamp, Gavin 154, 261
Starck, Philip 284
Steinberg, Sol 129
Stella, Frank 264
Stephen, Douglas 33, 39, 59, 64, 74,
  98, 121, 134, 281, 286, 288
Stephen, Margaret 64, 121
Stephen, Sandy *see* Boyle, Sandy
Stevens, Mary 62
Stevens, Thomas ('Sam') 60–3, 66,
  68, 72, 73, 74, 94, 167
Stirling, Ben (son) 170, 176, 179,
  182, 183, 255, 256, 266, 269,
  288–9, 291, 293; drawing of JS
  191, 192
Stirling, Christina (*née* Marshall)
  (great-grandmother) 1
Stirling, James (great-grandfather) 1
Stirling, James (grandfather) 1–2
Stirling, James ('Jim'):
  affairs/relationships with women
  25–6, 35, 68–71, 72, 96–8,
  99–102, 119, 120–3, 274–81,
  288–90; ancestry and parents 1–5;
  appearance and clothes xiii, 15, 34,
  66–7, 92, 93, 176–7, 185, 197,
  244, 258–9; at Architectural
  Association 71, 72; architectural
  beginnings 13–14, 26; architectural
  views and philosophy 27, 36,
  39–40, 79–84, 86, 114, 148–9,
  207, 208, 294–6; army career
  18–24; birth 1; and cats 171, 179,
  268–9; character xv, xvi, 67, 71,

74–5, 122, 139, 269, 270, 272–3, 277–8, 295, 296; childhood and schooling 2, 3, 4, 5–13; and his children 268, 269–70; death xv, 291–3; at Düsseldorf Art Academy 257–8, 274–5; entertaining at home 174–6, 268; exhibitions 85–6, 131, 186, 192; health problems 217, 262–3, 288; influences 32, 36–7, 38, 46, 47, 49, 70, 73–4, 90, *see also* Le Corbusier; interest in furniture xvii, 171–4, 197, 198, 254, 266–8; and 'International Circus' 184, 256; knighthood 261, 291; at Liverpool School of Architecture 27, 31, 32, 33–40, 47–9; his London office 242–6; with Lyons Israel Ellis 64, 86–9; marriage 165, 168–71; in New York xv, 40–6, 127–30, 134–6, 257; partnerships *see* Gowan, James; Wilford, Michael; poems 21–3, 122; prizes and awards xiv, 93, 184, 255–6, 281, 291; reading interests 17, 26, 36, 67, 69, 73, 92, 270; teenage years and friendships 14–17; in Venice 263–4, 281, 282–7; working methods 246–52; at Yale 99, 110, 116–20, 122–7, 131–4, 136, 192

Stirling, Joseph (father) 1, 2, 3–4, 5–6, 13, 24

Stirling, Kate (daughter) 170, 174–5, 176, 179, 182, 183, 266, 269–70, 275, 281, 288, 289, 293, 294

Stirling, Louise (*née* Frazer) (mother) 1, 2–3, 4, 5, 21, 24, 40, 170, 179

Stirling, Mary (*née* Shand) (wife): childhood 165–6; entertaining with JS 174, 175, 176, 268; as furniture designer 166–8, 171, 172, 175; holidays and trips with JS 181–4, 255–6, 264, 283; marriage to JS xiv, 165, 168–9, 170–1, 174,

176–7, 180, 269; and JS's affair with Marlies Hentrup 275, 280–1, 288; and JS's death 292, 293

Stirling, May (*née* Bett) (grandmother) 1

Stirling, Oonagh (sister) *see* Palin, Oonagh

Stirling, Sophie (daughter) xvi, 170, 176, 177, 179–81, 182, 183, 266, 268, 269, 270, 281, 288, 289, 291, 292, 293

Strand, Mark 264

Stuttgart: Neue Staatsgalerie xvi, 200–10, 211

Summerson, Sir John 237, 239

Sunday Times magazine 258–9

Surrealism 36

Swedish New Empiricism 31, 58

Tafel, Tommy 205

Tafuri, Manfredo 263–4, 294

Tange, Kenzo 144, 183, 184

Tate Gallery, London: Clore Gallery 212, 217–22, 260

Team X 84

Terragni, Giuseppe 38, 47

Terry, Quinlan 107, 108

This is Tomorrow (exhibition) 85–6

Thomas, Fred 39, 40, 41, 147

Thyssen, Baron von 231

Tigerman, Stanley 118, 119

Train, Kirk 259

Trescobear County Secondary School, Cornwall 88

Tuomey, John 209, 224, 249, 265

Turnbull, William 51

Valéry, Paul: 'Eupalinos or the Architect' 73

Vallebuona, Renzo 234

Van Eyck, Aldo 184

Venice 263–4; Biennale (1991) project 281, 282–7

Venturi, Robert 125; Venturi, Rauch

and Scott Brown 230, 231
Vernin, Alexander 112
Voelcker, John 85

Wade, Robin 167, 168, 169, 171
Walker, Megan 133
Wall Street Journal 215
Walpe, Cathy 51
Walsby, David 107
Wank Adams Slavin 229
Warhol, Andy and his Factory
  129–30
Warwick University 153
Watson, Professor J. Steven 149, 155,
  156
Waugh, Evelyn: *Decline and Fall* 197
Weese, Harry 99
Weinberg, David 163
Wells, Gerry 226
Wernik, Siegried (Sigi) 205, 226,
  233–4
Whitechapel Art Gallery: *This is
  Tomorrow* (exhibition) 85–6
Wickham, Cynthia *see* Manners,
  Cynthia
Wickham, Julyan 95
Wickham, Michael 93–6, 100, 154,
  281
Wilford, Michael 106, 107–8, 138–9,
  142, 144, 168, 193, 219–20, 293,
  294; in partnership with JS 142,
  164, 204–5, 212–13, 217, 222–3,
  226–36, 243, 244, 250, 252–3,
  260, 278, 281, 291; on JS 131,
  154, 179, 245–6, 247, 279, 287
Wilke, Ulla 132, 133, 242, 247–8,
  252, 280, 281, 293
Williams, A. A. 157, 159
Willink, Hugh 152
Wilson, Bernard 33
Wilson, Colin St John *see* Wilson,
  Sandy
Wilson, Muriel (*née* Lavender) 52,
  55, 70–1, 82

Wilson, Sandy 51–2, 58, 59, 69,
  70–1, 92, 93, 103, 104, 117, 139,
  219, 237, 239; marriages 55, 128;
  Sheffield University entry 75, 76;
  on JS 67, 72, 85, 86, 112
Wilton, Andrew 221, 222
Winter, John 79, 150
Wirral, the 9
Witherby, H. F.: *Handbook of British
  Birds* 7, 8
Wittkower, Rudolf 39, 48, 59;
  *Architectural Principles of the Age of
  Humanism* 58
Wolverhampton Civic Halls 86
Woolton Park, Liverpool 84–5, 89,
  187, 194
World War, Second 3, 11–13, 18–24
Wormfield, Mike 128, 129
Wright, Frank Lloyd 38, 45, 46, 72,
  77–8, 79, 236; Johnson Wax
  Building 79, 83, 113, 124

Yale School of Architecture 99, 100,
  110, 116–20, 122–7, 131–4, 192,
  256
Yorke, Rosenberg and Mardell 153

Zevi, Bruno 148; *Architecture
  Moderne* 77, 79
Zipatone 46–7